The
Real
Counties
of
Britain

The

Real

Counties

of

Britain

Russell Grant

Lennard Publishing
1989

LENNARD PUBLISHING
a division of Lennard Books Ltd.
Musterlin House
Jordan Hill Road
Oxford OX2 8DP

British Library Cataloguing in Publication Data
is available for this title

ISBN 1 85291 071 2

First published 1989
© Russell Grant, 1989

Typeset in Goudy Old Style
Design by Forest Publication Services, Luton
Cover design by Pocknell & Co.
Reproduced, printed and bound in Great Britain
by Butler and Tanner Limited, Frome & London

Contents

Introduction

Through ignorance, misconception or the facts being deliberately withheld, many of us are confused or indeed oblivious as to where we belong and actually live. Do **you** know in which county you really reside?

If, for instance, you came from Wraysbury, a small village-cum-parish on the banks of the Thames, you would pay your rates to Berkshire County Council and you would send your post via Middlesex, but you would actually live in Buckinghamshire. Confused? Of course you are, because county confusion which began in 1889, when they invented the administrative county (commonly known as the county council), was made worse in the mid 1960's and early 1970's by the huge upheaval in local government re-organisation.

The Royal Mail unwittingly added to the confusion when it introduced the 'postal county' purely for efficient delivery of the post, although the post office does make it quite clear that your postal address is not an accurate description or indication of your true geographical location. To make matters worse, the post office uses the administrative county in some addresses and the geographical county in others.

I was born in Hillingdon, Middlesex, but within a matter of months my roots were replanted in the Middlesex village of Harefield, the community that was to shape my character and provide me with the sense of belonging and protectiveness that the basic human nature demands. These formative years in a close-knit village community, where everything revolved around the church, local amateur dramatics and my junior school, gave me the happiest of childhoods and, as I was to find out in later years, fuelled a fierce love for and loyalty to the history, heritage and identity of the village and the county that had fostered my community spirit and cultivated my roots.

In 1965 the Greater London Council (the GLC) came into being and at the same time the Middlesex County Council was abolished. Nowhere, apart from in the local newspaper the Middlesex Advertiser and Gazette, was it made clear that *only* the administrative county was abolished, and that the historic geographical county of Middlesex continued to exist despite the local government changes.

By this time I had moved from the security of the red-brick Harefield Junior School, complete with school bell in its tower, to the soulless comprehensive Abbotsfield – ironically

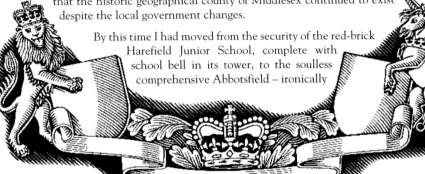

enough across the road from where I was born in Harvey Road, Hillingdon.

Not once in my education at the hands of the new local authority, the "London" Borough of Hillingdon or the GLC, were we taught or told about what had actually happened to Middlesex. We just assumed, quite wrongly, that our county home had been wiped off the map and we didn't belong anywhere anymore – certainly not to a bureaucratically devised local authority.

From the tender years of my teens right up until the late 1980's, I mourned the loss of Middlesex, and throughout my days on BBC 'Breakfast Time' I steadfastly remained loyal to geographical counties everywhere. Little did I realize I was correctly interpreting the Local Government Act as it had been properly defined by Parliament. People from all over Britain praised and applauded me for talking about Potters Bar, Middlesex, Grimsby, Lincolnshire and Beverley, Yorkshire. For these places were administered for local government by administrative counties that were different from their historic geographical county. As a result of this personal stand for our county roots, I was invited by 'Roots: County Heritage Conservation' to succeed Sir John Betjeman as Patron. I accepted with some trepidation; how do you follow Betjeman?

When my appointment was announced in the local press a number of letters were printed asking what was I going to do about my home County of Middlesex. It was then I realized that no society had been actually formed actively to promote the cause existence and identity of Middlesex, and other people's interest was the catalyst to motivate my own pride of place. My feelings were passionate, powerful enough to penetrate passion's greatest adversary, apathy.

I wrote to the Department of the Environment and 10, Downing Street to ask why they had abolished Middlesex, my home. The reply, which I hadn't expected, came back. From the Environment Department came this: "What makes you think of the abolition of a county that has lasted for 10 or 12 centuries .... of course Middlesex still exists and will continue to do so ...." The Downing Street reply was similar.

It was the information and ammunition I needed, for it was a fundamental fact that had escaped the majority of people. Some local authorities were perfectly aware of the situation; but it wasn't in their best interests to promote or publicize information that could potentially undermine their position politically or their standing in the community.

More research uncovered further facts which were complex and rather difficult to grasp but nonetheless confirmed that *all* our counties remained intact, and had never been affected by the invention of the administration/ local government county council. Indeed one Parliamentarian questioned whether Parliament could abolish the geographical county even if it wanted to, as it had not created it in the first place. But public ignorance and convenient political connivance had done what Parliament had never intended, and that was to abolish the real county in peoples' minds, even though in reality nothing of the sort had happened.

There are indeed three different types of county: the geographical county; the administration county and the 'postal county'. A government spokesman had gone so far as to say that "the new county boundaries are administrative areas, and will not alter the traditional (geographical) boundaries of counties, nor is it intended that the loyalties of people living in them will change, despite the curious names adopted by the administrative counties."

It was also confirmed that the re-structuring of local government was for efficiency only, and would not affect the cultural, social and local loyalties and associations or sporting ties based upon the identity of the geographical county. But it did.

Enter the villains: mapmakers, who only produce maps showing the administrative county; the media who brainwash with inappropriate regional descriptions, such as Bolton, near Manchester (BBC radio) or the administrative county of Avon; and the mail, though this is not *always* the villain. For instance, you still write to Middlesex but if you are in Southport, your 'address' is Merseyside, even though you live in Lancashire: a postal paradox.

Ignorance is far from bliss, for in some areas a total lack of the facts leads to all sorts of confusion. Take sport in Monmouthshire. For soccer you belong to Gwent F A but for rugby the Monmouthshire RU. Gwent County Council is the administrative county governing the geographical county of Monmouthshire. The government-sponsored Sports Council follows administrative boundaries but the vast majority of sporting associations follow the geographical counties, thus creating a ghastly cash dilemma and division of local loyalty. For example, children or sportsmen in Richmond (Surrey) and Barnet (Hertfordshire) must play for Middlesex, whilst these same people in Spelthorne and Potters Bar (both in Middlesex) must represent Surrey and Hertfordshire. Crazy, isn't it?

In education children are not taught where they actually live. Their school books are covered with the county council's identity, as it is not necessarily in the interests of the county council to teach too much about the geographical county it governs, if its title or boundaries are in conflict. This was borne out by 'Eastenders' actress Letitia Dean, who was recently asked "Do you come from London?" "No," she said, "Hertfordshire, Potters Bar" as her face broke into a kind of bemused grin. She was actually born in Middlesex. But who can blame Letitia, or any one else, for not knowing? Whose told them otherwise?

• • • • •

This book is the first of its kind to explain the difference between Britain's three types of county. It is dedicated to **the oldest and most important – the historic geographical county that dates back in many cases to Saxon times.** This is the parent county whose existence continues, whatever bureaucratic alterations are made to the ever-changing administrative county. For such an important county there has been a noticeable lack of books available; none in fact! The administrative county was formed to govern the territory of the geographical county; the postal county for Royal Mail delivery. But the importance placed upon these two by the public belies the simple reason for their existence. In the public's understandably wrong perception, it is "where I live".

In this age of conserving our history and heritage, let us protect our roots and the identity of our real county. It is our personal duty to promote the continuing existence of our county, for it is not just looking after our architecture, ancient monuments and the green belt, or those tangible objects of our heritage that matter, but also the land from which they grew and upon which they were built. Our county boundaries are very much a part of the natural world, following rivers, streams and mountain ranges, and have as much right to be protected as any tree, stately home or monastery. But English Heritage, The National Trust and other organisations dedicated to looking after our natural heritage continue to follow the arbitrary lines drawn by bureaucrats rather than the real county. The geographical county is a rich and valuable source of our nation's social development and growth of the local environment, for the whole structure of county and community is the basis of our roots and, along with the family, is at the core of our individual evolution. Lose our roots and we lose our identity, dignity, pride and that all important desire to belong.

The chance has come to find out, through the pages of this book, where you really belong, and to renew your sense of pride and county identity. No modern book has published the full facts as they are, so don't assume this book was written as a tribute to where we USED to live. It is written to create an awareness of what exists NOW. This is not only a history book but one of current, constant information. The only changing facts under each county are found in the administration section, for the county council area can be altered at the drop of a bureaucratic hat, but your real county home will remain unchanged in the future as it has done for a thousand years.

You will find surprises, I am certain. Did you know, to cite but two examples, that many cities in Britain are independent counties themselves with historic privileges? or that detached parts of one county are found within another? There are over 100 detached areas, many described in this book, although the 1844 Act deemed 110 of them to be part of the county by which they are surrounded. Even by 1895, it was noted that Worcestershire still had islands scattered about in Gloucestershire, Warwickshire, Oxfordshire, Staffordshire, Shropshire and Herefordshire. Indeed, I have no doubt that more will come to light as this book focusses attention on them. I have been amazed by how much I have unearthed, and I know it is an ongoing process. Every day I receive more news in my post, putting right further misconceptions. In a book of this size, we have had to omit many obvious pieces of information – there has been so much we could say about each county, but I offer this book as the first move in the campaign to reawaken the awareness in us all of our own county. No doubt further information will come to me once people have the opportunity to read this book. I will be only too delighted to receive it, so that we can continue to add to the true portrait of Britain.

I hope you enjoy re-discovering your roots and unravelling the county confusion as much as I enjoyed discovering the truth.

Russell Grant, 1989

The *Real* Counties of
Britain

Maps

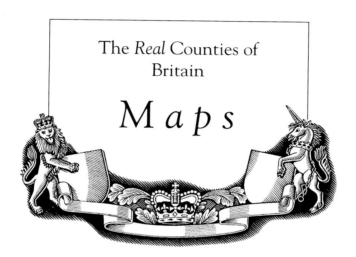

CAI

SUTHERLAND

Dornoch

ROSS

CROMARTY Cromarty

Dingwall Nairn

NAIRN M

Inverness

R. Spey

I N V E R N E S S

Glen Mor

R. Tay

PERTH

G R A M P I A N M O U N T

R. Tay

CLACKMANNAN

ARGYLL

R. Forth

Inverary Alloa Clackmann

Stirling

Loch STIRLING Li

Lomond WE

DUNBARTON LOTH

(LENNOX) DUN. (LINLITHG

Dumbarton

Renfrew Glasgow

Rothesay RENFREW

R. Clyde

BUTE Lanark

LANARK

Ayr AYR

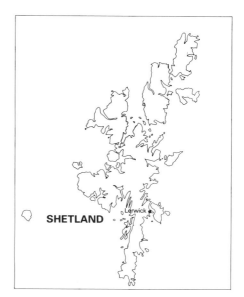

SHETLAND

Lerwick

Banff

NFF

ABERDEEN

Aberdeen

Stonehaven

KINCARDINE

Kincardine

ANGUS
(FORFAR)

Forfar

Dundee

Cupar

IFE

Haddington

EAST LOTHIAN
(HADDINGTON)

HIAN
RGH)

Duns

Berwick upon Tweed

BERWICK
(MERSE)

R. Tweed

Peebles

ES
LE)

Selkirk

Roxburgh

ELKIRK
RICK FOREST)

Jedburgh

ORKNEY

Kirkwall

The *Real* Counties of

England

BEDFORDSHIRE

COUNTY FACTS

Derivation of name: Anglo-Saxon, Beda's ford or the river crossing.
First Recorded: 1011 as Bedanfordscir
Motto: Constant Be
County Town: Bedford
Towns: Ampthill, Barton-in-the-Clay, Bedford, Biggleswade, Caddington, Clapham, Clifton, Cranfield, Dunstable, Eaton Socon, Flitwick, Henlow, Houghton Regis, Kempston, Leighton Buzzard, Luton, Maulden, Potton, Sandy, Shefford, Shillington, Stotfold, Toddington, Woburn Sands.

Local Government
Bedfordshire County Council and four district councils. The small town of Eaton Socon is under the control of Cambridgeshire County Council. Two tiny detached enclaves of the County around Ickleford and Gaddesden come under the administration of Hertfordshire County Council.

HISTORY

Two great roads passed through the county from earliest times – Watling Street, connecting north and south England, and the Icknield Way, connecting East Anglia with the west.

After the Roman occupation, the shire became part of the county of the Middle Angles, and then, in the 7th century, it was absorbed into the Kingdom of Mercia. Offa of Mercia ruled over Bedfordshire land and was buried there. In the 10th century it became a separate shire, with the name Bedfordshire.

The castle at Bedford was built by Payn de Beauchamp, the son of Hugo, who came over with the Conqueror. The barony of Bedfordshire was given to the Beauchamps, the most powerful family in the county. They sided with Empress Matilda in her fight against Stephen, and Bedford Castle was besieged several times. The story of the final siege forms the climax of Alfred Duggan's work, *Leopards and Lilies*.

A canon of Bedford was at the root of the quarrel of Henry II and Thomas à Becket. Accused of causing the death of a knight, the canon was acquitted by the bishop. The King's judiciary would not accept the acquittal, and ordered a retrial. The canon refused to appear. Henry was furious; Becket, the archbishop, held an inquiry and supported the canon – and the quarrel blazed out.

In the 16th century, Queen Catherine of Aragon lived at Ampthill mansion after being cast aside by Henry VIII, and her case was tried at Dunstable Priory by Cranmer.

During the civil war the county was roughly evenly divided in support for the king and support for parliament, and suffered much skirmishing, sequestration and plundering of estates by both sides. Negotiation between the parliamentary leaders and the defeated king took place in the county. The king was at Woburn, and the parliamentary leaders at Bedford. The meeting was in vain, however, as the king refused to abandon his loyalist friends to their enemies.

INDUSTRY PAST AND PRESENT

Agriculture, market gardening, brick-making, vehicle manufacture, engineering, cement, chemicals and printing.

The county, and especially Dunstable and Luton, were famous for straw-plaiting, and the associated industries of hat and bonnet making. Consequently, Luton Town F.C.'s nickname is 'The Hatters'. Wheat, barley, and oats were the main crops, and Bedfordshire onions and cucumbers were renowned. The county produced much butter, especially for the London market.

LANDMARKS

The Chiltern Hills
Dunstable Downs
Whipsnade Zoo Park is bigger than Monaco
Luton International Airport

MONUMENTS

Woburn Abbey, since 1539 home of the Russell family, later the Dukes of Bedford.

TOPOGRAPHY INCLUDING RIVERS

Bedfordshire, in the south-east midlands, is bordered by Hertfordshire in the south east and Buckinghamshire in the south west, Northamptonshire and Huntingdonshire in the north, and Cambridgeshire in the east.

The county rises and falls in gentle hills and valleys, from a rather flat, clay plain in the north, through a belt of sandy hills which stretch from Woburn to Sandy, to a rather higher ridge of chalk downs in the south. The highest point (on Dunstable Downs) is 801 feet.
Rivers: Flit, Ouse, Ivel, Hiz, Ouzel, Lea.

The monastic-style buildings were turned into a palatial country mansion in the 18th century. There is now a safari park in the grounds.

Wrest Park, formal gardens representing 150 years of garden design.

Luton Hoo, the Wernher family's mansion, housing a famous collection of tapestries, porcelain, paintings and Fabergé jewels.

Elstow Moot Hall, the meeting place of the followers of John Bunyan.

Maiden Bower, an ancient hill fort covering some 11 acres.

M1 Motorway, much-loved artery to the heart of the nation.

FAMOUS PEOPLE AND LOCAL CHARACTERS

John Leland, antiquary to Henry VIII, was born in Melchbourne.

John Bunyan was born in Harrowden in 1628. Having embraced Christianity he became a non-conformist preacher around Bedford, for which he was imprisoned for 12 years during the Restoration in Bedford Gaol. It was during his imprisonment that he wrote *The Pilgrim's Progress*.

Nicholas Rowe, the poet laureate, was born in Little Barford in 1673.

Admiral John Byng, son of Viscount Torrington, lived in Southill Park. He was court-martialled and executed in 1757 for his part in the loss to Britain of the island of Minorca. A tablet in Southill Church reads:

> 'To the Perpetual Disgrace of
> Public Justice
> The Honourable John Byng
> Vice Admiral of the Blue
> Fell a Martyr to
> Political Persecution
> on March 14, in the year 1757,
> when Bravery and Loyalty
> were insufficient securities
> For the Life and Honour
> of a naval officer.'

John Howard, the prison reformer, was born in the county in 1726.

THE **Pilgrim's Progress** FROM THIS WORLD, TO That which is to come:

Delivered under the Similitude of a

DREAM

Wherein is Discovered,
The manner of his setting out,
His Dangerous Journey; And safe
Arrival at the Desired Countrey.

I have used Similitudes, Hos. 12. 10.

By *John Bunyan*.

Licensed and Entred according to Order.

LONDON,
Printed for *Nath. Ponder* at the *Peacock* in the *Poultrey* near *Cornhil*, 1678.

TITLE PAGE OF THE FIRST EDITION.

ART AND LITERATURE

'I John of Gaunt
Do give and graunt
Unto Roger Burgoyne
And the heirs of his loine
Buth Sutton and Potton
Until the world's rotten.'

'*Bedford, as I have said, is a large, populous and thriving Town, and a pleasant well-built Place...it is full of very good inns, and in particular we found of good Entertainment here.'*
Daniel Defoe
Tour Through the Whole Island of Great Britain

'*In days of old, here Ampthill's towers were seen The mournful refuge of an injured Queen.'*
Horace Walpole
Memorial on the Gothic Cross

'*Bedfordshire is a brickworks in the middle of a cabbage patch'*
Local Saying

The Chiltern Hills of Bedfordshire are the Delectable Mountains of Bunyan's *Pilgrim's Progress.*

LOCAL FOLKLORE

Knocking Knoll, Shillington

Knocking Knoll is the remains of an ancient round barrow. A British Chieftain is said to be buried there with his treasure chest. At certain times, the old man can be heard knocking – whether to be let out of the barrow, or merely to make sure his treasure chest is still there, no one can say.

Maiden Bower, Houghton Regis

Maiden Bower is a small Iron Age fort. The legend of its origin is that a queen in the Iron Age cut a bull's hide into strips, which she joined end to end to form a circle on the ground. The King then ordered his men to dig the ditch and rampart of the fort following the line of the Queen's hide.

DISTINCTIVE FLAVOUR

The people of Dunstable used to go **Orange Rolling**.

The **Bedfordshire Clanger** was a suet dumpling filled with pork and onions. Sometimes the dumpling would be in the form of a long roll, with meat at one end and jam at the other, to give a complete meal within a single crust. You will go a long way in Bedfordshire before meeting anyone who admits to having eaten one of these.

Bedfordshire Wigs is a name given to a gingerbread cake which rises up over the rim of its container during cooking.

COUNTY DIARY

Easter Monday:
Pram Race, Ampthill

September:
Traction engine rally, Roxton

BERKSHIRE

COUNTY FACTS

Derivation of name: A mixture of both Brittonic (a branch of the Celtic language) and Anglo-Saxon source. Berkshire means a wooded hill district, originating from the great forest of birch trees called Bearroc, the Celtic word for 'hilly'. This the Saxons absorbed into their own language.
First Recorded: 860 as Beaurrucscir
County Town: Reading
Towns: Abingdon, Ascot, Bracknell, Cholsey, Cookham, Cumnor, Crowthorne, Didcot, Drayton, East Hendred, Faringdon, Harwell, Hungerford, Kennington, Lambourn, Maidenhead, Newbury, Old Windsor, Pangbourne, Reading, Sandhurst, Shrivenham, Sunninghill, Sunningdale, Thacham, Theale, Wallingford, Wantage, Wargrave, Windsor, Wokingham, Woodley.

Local Government
Berkshire County Council controls the central part of the county from Hungerford and Newbury to Windsor and Ascot. Oxfordshire County Council administers the Vale of the White Horse area in the north-west taking in Berkshire's old capital of Abingdon plus Wallingford, Wantage, Didcot and Faringdon. There are six district councils. There are two detached parts of Berkshire in Oxfordshire, the parishes of Shilton and Langford, controlled by Oxfordshire County Council.

HISTORY

The Saxons of the region of Berkshire were converted to Christianity by Berinus in AD 635.

Reading Abbey, one of the greatest in England, was founded in the reign of Henry I. Parliaments and royal festivals were held there: John of Gaunt married Blanche of Lancaster in its minster, and the festivities lasted fourteen days.

Berkshire has been known as the Royal County for 800 years. The connection with royalty goes back further than the building of Windsor Castle – Alfred the Great was born at Wantage, and there were royal palaces in Saxon times at Faringdon and Old Windsor. William the Conqueror established a castle at Windsor; the stone fortifications were built in the 12th or 13th centuries. It was captured by Simon de Montfort in 1263 during the Barons' Wars.

The Great Forest at Windsor was a favourite hunting ground of Kings.

In the time of Edward III, the county enjoyed peace, and Windsor Castle was rebuilt by William of Wykeham. The Order of the Garter was inaugurated at Windsor during his reign.

In AD 1389, at the Battle of Radcot Bridge, Robert de Vere, Earl of Oxford, was defeated by Henry, then Earl of Derby, and de Vere escaped by plunging into the Thames with his horse.

Berkshire was the scene of much fighting in the Civil War. The two battles of Newbury both ended in defeat for the Royalists.

INDUSTRY PAST AND PRESENT

Present industry includes electronics, biscuit making, dairying, engineering, boat building, fruit growing, racehorse training and nuclear research. Reading is one of the boom towns of the high-tech age. The Simonds, later Courage, brewing company is a major employer.

Corn and wheat are grown widely in the county, which also had more farm land until built upon. Huntley and Palmer's biscuits date from the 19th century.

THE WHITE HORSE AT UFFINGTON

TOPOGRAPHY INCLUDING RIVERS

Berkshire borders Oxfordshire and Buckinghamshire in the north, Surrey in the east, Hampshire in the south, and Wiltshire in the west.

Irregular in shape, due to the windings of the River Thames, the county has been likened to a shoe or slipper. John Betjeman describes Berkshire's shape as follows, "Berkshire is like a tattered old shoe, kicking out eastwards from Gloucestershire. Bits of the old shoe turn up in the most unexpected places, because the whole northern boundary of the county runs for 110 miles along the south bank of the Thames from Old Windsor, next door to Egham, by many convolutions through Henley, Reading, Wallingford and Oxford right up to Buscot, which is by Lechlade in Gloucestershire. The south boundary of the county and the sole of the shoe, stretches for the most part along the northern edge of Hampshire. And the uppers make a western border for the county on the Wiltshire downs. As for the toe, at the eastern end, that is Windsor Great Park. A range of chalk hills just south of the Thames form the northern boundary to the Vale of White Horse, named after the famous white horse scooped out of the side of the Berkshire Downs. These chalk downs form a ridge across central Berkshire over which runs the ancient track known as the Ridgeway, which formed part of the Icknield Way connecting east and west Britain. To the east of the county rolling heathland leads to Windsor Great Park." The highest point is Wadbury Hill, 974 feet.

Rivers: Thames, Kennet, Blackwater, Lambourn, Ock, Lodden.

LANDMARKS

Windsor Great Park
Inkpen Beacon, 954 feet high
Vale of White Horse
Berkshire Downs
White Horse Hill

MONUMENTS

Windsor Castle, home of British monarchs for almost 900 years. A castle was built on the site by William the Conqueror. St George's Chapel is one of the finest cruciform medieval churches in Britain.

Donnington Castle, the 14th-century gatehouse of a medieval fortified manor.

Abingdon has two major monuments. Its arcaded town hall is a masterpiece of 17th-century classical restraint; its almost vanished abbey was once as large as Wells Cathedral.

Reading Abbey, again almost completely destroyed has left a legacy of magnificent Romanesque carvings.

FAMOUS PEOPLE AND LOCAL CHARACTERS

Jack O'Newbury, the famous clothier and early factory entrepreneur, lived in Newbury in the time of Henry VIII.

King James I of Scotland was held captive at Windsor Castle for 19 years.

Thomas Howard, Earl of Surrey, was also imprisoned at Windsor before he was executed.

Archbishop Laud was born in Reading in 1573.

Alexander Pope lived in Binfield, and began writing there. He described the house in which he lived as, 'A little house with trees a-row, And like its master very low'.

Sir William Blackstone, the Judge and author of Legal Commentaries, lived in Wallingford. Thomas Hughes was born in Uffington on October 22, 1822. He describes the Vale of White Horse at the beginning of *Tom Brown's Schooldays*.

Oscar Wilde was moved to Reading Gaol, where he spent 2 years, in 1895. After being released from prison, the only thing he ever wrote was *The Ballad of Reading Gaol*.

Mary Russell Mitford moved with her family to a house in Reading, bought with a lottery prize of £20,000. They later moved to Three Mile Cross, on which she based her sketches of village life entitled *Our Village*.

Sir Stanley Spencer lived in the county. One of his most famous paintings is that of Cookham regatta.

ART AND LITERATURE

'...And then what a hill is the White Horse Hill! There it stands, right up above all the rest, nine hundred feet above the sea, and the boldest, bravest shape for a chalk hill that you ever saw.'

Thomas Hughes
Tom Brown's Schooldays

'Kennet, swift, for silver eels renowned.'
And but that Evsham is so opulent and great
That thereby shee herself holds in the Sovereign seat,
This White-horse all the Vales of Britaine would or'ebeare,
And absolutely sit in the imperiall Chaire...

Michael Drayton
Poly-Olbion

'In autumn, on the skirts of Bagley Wood -
....most the gipsies by the turf-edged way
Pitch their smoked tents.'

Matthew Arnold
The Scholar Gipsy

'In Reading goal by Reading town
There is a pit of shame,
And in it lies a wretched man
Eaten by teeth of flame,
In a burning winding-sheet he lies,
And his grave has got no name.'

Oscar Wilde
The Ballad of Reading Gaol

LOCAL FOLKLORE

Wayland's Smithy

Wayland, an invisible smith, had a smithy in a megalithic chamber tomb on the Ridgeway. If a rider's horse lost a shoe, all he need do was leave the horse outside the barrow for a short while, with a small sum of money. When he returned, the money would be gone, and the horse would be newly shod.

Wayland, or Weland to the Anglo-Saxons, was reputedly a smith of supernatural skill who had been captured by the king and lamed so that he could not escape.

Herne the Hunter

'There is an old tale goes that Herne the hunter,

Sometime a keeper here in Windsor Forest,
Doth all the winter-time, at still midnight
Walk round about an oak, with great ragg'd horns,
And there he blasts the tree, and takes the battle,
And makes milch-kine yield blood and shakes a chain
In a most hideous and dreadful manner.'

The Merry Wives of Windsor

Herne was a keeper in the forest in the time of Elizabeth. Having committed a great offence, for which he feared to lose his station and fall into disgrace, he hanged himself from an oak tree in the forest (known as Herne's Oak). His ghost is said to appear as a presage of misfortune: it has been claimed that his ghost was seen before the economic crisis of 1931, the abdication of Edward VIII in 1936, the outbreak of war in 1939, and the death of George VI in 1952.

DISTINCTIVE FLAVOUR

Berkshire Bacon Pudding was a suet roly-poly, with a filling of strips of home cured Berkshire bacon, flavoured with sage and onion, and boiled or steamed for two hours.

Flat racing and steeplechasing take place at Ascot and Newbury. Lambourn is the centre of horse racing in Berkshire, and is world renowned.

Aldermaston Atomic Weapons Research Station is a somewhat controversial feature of the county.

Berkshire has many military institutions, the most notable being the **Royal Military Academy** at Sandhurst.

COUNTY DIARY

Second Tuesday after Easter:
Hocktide Ceremony, commemorating the gift of fishing and grazing rights to the town of Hungerford by John of Gaunt in 1364.
May: Royal Windsor Horse Show
June: Royal Ascot Race Meeting
June: Garter Service, Windsor Castle
July: Royal Windsor Rose Show
September:
Newbury Show

BUCKINGHAMSHIRE

COUNTY FACTS

Derivation of name: The farm of Bucca's people.
First Recorded: 1016 as Buccingahamscir
Motto: Vestigia nulla retrorsum (No backward step)
County Town: Aylesbury
Towns: Amersham, Aylesbury, Beaconsfield, Bletchley, Bourne End, Buckingham, Burnham, Chalfont St Giles, Chalfont St Peter, Chesham, Datchet, Denham, Eton, Gerrards Cross, High Wycombe, Linslade, Marlow, Milton Keynes, Newport Pagnell, Princes Risborough, Slough, Stony Stratford, Wendover, Wolverton, Wraysbury.

Local Government
Buckinghamshire County Council controls most of the county except for the south-east corner around Slough and Eton, governed by Berkshire County Council, and the town of Linslade under Bedfordshire County Council. There is a detached part of Buckinghamshire in Oxfordshire – the parish of Caversfield, under Oxfordshire County Council. There are seven district councils, one shared with Berkshire.

HISTORY

Before the Roman conquest, the region was inhabited by the powerful Catuvellauni tribe. The ancient Icknield Way passes through the county, as does the Roman Watling Street. In AD 571 the region was included in the Kingdom of Wessex.

The people were converted to Christianity by St Birin.

In the 9th century, the region was included in the Danelaw. In the early 10th century, Edward the Elder defeated the Danes at Bledlow Hill, and cut out two crosses in the chalk of the hill to commemorate his victories. Edward the Confessor used to hunt in Bernwood Forest.

John Wycliffe, the founder of Lollardism, was vicar of Ludgershall, and the movement became very popular in the county.

Eton College, which is the second oldest public school in the county, was founded in 1440 by Royal Charter of Henry VI. Its original 70 pupils were educated there free of charge.

Buckinghamshire was strongly Puritan, and supported the Parliamentary cause in the Civil War. At least 30 of the men concerned with the trial and execution of the King were connected with the county.

INDUSTRY PAST AND PRESENT

Present industries include light manufacturing, dairy farming and lace making. High Wycombe and Slough are major centres of high-tech commerce.

The Vale of Aylesbury was rich in corn fields, pasture land and cherry orchards. Sheep, cattle, pigs, ducks, and geese were raised in great numbers. Lace-making was a flourishing industry, particularly in Buckingham, Stony Stratford, Newport Pagnell and Olney. The paper industry was based in High Wycombe and Chesham. Straw-plaiting and associated industries were carried on, especially in the villages towards the Hertfordshire border. There was a major railway works at Wolverton. The county has been responsible for many triumphs and travesties produced by the British film industry – the great studios of Pinewood at Iver, and Denham Studios nearby are both in Buckinghamshire.

LANDMARKS

Chiltern Hills, with Coombe Hill, the highest point
Burnham Beeches
Ivinghoe Beacon
Vale of Aylesbury

TOPOGRAPHY INCLUDING RIVERS

There are gently rising sandy hills in the north and east, below which stretches the fertile Vale of Aylesbury (famous for the intensive raising of ducks) rising in places to quite considerable hills. To the south, the long chalk ridge of the wooded Chiltern Hills rises to around 800 feet, with Coombe Hill at 852 feet. The famous stretch of woodland known as Burnham Beeches lies in the far south of the county, of which the Thames forms the southern boundary with Berkshire. Middlesex provides the south-east boundary along the River Colne and the eastern border is shared with Hertfordshire and Bedfordshire. To the north is Northamptonshire and to the west Oxfordshire.

The highest point is Coombe Hill, Wendover, 852 feet.

Rivers: Ouse, Ray, Thames, Coln, Chess, Wye, Lovat, Lyde.

HIGH WYCOMBE

They are said to have held secret revels in the underground caves excavated in the park.

FAMOUS PEOPLE AND LOCAL CHARACTERS

John Hampden, the parliamentarian and civil war leader, lived in the county.

John Milton's father retired to Horton in 1632, and Milton spent six years there after leaving Cambridge, producing *L'Allegro, Il Penseroso, Arcades, Comus,* and *Lycidas.* He came to Chalfont St Giles to escape the Great Plague of London, and spent two years there.

William Penn, the Quaker, and founder of Pennsylvania, lived in the county.

Thomas Gray spent summers at Stoke Poges with his mother, where he wrote his famous *Elegy.*

William Cowper came to live in Olney, where he wrote some of his finest poetry and most of his letters. He and John Newton together wrote many of the Olney Hymns, such as 'God moves in a mysterious way', 'How sweet the name of Jesus sounds', and 'Glorious things of Thee are spoken'.

Percy Bysshe Shelley attended Eton College from 1804. He was frequently unhappy there, and nicknamed 'mad Shelley', and 'Shelley the Atheist'. In 1817 he settled in Marlow, where Mary Shelley wrote *Frankenstein.*

Benjamin Disraeli lived at Bradenham Manor as a boy. He and his wife bought Hughenden Manor, north of High Wycombe, in 1847, where he lived until his death. He wrote *Lothair* and *Endymion* there. Queen Victoria

MONUMENTS

Bekonscot model village, the oldest model village in the world, first opened to the public in 1929; the brainchild of Roland Callingham.

Chenies Manor, owned by the Russell family from the 16th century. A whole wing was built by John Russell to accommodate Henry VIII and his court.

Chicheley Hall, built in 1719-23 for Sir John Chester. In the Library, hinged panels swing back to reveal the bookshelves behind.

Claydon House, a 16th-century manor house owned by the Verney family, where Florence Nightingale often came to stay.

Cliveden, the country home of Lord Astor in the 1930s, and a famous political centre. There are magnificent views over the River Thames from the house.

Dorney Court, a pink brick Tudor manor house. The first pineapple ever grown in England is said to have been produced here.

Hughenden Manor, the home of Benjamin Disraeli from 1848 until his death in 1881.

Milton's Cottage, the sole surviving home of John Milton, who came here for two years to escape the Great Plague of London.

Stowe, a mansion and landscaped park created and developed for the Dukes of Buckinghamshire in the 17th and 18th centuries by Vanbrugh, Robert Adam, Gibbons, and William Kent. There are 32 classical temples in the garden.

Waddesdon Manor, a 19th-century French style mansion built for Baron de Rothschild, which houses a magnificent collection of Sèvres porcelain, 18th-century furniture, and paintings.

West Wycombe Park and Caves, a Palladian style mansion, built in the 18th century by Sir Francis Dashwood, founder of the notorious Hell-Fire Club, whose members were known as the knights of St Francis of Wycombe.

FINGEST CHURCH

sent a wreath of primroses to his funeral, and the day of his death, April 19, has since been known as Primrose Day.

G.K. Chesterton lived in Beaconsfield from 1909 until his death in 1936. He is buried in the Church of St Teresa of the Child Jesus.

ART AND LITERATURE

'Come, friendly bombs, and fall in Slough
It isn't fit for humans now,
There isn't grass to graze a cow
Swarm over, Death!'

John Betjeman
Slough

'Oh God the Olney Hymns abound
With words of Grace which Thou didst choose
And wet the elm above the hedge
Reflected in the winding Ouse.

Pour in my soul unemptied floods
That stand between the slopes of clay
Till deep beyond a deeper death
This Olney day is any day.'

John Betjeman
Olney Hymns

LOCAL FOLKLORE

The Fingest Ghost

In the 14th century, Bishop Henry de Burghwash, chancellor of England, enlarged his park by encroaching on the Fingest village common, much to the dismay of the villagers. After his death, his ghost, troubled by this deed, used to walk abroad, until the cause of the haunting was explained to the canons of Lincoln, who restored the land to the Fingest villagers. The ghost was never seen again.

North Marston

Sir John Schorne was rector of North Marston from 1290 to 1314, and was revered as a saint. He is reputed to have struck the ground with his staff, and caused a spring to burst out, whose water had healing properties: a glass of water drunk at night was said to cure a cold by the following morning. A well was built around the spring, and many pilgrimages were made to it, until the practice was stopped during the Reformation.

Sir John is also reputed to have tricked the

EDMUND WALLER'S TOMB, BEACONSFIELD

devil and trapped him in a boot, as the rhyme tells:

'Sir John Shorne
Gentleman born
Conjured the Devil into a boot.'

Bulstrode Camp, Gerrard's Cross

Bulstrode Camp is the largest hillfort in Buckinghamshire. William the Conqueror gave the manor belonging to the Shobbington family to one of his followers. The Norman came to claim it with armed men, but the Saxon Lord Shobbington put up a stiff resistance. Eventually, having no horses, he and his followers mounted on bulls and put the Normans to flight. William, much impressed by this brave tale, sent for Shobbington. He and his seven sons came to court astride their bulls. William was delighted by this, and allowed him to keep his estate. He gave him, and his heirs for posterity, the name of 'Bulstrode'.

Cymbeline's Castle

Cymbeline's Castle, a motte and bailey earthwork at Great Kimble, is reputed to have been built by the British King Cunobelin, the original of Shakespeare's 'Cymbeline'. It is said that anyone who runs round the earthwork seven times will conjure up the devil.

The Ostrich Inn

In Medieval times the inn at Colnbrook (a village which is half in Buckinghamshire, half in Middlesex) then known as the Crane, was run by a wicked couple named Jarman. They used to murder rich travellers staying at the inn by tipping them, whilst asleep, through a trap door into a vat of boiling ale. They would then pocket the traveller's wealth

themselves, giving it out that the traveller had left very early in the morning, before anyone else was up. Their evil doings were finally discovered after they had murdered their 60th victim: they were arrested and hanged in Windsor Forest.

DISTINCTIVE FLAVOUR

The Olney Pancake Race takes place every Shrove Tuesday, and has survived since the 15th century. The race is between the market place and the church, and the first housewife to complete the race receives a silver cup, and a kiss from a bellringer.

Aylesbury Game Pie, hardly made nowadays, was a Victorian culinary creation of considerable richness, being a rough terrine of hare, chicken, pheasant, veal, bacon, brandy and spices. It could be eaten either hot or cold.

SHERINGTON CHURCH

COUNTY DIARY

May:
 Weighing the Mayor Ceremony, High Wycombe
June:
 Amateur Regatta, Marlow
September:
 Bucks County Show, Aylesbury
November 11:
 Firing the Fenny Poppers - a 6-gun salute, Fenny Stratford

CAMBRIDGESHIRE

COUNTY FACTS

Derivation of name: Cambridge is a mixture of both Anglo-Saxon and Brittonic origin. Originally called Grantebrige, the bridge over the River Granta. Possibly due to a misunderstanding the name of the river Cambridge city stands on has gradually changed from the Granta as it was before the Norman Conquest to the Cam. Granta is a Celtic name whose meaning is associated with swamps or marshes but by the 16th century it had become the Cam, with one of its tributaries becoming the Granta. Cam is a popular Celtic river name as the word means crooked or winding.

First Recorded: 1010 as Grantabrycgscir

Motto: Per undas, per agros (Through waves, through fields)

County Town: Cambridge

Towns: Burwell, Cambridge, Chatteris, Cottenham, Ely, Fulbourn, Girton, Great Shelford, Histon, Littleport, March, Soham, Wisbech, Whittlesey.

Local Government

Cambridgeshire County Council (including the whole of the county of Huntingdonshire together with Northamptonshire's Soke of Peterborough) and four district councils.

HISTORY

The region was inhabited by the Iceni tribe, who were defeated by the Roman invaders. After invasion by the Saxons, and then by the Danes, Cambridgeshire was created in the 10th century by Edward the Elder and Ethelfleda. Hereward the Wake established his refuge camp at Ely, and held out against the besieging Normans for a considerable time.

In the 13th century, schools were established which laid the foundations of Cambridge as a great seat of learning. They developed into the university. The first college, Peterhouse, was founded in 1254 through the gift of Bishop Hugh de Balsham of Ely.

During the Barons' Wars, the barons captured Cambridge Castle, driving out King John, who took refuge in Norfolk, losing first his baggage, in the Wash, and then his life.

Cambridge played a great part in the Reformation: Erasmus taught Greek there in 1511; Tyndale, Cranmer, Latimer and others, known as the Cambridge Reformers, used to meet at the White Horse Inn, discussing doctrines which were unacceptable to the Establishment.

Thomas Cromwell was Chancellor of the University.

After his defeat, Charles I was held prisoner in Cambridge.

A great fair was held annually at Sturbridge, which attracted merchants from all over Europe. In the 17th and 18th centuries it grew in importance to become one of the greatest in Europe.

ISLE OF ELY

An Act of Henry VIII described the Isle of Ely as a County Palatine, yet another of 1547 refers to the Isle of Ely in the County of Cambridge. The Isle's County status has never been clear, it had its own Lord Lieutenant under Edward VI, its own assizes, but *not* its own Sheriff which a county of a city like Bristol had. The historical facts are that the Isle was *not* a County let alone County Palatine. It was however a liberty or soke of great age, perhaps 8th century, certainly by 970. In 1889 it was made an administrative County, but still as a division of the County of Cambridge; therefore the Isle was never a real County but only a local government

TOPOGRAPHY INCLUDING RIVERS

Cambridgeshire, on the western border of East Anglia, is bordered by Lincolnshire and Northamptonshire to the north, Norfolk and Suffolk to the east, Essex and Hertfordshire to the south, and Bedfordshire and Huntingdonshire to the west.

Most of the county consists of the distinctive flat plain and fenland of East Anglia, drained by artificial rivers leading to the Wash. Ely Cathedral stands on a slight hill (the Isle of Ely was surrounded by water in medieval times, before the reclamation of the land by drainage). In the south, there are low, undulating chalk downs, which include the Gogmagog Hills. The highest point is Great Chishill, 480 feet.

Rivers: Cam, Ouse, Nene.

county. The creation and later abolition of the Isle of Ely County Council had no effect on this ancient area's name.

INDUSTRY PAST AND PRESENT

Tourism and a canny exploitation of the financial rewards of a world centre for scientific research are valued present industries. Before technology, the county had a flourishing wool industry in the 14th century, and became noted for its worsted cloth. In the 16th century, much barley was grown for malt, and willow baskets were manufactured in the fen district. The 18th century saw extensive cultivation of saffron, and paper was manufactured near Sturbridge.

LANDMARKS

The Fens
The Gog Magog Hills
Wandlebury Ring - an Iron Age hill fort on the crest of the Gog Magog Hills.

MONUMENTS

Cambridge University, the second oldest university in England. The first college, Peterhouse, was founded in 1254.
Ely Cathedral, towering above the flat fenland, was begun in 1083. In 1322 the Norman tower collapsed and was replaced by a grander, octagonal tower unique in medieval English architecture.
Anglesey Abbey, part medieval, part Tudor house, with 20th century additions by Lord Fairhaven, who purchased it in 1926. Amongst other treasures, it houses a collection of prints and drawings of Windsor Castle spanning 350 years.
King's College Chapel, founded in 1446 by Henry VI, was intended to be austere, but was completed by Tudor monarchs who were strangers to restraint, and thus is encrusted with stone Tudor roses the size of roundabouts..
Wimpole Hall, built by Sir Thomas Chicheley in the 17th century. The Hall was bequeathed to the National Trust by the last owner, Mrs Elsie Bambridge, daughter of Rudyard Kipling.

FAMOUS PEOPLE AND LOCAL CHARACTERS

Spenser, Milton, Wordsworth, Coleridge, Byron, and **Tennyson**, all went to Cambridge University.
Charles Kingsley was Professor of Modern History at Magdalene College for 9 years.
Sir Arthur Quiller-Couch became King Edward VII Professor of English Literature at Jesus College in 1912.
John Maynard Keynes, diplomat and economist, was born in Cambridge in 1883.
Rupert Brooke lived in Grantchester, made famous in his poem, for two years.

Local Characters

Thomas Hobson (circa 1544-1631) was a Cambridge carrier, who gave his name to the phrase 'Hobson's Choice', because he would only lend out his horses in strict rotation. He later became Mayor of Cambridge.

ART AND LITERATURE

'For Cambridge people rarely smile
Being urban, squat, and packed with guile
They love the Good, they worship Truth,
They laugh uproariously in Youth.'
      Rupert Brooke
      The Old Vicarage, Grantchester

'For England's the one land, I know,
Where men with splendid hearts may go
And Cambridgeshire, of all England,
The shire for men who understand.'
      Ibid

'The white of windy Cambridge courts, the cobbles brown and dry,
The gold of plaster Gothic with ivy overgrown,
The apple-red, the silver fronts, the wide green flats and high,
The yellowing elm-trees circled out on islands of their own –

Oh, here behold all colours change that catch the flying sky
To waves of pearly light that heave along the shafted stone.'
      John Betjeman
      Sunday Morning, King's Cambridge (1954)

LOCAL FOLKLORE

Wandlebury Ring

Tradition has it that if a warrior enters this hill fort alone at dead of night, crying 'knight to knight, come forth!', a mounted warrior will appear and fight him. One Osbert Fitzhugh tested out this legend, and on his issuing the challenge, a ghostly knight came out to meet him. In the ensuing fight, Osbert unhorsed his adversary, and seized the horse's bridle, to lead it away. At this, the ghostly knight leapt up, threw his spear at Osbert, striking him on the thigh, and vanished. Osbert led the beautiful horse home, but at day-break next morning, the horse broke free from its reins and galloped away, never to be seen again.
Every year, on the anniversary of the fight, Osbert's wound would start to bleed afresh.

Whirling Sunday

Whirling Sunday, the 5th in Lent, used to be celebrated in Leverington up to the last century, when whirling, or whirlwind, cakes were made for the village feast. This custom commemorated an old lady of the village who, while making cakes for a feast one Sunday in Lent, was whisked off over the church steeple in a whirlwind by the devil.

South Porch of King's College Chapel.

Cambridge University gained unfortunate renown as the breeding ground for spies – Philby, Blunt, Burgess and McLean all studied there before embarking on their infamous careers.

The mile along **the Backs at Cambridge** is said to be the most beautiful mile in the world.

Cambridge Science Park, the local equivalent of 'Silicone Valley' generates vast wealth from its high-powered, high-tech industries.

As befits a seat of learning, Cambridge has alcoholic traditions. **The Cambridge Ale Cup** dilutes water and spices with ale and sherry. It is presented to its startled consumer with a garnish of nutmeg-flavoured toast. **Cambridge Hot Milk Punch** is not as mild as it sounds, as it adds copious amounts of rum and brandy to its titular ingredient.

In a recent **guide for Canadian tourists**, the Cam is likened to a 'large irrigation ditch'.

COUNTY DIARY

July:	Rose Fair, Wisbech

Hereward the Wake

From his base at the Abbey of Ely, Hereward the Wake led a band of Saxon nobles holding out against William the Conqueror. Ely was on an island at the time, and three times Hereward foiled William's plans to build a causeway across the water. The third time, Hereward, riding towards William's camp, met a potter on the way and exchanged clothes with him. In this disguise, he entered the camp, and overheard the Normans' plans. Hereward's men were waiting in the reeds as William and his soldiers proceeded along the causeway and they set fire to these reeds, so that William's men were engulfed by the flames. Eventually the monks grew tired of the siege, and let the Normans in by a secret way. Hereward escaped with a small band of men, but he still had enemies: he was finally betrayed by a chaplain, and 16 Normans broke into his hiding place and attacked him. Nevertheless, Hereward slew them all, and only succumbed at last when four more soldiers arrived and stabbed him in the back.

The Wounded Swan

Seven swans used to fly over one of the Cambridgeshire fens, and the local people were afraid of them; anyone catching sight of them would run home and bar their doors. It happened that during a great famine in the countryside, a bold young fowler, desperate for food, shot one of the swans in the wing. When he went to pick it up, the other six attacked him and he fought them off with an iron knife. He took the swan home and bound up its wing. That night, the swan turned into a beautiful maiden, and he took her for his wife. Each night, the six swans flew round his hut and beat at his door. The fowler laughed, but secretly he was afraid. After seven days her wounded arm healed, and he realized that it was growing feathers. As he watched, his wife turned into a swan and attacked him. He ran out of the hut, and the other six were waiting for him. They flew with him to the middle of the fen, held him down and drowned him. The seven swans flew seven times round the fen, and then flew away and were never seen again.

CHESHIRE

COUNTY FACTS

Derivation of name: Chester means the camp or fort. The English originally called it Leganchester meaning the camp of the legions. This was then shortened to Chester, a corruption of the Latin word 'castra'.
First Recorded: 980 as Legeceasterscir
Motto: Jure et dignitate gladii (By the right and dignity of the sword)
County Town: Chester
Towns: Altrincham, Bebington, Birkenhead, Bramhall, Bromborough, Cheadle, Chester, Congleton, Crewe, Dukinfield, Ellesmere Port, Hale, Hazel Grove, Heswall, Hoylake, Hyde, Knutsford, Macclesfield, Marple, Nantwich, Neston, New Brighton, Northwich, Romiley, Runcorn, Sale, Stockport, Wallasey, West Kirby, Wilmslow, Winsford. Chester is a county of a city unto itself.

Local Government
A complex local government set up puts the greater area of the county under Cheshire County Council (which also includes Lancashire's Warrington and Widnes), but the two most populous areas around Wirral and the north-east of the county are split into a number of metropolitan boroughs. Wirral metropolitan borough encompasses all of Cheshire on the peninsula and once formed a part of the now defunct Merseyside County Council. To the north-east the metropolitan boroughs of Manchester, Tameside, Trafford and Stockport take in both Cheshire and Lancashire territory. All four boroughs once formed part of the Greater Manchester County Council which now, like Merseyside County Council, has been abolished. The only other large part of Cheshire under another county council control is the extreme north-east panhandle of Cheshire centred on Tintwistle and the Pennine peak of Black Hill which is controlled by Derbyshire County Council.

HISTORY
Battle of Chester 615: Aethelfrith, King of Northumbria, defeated Solomon, son of Cynan, King of Powys.
Richard II elevated the county to a principality, and styled himself Prince of Chester, although this ceased on his death in 1399.
1583 – Most of Nantwich was destroyed by fire. A nationwide collection was started to help rebuild the town. Queen Elizabeth I headed the subscription list with £2,000.
1642 – The Battle of Tarporley
1644 – The Siege of Chester, held by the Royalists.
1654 – The Battle of Rowton Moor, 24 September, was a defeat for the Royalists. King Charles rode off into Wales.
1659 – Cheshire rising of Royalists under Sir George Booth took place.

INDUSTRY PAST AND PRESENT
Today, Cheshire boasts dairying, market gardening, chemicals, high-tech activities and varied heavy industry.
In the past, the Wiches (Middlewich, Northwich, and Nantwich) were a major salt producing area – salt-pits were worked in Roman times. From the 17th century, mines were dug to extract the salt which is not yet exhausted.
Macclesfield and Stockport had coal seams, and a wet climate, which made them for a time the textile centre of the world.
In 1811 there were 17 houses in Birkenhead, and a total population of 105. By 1831 the population was 2,569, and by 1877, 77,000. The industries responsible for its growth were the docks, shipbuilding, boilermaking, flourmilling and tanning.
A silk mill was established in Macclesfield by Charles Roe in 1756.
Port Sunlight, built by Viscount Leverhulme, was named after Sunlight Soap, at which factory his employees worked.

LANDMARKS
Cheshire Plain
Delamere Forest
Alderley Edge
Frodsham Hill
Helsby Hill

MONUMENTS
Beeston Castle, magnificently sited on a sandstone escarpment overlooking the Cheshire Plain.

TOPOGRAPHY INCLUDING RIVERS
Cheshire is bordered by Lancashire to the north, Derbyshire to the east, Staffordshire to the south, Flintshire and Denbighshire to the west, with the Wirral peninsular in the north west sandwiched between the Mersey and the Dee. Mainly an alluvial plain, causing its rich pasture, Cheshire becomes surprisingly mountainous as it rises to the Pennines and Derbyshire's Peak District. Sandstone escarpments rise dramatically from the plain, most noticeably at Helsby, Frodsham and Beeston. Much of the northern border is composed of the basin of the Mersey, now drained and used for farming and industry. The highest point is Black Hill, 1908 feet.
Rivers: Dee, Mersey, Weaver, Dane.

Chester Cathedral, formerly the Benedictine Abbey of St Werbergh, most celebrated for its medieval choir stalls and misericords.

Chester Castle, surprisingly a severe 19th-century complex by the architect Harrison.

Chester City Walls, amongst the most complete in Britain, but lacking medieval gates.

Little Moreton Hall, the epitome of the 16th-century 'black and white' house.

Tatton Park, a National Trust property by Wyatt, in a restrained classical style.

Jodrell Bank, Britain's premier radio telescope, visible for 40 miles.

FAMOUS PEOPLE AND LOCAL CHARACTERS

Thomas Harrison was born in Nantwich. He was a Major General in the Parliamentary army, who led the saints in the Barebones Parliament. He was one of the signatories to Charles I's death warrant, and was in his turn executed for it.

Lady Emma Hamilton, mistress of Lord Nelson, was born in Ness in 1765.

Field Marshal Viscount Combermere, known as the 'Cheshire hero', died in 1865.

Mrs Elizabeth Gaskell (1810-1865) was brought up by her aunt on the Heath at Knutsford. Cranford is modelled on the town, and many of its inhabitants.

Dr James Prescott Joule (1818-1889) is buried in Sale Church. His work on the theory of heat gave us the 'Joule', Joule's equivalent, Joule's Law, and the Joule-Thomson effect. Before he died, Joule said, "I believe I have done two or three little things, but nothing to make a fuss about."

Charles Lutwidge Dodgson, better known as Lewis Carroll (1832-1898), was born in Daresbury. In All Saints church, the stained glass east window shows his characters from Alice in Wonderland - the white rabbit, the Dodo, the Mad Hatter, etc.

Local Characters

Robert Nixon, the 'Cheshire Prophet', was born circa 1467 at Over. The story goes that, while ploughing on 22 August 1485, he fell into a stupor, and when he awoke, told of a great battle, and that the King had been overthrown. That was the day of the Battle of Bosworth. The new king, Henry VII, commanded that Nixon be brought to court. He wept at the news, saying he would be starved to death at court. The King ordered

that he be kept in the kitchen so that he would never starve, but after a while the cooks were so irritated by his 'licking and picking at the meat' that they locked him in a cupboard – where he was forgotten, and starved to death.

At Thornton-le-Moors in the 16th century, the rector of the church, **Bernard Gilpin**, known as the 'Northern Apostle', was condemned to be burnt for his reformatory views. On his slow journey to the stake in London, the news came that Queen Mary had died. With a new queen came different religious circumstances, and Bernard was freed, so he returned home in triumph!

In Middlewich Church is the gravestone of **Anne Barker**, who died in 1778; the inscription reads:
> *'Some have children, some have none,*
> *But here lies the mother of twenty-one.'*

James Price, who robbed the Warrington Mail in 1790, was hanged on Trafford Heath and his remains stayed there for thirty years. In his skull was found a robin's nest - hence the rhyme:
> *'Oh! James Price deserved his fate,*
> *Naught but Robbing in his pate.'*

Maria Rathbone died in 1821 at the age of eight. An inscription on her gravestone at Prestbury reads:
> *'Having missed her way from a neighbouring shop she wandered the same day through various townships. Scoffed at by some and scoured by others till night, and a severe storm of thunder; snow; and wind put period to her travels and existence both: near the Crown Inn in Peover: being found in a plain open field, less than one mile whence she was last seen: after a painful search far and wide for 25 days.*
>
> *Well might Heaven's thunder rend the air*
> *To see such monsters dwelling there*
> *Thrice hapless child was doomed to roam*
> *And leave thy every friend at home.'*

ART AND LITERATURE

'Cheshire born, Cheshire bred, strong i' th' arm and quick i' th' head.'

(Traditional)

Delamere Forest in the 17th century:
'...a very delectable place for situation, and maintaineth not only a convenient being and preservation for his majesty's deer, both red and fallow, whereof there is no small store, but also a great relief to the neighbouring borders and

townships round about it; yielding plenty of pasture in the vales; wood upon the hills' fearn and heath...in the plains...'

'In her [Mrs Gaskell's] hours of childish sorrow and trouble she used to run away from her aunt's house across the Heath and hide herself in one of its many green hollows, finding comfort in the silence, and in the company of birds and insects and natural things.'

'An island farm, mid seas of corn
Swayed by the wandering breath of morn
The happy spot where I was born.'
Lewis Carroll, on Daresbury

'Middlewych is a pretty town
Seated in a valley
With a church and market cross
And eke a bowling alley.
All the men are loyal there;
Pretty girls are plenty;
Church and King, and down with the Rump,
There's not such a town in twenty.'

'Our ale here at Sandback being no less famous than that of Derby for a true nappe. And I have heard men of deep experience in the element conntend for the worth of it, that for true dagger stuff, it should give place to none.'
Webb, circa 1620

LOCAL FOLKLORE

Leon Gawer

According to medieval legend, Chester was built by 'Leon Gawer, a might strong giant; which builded caves and dungeons, many a one, No goodly buildings, ne proper, ne pleasant.'

Legend has it that two boys, aged ten and eight, the heirs of Prince Madoc, Lord of Dinas Bran, were drowned in the River Dee by Farndon Bridge, on the border with Wales. Travellers crossing the bridge late at night claim to hear the ghosts of the young boys:
> *Belated travellers quake with fear*
> *And spur their starting horse*
> *For childish shrieks they say they hear*
> *As Farndon's Bridge they cross.*

Beeston Castle tradition:
> *Though now in ruined heaps thy bulwarks lie,*
> *Revolving time shall raise those bulwarks high;*
> *If faith to ancient prophecies be due,*
> *Then Edward shall thy pristine state renew.*

Legend of Alderley Edge

A farmer was taking his fine white horse to market one day when he was waylaid by a wizard, who offered to buy it. The farmer refused, and continued on his way. But he couldn't sell the horse at market. On his way back home, he met the wizard again, who took him across the Edge to a large rock. He touched the rock with his wand, and 'immediately there arose before his eyes a ponderous pair of iron gates'. The gates opened, and inside the farmer saw a long succession of caves in which were lying a 'countless number of men and horses, the latter all milk white, fast asleep', waiting, as the wizard explained, to 'save their country in a future crucial battle' when 'George the son of George shall reign'. The farmer gave the wizard his white horse, and for reward received some of the treasure that was heaped in the caverns. He was then sent on his way home.

DISTINCTIVE FLAVOUR

Races were held at **Chester Racecourse**, formerly known as the Roodee, on St George's Day (23 April) from at least 1512, for a silver bell provided by the saddlers' guild. In 1612 it was enacted that 'the ryders shall not offer one to another any foule play in their ridinge upon payne of ymprisonment'.

Leasowe Races were held on the wastes of the Wirral peninsular in the 16th to the 18th centuries. In 1723 a consortium agreed to provide prize money of 20 guineas for the May races - making it then one of the most valuable events in the racing calendar. The races were subsequently moved to Melling near Liverpool, and then to Aintree.

The Heath, Bunbury village, used to be the site of the **Bunbury Wakes** held on the Sunday before the feast of St Boniface (5 June): 'Riot and dissipation' were 'always the order of the day on these occasions'.

There is a racing circuit at **Oulton Park**.

A CHESTER ROW

Chester is commemorated in a number of dishes. The most famous, **Chester buns**, are comparatively plain. **Chester pudding** is a suet confection, steamed and served with piquant blackcurrant jam.

Cheshire cheese comes in three colours, white, red and blue. The latter is particularly fine, combining a discrete 'blueness' with a mellow crumbly cheese.

The people of the **Wirral peninsular** dislike hearing it referred to as simply 'The Wirral'. As far as they are concerned it is Wirral *tout court*.

COUNTY DIARY

January:	Holly Holy Day (re-enactment of the Battle of Namptwyche)
May:	Royal May Day Festival, Knutsford
May:	Regatta, and Beating Retreat, Chester
June:	Cheshire County Show, Tabley, Knutsford
July:	South Cheshire Show, Nantwich
October:	Soul Caking Play, Antrobus village

CORNWALL

KERNOW

COUNTY FACTS

Derivation of name: The Welsh in Cornavia. From the latin 'Cornu', meaning horn. West of the Dunnoii (Devon) was the Corneu to the Britons – the land of the horn. The second syllable is derived from the Old English 'wahl', meaning foreign, as that was how the English called the Britons or the Welsh.

First Recorded: 891 as Cornwalam

Motto: One and all

County Town: Truro

Towns: Bodmin, Bude, Callington, Camborne, Falmouth, Fowey, Hayle, Helston, Launceston, Lostwithiel, Marazion, Mevagissey, Newlyn, Newquay, Penryn, Perranporth, Porthleven, Redruth, St Austell, St Blazey, St Ives, St Just, Saltash, Stratton, Tintagel, Torpoint, Truro, Wadebridge.

Local Government
Cornwall County Council and six District Councils.

HISTORY

As long ago as 445 BC, Cornish tin is known to have been worked, and traded as far afield as Greece and Phoenicia. The Roman occupation did not extend into Cornwall, and the Celtic inhabitants remained pagan until about the 5th century, when Irish and Welsh saints came to preach Christianity.

Cornwall was part of the British kingdom of Damnonia, which included Devon and Somerset, and the British resisted the English invasion for a considerable time, until in the 9th century, Egbert King of Wessex marched into Cornwall and it was merged into the powerful kingdom of Wessex. The Cornish then allied themselves with the Viking invaders to retain their independence, but were ultimately forced to surrender to Alfred the Great. After conquest by Athelstan in 936, English landowners were established throughout the region.

William the Conqueror made the shire an earldom, and in 1336 Edward III created it a Duchy, from which time it has been held by the heir apparent, or Prince of Wales, or, in the absence of such, by the Crown.

Stannary courts had existed in Cornwall since time immemorial, but they were confirmed under charter by King Edmund. The Stannary Parliament, as it was known, met at Truro, and its jurisdiction embraced the tin mines and all mining transactions carried on in the county.

After the Battle of Barnet in the Wars of the Roses, the Earl of Oxford fled and sought sanctuary on St Michael's Mount. There he raised the Lancastrian standard, and fought so bravely that the victorious Yorkists made peace with him and granted him a pardon.

Cornish opposition to the first English Book of Common Prayer introduced by Cranmer grew to armed rebellion in 1549, when the people of the county declared, 'We, the Cornyshe men, whereof certain of us understand no English, utterly refuse this new service'. Although the Prayer Book was introduced, concessions had to be made: even as late as 1640, the vicar of Feock had to administer the sacrament in Cornish, because his older parishioners had no English.

Two important battles in the Civil War were fought within the county, which was staunchly Royalist – Braddock Down and Shatton, at both of which the Royalists were victorious. Sir Bevill Grenville was the soul of the Royalist cause – 'the most generally loved man in Cornwall'.

In 1745 Hugh, Viscount Falmouth, raised a regiment of Cornishmen at his own expense to fight the Pretender. He was made Captain of the Yeomen of the Guard to George II and George III.

In 1981, the Penlee lifeboat, with a crew of

TOPOGRAPHY INCLUDING RIVERS

Cornwall, at the south-westernmost tip of England, is bordered in the east by Devon, and surrounded on all other sides by the sea. Eighty miles long, the county is like an irregular triangle or horn, becoming narrower towards the west until it is only 5 miles wide between Mounts Bay and St Ives. The underlying rock is mainly slatey, with four great masses of granite rising up from it. The hills and bogs of Bodmin Moor lie in central east Cornwall, with further hills running to the east. The coastline, which stretches for 250 miles, is rich and varied, with small rocky coves, known as 'porths', wide expanses of sandy beach popular with holiday-makers, and high, rugged cliffs, which are dramatic on the northern, Atlantic coast. The south coast is softer, and broken by inlets and river estuaries which wind inland from the sea. The Lizard, forming the 'heel' of Cornwall, is the most southerly point in mainland England, and Land's End the most westerly. The Isles of Scilly lie 30 miles west of Land's End. The highest point is Brown Willy, 1375 feet. Rivers: Tamar (forming the boundary with Devon), Camel, Fal, Fowey, Truro, Kenwyn, Allen.

Mousehole men, was lost attempting to save a freighter in difficulty. All hands were drowned.

INDUSTRY PAST AND PRESENT

Tourism, dairying, market gardening, fishing, china clay, mining, ship repairing, civil engineering all contribute to the current economy.

Tin and copper were mined in the county from earliest recorded times. In the 19th century Cornwall was known as the 'Copper Kingdom'. Fishing has long been the livelihood of the inhabitants of the coastal villages, and pilchards were the most important fish taken in Cornish waters. There was a huge pilchard industry until early this century. Smuggling was a flourishing industry in the 18th and 19th centuries; Mevagissey specialized in building fast sailing vessels for the trade.

LANDMARKS

Bodmin Moor

Land's End

The Lizard

St Michael's Mount, a rocky mount, around 250 feet high, cut off from the mainland at high tide. It is supposedly part of the lost kingdom of Lyonnesse.

'Rough Tow', 1,312 feet high

Dosmary Pool, an almost circular lake, a mile in circumference, and nearly 900 feet above sea-level, in the middle of Bodmin Moor. This is the lake into which Sir Bedivere is supposed to have flung King Arthur's sword Excalibur.

Cornwall coastal footpath, which follows the coast the full length of the county.

Falmouth dockyard

MONUMENTS

Tintagel Castle, supposedly the site of the birthplace of King Arthur. The earliest parts of the ruin date from circa 1145. By the 16th century, the central part connecting the inner ward with the lower ward had been washed into the sea.

Cotehele. One of the finest medieval and Tudor manor houses in England, dating from 1485-1539.

Lanhydrock. Begun in the 17th century by Lord Robartes, the house, overlooking the River Fowey, was largely rebuilt following a fire in 1881. There is a 116 feet long picture gallery.

Trerice. An Elizabethan manor house rebuilt by John Arundell in 1571, on the site of an older house.

Pendennis Castle, Falmouth, built in 1548 by Henry VIII as a link in his coastal defence system.

Restormel Castle. The remains of the 12th-century castle stand on a hill overlooking the River Fowey, surrounded by a 60 feet wide moat.

Truro Cathedral, a 19th-century Gothic pile.

FAMOUS PEOPLE AND LOCAL CHARACTERS

Sir Richard Grenville, MP for Cornwall in 1571 and 1584, was second-in-command of the Revenge, which in 1591, off the Azores, attempted to fight single-handed against a Spanish fleet of 53 ships. Sir Richard died of wounds sustained during the bravely fought battle.

Sir Johathan Trelawney, a member of a very old Cornish family, was born in Pelynt in 1650. He was consecrated Bishop of Bristol in 1685. He was one of the seven bishops imprisoned in the Tower of London by James II in 1688 for opposing the King. The support he received from his fellow Cornishmen is celebrated in Hawker's *Song of the Western Men*. The seven bishops were later triumphantly acquitted and released.

John Wesley, the founder of Methodism, visited Cornwall frequently from 1743; a huge number of Cornish folk became converts.

John Opie, historical and portrait painter, was born in St Agnes in 1761. He was known as the 'Cornish wonder'; Northcote, a rival, said of him, 'Other artists paint to live; Opie lives to paint'.

Richard Trevithick was born in Illogan in 1771. He went to school in Camborne, where he was a 'slow and obstinate scholar'. He invented the high-pressure steam engine.

Henry Trengrouse, a Cornishman, invented the rocket-firing apparatus for life-saving. He was known as the 'sailor's friend'.

Sir Humphry Davy, famous for his invention of the safety lamp, was born in Penzance in 1778.

Stephen Hawker was the poet vicar of Morwenstowe. A high churchman, he was yet much loved by his parishioners. Amongst his works are the *Cornish Ballads*.

Sir John Couch Adams, the astronomer, was born in Laneast in 1819. He was given credit for the discovery of the planet Neptune, simultaneously with the Frenchman, Leverrier.

Sir Arthur Quiller-Couch, who wrote under the pseudonym 'Q', was born in Bodmin in 1863, and lived in Fowey for many years.

The county has produced several statesmen: **Sir John Eliot**, 17th-century champion of Parliamentary government; **Sidney, Earl of Godolphin**, who became Lord High Treasurer under Queen Anne; and **Sir William Molesworth**, 19th-century Colonial Secretary.

Local Characters

Nancy Humphries lived in the neighbourhood of St Ives, and used to deliver fish to many of the surrounding parishes. She carried it in a basket on her head, and would travel up to 20 miles in a day, carrying over a hundredweight on her head. When she died, in 1826, her obituary notice read, 'Her passion for ardent spirits was extreme, and its indulgence is supposed to have hastened her end.'

ART AND LITERATURE

'St Michael's Mount, who does not know?
That wards the Western Coast.'
Spenser

'From Padstow Point to Lundy Light
Is a sailor's grave by day or night.'
(Local saying)

Most of Cornwall was Royalist during the Civil War. Charles I wrote a letter to 'ye inhabitants of ye county of Cornwall', full of praise for 'ye extraordinary merits of our county of Cornwall, of their Zeal for the Crown, and for ye defence of our person', as well as for their 'great and eminent courage'.

'The coast from Tintagel to Hartland is almost unrivalled for grandeur. The restless Atlantic is ever thundering on this iron-walled coast. The roar can be heard ten miles inland; flakes of foam are picked up after a storm at Holsworthy…the swell comes unbroken from Labrador to hurl itself against this coast and to be shivered into foam on its iron cuirass.'

Baring-Gould
Life of Hawker (1876)

'The Cornish love…the circuitous, shunning ever the direct statement, dealing much in qualifications and cautious ambiguities.'

Charles Lee

'There are more saints in Cornwall than in Heaven.'

(Anon)

Walter de la Mare thought Cornwall 'a haunted land', and vowed that he would 'never venture to stay there again'.

'You can imagine how the sea swings to and fro between the cliffs, foams, swells, beats and baffles itself against the steep faces of the rock. I should guess it must be unique in England.'

Swinburne, on Boscastle
(Letter to Mary Gordon, 2 September 1864)

'More than in gardened Surrey, nature spills A wealth of heather, kidney-vetch and squills Over these long-defended Cornish hills.

From today's calm, the lane's enclosing green Leads inland to a usual Cornish scheme – Slate cottages with sycamore between,

Small fields and tellymasts and wires and poles With, as the everlasting ocean rolls, Two chapels built for half a hundred souls.'

John Betjeman
Cornish Cliffs (1966)

'The general conditions in Cornwall for man, beast or crops are such as few countries are favoured with, and make our county a veritable Elysium, compared with less fortunate parts of the British Isles.'

Tregoning Hooper

'To Scrooge's horror, looking back, he saw the last of the land, a frightful range of rocks, behind them, and his ears were deafened by the thundering of water, as it rolled, and roared, and raged among the dreadful caverns it had worn, and fiercely tried to undermine the earth.'

Charles Dickens
Land's End, in A Christmas Carol

Queen Elizabeth I said of her Cornish Gentlemen that they were 'all born Courtiers, with a becoming confidence'.

'For my part I can make nothing of [the Cornish] at all. A division of races, older and more original than that of Babel, keeps this close, esoteric family apart from neighbouring Englishmen. Not even a Red Indian seems more foreign in my eyes. This is one of lessons of travel - that some of the strangest races dwell next door to you at home.'

Robert Louis Stevenson

'And have they fixed the where and when? And shall Trelawny die? Here's twenty thousand Cornish men Will know the reason why!'

Robert Stephen Hawker
Song of the Western Men

LOCAL FOLKLORE

The Padstow Mermaid

A greedy and blustering Padstow man fired a shot from his longbow and mortally wounded a mermaid who had been swimming in the bay. As she lay dying, she cursed the harbour, and foretold that its doom would be caused by sand. Even as she spoke, the sand began to drift in relentlessly from the sea, choking up the harbour and putting an end to the flourishing trade it had previously enjoyed.

St Petroc

St Petroc came to Padstow from Wales to preach Christianity. The local men working in the fields were hot and thirsty from their labours, and said they would listen to him once they had slaked their thirst, although they had no water. The holy man struck a rock with his staff, and a fountain of fresh water sprang out from it, to the astonishment of the labourers. It flows to this day.

The Giant Tregeagle

As punishment for his evil ways, the giant Tregeagle was doomed forever to crouch over Dozmary Pool on Bodmin Moor, emptying it with a limpet shell. His thankless task was compounded by being forced to use a shell with a hole in it; as fast as he emptied, the water trickled back into the dark pool…

King Arthur

Many tales are told in Cornwall of the legendary King Arthur. Tintagel Castle is said to be the place where he was conceived and born.

King Uther Pendragon fell in love with Ygraine, the wife of Duke Gorlois of Cornwall, who lived at Tintagel Castle. Declaring that Gorlois had been disloyal to him, Uther's army attacked Gorlois' army outside the castle, and during the battle, Uther, disguised by Merlin's art as Gorlois himself, slipped into the castle. There he found and made love to Ygraine: she conceived a son, Arthur. Meanwhile, Gorlois was killed in the battle, and Uther then married Ygraine. Although technically illegitimate, Arthur was acknowledged as Uther's heir, and under the guidance of the wizard Merlin, Arthur united the warring factions of the land into one Kingdom.

The Silken Shawl

After a series of lean years, the men of Newlyn took to piracy to earn a living. They forced all their victims to walk the plank. Aboard one of the ships they attacked was the Captain's wife, who was wearing a beautiful silken shawl. One of the pirates snatched it from her just as she fell overboard, and he took it home to his wife, who knew nothing of his piracy.

The next Sunday she was admiring the shawl in her mirror, when she saw reflected in the glass the pale and tragic face of the drowned woman, pointing at her shawl. The pirate's wife was so terrified by the apparition that she went quite mad, and died soon afterwards. No one knows what became of the silken shawl…

The Crowza Stones

St Just lived at Penwith, and, finding little to do there, except to offer prayers for the tinners and fishermen, he once went to visit St Keverne in his hermitage near the Lizard headland. The two saints feasted and drank together, and St Just's envy was aroused by the beauty of the chalice from which he was drinking his rich wine. With many professions of undying friendship, he pledged St Keverne to return his visit, and took his way home. Very soon St Keverne missed his famous cup and, after long search had been made, he could not but believe that his visitor had made away with it; so he decided to pursue him, punish him, and get the chalice back. As he passed over Crowza Down he picked up a few of the 'Ironstone' pebbles which lie on its surface, put them in his pockets, and hastened on his way. Soon afterwards, he caught sight of St Just and, raging inwardly, called to him to stop.

St Just only quickened his pace a little, but made no other sign of having heard. But at last St Keverne was within a stone's-throw, and, taking a stone from his pocket, he flung it at St Just. It fell so near that the saint was alarmed and took to his heels. But as he ran he untied the cup, which he had fastened to his girdle, and dropped it to the ground. St Keverne recovered it and, being wearied he abandoned his long pursuit. But he threw all the remaining stones after the vanishing figure of St Just, one by one, and a curse with each. There the pebbles remained, entirely unlike all the other stones about them, but clearly the same as the stones at Crowza, and so heavy that none but a saint could hope to life them. By day they have sometimes been removed, but they always return to their places by night.

Dando and his Dogs

In the neighbourhood of...St Germans formerly lived a priest connected with the old priory church of this parish...He lived the life of the tradition 'jolly friar'. He ate and drank of the best the land could give him, or money buy; and it is said that his indulgences extended far beyond the ordinary limits of good living. The priest, Dando, was, notwithstanding all his vices, a man liked by the people. He was good-natured, and therefore blind to many of their sins.

As a man increases in years, he becomes more deeply dyed with the polluted waters through which he may have waded...So was it with Dando.

The sinful priest was a capital huntsman, and scoured the country far and near in pursuit of game, which was in those days abundant and varied over this well-wooded district. Dando, in the eagerness of the chase, paid no regard to any kind of property. Many a cornfield has been trampled down, and many a cottage garden destroyed by the horses and dogs which this impetuous huntsman would lead unthinkingly over them. Curses deep though not loud, would follow the old man, as even those who suffered by his excesses were still in fear of his priestly power...

Dando worshipped the sensual gods which he had created, and his external worship of the God of truth became every year more and more a hypocritical lie. The Devil looked carefully after his prize and Dando was lured towards the undoing of his soul. Health and wealth were secured to him, and by and by

MANATON WELL.

the measure of his sins was full, and he was left the victim to self-indulgences – a doomed man. With increasing years, and the immunities he enjoyed, Dando became more reckless. His days were devoted to the pursuits of the field; and to maintain the required excitement ardent drinks were supplied him by his wicked companions. Even on the Sabbath, horses and hounds were ordered out, and the priest would be seen in full cry. One Sabbath morning, Dando and his riotous rout were hunting over the Earth estate; game was plenty, and sport first-rate. Exhausted with a long and eager run, Dando called for a drink.

"Whence can we get it?" cried one of the gang.

"Go to Hell for it, if you can't get it on earth," said the priest, with a bitter laugh at his own joke on the Earth estate.

At that moment, a dashing hunter, who had mingled with the throng unobserved, came forward, and presented a richly-mounted flask to Dando, saying:

"Here is some choice liquor, distilled in the establishment you speak of. It will warm and revive you, I'll warrant. Drink deep, friend, drink."

Dando drank deep and removed the flask, exclaiming, "By Hell, that was a drink indeed. Do the gods drink such nectar?"

"Devils do," was the reply.

"An they do, I wish I were one," said Dando. "Methinks the drink is very like –" The impious expression died upon his lips.

Looking round Dando saw that his new friend had appropriated several head of game. Notwithstanding his stupid intoxication, his selfishness asserted its power, and he seized the game, exclaiming, "None of these are

thine."

"What I catch, I keep," said the hunter.

"By all the devils, they're mine," stammered Dando.

The hunter quietly bowed.

Dando's wrath burst at once into a burning flame, uncontrolled by reason. He rolled himself off his horse, and rushed, staggering as he went, at the steed of his unknown friend, uttering most frightful oaths and curses. The strange hunter's horse was a splendid creature, black as night, and its eyes gleamed with unnatural lustre. The horse was turned adroitly aside, and Dando fell to the earth with much force. Aided by his attendants, he was speedily on his legs, and again at the side of the hunter, who shook with laughter, shaking the game in derision, and quietly uttering "They're mine."

"I'll go to Hell after them, but I'll get them from three," shouted Dando.

"So thou shalt," said the hunter, and, seizing Dando by the collar, he lifted him from the ground, and placed him, as though he were a child, before him on the horse.

With a dash, the horse passed down the hill and the dogs, barking furiously, followed impetuously. These strange riders reached the banks of the Lynher, and with a terrific leap, the horse and its riders, followed by the hounds, went out far in its waters, disappearing at length in a blaze of fire, which caused the stream to boil for a moment, and then the waters flowed on as tranquilly as ever over the doomed priest.

Dando never more was seen, and his fearful death was received as a warning by many, who gave gifts to the Church. One amongst them carved a chair for the bishop, and on it he represented Dando and his dogs, that the memory of his wickedness might be always renewed.

DISTINCTIVE FLAVOUR

The Isles of Scilly are said to be all that remains of **Mark's Lyonnesse**, overwhelmed by the sea one fateful Sunday morning. They were the favourite holiday spot of Sir Harold Wilson, where *Private Eye* alleged, he drank at a pub called 'The Scilly Cow'.

Due to its geographical position, the Celtic origins of its people, and their history of trade with overseas, Cornwall has always retained a strong individuality, and a very separate identity from the rest of England. It is said that travellers into the county leave England to enter Cornwall.

Cornish was spoken until the 18th century,

and many words still survive in the names of people and places; a local saying runs:

'By Tre, Ros, Car, Lan, Pol, and Pen,
You may well know all Cornishmen'

The following words are frequently to be seen as prefixes or suffixes in place-names:

tre	=	homestead
ros	=	heath
car, caer	=	camp
lan	=	monastery
pol	=	pool
pen	=	headland
maen	=	stone
bron	=	hill

Many dialect words and phrases still survive, too:

'Tez a wisht ole job i'it' means 'It's a great pity'.

If a man says he 'scat', he means he hasn't any money.

'Do 'ee give'n a dinky bit, co!' means 'Do give him a tiny piece, there's a dear!'

The words for 'up' and 'down' are often followed by '-along': 'I'm going up-along to Truro' – a clue to the undulating terrain characteristic of the county.

Other dialect words include: hekkymowl (blue tit); aglets (hawthorn berries); airy-mouse (bat); angle-twitch (earthworm).

To some city-dwellers, the unhurried pace of Cornish life may seem slow, but the Cornish are unperturbed: they 'will be slocked [persuaded] but won't be drove'. The Cornishman is also noted for his common sense, and for being reserved towards strangers: as Mrs Pengilly says in H Elli's *My Cornish Neighbours*, 'It do take years with we to treat a stranger like one of our own.'

The most well-known food in Cornwall is the **Cornish pasty**, traditionally a mixture of meat and vegetables (often turnip) in a half-moon shaped pastry case. The pasty is held by the thick ridge of pastry on the side. The ingredients can vary, and Cornish children were always told that the devil never dared cross the Tamar from the English side into Cornwall, lest some enterprising Cornishwomen should catch him and put him in a pasty.

Saffron Cake is a bread cake flavoured with saffron, candied peel and currants. A receipe from 1929 specifies '^{1}/$_2$d worth of saffron'...

Star-gazy Pie is a traditional fish pie, with the heads of pilchards, mackerel, or herring, protruding through the pastry lid, 'gazing at the stars'!

Cornwall has been called the 'Land of pilchards and cream', pilchards and clotted cream (not necessarily together!) being local specialities. **Marinated pilchards** are a favourite hors d'oeuvre: a local man is quoted as declaring, "tes ridiculous to ate pilchers onless they'm cold as paddicks. 'Tedden fair to yerself to ate 'em hot, and 'tedden fair to the pilchers'.

Mahogany was a drink made of two parts gin and one part treacle. Dr John referred to it as 'a curious liquor...which the Cornish fishermen drink'.

Cornish piskies are renowned for being mischievous and humorous, playing tricks on householders, but without any malice.

On May 8th, the **Helston Flora** or **Furry Dance**, believed to be of Celtic origin, is held, when the people gather flowers and branches, and dance through the streets and in and out of the houses.

The Padstow Hobbyhorse ceremony is held on May day.

Wrestling was a highly popular sport in the county from olden times, and the Cornish were renowned for their skill. Henry VIII commanded that Cornish wrestlers be sent to the great sporting tourney at Calais; Charles II declared that 'the Cornish are masters in the art of wrestling'. Although it declined in Victorian times, wrestling is still popular in the county today.

Hurling was a traditional local sport, played with a wooden ball, encased in silver. The goals were two miles apart. Three centuries ago, the game ended in players 'retyring home as from a pitched bataille, with bloody pates, bones broken and out of joint, and such bruises as serve to shorten their days'.

COUNTY DIARY

Shrove Tuesday:
    Hurling, St Colomb Major
May 1: Hobbyhorse Ceremony, Padstow
May 8: Furry Dance, Helston
June: Royal Cornwall Agricultural Show, Wadebridge
August: Blessing of the Sea, Bude
September:
    Gorsedd (Celtic traditional ceremonies)

CUMBERLAND

HISTORY

AD 121 marked the beginning of the construction of the great wall by the Roman Emperor Hadrian, which formed the boundary between Roman England and the heathen Scots.

In the year 573, St Mungo came to Carlisle from Scotland and preached Christianity. In the same year was fought the Battle of Ardderyd (or Arthuret), in which the British clans conquered the English and established their kingdom of the Strathclyde Britons from the Mersey to the Clyde.

By 685, most of the land was ruled by the English. St Cuthbert came to Carlisle and a monastery and a school were established in the city.

The district then became known as the Land of the Cymri - Cymbriland, or Cumberland. In the 10th century, Cumberland belonged to Scotland, until William Rufus in 1092 once more gained it for England, bringing in some displaced English-folk from Hampshire to swell the sparse population. The county was the scene of frequent raids, disputes, and battles with the Scots across the border. Edward I died in Burgh-by-the-Sands during the Scottish Wars.

In the Wars of the Roses, Cumberland supported the House of Lancaster, but wisely adopted a policy of conciliation on the triumph of the Yorkists.

In 1644, the Parliamentarians, led by David Leslie, put Carlisle under seige for more than a year. After enduring much hardship, the Governor eventually capitulated, and the garrison marched out with all the honours of war. The city had its own mint.

In 1745, the city of Carlisle was briefly captured by Charles Edward Stuart, the Young Pretender, on his abortive march on London.

INDUSTRY PAST AND PRESENT

Tourism, sheep farming and forestry are currently important.

Oats, turnips and swedes were the main crops grown. The principal resource of the farmers has always been sheep-farming. Coal mining was the most important industry around Whitehaven, Workington and Maryport, together with the raising of iron ore. Cotton and wool were also manufactured, and there

TOPOGRAPHY INCLUDING RIVERS

Cumberland, in most north-west England, is bordered by the Solway Firth and Dumfries and Roxburgh in the north, Northumberland and Durham in the east, Westmorland and Lancashire in the south, and the Solway Firth and Irish Sea in the west.

The far north of the county is a flat plain below the Cheviot Hills of Scotland, which soon rises to mountainous country. The western part of the Pennine Chain lies in the north east, rising to 2,890 feet at Cross Fell, and the Cumbrian mountains form a roughly circular area in the south west. Here are Skiddaw, at 3,166 feet, and Scafell Pike, the highest mountain in England at 3210 feet. The region is known as the Lake District, and the mountains, or fells, are intersected by valleys and large lakes such as Derwentwater, Buttermere, Ennerdale Water and Wastwater, and smaller, higher lakes known as tarns. The land drops in the west to low coast bordering the Irish Sea.

Rivers: Eden, Derwent, Esk, Duddon.

were pencil mills at Keswick and iron shipbuilding yards at Whitehaven.

LANDMARKS
The Bowder Stone
Hadrian's Wall
Scafell Pike, the highest mountain in England.

MONUMENTS
Carlisle Cathedral was built between the 11th and the 15th centuries, and is one of the smallest and most battle-scarred cathedrals in England.

Carlisle Castle, built by William Rufus in circa 1092. Only the main gate, Queen Mary's tower, and the central keep remain.

Calder Abbey, the remains of a 12th-century Cistercian Abbey.

Lanercost Priory, founded in 1169 for Augustinian canons. It is approached over a Tudor bridge.

Naworth Castle, a 14th-century castle, used by Sir Walter Scott as the setting for his 'The Lay of the Last Minstrel'.

Sellafield Nuclear Power Station, formerly called Windscale. Controversial plant for reprocessing nuclear waste.

FAMOUS PEOPLE AND LOCAL CHARACTERS
William Wordsworth was born on 7th April 1770 in Cockermouth. His father was law agent to the first Earl of Lonsdale.

Sir Walter Scott visited Gilsland, where he met and fell in love with Charlotte Mary Charpentier. They were married in Carlisle Cathedral.

Samuel Taylor Coleridge lived at Greta Hall in Keswick from 1800. His brother-in-law, Robert Southey, also settled in Keswick, and in 1809 Greta Hall became his. He was made poet laureate in 1813.

John Peel, the famous hunter (D'ye ken John Peel?) was born in Caldbeck in 1776 - and was buried there 78 years later. He was master of hounds in the region for 55 years.

Sir Hugh Walpole lived in Borrowdale, which was the main setting for his *Herries Chronicles*.

Melvyn Bragg, the novelist, was brought up in Cumberland.

ART AND LITERATURE
*'Much favor'd in my birthplace, and no less
In that beloved Vale to which, erelong,*

*I was transported. Well I call to mind
('Twas at an early age, ere I had seen
Nine summers) when upon the mountain slope
The frost and breath of frosty wind had snapp'd
The last autumnal crocus, 'twas my joy
To wander half the night among the Cliffs
And the smooth Hollows, where the woodcocks ran
Along the open turf.'*
William Wordsworth
The Prelude

*'There was an Old man of Whitehaven
Who danced a quadrille with a raven;
But they said 'It's absurd
To encourage this bird',
So they smashed that old man of Whitehaven.'*
Edward Lear

'We have no fear of injury, moral or economical, from the great recent change, the introduction of railways. The morals of rural districts are such as cannot well be made worse by any change. Drinking and kindred vices abound wherever, in our day, intellectual resources are absent: and nowhere is drunkenness a more prevalent and desperate curse than in the Lake District.'
Harriet Martineau
A Complete Guide to the English Lakes (1885)

*'That ancient woman seated on Helm Crag
Was ready with her cavern: Hammer Scar,
And the tall steep of Silver Hows, sent forth
A noise of laughter; southern Loughrigg heard,
And Fairfield answered with a mountain tone:
Helvellyn far into the clear blue sky
Carried the lady's voice; old Skiddaw blew
His speaking trumpet; back out of the clouds
Of Glaramara southward came the voice;
And Kirkstone tossed it from his misty head.'*
William Wordsworth

*'Till Skiddaw saw the fire that burned on Gaunt's embattled pile,
And the red glare on Skiddaw roused the burghers of Carlisle.'*
T.B. Macauley
The Armada

LOCAL FOLKLORE
The Solway Worm
The people of Workington used to tell of a great sea-snake or worm that would come up the Solway Firth and eat the fish – and the fishermen, too, if they weren't careful. It even gobbled up the cattle that sometimes strayed down to the shore to feed on the seaweed. So the people, deprived of their livelihoods, and half starving, decided to rid themselves of the worm once and for all. They took a hundred stakes, sharpened at one end, and at low tide went out in their coracles and drove the stakes into the sea bed, so that the sharp ends were just covered when the tide came in. Sure enough, with the tide came the Solway Worm, intent on his next meal, and the tide drove him onto the stakes, where he was impaled. He struggled to get free for three days, and his roaring was terrible to hear. Eventually he died, and the gulls and the fish feasted on the remains.

The Abbey of St Bees
One stormy night, a ship was wrecked on the coast near Whitehaven. Amongst its passengers were St Bega and some of her sister nuns. The Lady of Egremont took pity on the nuns and begged her husband to grant them a dwelling place, which he duly did. The abbess, St Bega, later besought the Lady of Egremont to persuade her husband to build them a proper abbey. When she broached the subject to him, pointing out that he had a good deal of land and to spare, he laughed, and vowed that he would grant the nuns as much land as should be covered by snow the following day – which was Midsummer Day. To their amazement, when they awoke next morning, the ground was white with snow from Egremont to the sea. True to his word, the Lord of Egremont ordered the building of an abbey, and granted it all the land upon which the snow had miraculously fallen.

The Horn of Egremont
It was said that the horn which hung by the gateway of Egremont Castle could only be sounded by the rightful heir of Egremont. One day, Sir Eustace de Lucy, the Lord of Egremont, and his brother Hubert, set off on a Crusade to the Holy Land. Sir Eustace told his brother that if he were to die in the Holy Land, Hubert was to return home, blow the horn, and take possession of the castle, so that Egremont should not be without its rightful Lord. The wicked Hubert bribed a band of ruffians to seize his brother and throw him into the River Jordan. He then returned home and took possession of the castle, although he did not dare blow the horn.

One evening, he was giving a banquet at the castle when he heard the horn being blown at the castle gate. Realizing that only the rightful owner could sound the horn, and that his brother must be alive, Hubert fled by the back gate. Sir Eustace returned in triumph and once more took possession of Egremont. Hubert, in remorse, repaired to a monastery, where he later died.

Adam Bel, Clym of the Clough and William of Cloudesley

Merry and joyous it is in the green forest, when the leaves are full and broad, to walk beneath its breezy shade and hearken to the wild birds' song.

It is of three good yeomen of the north country that I seek at present to tell you all: Adam Bel, Clym of the Clough, and William of Cloudesley. Archers of approved skill were they, and outlawed for venison; and in the town of Carlisle where they dwelled, they sware brotherhood, and to the forest betook them. Whereof twain were single men; but Cloudesley had taken unto him a wife, and with moist eyes he brake from fair Alice, and the children clasped to his knee, to lead a strange new life in Inglewood with his two comrades, their hand against every man, and every man against them.

So they made such shift as they could, and passed their days amid the forest glades and lawns, sustaining themselves on the king's venison and the water of the brook; and ever and again a little boy, who had served Cloudesley as his swineherd, was sent to him privily, and brought him and the others victuals and raiment and news withal.

Till, after a certain space of time, Cloudesley waxed homesick, thinking often on his young wife Alice and his sweet little ones, whom he had left behind him; and he said to the others, that he would fain make his way to Carlisle, to gladden his eyes with the sight of them all once more. For Alice, while she caused the little swineherd to pass to and fro with meat for the foresters, held it unwise to charge the boy with any message praying Cloudesley to come unto her, seeing that she was so straitly observed.

Then said Adam Bel to him: "Ye go not, brother, by mine advice; for if ye be marked and the justice take ye, your life is even at an end. Stay, prythee, where ye are, and be content."

But Cloudesley replied: "Nay, wend thither I must; and if so I return not to you and Clym by noon, ye may augur that I am taken or slain."

And when his brethren saw that they might nowise prevail upon him they said no more, and he departed on his way, as it drew toward evening.

With a light step, and an anxious heart, he sped along till he came to the gates of Carlisle, and he passed in thereat disguised, that no man might discern who he was; and he paused not till he was at his own window, and called on Alice his wife to undo the door, for it was her own William who stood without.

Then when the joy of the meeting had a little abated, fair Alice gazed at him pensively, and said: "William, it is so that this house has been watched and beset for you this half-year or more."

But he replied to her: "Now I am here, bring me to eat and drink, and let us make good cheer while we may."

Now there was an old wife in the chimney corner, that Cloudesley had harboured for charity's sake some seven years, and that had not of long time set foot on ground. This shrew and cursed crone, albeit she had eaten his bread so long, seized her occasion, and crept privily to the sheriff, where he lived, and warned him that that very night William the outlaw had by stealth come into the town, and was even now securely at home, where they might have him.

The sheriff caused the bell to be rung, and the justice and the sheriff getting their men together, they soon encompassed the house round on every side. Then Cloudesley made all the doors fast, and took his sword and buckler and bow, and with his three children and fair Alice his wife mounted the stair to an

THE BOWDER STONE

upper chamber, where he imagined that he might withstand them all; and by his side his true wedded wife held a poleaxe in her hand. Cloudesley bent his bow, and the arrow shivered in two against the justice's breastplate. "Beshrew the varlet," muttered Cloudesley, "that dressed thee in that coat; if it had not been thicker than mine, thou hadst not spoken more."

"Yield, Cloudesley," cried the justice, "and give up thy arms."

"A curse light on him," cried Alice, "who lendeth us such counsel!"

And they kept them all at a distance, for Cloudesley was at the window, with his bow ready bent, and none durst break the doors, so true an archer was he.

"Set fire to the house, since there is no other way," shouted the sheriff; and they did as he bad, and the flames quickly rose. Cloudesley opened a back window, and let down his wife and children, and said to the sheriff, "For Christ's love, hurt them not, but wreak all your ire on me." And he kept his bow busy till all his arrows were spent and the fire night burnt his bowstring in twain.

"This is a coward's death," he explained, "and liever had I fallen sword in hand than thus." And he cast down his bow, and taking his sword and buckler, leaped down among the throng, and smote them on every side, till only by hurling doors and windows at him could they make prisoner that stout and bold yeoman.

Then they bound him hand and foot, and led him to prison and the justice commanded that he should be hanged the next morning, and that the gates should be shut, so that none might enter thereat. For the justice doubted that Adam Bel and Clym of the Clough might gain tidings of their fellow, and might essay to rescue him from the gallows.

"Not Adam Bell, nor Clym, nor all the devils in Hell," quoth the justice, "shall save thee from the rope this time."

Early in the morning a pair of new gallows was erected in the market place, nigh the pillory, and the gates of Carlisle were locked.

Now Alice, seeing no other remedy, had that same night that Cloudesley was taken despatched with all speed to Inglewood the little swineherd, who crept unobserved through a crevice in the wall after dusk, and lost not a moment in finding the two foresters, where they lay under the greenwood shade. "Too long, too long," cried he, "tarry ye here, ye good yeomen. Cloudesley is taken, and tomorrow betimes he shall be hanged on a new gallows in the market-place."

"He might have dwelled with us in peace," said Adam Bel, "as I prayed him heartily to do, and now here is a shrewd pass." And he took his bow in his hand, and a buck that bounded by was stretched suddenly on the ground. "That will serve us for our breakfast," said he, "ere we go. Fetch me my arrow again, boy, for we shall have need enough."

Now when these yeomen had eaten their meal hastily, they girded on their swords, and took their bows and arrows and bucklers, and sped on their way, for time pressed, and it was a fair May morning when they reached the gates of Carlisle.

"We must devise some sleight," said Clym of the Clough, "to get in. Let us say that we are messengers from the king."

"I have a fair letter," quoth the other; "we will declare that we have the king's signet; the porter is, I warrant, no clerk."

They beat hard at the door, and when the porter heard that they had the king's seal, he unlocked the gate, and let them enter.

"Now we are in," whispered Adam Bel; "but by Heaven! I do not know how we shall make our way out again."

"Let us seize the keys," whispered Clym.

They beckoned the porter to them, and wrang his neck, and cast his body into a corner.

"Now am I porter in his room," cried Adam, "the worst they have had here in Carlisle this hundred year."

And without more ado they hastened to the market-place, placing themselves where they might not be noted. They espied the gallows, and the justice with his inquest, that had ajudged Cloudesley to die, and Cloudesley hard by in a cart, bound hand and foot, with a rope around his neck.

The justice called a boy, and promised him the outlaw's clothes, if he would dig his grave against the time for despatch. Cloudesley cast his eye aside, where his two brethren stood, and he said to the justice: "Such wonders have happened ere now as that a man who diggeth a grave for another lieth in it himself."

But the justice answered and said: "Ah! thou talkest proudly. I will hang thee, fellow, with my own hand."

Scarce had the words fallen from him, when an arrow pierced his breast, and a second the sheriff's; the rest began to scatter, and Adam, running up to the cart, loosed Cloudesley, who wrenched an axe from a man near him. There was a panic; the bells were rung backward, the outhorns were blown, and the mayor with a strong force behind him arrived with their bills and their swords.

The foresters, when they saw them, were dismayed by their numbers, and retreated towards the gate; and when they could no longer use their bows, they cut down all that came near with their swords, till at last they reached the gate, and unlocked it; and when they were without, Adam Bel threw the keys at the heads of the mayor's men, and cried: "I give up my office. Prythee, elect a new porter." And they waited not to see what further befell but took their way back to Inglewood, where Cloudesley found fair Alice and his children three, that had thought him dead; and there was great rejoicing among them all and they feasted to their heart's ease.

Then, when those three bold foresters, with Alice and her children three, had supped merrily together, and they had rested somewhat after that notable work at Carlisle, quoth Cloudesley to the others: "Brethren mine, let us even go straightway to London to our king to seek his grace, ere the tidings come to his ear, how the justice and sheriff be slain, with many more; and Alice and two of my children shall repair to a nunnery hereby, and my eldest son I shall take with me.

So, when they came to London, they sought our lord the king, pushing bluffly past the porter at the palace gate, and the usher, and all, who pressed after them in a body to know what they would have; and they said they had travelled far to obtain from the king a charter of peace.

When they were brought into the presence of our lord the king, they fell on their knees, as the law of the land was, and each held up his hand; and they said: "Lord, we beseech thee to grant us grace, for we have slain your highness's deer."

"What are your names?" asked the king.

"Adam Bel, Clym of the Clough, and William Cloudesley."

"Ah! ye be those thieves," returned the king, "that men have reported so oft to me? Gramercy, sirs, I shall see well that ye be hanged without more ado."

"We pray your highness," said they again, "that you will suffer us to leave you with our arms in our hands till we are out of this place, and we will seek no farther grace."

"You talk rather proudly," quoth the king, "Nay, nay; ye shall be of a surety hanged all three."

Now the queen, hearing the news of these archers having made so long a journey to see her lord the king, came to him, praying him, as he had made promise to her on their marriage to grant the first boon she should ask, to yield unto her the lives of those three

COINS FROM CARLISLE'S MINT DURING THE CIVIL WAR

yeomen; and the king, albeit he was wroth that she should have begged so mean a thing, when she might have had market-towns, castles and forests to her use and pleasure, said unto her: "I depart not, madam, from my words; they are yours."

"My lord," she said, "much thanks. I undertake that they shall become to your grace good men and true. But, prythee, speak a word to them, that they may know your bounty to them."

"You are pardoned, fellows," our lord the king said thereupon. "Go now, wash, and sit to meat."

A crafty man was William of Cloudesley, who thought of fair Alice and his sweet children, and wist well that the men of Carlisle would send messengers to London without delay to apprise our lord the king of what had there befallen; and, certes, scarcely were those three yeoman assailed by our lady the queen's favour, when, as they sat at meat in the king's kitchen, there came a post from the north country to disclose the whole thing as it was. The messengers kneeled, and presented their letters, saying, "Lord, your officers of Carlisle in the north country greet you well." And when our lord the king crake the seal, he was a sad man; for he found that those three yeomen, to whom he had granted grace, and leave to wash and eat at his board, had slain three hundred and more, with the justice and the sheriff, and the mayor and many other, and had ravaged his parks, and killed his deer, and by all that country were held in dread. "Take away the meat," cried the king. "I can touch no more. What archers be these, that can do such feats with their bow? Marry, I have none such. Methinks I will see them shoot." And his grace commanded that his bowmen, and the queen's should forthwith hold a meeting, and set up butts. Whereto Adam Bel, Clym of the Clough and William

of Cloudesley were summoned to come. They all took their turns, and the king's bowmen, and the queen's put out their whole strength and skill before those three yeomen of the north country; but those three yeomen carried everything; and there was much marvelling at such archery.

But William of Cloudesley spake and said: "Gramercy, I hold him no archer that shooteth at such wide butts."

"What wouldest thou, then?" demanded the king.

"Such a butt, lord," he answered, "as men use in my country."

And the king gave him leave that he should shew his meaning.

Then Cloudesley took two hazel wands in his hand, and set them up two hundred paces apart, and said to the king: "Whoso cleaveth them both in twain, I hold him an archer indeed."

No man that was with the king raised his voice or made a sign, but all were still and silent; and the king said: "There is none here who can do such a thing."

"I shall try then," said Cloudesley, stepping forward suddenly; and fixing a bearing arrow in his bow, he drew it to the head, and split both the wands in two.

"Thou art the best archer," exclaimed the king, delightedly, "that I ever beheld."

"Wait a moment, lord," said Cloudesley, "and I will shew your grace even more. Here is my little son, seven years old; dear enough to his mother and to me he is. Grieved in our hearts were we if any misadventure should befall him; yet, lo! I will bind him to a stake, and place an apple on his head, and at sixscore paces I will cut the apple in two."

None believed that even Cloudesley had the courage and steadfastness to achieve such a deed. But he called his son to him and fastened him with his back towards him, lest

he might wince, to a post, and the apple was laid upon the child's head, and sixscore paces were measured out. Cloudesley stood motionless for an instant, not a breath was heard throughout all that meeting, and many prayed for the yeoman that God would protect him in his task, and some wept. He drew out a broad shaft, fixed it in his good bow, and the next moment the apple fell from the child's head, and not a hair was stirred.

"God forbid," cried the king, "that thou shouldest shoot at me! I perceive how my officers in Carlisle sped so ill when they had such a foe. But I have tried thee sorely, William, and thou art an exceeding good archer. I give thee eighteenpence a day, and thy clothing, and make thee a gentleman, and chief forester of my north country; and thy brethren twain shall be yeomen of my chamber. Thy little son, whom thou so lovest, I will place in my wine cellar, and when he cometh to man's estate, he shall be farther preferred."

So said the king; and our lady the queen commanded that Alice should be brought to London to the court, and should be set over her nursery.

So fared these three yeomen excellently well through the mastery of William of Cloudesly and the gracious offices of our lady the queen; and when they had gone on pilgrimage to Rome, to our holy father the Pope, to obtain remission of their sins against God, they returned to their own land, and lived ever after in ease and worship.

W. Carew Hazlitt
National Tales and Legends

DISTINCTIVE FLAVOUR

Cumberland Sauce, a cold sauce for meats, made from redcurrant jelly flavoured with orange, lemon and port.

Cumberland Currant Cake is made with currants and candied peel, sandwiched between two layers of pastry.

Cumberland Sausage, a long, coiled sausage, highly flavoured with herbs and spices.

COUNTY DIARY

July:	Cumberland Show, Carlisle
September:	Crab Fair and World Gurning championships, Egremont

DERBYSHIRE

COUNTY FACTS

Derivation of name: Formerly known as Northworthy it was re-named Derby by the Danes from the concentration of deer, possibly in some sort of enclosure. Derby therefore means deer village or village with a deer park or enclosure. It would therefore translate into Persian as 'Paradise'.

First Recorded: 1049

Motto: Bene consulendo (By good counsel)

County Town: Derby

Towns: Alfreton, Ashbourne, Bakewell, Belper, Bolsover, Buxton, Chapel-en-le-Frith, Chesterfield, Clay Cross, Derby, Dronfield, Eckington, Glossop, Hadfield, Heanor, Ilkeston, Killamarsh, Long Eaton, Matlock, Mickleover, New Mills, Ripley, Sandiacre, Shirebrook, South Normanton, Staveley, Swadlincote, Whaley Bridge.

Local Government

Derbyshire County Council (including Cheshire's Tintwistle) and nine district councils, with a detached part of Derbyshire around Measham under the control of Leicestershire County Council.

HISTORY

In about the 7th century, English settlers came to the region and became known as Pec-setan, or Peak dwellers. The district became part of the great kingdom of Mercia, and then, on the arrival of the Danes in the 9th century, Derby was included in the Danelaw, the confederacy of Lincoln, Leicester, Stamford, Nottingham and Derby. William de Peveril, natural son of William the Conqueror, built a castle named Peak near the village of Castleton.

Robert de Ferrers, Earl of Derby, fought on the side of the barons against Henry III. He and his men were attacked at Chesterfield, and he was forced to flee. He hid in the church, among some happily placed bags of wool. However, his presence was revealed by a girl whose lover had been compelled against his will to fight, and had been killed. The Early of Derby was imprisoned at Windsor.

The men of Derby were renowned fighters, and were often called to aid in the Scottish and Welsh wars.

Mary Queen of Scots was a prisoner at Chatsworth and Wingfield Manor. She also visited Buxton for her health. Her jailor was George Talbot, Earl of Shrewsbury, to whom it also fell to arrange her execution.

William Cavendish, Earl of Devonshire, was one of the leading spirits in bringing over William of Orange to England. The Earl and his conspirators used to meet in the 'Plotting Parlours' of an inn on Whittington Moor.

Dr Sacheverell preached his famous assize sermon in Derby in 1710, in which he attacked the 'Glorious Revolution' of 1688, and all who had taken part in it. The people of Derby supported him.

In 1745 the Young Pretender, Charles Edward Stuart, was proclaimed King in Derby.

The 18th century saw the rise of many manufacturers, with improved machines for silk throwing and stocking ribbing. The Luddites in the 19th century did much damage in the county.

As a result of the wars with France, great distress was caused by high food prices, and the county was the scene of the Pentrich Rising by a few half-starved peasants. Three of them were executed and around 40 transported.

INDUSTRY PAST AND PRESENT

Coal, engineering, man-made fibres and Rolls-Royce are important in Derby. Now the Japanese car industry is a major factor.

The county was famous for the manufacture of silk, especially in Derby, Belper and Duffield. Cotton and lace-making were also

TOPOGRAPHY INCLUDING RIVERS

Derbyshire in the north midlands is bordered by the West Riding of Yorkshire in the north, Nottinghamshire in the east, Leicestershire to the south, Staffordshire to the south and west and Cheshire to the north-west.

It is a hilly country, rising in the north east to the mountain mass of the Peak District, at places 2,000 feet high. The Pennine Way begins at Edale in the Hope Valley. Of the several waterfalls in this craggy country, the highest is Kinder Downfall, on Kinder Scout, with a drop of some 400 feet. Around Castleton are a series of vast limestone caverns, which are a popular centre for potholing. Further south is moorland country, cut by gorges or dales, of which Dove Dale is considered the most beautiful. The highest point is Kinder Scout, 2088 feet.

Rivers: Derwent, Dove, Trent, Wye.

thriving industries. Coal has been mined in the east of the county for many years. Lead was mined by the Romans. The waters of Buxton were famous in the 17th century.

LANDMARKS

The Peak District
The Pennines
The Derbyshire Dales
Black Rock
Kinder Scout
Mam Tor
High Tor
Creswell Crags
Dove Dale
Caverns - Speedwell Cavern, Peak Cavern, Treak Cliff Cavern, Blue John Caves

MONUMENTS

Bolsover Castle, a 17th-century castle built by Sir Charles Cavendish, on the site of an older, Norman castle.
Chatsworth House, a classical mansion built between 1687 and 1707 by William Talman for the 1st Duke of Devonshire.
Haddon Hall; the building was begun by William de Peveril, or Pevensey, the natural son of William the Conqueror. The present building was completely and faithfully restored in the 20th century.
Hardwick Hall was begun in 1591 by Elizabeth of Shrewsbury (also known as Bess of Hardwick), as her 'retirement home', after the death of her fourth husband. The huge windows increase with size the higher up the building they are, giving rise to the saying,
> 'Hardwick Hall,
> More glass than wall.'
Kedleston Hall; the Curzon family have lived on the site for over 800 years. The present mansion, built in the 18th century, was Robert Adam's first great work.
Melbourne Hall, a country mansion developed between 1563 and 1644 by Sir John Coke, further developed by his great grandson, the Vice Chamberlain to Queen Anne and George I.
Cromford Old Mill; it was at this mill that Richard Arkwright in 1771 first used water power to drive a cotton mill.

FAMOUS PEOPLE AND LOCAL CHARACTERS

Bess of Hardwick was born circa 1527 (although this is disputed). She had a knack of marrying wealthy men and surviving them: after the death of her fourth husband in 1590, she returned to Hardwick Hall, where she was born, and set to work to begin a new house not far from the Old Hall. Although 70 years old by this time, she was still a very vigorous and powerful lady, and her energy inspired the architect to complete the building of Hardwick Hall within seven years. She left her mark on the house in many ways, including her initials, ES (Elizabeth of Shrewsbury), 6 feet high on the parapets of the towers. She is the ancestress of the Dukes of Devonshire and the Dukes of Newcastle, (later Portland).
Thomas Hobbes, the philosopher, was tutor and secretary to the 2nd and 3rd Earls of Devonshire at Chatsworth and Hardwick, from 1610. He died at Hardwick Hall in 1679, at the age of 91.
Dr Samuel Johnson married Mrs Elizabeth Porter in Derby on July 9, 1735.
Adam Bede, which established **George Eliot** as a novelist, was set in Derbyshire, although she changed the names of the towns. 'Stoniton' is Derby, 'Snowfield' is Wirksworth, 'Oakbourne' is Ashbourne, 'Norbourne' is Norbury, and 'Eagledale' Dovedale.
Florence Nightingale was the daughter of a Derbyshire gentleman, and spent her early childhood at Lea Hurst near Crich.
Sir Osbert and Dame Edith Sitwell lived at Renishaw Hall, south of Eckington.

Local Characters

William Mompesson was rector of Eyam in the 17th century. It was the time of the Great Plague, and the infection was brought to the village in a box of clothes. Soon, it had claimed more than 80 per cent of the village inhabitants. William Mompesson, by his strength of character, persuaded the remaining villagers not to flee, and thus prevented the plague from spreading throughout the county. Goods were delivered to them from outside the village, for which they paid by leaving money in the water of a well, which stopped the spread of any infection. A memorial service is held every year in the village to commemorate the selflessness of the villagers during their self-imposed siege.

ART AND LITERATURE

'She dwelt among the untrodden ways
Beside the springs of Dove
A maid whom there were none to praise
And very few to love.'
William Wordsworth
Lucy

'Life here is as dank as ditch-water and has some of the other qualities of ditch-water; at least I know that I am reduced to a great weakness by diarrhoea, which lasts too, as I were poisoned.'
Gerard Manley Hopkins
of Chesterfield in a letter to Robert Bridges

'From Matlock Bath's half-timbered station
I see the black dissenting spire –
Thin witness of a congregation
Stone emblem of a Handel choir;
In blest Bethesda's limpid pool
Comes treacling out of Sunday School.

By cool Siloam's shady rill –
The sounds are sweet as strawberry jam:
I raise mine eyes unto the hill
The beetling HEIGHTS OF ABRAHAM:
The branchy trees are white with rime
In Matlock Bath this winter-time...

And from the whiteness, grey uprearing,
Huge cliffs hang sunless ere they fall
A tossed and stony ocean nearing
The moment to o'erwhelm us all:
Eternal Father, strong to save,
How long wilt thou suspend the wave?

How long before the pleasant acres
Of intersecting LOVERS' WALKS
Are rolled across by limestone breakers,
Whole woodlands snapp'd like cabbage stalks?
O God, our help in ages past,
How long will SPEEDWELL CAVERN last?'
John Betjeman
Matlock Bath (1966)

'Oh my beloved nymph! Fair Dove,
Princess of rivers, how I love
Upon thy flow'r'y banks to lie
And view thy silver stream
When gilded by a summer's beam!'

Charles Cotton
The Retirement

LOCAL FOLKLORE

Haddon Hall

Dorothy Vernon was the younger daughter of Sir George Vernon, and heiress to Haddon Hall. She fell in love with (Sir) John Manners, the second son of the Earl of Rutland, but was unable to meet him, as her family kept her confined to the house, where she was ill-treated. John therefore used to disguise himself as a forester in order to be able to see her.

The couple planned that Dorothy should escape one night and they would elope together. During a ball given in honour of her sister's marriage, Dorothy slipped away into an anteroom and down the stairs (now named after her) to where John Manners was waiting for her. They eloped together, and as a result Haddon Hall passed from the Vernon family to the Dukes of Rutland.

Winlatter Rock

The Devil came out of the north. He turned himself into a fiery dragon and laid waste all the land, crawling over hills and dales and woods and farms.

He had got as far as the hills above Chesterfield when he saw a man, just one man with bare feet and a tattered gown, and he didn't run away. He climbed to the top of Winlatter Rock and spread his arms wide so that he made a cross of himself and the Devil was afraid of him and sent a tempest to blow him away – but he never moved.

Three times the Devil tried and the priest stood so firm his feet sunk into the rock and it held him up. Then the Devil ran away back to the north and the priest got down and told the people of Chesterfield how he had saved them and the town.

The Three Valiant Lads

Many years after the monk had driven him away, the devil came again in the guise of a dragon, bringing fire and thunder and tempest with him. All the people were terrified, and at their wits' end to know what to do.

Then three brave young lads persuaded a blacksmith to forge them a mighty iron sword. They struggled with this sword to the top of Winlatter Rock, and stood it upright in the holes made years before by the monk's feet. They hammered it securely in the rock, and looking northwards, saw the smoke that announced the imminent arrival of the dragon.

One of the lads stayed with the sword, and the other two ran to warn the folk of Chesterfield.

The dragon advanced burning everything in his path, till he came to the mighty sword standing up like a cross. He was powerless against the cross, and as he stood fixed to the spot, the bells rang out and he saw an army of men climbing the hill, with their swords held up like crosses. In despair, the dragon fled down the first dark cavern he came to and took refuge at the bottom of the Blue John Mines before vanishing from the region for ever.

DISTINCTIVE FLAVOUR

The Arboretum, the oldest Park in Derby, contains a monument to the car-maker, Sir Henry Royce. The firm of Rolls Royce has been connected with Derby since 1908. Rolls Royce aero engines have been made there since 1915.

Bakewell Tart consists of a pastry case covered with a layer of jam, topped with a sponge mixture, and was derived from a misunderstanding. In 1859, a Mrs Greaves, the mistress of the Rutland Arms Hotel in

BOLSOVER CASTLE.

Bakewell, asked her cook to prepare some jam sponge tarts. Instead of stirring the egg mixture into the pastry and then filling the tart with jam, the cook put the jam in first and then poured the egg mixture over it. The result was so successful that Bakewell Tarts have been produced to that recipe ever since.

The famous Derbyshire custom of **well-dressing** is believed to have begun in the village of Tissington, circa 1350. There are five wells in Tissington, which the locals 'dress' or decorate with flowers on Ascension Day. Other well-dressing ceremonies take place within the county on other days.

COUNTY DIARY

May:	Well-dressing, Tissington
June:	Derbyshire County Show, Derby
July-August:	Festival of Music and Arts, Buxton
August:	Plague memorial service, Eyam

D^{EVO}N

COUNTY FACTS

Derivation of name: The district of tribe of the Dumnonii.

First Recorded: 851 as De Fenascir

County Town: Exeter

Towns: Ashburton, Axminster, Barnstaple, Bideford, Bovey Tracey, Brixham, Budleigh Salterton, Crediton, Cullompton, Dartmouth, Devonport, Exeter, Exmouth, Great Torrington, Honiton, Ilfracombe, Kingsbridge, Kingsteignton, Newton Abbot, Okehampton, Paignton, Plymouth, Plympton, Seaton, Sidmouth, South Molton, Tavistock, Torquay, Totnes. Exeter is historically a city of a county unto itself.

Local Government

Devon County Council. A small part of Devon (namely the parishes of North Petherwin and Werrington, protruding like a beckoning finger into Cornwall) is administered by Cornwall County Council. There are eleven District Councils.

HISTORY

In 710, King Ine of the West Saxons conquered Geraint, Prince of Devon, and began the Saxon conquest of Devon which was complete by 823.

William the Conqueror besieged the city of Exeter for 18 days, until it fell to him.

In the time of Edward III, Dartmouth, Plymouth and Fowey in Cornwall were among the most thriving ports in the country.

The tin miners had their own Stannary courts for the regulation of mining matters. At the end of the 15th century, 96 members from the four stannary towns (Ashburton, Chagford, Plympton and Tavistock) formed the Stannary Parliament to decide on legislation and all questions relating to the tin trade.

The Prayerbook Rebellion began in Sampford Courtenay in 1549. 10,000 rebels marched on Exeter, protesting against the new, English prayerbook; they were ultimately defeated, and 4,000 peasants died in the uprising.

Plymouth and Dartmouth were centres of maritime adventure, from which many ships sailed for colonization in the Americas, and on expeditions to the South Seas and the Bay of Mexico.

Most of the county supported the Parliamentary cause during the Civil War, although Exeter was staunchly Royalist.

In 1688 the Prince of Orange landed at Brixham and marched to Exeter, initially receiving a very cool welcome. However, after three days, realizing that this foreigner was likely to become their next sovereign, the gentlemen of Devon rallied to his standard. Plymouth was devastated by a Luftwaffe raid during the Second World War.

In August 1952, in a freak flood, the river Lyn swept down the valley, claiming 30 lives in what became known as the Lynmouth Disaster.

INDUSTRY PAST AND PRESENT

Today, Devon has tourism, mixed farming, ship-building and fishing as major industries. Tin mines were worked in the county from time immemorial. By the 14th century, tin, copper, lead and silver were being worked. Wool was a flourishing trade from early days. The county has been famous for its cider since the 16th century. Honiton used to be famous for its lace, as also was Ottery St Mary.

LANDMARKS

Dartmoor

Exmoor

Kent's Cavern, limestone caves dating from the Stone Age, where many prehistoric relics

TOPOGRAPHY INCLUDING RIVERS

Devon is bordered by the Bristol Channel in the north, Somerset and Dorset in the east, the English Channel in the south, and Cornwall in the west.

From Exeter to the boundary with Cornwall in the west extends the wide, barren tract of Dartmoor, scattered with granite rocks, known as tors. To the north, the moorland rises to hills, and in the north-east are the higher hills of Exmoor, leading into Somerset. Here are the gorges of the East and West Lyn. The Atlantic coast is one of steep cliffs and rugged headlands. The south coast is broken by many wooded river estuaries. Inland the many rivers pass through beautiful wooded valleys known as combes. the highest point is High Willihays, 2039 feet.

Devon has more rivers and streams than any other English county. They include the Plym, Lyd, Tavy, Bovey, Dart, Avon, Teign, Exe, Taw, Torridge, Mole, Bray, Culm, Otter, Yarty, Axe, Tamar, Hamoaze, Yealm, Erme. The name Tavy means 'the lesser water', and Tamar means 'the greater water'.

have been found.
Lydford Gorge, 200 feet deep, which once
hid the notorious Gubbins gang.

MONUMENTS

Compton Castle, a fortified manor house,
built by Geoffrey Gilbert in 1329.
Dartmouth Castle; this harbour fortress was
built by Edward IV in 1481.
Powderham Castle, built circa 1390, and
converted to a manor in the 18th century,
this has been the home of the Courtenay
family for 600 years.
Exeter Cathedral, established in 1050. The
roof of the nave and choir, at 300 feet, is the
longest single run of Gothic vaulting in the
world.
Buckfast Abbey; the original abbey, founded
in 1018, fell into decay after the Dissolution
in 1539. In 1907 six Benedictine monks
started recreating the Cistercian Abbey. It
took them 31 years.
Buckland Abbey; this Cistercian Abbey,
founded in 1278, became the home of Sir
Francis Drake for the last 15 years of his life.
Killerton House, built in 1778, houses a
costume collection of some 3,000 articles
from the 18th to the 20th century, started by
the theatrical designer, Paulise de Bush.
Saltram; Georgian classical façades were
added to the Tudor house in the 1740s. In
1789 Fanny Burney wrote of it: 'The house is
one of the most magnificent in the kingdom;
its view is noble.'
Exeter Underground Passages; these are a
system of conduits built to bring water to
Exeter from the springs at the head of the
Langbrook Valley.

FAMOUS PEOPLE AND LOCAL CHARACTERS

Sir Francis Drake, sailor and adventurer,
was born near Tavistock in 1540. He was the
first Englishman to sail his ship around the
world.
Sir Walter Raleigh, explorer and colonizer,
was born at Hayes Barton around 1552. He
enjoyed the favour of Queen Elizabeth I for a
while: he is said to have thrown his cloak over
a puddle for her to walk over. He was executed
for treason in 1618.
John Ford, the dramatist, was born around
1586 in Ilsington.
Robert Herrick, the poet, lived in Dean
Prior as vicar for many years, with an interval
of 15 years when, being a Royalist, he was

EXETER

ejected by the Parliamentarians.
John Gay was born in Barnstaple in 1685,
and educated at the grammar school there.
Samuel Taylor Coleridge was born on
October 21st 1772 in Ottery St Mary. He was
the thirteenth child of the rector.
William Makepeace Thackeray stayed in
Ottery St Mary during his school holidays.
Charles Kingsley was born on June 12th
1819 in Holne. He spent much of his boyhood
in Clovelly. During a stay in Bideford he
wrote *Westward Ho!* The village is named
after his book. He died in Salcombe in 1894.
R D Blackmore, author of *Lorna Doone*, went
to school in Tiverton, where bullying by
other boys was the cause of his epilepsy later
in life. Doone Valley, in Exmoor, is named
after his book.
Elizabeth Barrett Browning came to Torquay
in 1834 for her health. Her brother was
drowned in Babbacombe Bay.

ART AND LITERATURE

'Dean-bourn, farewell; I never look to see
Dean, or thy warty incivility.'
   Robert Herrick,
    To Dean Bourn

John Keats called Devon 'a splashy, rainy,
misty, snowy, foggy, haily, muddly, slip-shod
country.'

'A false step yonder means death to man or beast.
Only yesterday I saw one of the moor ponies
wander into it. He never came out. I saw his
head for quite a long time, craning out of the bog
hole, but it sucked him down at last. Even in dry
seasons it is a danger to cross it, but after these
autumn rains it is an awful place.'
   Sir Arthur Conan Doyle,
   on Dartmoor, in *The Hound of the Baskervilles*

'Far to the south, in sunset glow'd
The peaks of Dartmoor ridge,
And Tamar, full and tranquil, flow'd
Beneath the Gresson Bridge.'
   Coventry Patmore
   Devonshire Scenes

'Over the hill and over the dale,
And over the bourne to Dawlish –
Where gingerbread Wives have a scanty sale
And gingerbread nuts are smallish.'
   John Keats (1818)

'Plymouth is beautiful.'
   Queen Victoria

'Brave, beautiful, hanging woods be they which
fall about Dart where she runneth out of the
moor.'
   Eden Philpotts

'In everything, except the accident of my birth, I
am Devonian; my ancestry were all Devonians;
my sympathies and feeling are all Devonian, and
I now actually possess in Devonshire a nearly
perpendicular wood that unfortunately has to pay
out more in rates and taxes than it buys in profit
to me…'
   Richard Doddridge Blackmore

'For there's Bishop's teign
And King's teign
And coomb at the clear teign head
Where close by the stream
You may have your cream
All spread upon barley bread.'
   John Keats

LOCAL FOLKLORE

Devon is well known for its **pixies**, who need
to be treated with respect.
Anyone who ventures near Sheepstor drops
a pin as an offering to the pixies.
No miner will whistle underground for fear of
offending the pixies.

Dartmeet
A farm hand at Rowbrook Farm one winter's
evening heard a voice calling him from a

distance – 'Jan Coo! Jan Coo!' He brought the other farm hands to listen, but at first they heard nothing but the sound of the river. Then they too heard the voice: 'Jan Coo! Jan Coo!'

The lad cried out in answer – and the voice was silent.

The same thing happened each evening around suppertime – the voice would cry his name, but as soon as he answered, it was silent.

Some weeks later, he was on his way home with another farm hand when he heard the voice from across the river. He answered, and this time the voice kept on calling. He started running towards the voice, despite his companion begging him to come on home. The friend went on alone to the farm, still hearing the calling, until it suddenly stopped. They never saw Jan again, nor did they ever again hear the voice calling. Folks in the neighbourhood assumed he had been pixy-led.

Sir Francis Drake

Many legends sprang up about the great deeds of Sir Francis Drake, most of them crediting him with magical powers.

Drake and the River:

Sir Francis Drake had an artificial channel, or leet, constructed, to bring water from Dartmoor to Plymouth. Legend tells that he brought the water by more magical means: he rode out to the moors, hunting for a suitable stream, then, with magical words, he bid the stream follow him, and he galloped back to town with the water at his heels.

Drake and the Armada:

One day Sir Francis Drake was playing at bowls on Plymouth Hoe when he had news that a foreign fleet was sailing into the harbour. He finished his game and then took a hatchet and ordered a large block of wood to be brought to him. He chopped this up into small pieces and threw them into the sea with magic words. As they touched the water each one became a fire-ship and sailed against the foreign fleet so that it was utterly destroyed.

Drake and his Lady:

When Drake sailed away to circumnavigate the world, and 'shot the gulk', he was away so long that his lady despaired of ever seeing him again. After seven years she decided to re-marry; the bridal day came, and the bridal party were in the church.

At that moment one of the spirits who served Sir Francis brought him news, as he sailed in the Antipodes, of what was happening in England. At once he took a cannon and fired right down into the sea. So powerful was the shot and so true was his aim that the ball sped straight through the earth and landed with a loud explosion between the bride and bridegroom just as they reached the altar. 'That is Drake's shot,' said his lady, 'I am still a wife.' And she went home and waited patiently for his return.

Lady Howard's Coach

Around Okehampton and Tavistock, folk claim to have seen the death-coach, all black, with black horses drawing it, driven by a headless coachman. A black hound runs before it, and within sits a lady supposed to be a certain Lady Howard, but she is assuredly an impersonification of Death, for the coach halts to pick up the spirits of the dying.

'Now pray step in! my lady saith;
Now pray step in and ride.
I thank thee, I had rather walk
Than gather at thy side.

The wheels go round without a sound
Or tramp or turn of wheels.
As cloud at night, in pale moonlight,
Along the carriage steals.

I'd rather walk a hundred miles
And run by night and day,
Than have that carriage halt for me,
And hear my lady say —

Now pray step in, and make no din,
Step in with me to ride;
There's room, I trow, by me for you,
And all the world beside.'

The people round Combe Sydenham still believe that Drake's cannon ball rolls up and down in time of national danger.

Drake's Drum stands in the great hall of Buckland Abbey. At the beating of this drum, his sailors mustered on the decks of the *Revenge* in preparation for the battle with the Spanish Armada. Tradition has it that when the drum is beaten, Drake will return. It was said to sound during the Second World War. A poem by Henry Newbolt refers to the legend:

'Take my drum to England, hang it by the shore,
Strike it when your powder's runnin' low
If the Dons sight Devon I'll quit the port o'
Heaven
An' drum them up the Channel as we drummed
them long ago.'

The River Dart is said to be 'cruel', and demands the annual tribute of a human heart.

Legend of Berry Pomeroy

The young Lord Berry and his cousin Genevieve were attacked one day by robbers. She was taken to a cave, and awoke to find the robbers dead, killed by Lord Berry's standard bearer, Raby Copeland. He was badly wounded; she bound up his wound with her scarf. When he recovered, he admitted his love for her, and she returned his love. Lord Berry, who had hoped to marry her himself, gave his consent, and the couple were married.

A different version of the story says that in his jealousy Lord Berry killed them both in a room in the gatehouse, and that their ghosts can be seen on certain nights, trying to touch each other.

DISTINCTIVE FLAVOUR

Devon is a county of **hedgerow banks**, some of them 6 or 8 feet high.

Dartmoor is famous for its ponies which roam wild there, and for its tors, which are large stones, often in piles, scattered over the moor. The featureless bogs and marshes up on Dartmoor can lead the walker to go round and round in circles; he is then said to be 'pixy-led'.

Devon is famous for its clotted cream, which is served in the classic **Devonshire Cream Tea**, with home-made scones and jam.

Devon Rex cats have short, crinkly fur, and crinkly whiskers.

Devonshire Squab Pie consists of layers of mutton chops, cooking apples and onion, flavoured with allspice, and topped with shortcrust pastry.

The most well-known beverages in the county are **Cider** and **Scrumpy**, both made from apples; the uninitiated can be quite misled by the strength of these two local drinks.

COUNTY DIARY

May:	Devon County Show, Exeter
August:	Air Show, Exeter
August:	Navy Days, Plymouth

Dorset

COUNTY FACTS

Derivation of name: West Saxon settlers who made their home around the Roman city of Dorchester became known as the Dornsaete the root of Dorset. Seatan is Old English for settlers.

First Recorded: 940 as Dorseteschire

County Town: Dorchester

Towns: Blandford Forum, Bridport, Dorchester, Ferndown, Gillingham, Lyme Regis, Melcombe Regis, Poole, Portland (inc. Easton and Fortuneswell), Shaftesbury, Sherbourne, Sturminster Newton, Swanage, West Moors, Weymouth, Wimborne Minster, Wool.

The Isle of Purbeck once had its own Lord Lieutenant separate to that of Dorset.

Poole is a county of a town unto itself.

Local Government

Dorset County Council and six district councils. Two small areas around Stockland, Dalwood and Chardstock in the far west fall under Devon County Council and Wambrook is controlled by Somerset County Council.

HISTORY

Before the Roman invasion, the region was occupied by a race of Celts, who had adopted Christianity, and who co-existed with the Roman settlers. In the 7th century, the West Saxons gradually overcame the Celts, and Dorset became part of Wessex. The Wessex settlers in Dorset called themselves 'Dornsaete', or 'Dorsaete', from which the county name comes.

During the Wars of the Roses, Margaret, wife of Henry VI, landed at Weymouth with her small son Edward, and a band of French supporters. She sought sanctuary at Cerne Abbey, before leaving for ultimate defeat at Tewkesbury.

During the Civil War sieges were laid at Lyme, Corfe Castle, and Sherborne Castle. In the north of the country, there gathered together a band of rustics known as 'clubmen', who cared little about either cause, but thoroughly resented the repeated plunder of their land carried out by both armies. Having assembled on Hambleton Hill, they unwisely began to fire on Cromwell's army. They were soon overcome and put to flight -and the plunder continued unabated.

In 1651 Charles II, after his defeat at Worcester, arrived in Charmouth, disguised as a groom, with the intention of escaping to France. The plan misfired, and the secret party had to press on to Bridport, only to find it full of soldiers. Charles went among them, chatting and joking, in his disguise, and they then managed to escape to Trent, the home of Col. Wyndham. Charles later managed to leave England via Sussex, in a collier brig skippered by a Dorset man named Tattersal. In 1685, the Duke of Monmouth landed at Lyme Regis at the start of his ill-fated rebellion. After his ultimate defeat at Sedgemoor, he was captured in Dorset and the recorder of Poole sent him under escort to London, and execution.

In 1834, six labourers from Tolpuddle were transported for their part in illegal union activities. They became known as the 'Tolpuddle martyrs'. Their seven-year sentence was cut short after two years, and they were brought back to England at great expense.

In the 19th century, fear of an invasion by Napoleon caused Dorset folk to build beacons on the downs, ready to flash news of his coming. The panic was ill-founded, as he never came, but the excitement of the time is vividly described in Hardy's *The Trumpet Major*.

TOPOGRAPHY INCLUDING RIVERS

Dorset, on the south coast of England, is bordered by Somerset and Wiltshire in the north, Hampshire in the east, the English Channel in the south, and Devon in the west. In the south, a narrow, broken ridge of chalky hills roughly follows the coast, the easterly ridge being known as the Purbeck Hills. Further north, a region of sandy heathland (Hardy's Egdon Heath), extends from the Hampshire border to the centre of the county, and another range of chalky downs runs east-west towards Salisbury Plain in Wiltshire. Central Dorset is traversed by the wide, rolling expanse of Blackmore Vale, and in the north is the densely wooded chalk mass of Cranborne Chase, shared with Wiltshire. Portland Bill is a rocky peninsular extending south into the channel, connected to the mainland by the long pebble ridge known as Chesil Bank. The highest point is Pilsden Pen, 909 feet.

Rivers: Axe, Frome, Stour.

INDUSTRY PAST AND PRESENT

Present industry includes tourism, Portland stone quarrying, arable dairy and sheep farming, cement making, brickworks, potteries and sand and gravel quarries.

In the 14th century, large quantities of wheat and wool were produced, and the clothing trade flourished in the county, until the Great Plague, from which time it declined. In the 17th century, saltpetre was produced in large quantities, and the first Portland stone was quarried. The towns of Blandford, Lyme Regis and Sherborne were famous for lacemaking in the 18th century, but this industry declined in the 19th.

LANDMARKS

Purbeck Hills
Cranborne Chase
Lulworth Cove
Chesil Beach
Hambledon Hill
Portland Bill
Brownsea Island

The Cerne Abbas Giant, an 180 foot tall chalk figure cut in the hillside during the Roman occupation, or earlier.

MONUMENTS

Corfe Castle, ruins of a Norman castle where Prince Edward was murdered in AD 978. Destroyed during a siege in the Civil War.

Athelhampton Hall, a 15th-century mansion, with additions from the 16th century. The stables have a thatched roof.

Clouds Hill, home of T.E. Lawrence, 'Lawrence of Arabia'.

Hardy's Cottage, the thatched cottage where Thomas Hardy was born in 1840.

Kingston Lacy, the only surviving example of a country house designed by Sir Roger Pratt in 1663-5. The owner, Sir Ralph Bankes, had it built after his previous home, Corfe Castle, was destroyed in the Civil War.

Maiden Castle, the most famous Iron-Age hillfort in England.

Milton Abbey, a former Benedictine monastery. The Gothic abbey church was built in the 15th century.

Parnham, a mainly Elizabethan house, where Sir Arthur Conan Doyle is said to have had his inspiration for *The Hound of the Baskervilles*.

Forde Abbey is a Tudor country house created from a monastery.

Sherborne Abbey, built between the 12th and the 15th centuries. 'Great Tom', a tenor bell given by Cardinal Wolsey, hangs in the

PANEL FROM CLOISTERS. FORDE ABBEY

tower.

Wimborne Minster dates from the 12th century. The two stone towers, one central, the other at the west end, are a famous landmark in the county.

Sherborne Old Castle, a 12th-century castle leased by Elizabeth I to Sir Walter Raleigh. He built the existing Sherborne Castle, which passed to the Digby family in 1617.

Winfrith Atomic Power Station is a more recent adornment.

FAMOUS PEOPLE AND LOCAL CHARACTERS

Thomas Fuller was rector of Broadwindsor from 1634 to 1641. Here he wrote his *Holy and Profane State*.

William Barnes, the poet, was born on March 20 1801 in the hamlet of Rushay. He ran a little school in Dorchester.

Thomas Hardy was born at High Bockhampton, near Dorchester, on June 2, 1840. The son of a stonemason, he was educated at the village school and then in Dorchester. He became an architect, but the success of his fourth published novel, *Far From the Madding Crowd*, enabled him to give up architecture and concentrate on his writing. His novels and poems depict the Wessex countryside, and Dorset towns are recognizable, although given different names: 'Casterbridge' is Dorchester, 'Kingsbere' is Bere Regis, and 'Sherton Abbas' Sherborne. Hardy died at his home, Max Gate, on 11 January 1928.

Local Characters

John Tregonwell was lord of the manor of Middleton. As a baby, he had a miraculous escape when he fell from the roof of Milton Abbey. So swaddled was he in voluminous clothes that these acted as a parachute, and he came to land unhurt.

ART AND LITERATURE

'..as there is nothing to admire in the buildings themselves, the remarkable situation of the town, the principal street almost hurrying into the water, the walk to the Cobb, skirting round the pleasant little bay, which in the season is animated with bathing machines and company, the Cobb itself, its old wonders and new improvements, with the very beautiful line of cliffs stretching out to the east of the town, are what the stranger's eye will seek; and a very strange stranger it must be, who does not see charms in the immediate environs of Lyme, to make him wish to know it better. The scenes in its neighbourhood, Charmouth, with its high grounds and extensive sweeps of country, and still more its sweet retired bay, backed by dark cliffs, where fragments of low rock among the sands make it the happiest spot for watching the flow of the tide, for sitting in unwearied contemplation; — the woody varieties of the cheerful village of Up Lyme, and, above all, Pinny, with its green chasms between romantic rocks, where the scattered forest trees and orchards of luxuriant growth declare that many a generation must have passed away since the first partial falling of the cliff prepared the ground for such a state,…These places must be visited, and visited again, to make the worth of Lyme understood.'

Jane Austen
Persuasion (1815)

'Rime Intrinsica, Fontmell Magna, Sturminster Newton and Melbury Bubb,
Whist upon whist upon whist upon whist drive, in Institute, Legion and Social Club,
Horny hands that hold the aces which this morning held the plough —
While Tranter Reuben, T S Eliot, H G Wells and Edith Sitwell lie in Mellstock
  Churchyard now.

Lord's Day bells from Bingham's Melcombe, Iverne Minster, Shroton, Plush,
Down the grass between the beeches, mellow in the evening hush,
Gloved the hands that hold the hymn-book, which this morning milked the cow —
While Tranter Reuben, Mary Borden, Brian Howard and Harold Acton lie in
  Mellstock Churchyard now.'

John Betjeman
Dorset (1937)

'…the gorgeous autumn landscape of White-Hart Vale, surrounded by orchards lustrous with the reds of apple-crops, berries and foliage, the whole intensified by the gilding of the declining sun.'

Thomas Hardy
The Woodlanders (1887)

'Norcombe Hill – not far from Lonely Toller-Down – was one of the spots which suggest to a passer-by that he is in the presence of a shape approaching the indestructible as nearly as any to be found on earth. It was a featureless convexity of chalk and soil – an ordinary specimen of those smoothly – outlined protruberances of the globe which may remain undisturbed on some great day of confusion, when far grander heights and dizzy precipices topple down.'

Thomas Hardy
Far from the Madding Crowd (1874)

LOCAL FOLKLORE

Cerne Abbas Giant

The huge chalk-cut figure on the side of the hill is said by some to be the outline of a real giant who had killed some sheep in Blackmoor, and, having made a feast of them, had laid down to sleep. The local people, furious at the slaughter, and finding him fast asleep, killed him on the spot and traced out his shape on the hillside as a memorial.

He is believed by many to have been a fertility symbol, and as late as the 19th century, it was said that a barren woman could be cured by sitting on the giant. Another school of thought claimed, however, that the woman must engage in sexual intercourse there for the power of the giant to be effective. A local vicar put a stop to the 'scourings' that were held there every seven years, as he discovered that those taking part were testing out the tradition....

Edward the Martyr

On the death of his father Edgar in AD 975, Edward became King, to the disgust of his step-mother Elfryth, who hoped that her son Ethelred would reign. One day, three years after his accession, Edward had been out hunting with his jester Wulfstan, and had sent him off to find food. Wearying of waiting for Wulfstan's return, Edward rode to Corfe Gate alone. It was evening, and he remained on horseback while he took a cup of wine. As he was drinking, a man crept up behind him and stabbed him in the back. The horse took fright and bolted, and Edward, his foot caught in the stirrup, was dragged off down the hill. A group of peasants finally stopped the terrified horse, and although they didn't recognize the body of the king, they saw from the cloak that it must be that of some rich noble. However, they heard horsemen approaching, and fled from the body. It is assumed that the horsemen hastily buried the body on the spot. The King of England had disappeared, and word was given out that he had been killed by a fall from his horse. Ethelred, who is supposed to have cried for his dead brother, whom he greatly loved, was proclaimed King by St Dunstan, but the saint prophesied evil for him, because he had climbed to the throne through the death of his brother. The reign of Ethelred the Unready was indeed a troubled one.

A ghostly horse can sometimes be heard galloping down the hill from Corfe Castle, following the route that Edward's horse took in its flight. Not long after the disappearance of Edward, tales began to be told of miracle cures being effected at a certain place on the Wareham Road. Elfryth set out to see the place for herself, but her horse refused to move under her; a second horse did the same. Rumours of Elfryth's plotting against her step-son were rife. St Dunstan sent men to dig on the spot where the miracles were happening, and they there found the body of the dead king, with a dagger wound which proved that death was not only due to a fall from his horse. It was clear that he had been murdered, and although no one was actually accused, Elfryth has long been held to be the instigator of the murder. Because of his murder and the miracles that had been wrought at his grave, Edward was revered as a saint, and became known as Edward the Martyr.

The Lyme Regis Black Dog

A farmer in Lyme Regis lived in a farmhouse, part of which dated back to before the Civil War. At the end of a long day the farmer used to sit in his favourite seat in the large inglenook fireplace to rest, and a large black dog would seat himself down on the other side of the fire. At first the dog's presence unsettled the farmer, but after a while he began to look on him as one of the family. His friends told him he should get rid of the dog, but the farmer retorted that it was a quiet animal, cost him nothing, and ate nothing, so he had no cause for complaint. However, one night, when the farmer had been drinking a little too much, and a neighbour had been taunting him about the black dog, he decided to prove that he had no fear of it and rushed at it with a poker. The dog bolted to the attic, where it sprang up and disappeared through the ceiling.

The enraged farmer struck the ceiling with the poker on the spot where the dog had seemed to pass through, and down fell an old box. The farmer looked inside, and found a large sum in gold and silver from the reign of Charles I.

Some believe that the dog was the ghost of a person who had hidden the treasure and died before he could tell of it, but to this day a black dog is said to haunt the lane which leads to the house; the lane is appropriately called Dog Lane.

DISTINCTIVE FLAVOUR

Lyme Regis and its chalky cliffs are renowned for their abundance of fossils: in 1811, Mary Anning, then 12 years old, found a fossilized ichthyosaurus in the rocks.

The dialect of Dorset is most distinctive, and even has its own grammar: nouns are divided into two classes, personal (for formed things, such as man, tree, book), and impersonal (for unformed quantities, such as wood, water, hair). The pronoun for personal things is 'he', and that for impersonal things is 'it'. The demonstratives of personal things are 'th_ase' and 'thic' - th_ase tree; thic cow.
To a Dorset man a mole hill is a 'wont-heave', and a cantankerous person is 'thirtover'.

Dorset Apple Cake is a deliciously moist delicacy, in which apples are complemented by currants and mixed peel. The finished cake is served sprinkled with brown sugar.

Blue Vinney is a Devon cheese of some repute.

COUNTY DIARY

June:	Pitchfork Rebellion pageants, to commemorate the landing of the Duke of Monmouth in 1685, Lyme Regis
August:	Dorset County Fair, Dorchester
September:	Dorchester Agricultural Show

DURHAM

COUNTY FACTS

Derivation of name: Island with a hill. Only English county with an ecclesiastical origin. After the Danish raids on Holy Island where St Cuthbert died, the monks fled carrying his coffin with them to find a safe resting place. They chose the secure rockly 'outcrop' where the cathedral of Durham now stands. Hence Durham never has had the 'shire' suffixed as the Bishops ruled with unique powers over the area until 1836 when their powers were handed over to the crown. Hence County Durham never Durhamshire. Under Norman influence Dunholme which led to Dunham and then the 'n' mutated to an 'r' hence Durham.

First Recorded: 1000 as Dunholme

County Town: Durham

Towns: Barnard Castle, Billingham, Birtley, Blaydon, Boldon, Brandon, Chester-le-Street, Consett, Darlington, Durham, Easington, Felling, Ferryhill, Gateshead, Hartlepool, Hebburn, Hetton-le-Hole, Houghton-le-Spring, Jarrow, Newton Aycliffe, Peterlee, Ryton, Seaham, Shildon, South Shields, Spennymoor, Stanley, Stockton-on-Tees, Sunderland, Washington, Whickham.

There are two large chunks of Durham within Northumberland. Bedlington or Bedlingtonshire up until Henry VIII time had its own courts and justices of the peace as it was owned by the Bishops of Durham. At the very far tip of Northumberland dividing Berwick-upon-Tweed from Northumberland is a large area of Durham detached containing the suburbs of Berwick-upon-Tweed south of the river, Tweedmouth and Spittal plus the villages of Cornhill-on-Tweed at its far eastern edge, Norham, Ancroft, Kyloe, and Elwick at its most southern tip, plus the sacred church land, Holy Island, containing Lindisfarne Castle.

Local Government
Durham County Council, Northumberland County Council, three Metropolitan Boroughs and ten District Councils.

HISTORY

In the 6th century, the kingdom of Northumbria was divided into the two states of Bernicia and Deira, the region which later became County Durham being included in the latter. The county was converted to Christianity in the 7th century, and from this time and well into the 8th century, there was a great flourishing of religion, art and literature in the county. The Venerable Bede, or Baeda, is the most well known writer from this Golden Age of the county.

After the monks on Lindisfarne had been driven out by the Danes, the body of St Cuthbert was taken to rest at Chester-le-Street, which became as a result a place of pilgrimage: the Christian metropolis of the north. In 995, his remains were finally taken to Dun-holm, or Durham, and Durham City became the centre of the expanding Bishopric. The 11th century saw resistance in the county to the Norman invasion, and as a result the county was duly laid waste by the invaders. The same century saw the beginnings of the great cathedral in Durham.

During the reign of Henry II, his cousin Pudsey was Bishop of Durham, and under him the Bishopric, or Palatinate of Durham was established, as a separate 'kingdom', with the Bishop as sovereign.

In the Battle of Neville's Cross in 1346, the English were victorious against the invading Scots. In the same century, the county was ravaged by the Black Death.

Feeling ran high against the Reformation, and in 1569 there was an uprising against the new regime in church and state. For a time, the Old Order was restored in Durham Cathedral.

In 1640 the Scots occupied Durham and the high sheriff of the palatinate guaranteed to supply the Scots army with provisions. The county was, however, mainly Royalist during the Civil War.

In the 17th century, the great development of shipping at Sunderland and Hartlepool increased the trade in coal, lead and salt which had flourished for centuries.

The Industrial Revolution accelerated the growth of prosperity of the county, and the population increased dramatically. The Wesleyan movement took hold in the county and exerted a strong influence.

During the reign of William IV, the University of Durham was founded, and the Palatinate of Durham was annexed to the Crown.

The 20th century has seen the dramatic economic decline of the county: in 1936 the famous 'Jarrow Marchers' went on a hunger march to London, with their numbers swelling as they travelled south.

TOPOGRAPHY INCLUDING RIVERS

Roughly triangular in shape, with the coast as the base, the western angle of County Durham is crossed by the high, barren ridge of the Pennines. The Wear and the Tees (which forms the southern boundary of the county) wind down from these heights between undulating hills towards the (now largely worked out) coalfields of the eastern lowlands and the coast. A meander of the River Wear forms a peninsular in the centre of Durham City, on which hilly ground stands the cathedral and the castle. Hamsterley Forest stretches for some 5,000 acres roughly in the centre of the county. The highest point is Burnhope Seat, 2452 feet.

Rivers: Wear, Tees.

INDUSTRY PAST AND PRESENT

Engineering, Nissan cars, coking coal and chemical products are important. The coal and shipbuilding industries have declined. Coal was mined in the county from Norman times, and was the centre of the county's economy until the 20th century. There was lead-mining in the west, and mustard was extensively cultivated. The shipyards on the Tyne, at Sunderland, and Hartlepool, saw a booming trade in the 19th century. The output of limestone used to be greater than in any other part of the country. Lead was also worked in Weardale.

LANDMARKS

The Pennines
Marsden Cliffs and Marsden Rock
Hamsterley Forest
High Force Waterfall
Holy Island, or Lindisfarne, on which St Aidan, Bishop of Iona, founded a priory, AD 635 (a detached part of Durham)

MONUMENTS

Durham Cathedral, founded in the 11th century, is one of the most outstanding examples of Romanesque architecture in Europe.
Durham Castle, the palace of the Prince-Bishops of Durham from its beginnings in 1072 up till 1836. It is the only castle in northern England never to be captured by the Scots.
Durham University, created as the third university in England in 1832.
Auckland Castle, the residence of the Bishops of Durham for 800 years.
Raby Castle, a 14th-century fortress, with a great hall large enough to hold 700 knights.
Gulbenkian Museum, the only museum in Britain devoted wholly to Oriental art.
Finchale Priory; the ruins of the 13th century priory stand on the banks of the River Wear. In the 14th century, the priory became the 'holiday home' of the monks of Durham Cathedral priory.

FAMOUS PEOPLE AND LOCAL CHARACTERS

Bede, the English historian and theologian, was head of the Jarrow school of 600 monks. He was born in the territory of the monastery at Jarrow in AD 672 or 673. He is famous for his histories and his translation of the Gospel of St John into English.
Christopher Smart, the poet, was educated at Durham School. The Duchess of Cleveland gave him £40 a year until her death in 1742.
Robert Surtees, the journalist and novelist, was born in Durham in 1805. He was educated at Durham School. On the death of his father he succeeded to the estate of Hamsterley Hall, where he indulged in his favourite pursuits of hunting and fishing. He wrote several novels on the theme of foxhunting society.
Elizabeth Barrett Browning was born on 6 March 1806 in Coxhoe Hall in Kelloe.

ART AND LITERATURE

'The road to it is steep:
It is surrounded with rocks
And with curious plants:
The Wear flows round it
A river of rapid waves

There is in this city
Also, well known to men
The venerable St Cudberth.'
    Anglo-Saxon poem
    (about Durham City)

'The Cathedral has a massyness and solidity such as I have seen in no other place…It rather awes than pleases, as it strikes with a kind of gigantick dignity, and aspires to no other praise than that of rock solidity and indeterminate duration.'
    Dr Samuel Johnson

'I have one of the most beautiful vales in England to walk in…all rude and romantic, in short, the sweetest spot to break your neck or drown yourself in that ever was beheld.'
    Thomas Gray,
    on the environs of Durham, (1753)

'…after many wanderings past,
He chose his lordly seat at last,
Where his Cathedral huge and vast
Looks down upon the Wear;
There, deep in Durham's Gothic shade
His relics are in secret laid.'
    Sir Walter Scott
    Marmion

John Ruskin thought the combination of river, cathedral, and castle in Durham city *'One of the seven wonders of the world'*.

'…spieth near her banke
(That from their loathsome brims do breathe a
sulphurous sweat)
Hell-kettles rightly cald…'
    Michael Drayton
    Poly-Olbion

'Grey towers of Durham…
Yet well I love thy mixed and massive piles…'
    Sir Walter Scott
    Harold the Dauntless

Durham cathedral is *'Half Church of God, half castle 'gainst the Scot'*.
    (Anon)

LOCAL FOLKLORE

The Staindrop Cat
One night, a farmer was on his way home to Staindrop when a cat jumped out in front of him and spoke the following words:
    'Johnny Reed! Johnny Reed!
    Tell Madam Monfort
    That Mally Dixon's dead!'
The farmer, much bemused, went on home, and related the tale to his wife. Suddenly their own cat leapt up, crying, 'Is she?!', and disappeared. They never saw her again.
It was believed that the cat was really a fairy in disguise, and had gone off to her sister's funeral.

Hell Kettles
The Hell Kettles are three small, round ponds, about 17 feet deep.
One day, the farmer who owned the land where they now lie was carting his hay on St Barnabas' Day. His neighbours rebuked him for his impiety, to which he retorted,
    'Barnaby yea, Barnaby nay,
    A cartload of hay,
    Whether God will or nay.'
As he finished uttering these words, he, his haycart, and the horses, were all swallowed up by the pools. It is said that on certain fine days, they can be seen, floating deep down in the water.
The ponds were given the name Hell Kettles because they were believed to be bottomless, and because the water in them was hot - giving rise to the further belief that they were used by the devil to boil the souls of sinners.

The Lambton Worm
The heir to Lambton Castle went fishing one Sunday, ignoring the sanctity of the Sabbath. Having caught nothing all day, he was preparing to return home, thoroughly vexed, when he suddenly got a bite. He struggled with the catch, and eventually pulled up – a very small, but nonetheless hideous worm!

THE CLOISTERS, DURHAM CATHEDRAL

He showed it round the neighbourhood as a curiosity, and the jester declared that it was the devil. Lambton retorted that since it was the devil, it could go straight back down to hell, and threw it down a well.

Shortly after this, the young man renounced his wild ways and set off on a crusade to the Holy Land.

Meanwhile, the tiny worm grew and grew until eventually a huge serpent crawled out of the well and made its way to a hill, where it wound itself round and round the base, and preyed on the livestock in the vicinity till the local farmers were in despair.

Knights came from far and wide to try to destroy the evil worm, but each time it was hacked to pieces, these pieces would join together again; the serpent would then coil its loathsome body round and round the luckless knight, and crush him to death.

Some years later, Lambton came home from the crusades, and he swore to kill the worm. He paid a visit to a local witch to ask her for help. Unknown to the young man, this witch had a long-standing grudge against his father, but she promised to help him in his self-appointed task - provided he swore to kill the first living thing he met after the worm was dead. Lambton duly swore his oath, and the witch furnished him with a suit of armour covered all over with sharp knives. Thus clad, he set off to kill the worm.

As before, each time he hacked at the worm, the pieces joined together again; but when it curled around his body to crush him to death, the knives on his armour cut it to pieces. The witch shouted to Lambton to make for the river, and the worm, infuriated, hurled itself after him. Once in the fast-flowing river, Lambton attacked the worm again, and this time, whenever a piece of the worm was hacked off, the river carried it swiftly away, preventing the creature from reassembling itself. Finally, even the head was gone, and the Lambton Worm was dead.

Lambton blew his horn, to signal to his father that the deed was done, and that he would release one of the hounds, that he might fulfil his oath to the witch by slaying it. But his father, in his great joy at his son's success, rushed up to congratulate him. Lambton, horrified, refused to kill his father, thereby going back on his oath. The witch, furious at being foiled of her revenge on Lord Lambton, cursed the family, prophesying that no heir to the Lambton estates would die in his bed for nine generations.

The witch's curse was fulfilled, as every one of the nine succeeding Lords Lambton died a violent death. The 10th Lord Lambton ensured that the curse was at an end: feeling slightly unwell one day, he took to his bed, and remained there, obstinately refusing to move, until he finally died peacefully between the sheets.

DISTINCTIVE FLAVOUR

Durham County has been severely hit by the decline in its main industries – coal, steel and shipbuilding, and unemployment in the county is amongst the highest in the country.

The Durham Miners' Gala is held annually on the 3rd Saturday of July, and the streets of the city of Durham are filled with bands and marchers.

Stotty Cake is a locally baked bread cake.

Durham Lunch Cake is a rich mixture characterised by the use of dried fruit and spices baked in a loaf tin.

COUNTY DIARY

April:	Teesdale County Show, Barnard Castle
May 1:	Riding the Bounds, Berwick-upon-Tweed
June:	Northumberland miners' picnic, Bedlington
June:	Regatta, Durham City (claimed to be the oldest in the country)
July:	Miners' Gala, Durham City
July:	Durham County Show, Lambton Park, Chester-le-Street

E^{SSE}X

COUNTY FACTS

Derivation of name: Essex comes from the Old English, 'the land of the East Saxons'

First Recorded: 604 as East Seaxe

County Town: Chelmsford

Towns: Barking, Basildon, Billericay, Braintree, Brentwood, Chelmsford, Chingford, Clacton-on-Sea, Colchester, Dagenham, East Ham, Epping, Grays Thurrock, Harlow, Harwich, Hornchurch, Ilford, Leyton, Loughton, Maldon, Romford, Saffron Walden, Southend-on-Sea, Tilbury, Tiptree, Walthamstow, Wanstead, West Ham, Woodford, Witham.

Local Government

Essex County Council, five London Boroughs, and fourteen District Councils.

HISTORY

The Trinobantes tribe inhabited the region before the Roman conquest.

Colchester was the first Roman British colony. After the Romans, the northern tribes of Angles, Saxons, and Jutes invaded, and the Kingdom of East Saxony was founded circa AD 527.

Although Christianity had begun to spread in Roman times, it was not until circa 643 that the county was fully converted, by Cedd, brother of St Chad.

In 933 the Battle of Maldon occured, when the Danes defeated the Saxons. This incident gave rise to the poem 'The Battle of Maldon'. The Danish invasion culminated in their victory at Assandune, near Rochford, in 1016, when Essex came under the rule of Canute. King Harold was governor of Essex. William the Conqueror, after his coronation, retired to Barling Abbey, awaiting the building of the Tower of London.

Essex was the birthplace of the Peasants' Revolt in 1391, when the men of Essex rose with the men of Kent and marched to Mile End. There they petitioned the King and Queen for the abolition of slavery, fixed rents, freedom to buy and sell in market towns, and a free pardon. Their requests were granted, but the king's army were then ordered out to suppress the revolt, which resulted in much slaughter and cruelty.

The county was pre-eminent in Protestant Non-conformity – 71 people of Essex were persecuted during the reign of Mary Tudor. Tilbury was the setting for Queen Elizabeth I's famous address to her 'faithful and loving people' for the defence of the realm against the Spanish Armada.

The letter which led to the discovery and frustration of the Gunpowder Plot was sent to an Essex landowner, Lord Monteagle, who disclosed the warning to the Secretary of State.

Prior to the Restoration, Matthew Hopkins, from Manningtree, was the 'Witchfinder General', and was responsible for the deaths of hundreds of innocent men and women.

The county was divided during the Civil War, but the Restoration was hailed with gladness throughout the county.

In 1803, when a French invasion was anticipated, Sir William Hilary of Essex raised a force of 17,000 men, the largest private army in the kingdom.

INDUSTRY PAST AND PRESENT

Nowadays, Essex boasts docks, car manufacture, oil refineries, Bradwell nuclear power station, agriculture and market gardening. Tilbury is Britain's largest port.

Essex was always mainly an agricultural county; Domesday Book also mentions salt-making, wine-making, bee-culture and cheese-making. Oyster fisheries were famous from earliest recorded times. The woollen industry grew in Saxon times and ranked as the most important trade for many centuries. In the 16th century, the county was exceptionally wealthy and prosperous, with flourishing weaving and leather industries. The 17th century saw much saffron culture and silk-weaving, and later, malting and brewing, and potash-making grew in importance.

LANDMARKS

The Naze

Epping Forest

Mudflats and saltmarshes along the coast

TOPOGRAPHY INCLUDING RIVERS

Essex, in the southern part of East Anglia, is bordered by Suffolk and Cambridgeshire in the north, the North Sea in the east, Kent, and the Thames Estuary in the south, and Middlesex and Hertfordshire in the west. The River Lea is the boundary with Middlesex.

The coastline which stretches for 310 miles in the east and south-east, is very flat, and marshy, with many rivers and creeks projecting inland. Further west the land rises and becomes undulating, although it remains flat and marshy along the Thames. In the south west, the ancient forest of Epping extends in a crescent shape over 6,000 acres. The highest point is High Wood, near Langley, 480 feet.

Rivers: Stour, Lea Colne, Blackwater, Chelmer, Crouch, Roding.

MONUMENTS

Audley End, one of the largest Jacobean houses in England, built by the Lord Treasurer, Lord Howard of Walden, Earl of Suffolk, in 1603. James I said of it: 'Too large for a king, but might do for a Lord Treasurer'.

Bourne Mill, built in 1591 by Sir Thomas Lucas as a fishing lodge, and later converted to a mill.

Colchester Castle; the castle keep, built circa 1085, and now a museum, was built over a former Roman temple.

Harwich Redoubt is a huge fortress, built circa 1810, against the threat of Napoleonic invasion.

Layer Marney Towers; this enormous gatehouse, 90 feet high, and the largest of its kind, is the only completed part of a magnificent 16th century mansion, built by Henry, 1st Lord Marney. He died before it was completed.

Waltham Abbey, founded in 1030, was built by King Harold. Only the Romanesque nave remains, but it is a work of the highest quality.

FAMOUS PEOPLE AND LOCAL CHARACTERS

Daniel Defoe lived in Chadwell St Mary. He was manager of a tile works in West Tilbury.

Arnold Bennett owned a house in Thorpe-le-Soken.

ART AND LITERATURE

'The vagrant visitor erstwhile,'
My colour-plate book says to me,
'Could wend by hedgerow-side and stile,
From Benfleet down to Leigh-on-Sea.

And as I turn the colour-plates,
Edwardian Essex opens wide,
Mirrored in ponds and seen through gates,
Sweet uneventful countryside.

Far Essex, – fifty miles away
The level wastes of sucking mud
Where distant barges high with hay
Come sailing in upon the flood.

Near Essex of the River Lea
And anglers out with hook and worm
And Epping Forest glades where we
Had beanfeasts with my father's firm.'
      John Betjeman
      Essex (1954)

'For since the plague, hundreds of couples have married, yet the only fruit they have brought forth are foul words; they live in jealousy, without happiness...If they went to try for the Dunmow Flitch, they wouldn't stand a chance without the Devil's help...'
      William Langland
      Piers Plowman

LOCAL FOLKLORE

Waltham Abbey

It is believed by many that the body of King Harold, killed by William the Conqueror at the Battle of Hastings, was interred in Waltham Abbey. One legend has it that, the night after the battle, a peasant and his wife came to strip the bodies of the dead of the battlefield, and found that Harold was still alive. They took him home with them. Heming, a Norwegian who had been in Harold's service, came to see him and offered to help him win back his kingdom. Harold refused, saying that many of the English had sworn fealty to William and that he would not be the cause of them breaking their oaths. Instead he became a hermit near Canterbury, from where he would watch William as he went to Church.

Three years later he died, and all the bells of Canterbury rang out. William asked the reason for the ringing, and then asked to see the body of the hermit. He recognized Harold and had him clothed in royal robes and buried at Waltham Abbey with great ceremony.

Little Dunmow

Legend has it that Matilda the fair, or Robin Hood's Maid Marian, is buried in the former Priory Church of Little Dunmow.

After the death of Robin, she took refuge in the priory. King John, whose suit she had previously rejected, sent one of his men, Robert de Medewe, with a bracelet for her, seemingly as a token of his affection. Although no longer young, Matilda was still beautiful, and Robert fell in love with her. He set off to return to London, but turned back in order to see her again. He reached the priory at nightfall, as a funeral was taking place. On making enquiries, he learned that it was the funeral of Matilda; the bracelet he had given her had eaten into her flesh and poisoned her.

In an agony of remorse, he flung himself on her bier. He never returned to court, but instead lived the rest of his days as a monk.

DISTINCTIVE FLAVOUR

The Dunmow Flitch: an old custom attaches to Little Dunmow, dating from the 15th century, by which a flitch of bacon can be claimed by any married couple who have 'not repented them, sleeping or waking, of their marriage in a year and a day'. Couples may come from all over the country, and they must kneel on two stones at the door of the Church of Little Dunmow and take a solemn oath that they have not quarrelled, offended each other by word or deed, nor been guilty of any infidelity, and that they have never once wished themselves unmarried.

The Essex coastline contains one-fifth of Britain's mudflats, and one-sixth of its saltmarshes.

The county provides an almost unique habitat for several species of flora and fauna: The **Sickle-leaved Hare's Ear** within Britain is found only on one Essex roadside verge. The **Mersea Pea**, very rare in Britain, has its stronghold on Mersea Island. The main locality in Britain of the **Sea Hog's-fennel** is in north-east Essex. **Lesser Calamint**, rare in other parts of Britain, is locally common.

In early winter, up to 50% of the British wintering population of the **Dark-bellied Brent Goose** are to be found on the Essex coast.

The Essex Skipper butterfly and the **Essex Emerald moth** were first discovered in Britain on the Essex coast. Essex is the world stronghold of the **Matthew's Wainscot moth**, unknown outside Britain.

COUNTY DIARY

June:	Essex County Show, Chelmsford
August:	Jousting and county fair, Layer Marney Tower
August:	Regatta week, Burnham-on-Crouch
October:	Oyster Feast, Colchester

GLOUCESTERSHIRE

COUNTY FACTS

Derivation of name: From the Brittonic Glouiu, meaning bright place or shining fortress. Its Roman name is Glevum.

First Recorded: 1016 as Gleaucestrescir

Motto: Prorsum Semper (Ever Forward)

County Town: Gloucester

Towns: Avonmouth, Bristol, Brockworth, Chipping Campden, Chipping Sodbury, Cheltenham, Cinderford, Cirencester, Coleford, Dursley, Gloucester, Hucclecote, Kingswood, Lydney, Mangotsfield, Nailsworth, Shirehampton, Stow-on-the-Wold, Stroud, Tetbury, Tewkesbury, Thornbury, Wootton under Edge, Yate. Gloucester is a county of a city unto itself.

The city and county of Bristol: In 1373, Edward III declared that Bristol was 'a county by itself separated (from the) Counties of Gloucester and Somerset equally and in all things exempt...(to be) called the County of Bristol for ever'.

Local Government

Gloucestershire County Council and Avon County Council. There are nine District Councils.

The parish of Kemerton protrudes into Worcestershire, administered by Hereford and Worcester County Council. There are detached parts of Gloucestershire as follows: Tidling Corner, near Minety in Wiltshire (Wiltshire County Council); Shennington (Oxfordshire County Council) and Little Compton and Sutton-under-Brailes in Warwickshire (Warwickshire County Council).

The geographical boundaries of Gloucestershire , Worcestershire and Warwickshire are probably the most complex in Britain, as detached areas and indentations for individual parishes leave a very convoluted pattern. It is not therefore possible to give a complete explanation of all these boundaries in a book of limited pages.

HISTORY

Before the Roman occupation, the Celtic tribe of Duboni inhabited the west of the region, and the Cattuvellani tribe the east. With the Roman invasion, Corinium (Cirencester) became one of the most important towns in Britain. Several Roman roads passed through the county – Ermin Street, Acman Street, and Icknield Street (the ancient Icknield Way).

In AD 577, in a battle on the hill of Dyrham, the West Saxons defeated the Britons and completely established their rule in the Severn Valley. By AD 650 the northern part of the region was included in the Kingdom of Mercia. Christianity was brought to the region by Wulfhere and Osric.

After invasion by the Danes, Bristol sprang into being as a port for (slave) trade with the Danes in Ireland.

Circa 910, the Kingdom of Mercia was divided up, and the region took the name of Gloucestershire.

William the Conqueror hunted in the Forest of Dean, and he held his Witan at Gloucester. It was there that he arranged for the compilation of Domesday Book.

The county was the great theatre of the war between Stephen and Matilda. The castles of Bristol, Gloucester and Cirencester were all garrisoned on Matilda's behalf.

TOPOGRAPHY INCLUDING RIVERS

Gloucestershire, in the west of England, around the Severn basin, is bordered by Herefordshire, Worcestershire and Warwickshire in the north, Oxfordshire in the east, Wiltshire and Somerset in the south, and Herefordshire and the Bristol Channel in the west.

The high sweep of the Cotswolds fills the eastern half of the county, the highest point being Cleeve Cloud at 1,000 feet. They form a border to the Severn Valley. The Severn enters the county at Tewkesbury in the north, and the tide-wave from the Atlantic, the

Severn bore, is felt even there, 70 miles from the sea. The Severn Valley is about 8 miles wide in the north and is known as the Vale of Gloucester. South of the city, it narrows, and is known as the Vale of Berkeley. West of the Severn lies the Forest of Dean. The highest point is Cleever Hill near Cheltenham, 1083 feet (the nearest place to London over 1000 feet).

Rivers: Severn, Windrush, Coln, Leadon.

In the 12th century the county became prosperous, and Bristol was a thriving port with a wealthy colony of Jews.

King John is buried in Gloucester, and his successor, Henry III, was crowned there.

In 1278, the Statutes of Gloucester were passed, for enquiring into the powers and rights exercised by the great lords in their domains.

Berkeley Castle was the scene of the foul murder of Edward II in 1327.

The Battle of Tewkesbury on 4 May 1471, was the fiercest battle of the Wars of the Roses. The defeated Lancastrians were pursued into Tewkesbury Abbey Church and blood was spilt within it.

The county was strongly on the side of Parliament in the Civil War, and there were sieges at Gloucester and Bristol. The decisive battle at Stow-on-the-Wold ended in defeat for the King.

In the 18th century, Cheltenham became the fashionable centre of the beau monde, vying in importance with Bath.

INDUSTRY PAST AND PRESENT

Nowadays, the county practises engineering, aircraft manufacture, sheep-rearing, dairying and fruit-farming (apples, plums and pears). The forest district was the chief iron-producing area of the kingdom until the 16th century; the mines were worked in Roman times. The timber from this district gave rise to numerous tanneries and the shipbuilding trade. The woollen trade flourished first in the major towns and then, as they became increasingly involved in foreign trade, moved to the smaller towns of the Cotswolds. Silk-weaving, which began in the 17th century, flourished particularly in the Stroud valley. Brick, tiles, and pottery were also produced, from the abundance of clay and building stone to be found in the county. In the 17th and 18th centuries, a thriving trade grew in the manufacture of pins, buttons, lace, and stockings.

LANDMARKS

Forest of Dean
Cotswolds
Clearwell Caves
Puzzle Wood
Birdlip Hill
Westonbirt Arboretum, begun in 1829.
The Severn Road Bridge

MONUMENTS

Badminton House, a Palladian mansion, the home of the Dukes of Beaufort since the 17th century. The annual horse trials are held at Badminton.

Gloucester Cathedral, begun in 1089 and finished in 1128. The murdered King Edward II was buried here in 1327. The east window is the size of a tennis court!

Berkeley Castle, a well preserved stronghold overlooking the River Severn, which has been the home of the Berkeley family since its beginnings in 1153.

Chedworth Roman Villa – one of the best preserved Roman villas in the country.

Littledean Hall, the home of the Lords of Dene since before the Norman Conquest.

Prinknash Abbey, the Old Abbey dates from the 14th century. In 1928 it was given back to the Benedictine monks as an abbey. The New Abbey was consecrated in 1972.

Snowshill Manor, a manor house dating from the 16th and 17th centuries, which houses a fantastic collection of curios amassed by a former owner, Charles Wade – including Samurai armour, firefighting equipment, clocks and mousetraps.

Tewkesbury Abbey dates from the early 12th century. One of the largest Parish Churches in England, it was bought by the townspeople on the dissolution of the monasteries for £400.

Sudeley Castle; Queen Catherine Parr lived here after the death of Henry VIII.

FAMOUS PEOPLE AND LOCAL CHARACTERS

Edward II was murdered at Berkeley Castle with a red-hot poker.

Bishop Hooper was burnt at the stake as a heretic in the city of Gloucester.

John Taylor, the 'water poet', was born on August 24 1580, in Gloucester, and attended the Grammar School there.

Robert Raikes, the educational pioneer, taught children in Gloucester on Sundays, and started the Sunday School tradition.

Edward Jenner, who was born in the county in 1743, discovered the smallpox vaccine, and helped to lay the foundations of modern immunology.

Tennyson came to Cheltenham for his health, and is said to have written part of 'In Memoriam' during his stay there.

W G Grace, the cricketer, was batsman for Gloucestershire and England. Amongst other memorable achievements was his scoring of 1,000 runs within one month, May 1885.

Ivor Gurney, the poet and composer, was born in Gloucester in 1890. After the First World War, he became increasingly unsettled, and died in a mental hospital in 1937.

Sir Peter Scott, the artist and ornithologist, was responsible for the setting up of the Slimbridge Wildfowl Trust.

Laurie Lee, the writer, was born in the county in 1914, and educated at Slad Village School and Stroud Central School. His best known work, *Cider with Rosie*, is a nostalgic account of his boyhood in a peaceful valley in the Cotswolds.

ART AND LITERATURE

'The village to which our family had come was a scattering of some twenty to thirty houses down the south-east slope of a valley. The valley was narrow, steep and almost entirely cut off; it was also a funnel for winds, a channel for the floods, and a jungley, bird-crammed, insect-hopping sun-trap whenever there happened to be any sun. It was not high and open like the Windrush country, but had secret origins, having been gouged from the Escarpment by the melting ice-caps some time before we got there. The old flood-terraces still showed on the slopes, along which the cows walked sideways. Like an island, it was possessed of curious survivals – rare orchids and Roman snails; and there are chemical qualities in the limestone springs which gave the women pre-Raphaelite goitres. The sides of the valley were rich in pasture and the crests heavily covered in beech woods...Most of the cottages were built of Cotswold stone and were roofed by split-stone tiles. The tiles grew a kind of golden moss which sparkled like crystallized honey. Behind the cottages were long steep gardens full of cabbages, fruit-bushes, roses, rabbit-hutches, earth-closets, bicycles and pigeon-lofts...'

Laurie Lee
Cider with Rosie (1959)

'I am a stranger here in Gloucestershire:
These high wild hills and rough uneven ways
Draw out our miles and make them wearisome.'

William Shakespeare
King Richard II

'When I go down the Gloucester lanes
My friends are deaf and blind.
Fast as they turn their foolish eyes

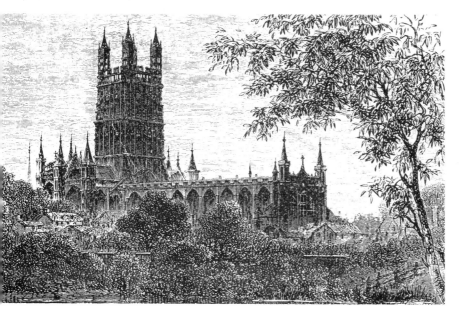

GLOUCESTER CATHEDRAL

*The Maenads leap behind.
And when I hear the fire-winged feet,
They only hear the wind.'*

James Elroy Flecker

*'Yes. I remember Adlestrop –
The name, because one afternoon
Of heat the express train drew up there
Unwontedly. It was late June.*

*And willows, willow-herb, and grass
And meadowsweet, and haycocks dry
No white less still and lonely fair
Than the high cloudlets in the sky.'*

R S Thomas
Adlestrop

LOCAL FOLKLORE

The Nine Witches of Gloucester

Peredur, whilst wandering in the mountains, came to a castle, in the Great Hall of which he found the countess, a beautifull, tall woman, seated with her handmaids. They invited him to dine with them, but afterwards bade him leave, explaining that the nine witches of Gloucester were coming; these witches, they said, had already conquered all of the Countess's lands except for this one castle, and they believed that the witches would now come and kill them all.

Peredur vowed to protect them, or die in the attempt.

At daybreak, he was roused by a great cry. He leapt up and found a witch attacking one of the watchmen. He dealt the witch a mighty blow with his sword, which flattened out her helmet like a dish. The witch cried out to him by name, and begged his protection. Peredur demanded to know how she knew his name, and the witch told him that it was their destiny to suffer at his hands, and also that he should learn from them how to be a knight and handle weapons.

Peredur agreed to spare them, if they vowed to do no wrong in the realm of the Countess. They swore an oath to him, and he took his leave of the Countess and went with the witch to the court of the Witches of Gloucester. He remained there for three weeks, learning the skills of a knight. The witches then provided him with arms and a horse, and he set off to ride abroad.

Some time later, the knight Peredur heard that the witches had been engaged in evil-doings in the realm of King Arthur. Peredur vowed to take vengeance on them, and, with the help of King Arthur's men, he went to fight the witches. One of Arthur's men was slain by a witch in Peredur's presence, although Peredur forbade her; again the witch killed one of Arthur's men in Peredur's presence, despite Peredur's warning; when she killed a third man, Peredur took his sword and struck the witch a mightly blow on the head that all but severed it from her body. As she died, she cried to the other witches to flee, saying that this was the knight who had learnt his skill amongst them, and who was destined to bring about their end. After this, King Arthur and his men renewed their attack, and the Witches of Gloucester were slain.

The Campden Wonder

William Harrison of Chipping Campden was steward to Viscountess Campden. One day, in August 1660, he set off as usual to collect rents on the estate – and never returned home. That evening, his wife, anxious for his safety, sent their servant, John Perry, to look for him. Perry wandered the streets asking for news of his master from passers-by, but returned the next morning with no clues to his whereabouts. That same day, Harrison's hat, neckband, and comb were discovered under a bush. No trace of Harrison could be found, and people grew suspicious that John Perry had somehow made away with his master. He was arrested and detained for questioning.

At first, he stuck to his story that he had no idea what had happened to Harrison; then he claimed that Harrison had been murdered by a tinker; next he said he had been killed by a gentleman's servant; finally, he broke down and promised to tell the truth. He confessed that his mother and brother had murdered Harrison, but that his only part in the deed was to tell them on what day he would be abroad.

All three were taken to be hanged, the mother and the brother screaming out their innocence the whole time. Folk muttered that Joan Perry had long been known as a witch, and there was little sympathy for her. At the last minute, John Perry screamed out that he too was innocent, and that Harrison would return to the village within seven years. He was silenced by the noose.

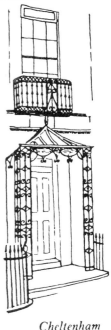

Cheltenham

Two years later, Harrison did indeed return, telling a fabulous tale of having been attacked and robbed, carried off and transported to Algiers, where he had been sold into slavery. His master, a Moorish doctor, had been so impressed with his knowledge of the world that he had arranged for him to buy his passage home.

The townsfolk felt that this tale confirmed the witchery of Joan Perry, and that by her arts she had spirited Harrison over the sea. The truth was somewhat more prosaic: Harrison had been embezzling his employer, the Viscountess Campden, for years, and had staged his own murder with the connivance of his servant. Not long after his return, his wife committed suicide. She was unable to live with the knowledge that she had been party to the hanging of three innocent people.

The Witch of Berkeley

In Norman times there lived a woman in the village of Berkeley, a very gluttonous and lazy witch, who led a life of riot and pleasure, although she was getting on in years. One day, as she was eating, her pet raven suddenly cried out loudly. At the sound the witch's knife dropped from her hand. 'To-day my plough has reached its last furrow; there is nothing but grief before me from this day.' No sooner had she spoken than a servant came running in with news of the death of her eldest son and all his family. This news struck her to the heart, and grief brought her to her death-bed.

When she knew that she had no hope of recovery she sent for her two surviving children, a monk and a nun, both of great piety. When they had come she said to them: 'My children, I have to confess to you that all my wealth has been gained by diabolical arts; all these years I have practised every wickedness, and have had no hope of salvation except in your piety. Even that has failed me now and I despair of my soul, but it may yet be that you can save my body from the Devil's clutches. Sew up my corpse in the skin of a stag, lay it on its back in a stone coffin and bind it with three great chains, curiously wrought. Let there be psalms sung for my soul for fifty nights, and masses said for fifty days. If I lie secure for three nights you may bury me on the fourth day.'

With that she died, and her children did all they could to save her body from the Devil. On the first night, whilst the monks were singing their psalms, the bolted door of the church burst open, and a crowd of devils broke one of the chains. On the second night

STANWAY

they broke another, but the third was more artfully made and resisted their efforts. On the third night, however, just before cock-crow, there was a tremendous rumbling like an earthquake, the foundations of the church shook, the door was shivered into splinters, and a great devil, more terrible than any of the rest, came up to the coffin. The monks' singing died on their lips, and their hair stood on end. The fiend called on the woman by name, and from the coffin she answered him: 'I cannot come, I am chained.'
'You shall be loosed,' he said, and broke the massive chain like a piece of flax. He shattered the lid of the coffin with one thrust of his foot, and plucked out the woman. He led her through the door. A black charger was neighing outside, its back covered with iron hooks. He flung the woman on them and vanished with her from men's sight. But pitiable lamentations and cries for help were heard from the air for four miles.

DISTINCTIVE FLAVOUR

A local delicacy in the county are **elvers**, baby eels which come up the River Severn.

Gloucester Cheese and Ale is a delicious traditional snack: a slice of Gloucester cheese, spread with mustard and covered with ale, is melted and poured over hot, ale-soaked toast.

A **Clipping the Yews Ceremony** is held in Painswick on or near the 19th September, which dates back to the 14th century. The 'clipping' actually comes from an early English word meaning 'to enclose', and has nothing to do with the clipping of yew trees.

The prefix **'Chipping'**, in Chipping Campden, and Chipping Sodbury, comes from an Old English word for market.

Gloucestershire County Cricket Club was founded in 1871. Their main ground is Ashley Down in Bristol, although they sometimes play at Gloucester or Cheltenham. Their crest is the coat of arms of the City and County of Bristol.

COUNTY DIARY

HAMPSHIRE

(SOUTHAMPTONSHIRE)

COUNTY FACTS

Derivation of name: A Homm of Hamm was in Old English, a water meadow. The original name for Southampton was Homtun or Hamtun, meaning 'the farm on the river land'. The county's abbreviation Hants shows its descent from an earlier form.

The Isle of Wight means the island risen or heaved out of the sea. Its Roman name was Vectis.

First Recorded: 755 as Hamtunscir

County Town: Winchester

Towns: Aldershot, Alton, Andover, Basingstoke, Bournemouth, Christchurch, Cowes, Eastleigh, Emsworth, Fareham, Farnborough, Fleet, Gosport, Havant, Lymington, New Milton, Newport, Petersfield, Portsmouth, Ringwood, Romsey, Ryde, Sandown, Shanklin, Southampton, Southsea, Swaythling, Totton, Ventnor, Waterlooville, Winchester. Southampton is a county of a city unto itself.

Local Government

Hampshire County Council, Dorset County Council and the Isle of Wight County Council. There are eighteen District Councils.

There is a long strip of detached Hampshire in Sussex, stretching for nearly ten miles from Baldwins and Wades Marsh on the borders of Hazlemere right down to South Ambersham near Midhurst, cutting through Redlands and part of Cowdray Park on the way. This is administered by West Sussex County Council.

The Isle of Wight was designated an administrative county in 1890 and again in 1974. It is however a part of the geographical county of Hampshire and has never been separated from it.

HISTORY

In the 5th and 6th centuries, Saxons, and later Jutes, invaded Southampton Water, and gradually defeated the Britons until in 519, the Kingdom of Wessex was formed, of which Hampshire was the centre.

In 686, Winchester became the seat of the Wessex Bishop Haedda, and thus the capital of Wessex.

In the reign of Alfred the Great, the Peace of Wedmore divided England between Alfred and Guthrum of Denmark; Winchester became the capital of all England not included in the Dane Law.

Under the Danish King Canute, Winchester was capital of all England.

After the Norman Conquest, William reserved the New Forest as a royal hunting domain.

On 2 August, 1100, William Rufus was shot dead whilst hunting in the New Forest. Whether it was an accident or not has never been satisfactorily proven; one of his companions, Walter Tirel, immediately fled to France, and his brother Henry, who happened to be in the forest at the time of the incident, made haste to have himself proclaimed King.

In 1141, the Bishop of Winchester, Henri de Blois, sided with Stephen, and garrisoned Wolvesey Castle in his interest. Winchester

TOPOGRAPHY INCLUDING RIVERS

Hampshire, in the south of England, is bordered by Berkshire in the north, Surrey and Sussex in the east, the English Channel and the Solent in the south, and Dorset and Wiltshire in the west.

The county is crossed by the chalk uplands of the North and South Downs, running roughly parallel with each other, and connected by the Alton Hills in the east. Some wooded areas in the east are all that remain in Hampshire of the ancient Wealden Forest, which stretched across Sussex. The coast, in the south, is indented and low-lying, with some parts, such as Hayling Island and Gosport, cut off from the mainland by narrow fingers of sea. Southampton and Portsmouth stand on two great natural harbours. In the south-west of the county is the large expanse of the New Forest. The Isle of Wight is separated from the mainland by the Solent. The highest point is Pilot Hill, 938 feet.

The rivers of Hampshire include the Meon, the Itchen, the Test, the Hamble, the Beaulieu, and the Avon.

ST CROSS HOSPITAL

Castle was garrisoned for the Empress Matilda. In the ensuing struggle, many churches and beautiful buildings in the city were destroyed. In 1545, Henry VIII's flagship, the *Mary Rose*, set off from Portsmouth to engage the French invasion fleet off the Isle of Wight. Too heavily laden with men, she heeled over and sank in the bay in full view of all the watchers on the shore. The hull was raised from the sea bed in 1982.

In 1603, the trial and sentencing of Sir Walter Raleigh took place at Wolvesey Castle in Winchester.

During the Civil War, the Battle of Alresford was fought on 29 March 1644, at which the Royalists sustained a serious defeat, which laid Winchester open to the Parliamentarians. The Parliamentarians were also victorious at the Siege of Basing House, after the storming of which many royalists were executed; the house was burned to the ground.

Lady Lisle of Moyles Court sheltered two fugitives from the Monmouth Rebellion. She was tried at Winchester Assize. The Hampshire jury found her not guilty at two separate trials, but Judge Jeffreys had determined to make an example of her, and bullied the jury into bringing in a guilty verdict. He sentenced her to be burnt alive, but the Hampshire men refused to do this. She was executed in 1685.

INDUSTRY PAST AND PRESENT

Ports, dockyards, tourism, light industry and strawberry growing are amongst the county's present day activities. Enterprises connected with the Naval bases in the county are still major employers. There is a vast oil refinery near Southampton.

Shipbuilding and foreign trade grew up with Hampshire's ports. Many famous warships were constructed at Southampton docks from the 15th century. Salt-making, and iron manufacture, dated from before the Norman Conquest. In the 17th century, French refugees set up silk-weaving mills at Southampton. Paper was manufactured from the 17th century in Laverstoke, and bank-

note paper was supplied from there to the Bank of England. A large proportion of the county was used for agricultural pursuits: sheep, dairy cattle, horses, and pigs being widely raised.

LANDMARKS

New Forest
Butser Hill
The Needles, Isle of Wight

MONUMENTS

Broadlands, originally built in the 16th century, was the home of Earl Mountbatten of Burma, last Viceroy of India.

Breamore House; this pink Elizabethan manor house was bought in 1748 by Sir Edward Hulse, physician to Queen Anne. His descendants still live there.

Porchester Castle, built in the 3rd century, is probably the best surviving Roman fort in England.

The Vyne, a Tudor house built by Lord Sandys, Lord Chamberlain to Henry VIII.

Beaulieu; the Palace House was originally the 14th-century gatehouse of a Cistercian Abbey, and subsequently extended into the present manor house. Nearby is the **National Motor Museum**.

Marwell Zoological Park, where Victor the giraffe slipped and fell, and subsequently died, in 1977.

Beaulieu Abbey, the remains of a Cistercian Abbey completed in 1246.

Osborne House; this Italianate Palace on the Isle of Wight, overlooking the Solent, was designed by Thomas Cubitt and the Prince Consort in the 1840s. Queen Victoria retired here after the death of Prince Albert, and died here in 1901.

Appuldurcombe House, the remains of a Baroque house which was the seat of the Worsley family for 300 years.

Carisbrooke Castle; the keep is Norman, and the rest of the castle dates from the 12th century. Charles I arrived here as a visitor and remained as a prisoner, although he tried to escape three times.

Winchester Cathedral is the longest medieval church surviving in Europe. Its nave gives the impression of being a 14th-century Perpendicular structure, but is in fact a somewhat drastic reworking of Norman masonry.

HMS Victory, arguably the most famous warship in the world, is preserved at Portsmouth. Nelson's flagship is not the only naval antique there – **HMS Warrior** is also on display.

ROMSEY ABBEY

FAMOUS PEOPLE AND LOCAL CHARACTERS

Izaak Walton, author of *The Compleat Angler*, came to Winchester in 1662 at the age of 70, where he lived happily for the last 20 years of his life; fishing the Itchen and the Test was his particular pleasure.

Gilbert White, famous for his Natural History and Antiquities of Selborne, was born at the parsonage in Selborne on January 18th, 1720. His father was a barrister. In his later years he was Vicar of Selborne. He lived at 'The Wakes' for most of his life.

Edward Gibbon lived in Buriton. He joined the Hampshire militia.

William Cobbett was born in Farnham in 1763.

Jane Austen was born on December 16th, 1775, in Steventon, the youngest of seven children. She spent the first 25 years of her life there. Her formal education ended at the age of 9. She died in Winchester of Addison's Disease at the age of 41.

Lord Palmerston, Prime Minister to Queen Victoria, was born at Broadlands in 1784.

Captain Frederick Marryat often stayed with his brother at Chewton Glen House during the 1840s, where he gathered material for his ever popular *Children of the New Forest*.

Charles Dickens was born on February 7th, 1812, in Portsmouth, where his father was a clerk in the Navy Pay Office.

Swinburne was born on the Isle of Wight in 1837. His sons played with Charles Dickens's sons on holiday in Bonchurch.

Mary Shelley, and her husband's heart, are buried in Bournemouth.

Mrs Gaskell bought a house in Holybourne with the proceeds from *Wives and Daughters*. She died there on November 12th, 1865.

Alfred Lord Tennyson lived in Harringford on the Isle of Wight, for 30 years.

Captain Lawrence Oates, born in the county in 1880, was a member of Scott's expedition to the Antarctic in 1911. On the return journey, crippled with frostbite, he walked out into a blizzard to die.

Sir Arthur Conan Doyle lived in Portsmouth, where he wrote his first Sherlock Holmes story, 'A Study in Scarlet'.

On July 16th, 1967, a local shopkeeper set off from Southsea in his boat *Lively Lady*, and sailed round the world, in just under a year. **Alec Rose** was knighted a week after his return.

Local Characters

William Walker, a diver, was known as 'the man who saved Winchester Cathedral'. In

OLD HOUSES IN CLOSE, WINCHESTER

1905 it was discovered that the timber foundations of the cathedral were flooded and rotting, and that the building was sinking. Walter worked under water to repair the foundations. The work took over 6 years. The 'biggest sculptured table in the world', which is 18 feet long and weighs nearly 2 tons, was made by **Maxie Lane**, of Furzey in the New Forest, a sculptor of stools, tables and other furniture carved entirely without joints, from one great piece of sycamore, or wych elm.

ART AND LITERATURE

'Yes, weekly from Southampton
Great steamers, white and gold
Go rolling down to Rio
(Roll down – roll down to Rio!)
And I'd like to roll to Rio
Some day before I'm old!'
Rudyard Kipling
Beginning of the Armadillos

'Ye, through the pass the Autlone [Alton]
Poverte inyght pass
Withouten peril of robbynge.'
William Langland
Piers Plowman (14th century)

'Having partaken of a copious breakfast, with fish, and rice, and hard eggs, at Southampton, he had so far rallied at Winchester as to think a glass of sherry necessary.'
W M Thackeray
Vanity Fair

'Should all our churchmen foam in spite
At you, so careful of the right,

Yet one lay-hearth would give you welcome
(Take it and come) to the Isle of Wight.'
Alfred Tennyson
At Farringford

'Early sun on Beaulieu Water
Lights the underside of oaks
Clumps of leaves it floods and blanches
All transparent glow the branches
Which the double sunlight soaks.'
John Betjeman
Youth and Age on Beaulieu River, Hants (1945)

'Hampshire, long for her, hath had the term of Hogs.'
Michael Drayton
Poly-Olbion (1622)

'Botley is the most delightful village in the world…It is in a valley. The soil is rich, thick set with woods; the farms are small, the cottages are neat…'
William Cobbett
The Isle of Wight:
'Of all the Southern Isles she holds the highest place,
And evermore hath green the great'st in Britain's grace.'

LOCAL FOLKLORE

There has been a brewery in Romsey since the 16th century, renowned for its strong ale: from which came the saying that, if a man had drunk so much liquor that his legs could no longer support him, he was 'So drunk, he must have been to Romsey'.

St Swithun

Swithun was Bishop at the Old Minster in Winchester. Before he died, in 862, he expressed a wish to be buried in a grave under the open sky, so that his country men could walk freely over it, and the rain could fall on it. This was duly done, but about 100 years later, when he was canonized, his bones were moved inside the minster, which was considered a more fitting shrine to such a saintly man. Legend has it that his sadness at being thus confined takes the form of 40 days of rain, starting from July 15, St Swithun's Day.

The Gipsy's Curse

A gipsy called at the house of the Tichborne family begging, and was turned away. She put a curse on the baby of the family, saying that he would die by drowning, and naming the fateful day. When the appointed day arrived, his parents took extra precautions, and sent him out with the maids to the Downs, well away from the river. As the maids walked on the Downs, the baby carriage toppled over, and the baby fell out and drowned in rainwater collected in the ruts of a cart track.

In the Tichborne's chapel there is a statue to a small boy, Richard Tichborne, who died in 1619 aged 'one yeare, six monthes and too daies'.

Sir Bevis of Hamtoun

Bevis was the son of Sir Guy of Hamtoun and his wife, daughter of the King of Scotland. Bevis's mother and her lover killed Sir Guy, and sent Bevis away to be sold into slavery in foreign lands.

There, Joisyan, the daughter of a heathen king, fell in love with him, and after a series of adventures, including a fight with a mighty dragon, the couple escaped and fled to England.

On their travels, they met a giant, whom Bevis defeated in a fight. After this the giant became their faithful friend.

On his return to Hamtoun, Bevis took his revenge. He boiled his mother's lover down to dog meat in a cauldron, and his mother, terrified at what she had done to her son and her husband, leapt off the top of a high tower to her death.

The people of Hamtoun rejoiced at the homecoming of the rightful heir.

Tichborne Dole and the Crawles

Lady Isabella was the wife of Sir Roger Tichborne, and was renowned for her charitable works. As she lay dying, she begged her husband to grant her enough land to enable her to distribute bread to the poor and needy who came to the gates of Tichborne on Lady-day. Sir Roger in reply took a flaming brand from the fire, and agreed to grant her as much land as she could encircle whilst the brand burnt. She ordered that she be carried from her bed, and once outside, she started to crawl on her hands and knees; before the brand went out, she had crawled round nearly 23 acres. These are still known today as the 'Crawles'. Sir Roger and his descendants kept to the promise, and every Lady-day, nearly 2,000 small loaves of bread were distributed to the poor, until the practice was stopped at the end of the 18th century, as the crowd it attracted were becoming too unruly. The Tichborne Dole is now given to the poor of the parish in the form of money. Tradition has it that the house will fall, and Tichborne family will die out, if Lady Isabella's request is ever disregarded.

DISTINCTIVE FLAVOUR

Aldershot is the 'Home of the British Army'.

The **Royal Aircraft Establishment** is based in Farnborough.

The Knightwood Oak in the New Forest is said to be the largest and oldest oak in all England.

The River Test is said to be the finest trout stream of its kind in the world.

In the Church of St Mary Bourne is the 'Vinegar Bible' of 1717, open at the error which gives it its name – the printing of the word 'vinegar', instead of 'vineyard' in the parable in Luke 20.

Hampshire County Cricket Club was founded in 1863. Their grounds include Southampton, Portsmouth and Bournemouth. Their badge is the Tudor Rose and Crown.

Hambledon cricket team play at Broad Halfpenny Down. They played England's finest cricket at the end of the 18th century.

There is a race track at **Thruxton**.

Cowes, on the Isle of Wight, is a great sailing centre. The Royal Yacht Squadron has its headquarters here.

The **New Forest** ponies are a small, hardy breed, who wander freely through the villages within the forest. The verderers' court in Lyndhurst has had charge of that part of the forest belonging to the Crown since 1887. The New Forest was subject to the strict forest laws from Norman times until 1640.

WINCHESTER CATHEDRAL

COUNTY DIARY

January:	Boat Show, Southampton
March:	Dole Ceremony, Tichborne
June:	Round the Island Race, Isle of Wight
July:	Balloon Festival, Southampton
July:	New Forest and Hampshire County Show, Brockenhurst
July:	Royal Isle of Wight County Show, Cowes
August:	Cowes Week, Cowes
August:	Admiral's Cup Race, Cowes (alternate years)
August:	International Power Boat Race, Cowes
August:	Navy Day, Portsmouth

HEREFORDSHIRE

COUNTY FACTS

Derivation of name: Herefordshire comes from the Old English for army ford, i.e. one wide enough for an army to cross.
First Recorded: c. 1038 as Herefordscir
Motto: Pulchra Terra Dei Donum (This Fair Land is the Gift of God)
County Town: Hereford
Towns: Bromyard, Hereford, Kington, Ledbury, Leominster, Lugwardine, Ross-on-Wye, Weobley, Whitchurch.

Local Government

Herefordshire and the detached part of Herefordshire in Worcestershire, Rochford, is administered by Hereford & Worcester County Council. There are three other detached parts of Herefordshire; within Monmouthshire (Fwthog) under Gwent County Council control; within Radnorshire (Litton) administered by Powys County Council; within Shropshire (Farlow) governed by Shropshire County Council. There are four district councils one of which is shared with Worcestershire.

HISTORY

The region was occupied by the Silurian tribe and by the Celts before the Roman invasion. Thereafter it became part of the Saxon Kingdom of Mercia.

In the 8th century, Offa, the King of Mercia, built the wall and rampart which stretched from sea to sea and served as a fortification against the Welsh, known as Offa's Dyke, part of which passes through the county of Herefordshire.

After the Norman Conquest, a chain of castles was built along the border with Wales, known as the Welsh Marches, to ward off attack from the Welsh. The barons who held these castles were known as the Lords' Marchers.

In the 15th century, the county was raided again and again by the Welsh under Owen Glendower, and was seriously impoverished. On the 2nd or 3rd February 1460, at the hamlet of Mortimers Cross, five miles to the north-west of Leominster, the Yorkists under Edward Mortimer, Earl of March (later Edward IV) defeated the Lancastrians under Jasper, Earl of Pembroke and James, Earl of Wiltshire in one of the most important and decisive battles of the War of the Roses. It was here that Owen Tudor, husband of Catherine, Henry V's widow, was taken and executed by the Yorkists.

The Battle of Mortimer's Cross was one of the decisive battles marking the end of the Wars of the Roses.

In general, the north of the county was on the Parliamentarian side, and the south was for the King, in the Civil War, although many houses were divided. Lady Harley staunchly defended Brampton Bryan castle in her husband's absence, through a long and tense siege by the Royalists. Eventually, however, the besiegers burnt the castle down, and Lady Harley lost her life.

INDUSTRY PAST AND PRESENT

Present industry includes agriculture, beef cattle, dairying, fruit farming, orchards and hops. Bulmers cider is produced in Hereford. The county has always been an exceptionally rich agricultural area. The woollen and cloth industries flourished in Norman times; during the reign of Henry VIII the towns declined in prosperity, and Elizabeth I insisted on her subjects wearing caps made in a factory in Hereford, in order to stimulate local trade. Hops were introduced to England in 1524, and were widely grown in the county from then on. The apple and pear orchards, and the resultant cider and perry industries, began to flourish in the 17th century.

TOPOGRAPHY INCLUDING RIVERS

Herefordshire, in the west midlands of England, is bordered by Shropshire in the north, Worcestershire in the east, Gloucestershire in the south, and Monmouthshire, Breconshire, and Radnorshire in the west.

Four ranges of the Black Mountains of Wales enter the south-west corner of the county, with valleys between them, the widest and most scenic being the Golden Valley. The River Wye crosses the county from the west to Hereford, flowing between high rocks and woods. The Malvern Hills rise in the east. The highest point is in the Black Mountains, 2306 feet.

Rivers: Wye, Frome, Lugg, Teme.

LANDMARKS

Wye Valley
Golden Valley
Herefordshire Beacon
Offa's Dyke
Symond's Yat

MONUMENTS

Hereford Cathedral dates from the 12th century, but was much altered subsequently. It houses the famous Mappa Mundi, one of the largest and most elaborate medieval maps in Europe, which shows the world as flat, with Jerusalem at the centre.

Croft Castle, on the Welsh border, was owned by the Croft family from Domesday until 1957, except for a gap of 173 years from 1750.

Goodrich Castle, a Welsh border castle, the remaining parts of which were built in the

HEREFORD CATHEDRAL FROM THE EAST AND (Right) WINDOW TRACERY FROM ITS CLOISTER

12th and 13th centuries.

Berrington Hall, a country mansion built between 1778 and 1781 by Henry Holland. The park was landscaped by Capability Brown in 1780.

Abbey Dore is a very rare survival – a Cistercian church still in use. Viscount Scudamore restored the then derelict eastern parts of the monastic church to serve his parish.

FAMOUS PEOPLE AND LOCAL CHARACTERS

John Kyrle lived in Ross-on-Wye, and was known as the 'Man of Ross'. He lived a very simple life, and gave all his spare income to charitable works and to the planning and building of the town.

Nell Gwynn, actress and mistress of Charles II, was born in Hereford.

Robert Harley, one of the great county family of Harley, became the first Earl of Oxford. Harley Street in London is named after him.

Elizabeth Barrett Browning was brought to a house on Oyster Hill, north of Ledbury, as a baby, and lived there for the first 28 years of her life.

John Masefield, the poet laureate, was born in Ledbury on 1 June, 1878.

Local Characters

Tom Spring, whose real name was Thomas Winter, was a Herefordshire man, who became champion boxer of all England from 1823 to 1824.

ART AND LITERATURE

'Acton Beauchamp, the poorest place in all the nation,
A lousy parson, a nitty clerk, and a shabby congregation.'

Anon

'The copse-checkered slopes of rolling Hereford, white with the blossom of apples.'

Henry James
A Passionate Pilgrim

LOCAL FOLKLORE

The Battle of Mortimers Cross

At the Battle of Mortimers Cross in February 1460, Edward's first victory in the War of the Roses over Jasper, Earl of Pembroke and James, Earl of Wiltshire, an astronomical phenomenon appearing to be three Suns appeared in the heavens. This mystical event helped Edward encourage his troops with this auspicious omen and the 'Sun in Splendour' as it was known, became one of his favourite and most famous badges.

Black Vaughan

Perhaps the most notorious and troublesome of Herefordshire ghosts was Black Vaughan, of Hergest Court, said to be the ghost of the Vaughan whose monument stands in Vaughan chapel of Kington Church. He was a very wicked man, so after his death he could not rest, and came back 'stronger and stronger all the while.' At last he came in broad daylight, and would upset the farmers' waggons, loaded with hay or corn; he would jump up behind their wives riding to Kington market. He sometimes took the form of a fly, in order to 'torment (tease) the horses!' Finally, he came into the church itself, in the form of a bull. It was decided that something must be done; people went so much in fear of Black Vaughan that attendance at Kington market was affected, and the prosperity of the town suffered. So they got twelve parsons, with twelve candles, to wait in the church to try and read him down into a silver snuff-box. For 'we all have a spirit inside us, and that spirit can go large or small, or down, down, quite small, even into a snuff-box'. There were present, to help lay the spirit, a woman with a new-born baby, whose innocence and purity were held powerful in exorcism.

Well, they read, but it was no use; they were all afraid, and all their candles went out but one. The parson that held the candle had a stout heart, and he feared no man nor spirit. He called out 'Vaughan, why art thou so fierce?' 'I was fierce when I was a man, but fiercer now, for I am a devil!' was the answer. But nothing could dismay the stout-hearted parson. He read, and read, and read, and when Vaughan felt himself going down, and down, and down, till the snuff-box was nearly shut, he asked 'Vaughan, where wilt thou be laid?' The spirit answered 'Anywhere, anywhere, but not in the Red Sea!' So they shut the box, and took him and buried him for a thousand years in the bottom of Hergest pool, in the wood, with a big stone on top of him.

Two footmarks were formerly to be seen in the grass under an oak tree near Hergest, which were pointed out as the spot where Black Vaughan was wont to stand, to watch the deer in the park. So wicked was he that grass never after grew on the spot where he stood. The oak tree was cut down some years ago, and it was said that the man who felled it went mad afterwards, and died in an asylum.

King Herla

Herla was king of the Ancient Britons, and was challenged by another king, a pigmy no bigger than an ape, and of less than half human stature. He rode on a large goat; indeed, he himself might have been compared to Pan. He had a large head, glowing face, and a long red beard, while his breast was conspicuous for a spotted fawnskin which he wore on it. The lower part of his body was rough and hairy, and his legs ended in goats' hooves. He had a private interview with Herla, in which he spoke as follows: "I am lord over many kings and princes, over a vast and innumerable people. I am their willing messenger to you, although to you I am unknown. Yet I rejoice in the fame which has raised you above other kings, for you are of all men the best, and also closely connected with me both by position and blood. You are worthy of the honour of adorning your marriage with my presence as guest, for the King of France has given you his daughter, and indeed the embassy is arriving here to-day, although all the arrangements have been made without your knowledge. Let there be an everlasting treaty between us, because, first of all, I was present at your marriage, and because you will be at mine on the same day a year hence." After this speech he turned away, and moving faster even than a tiger, disappeared from his sight. The King, therefore, returned from that spot full of surprise, received the embassy, and assented to their proposals. When the marriage was celebrated, and the king was seated at the customary feast, suddenly, before the first course was served, the pigmy arrived, accompanied by so large a company of dwarfs like himself, that after they had filled all the seats at table, there were more dwarfs outside in tents which they had in a moment put up,

than at the feast inside. Instantly there darted out from these tents servants with vessels made out of precious stones, all new and wondrously wrought. They filled the palace and the tents with furniture either made of gold or precious stones. Neither wine nor meat was served in any wooden or silver vessel. The servants were found wherever they were wanted, and served nothing out of the king's or anyone else's stores, but only from their own, which were of quality beyond anyone's thoughts. None of Herla's provisions were used, and his servants sat idle.

The pigmies won universal praise. Their raiment was gorgeous; for lamps they provided blazing gems; they were never far off when they were wanted, and never too close when not desired. Their king then thus addressed Herla: "Most excellent King, God be my witness that I am here in accordance with our agreement, at your marriage. If there is anything more that you desire, I will supply it gladly, on the condition that when I demand a return, you will not deny it." Hereupon, without waiting for an answer he returned to his tent and departed at about cock-crow with his attendants. After a year he suddenly

came to Herla and demanded the observance of the treaty. Herla consented, and followed at the dwarf's bidding. They entered a cave in a very high cliff, and after some journeying through the dark, which appeared to be lighted, not by the sun or moon, but by numerous torches, they arrived at the dwarf's palace, a splendid mansion.

There the marriage was celebrated, and the obligations to the dwarf fittingly paid, after which Herla returned home loaded with gifts and offerings, horses, dogs, hawks, and all things pertaining to hunting and falconry. The pigmy guided them .... and there gave them a (small) bloodhound (*canem sanguinarium*) small enough to be carried (*portabilem*), then, strictly forbidding any of the king's retinue to dismount until the dog leapt from his carrier, he bade them farewell, and returned home. Soon after, Herla reached the light of day, and having got back to his kingdom again, called an old shepherd and asked for news of his queen, using her name. The shepherd looked at him astonished, and said, "Lord, I scarcely understand your language, for I am a Saxon, and you a Briton. I have never heard the name of that queen, except in the case of one who they say was

THE DOVE COTE AT RICHARD'S CASTLE

67

Herla's wife, queen of the earliest Britons. He is fabled to have disappeared with a dwarf at this cliff, and never to have been seen on earth again. The Saxons have now held this realm for two hundred years, having driven out the original inhabitants." The king was astonished, for he imagined that he had been away for three days only. Some of his companions descended from horseback before the dog was released, forgetful of the dwarf's commands, and were instantly crumbled to dust. The king then forbade any more of his companions to descend until the dog leapt down. The dog has not leapt down yet. One legend states that Herla for ever wanders on mad journeys with his train, without home or rest. Many people, as they tell us, often see his company. However, they say that at last, in the first year of our (present) King Henry (the second) it ceased to visit our country in pomp as before. On that occasion, many of the Welsh (*Wallenses*) saw it whelmed in the Wye, the Herefordshire river (*Waiam Herefordiae flumen*). From that hour, that weird roaming ceased, as though Herla had transferred his wandering (*Errores*, a pun containing the idea of error) to us, and had gained rest for himself (a hit at contemporary politics).

The Shepherd and the Crows

Years ago, on the Black Mountain above Longton, there lived a hired shepherd, who managed a little farm for his master. There were on either side of this farm two brothers, farming for their father, and they hated the hired shepherd.

He stuck to his master, and they to their father. At last one day they got him alone on the mountain, and caught him, and said they would murder him. They told him there was no one about, and it would never be known. 'If you kill me,' he said, 'the very crows will cry out and speak it.'

Yet they murdered and buried him. The body was found after some time, but there was no evidence to show who the murderers were. However, not long after that, the crows took to wheeling round the heads of those two brothers, and crowing loudly all day long – when they were together, and when they were apart. At last they could scarcely bear it, and one said to the other, 'Brother, do you remember when we killed the poor shepherd on the mountain top there, he said the very crows would cry out against us?' These words were overheard by a man in the next field, and the matter was looked into, so that in the end the brothers were both hanged for murder.

PEMBRIDGE OLD MARKET PLACE

Jack o'Kent was a major figure in Herefordshire legend:–

Jack's Funeral

Jack was a wizard in league with the Devil, and when still a boy he sold his body and soul to the 'old un' in exchange for supernatural power in this world; whether he were buried in the church or out of the church, that was the bargain. He was therefore buried at Kentchurch, or some say at Grosmont, in the wall of the church, so that he should be 'neither in nor out.'

The Bridge at Kentchurch

Jack and the Devil built the bridge over the Monnow between Kentchurch and Grosmont in a single night. What they built by night fell down by day, as long as the bridge remained incomplete; hence the need for haste. The first passenger to pass over the bridge was to belong to the Devil, so Jack threw a bone across and a poor dog ran after it. That dog was all the Devil had for his pains.

The White Rocks, Garway

The Devil was helping Jack to stop up the weir, at Orcop Hill, in order to flood the valley, and make a fishpool. But as the Devil was coming over Garway Hill his apron strings broke, and down fell all the stones he was carrying. Then the cock crew, and he had to go home, so there are the stones to this day.

Jack and the Pigs

Jack and the Devil agreed that Jack should go to market and buy some pigs. "Which will you have," said Jack, "the curly-tailed pigs, or the straight-tailed pigs?" "Straight tails," said the Devil. So on the way home Jack gave them all a feed of beans, and their tails all curled, every one of them; they were as curly as pigs' tails could be. Next time Jack went to the market, the Devil said he would have all the curly-tailed pigs. That time Jack drove them through a pool of water, by the roadside, on the way home; all their tails became straight

then, because they were so wet and cold.

The Tops and the Butts

One day, Jack took the Devil into a field of wheat, when it was springing up. He said, "Which will you have, the tops or the butts?" There was not much top to be seen, so the Devil said he'd have the butts. At harvest time, Jack accordingly had the wheat, the Devil the straw; naturally he grumbled a good deal over such a bad bargain. Next year the field was sown with turnip seed, and Jack said "You shall have tops this time"; the Devil agreed to this, and in due time Jack had the turnips, leaving for his partner the green tops. After that they went to mow a field of grass, each one to have all the hay he could cut: they were to begin together in the morning. Jack got up in the night and put harrow tynes in the grass, on the side of the meadow where the Devil was to mow. In the morning these notched and blunted the scythe, which was continually catching in them; but the 'old un' thinking they were only burdocks, kept muttering, "Bur-dock, Jack! Bur-dock, Jack!" Jack took no notice, and moving diligently, secured nearly all the crop for himself once more. Then they went to threshing; Jack was to have bottoms this time, so he got the barn floor, and the Devil went on top; he put up a hurdle for the Devil to thresh on, and as he battered away Jack collected the corn on the floor.

DISTINCTIVE FLAVOUR

Herefordshire people are said to be generally placid and easy-going, but dangerous when roused. These are characteristics shared by the **Herefordshire Bulls**, bred in the county. They are a reddish-brown, with mottled or white faces, and are renowned for the quality of their beef.

Cider and perry are the staple beverages of the county.

Herefordshire joins with Worcestershire and Gloucestershire for the **Three Counties Show**, which is held in Great Malvern, Worcestershire in June.

COUNTY DIARY

August: Three Choirs festival, held alternatively at Hereford, Gloucester and Worcester

HERTFORDSHIRE

COUNTY FACTS

Derivation of name: Hertfordshire comes from the Old English, 'ford where hart, stag or deer came to drink'.
First Recorded: 866 as Heortfordscir
Motto: Trust and Fear Not
County Town: Hertford
Towns: Abbots Langley, Barnet (partly in Middlesex), Berkhamsted, Bishop's Stortford, Borehamwood, Bushey, Cheshunt, Chorleywood, Elstree (partly in Middlesex), Harpenden, Hatfield, Hemel Hempstead, Hertford, Hitchin, Knebworth, Kings Langley, Letchworth, London Colney, Oxhey, Radlett, Redbourn, Rickmansworth, Royston, St Albans, Sawbridgeworth, Stevenage, Tring, Ware, Watford, Welwyn Garden City, Wheathampstead.

Local Government
Hertfordshire County Council and part of a London Borough and ten District Councils. The detached part of Hertfordshire centred upon Coleshill is administered by Buckinghamshire County Council.

HISTORY

In AD 61 the East Anglian tribe of the Iceni, led by Queen Boadicea, attacked and captured Verulamium (St Albans), in revolt against the Roman conquerors, and massacred the inhabitants.

The Roman roads Ermin Street, Icknield Street, and Watling Street all pass through Hertfordshire.

St Alban was martyred in AD 303. The event was commemorated by the repentant King Offa of Mercia, who is responsible for the beginnings of St Albans Abbey.

Under the Saxon heptarchy, part of Hertfordshire was included in East Saxony, and part in Mercia.

A great battle was fought in 896 between Alfred the Great and the Danes, in the area now called Watford. There was a huge death toll, but Alfred was victorious.

In the 14th century, the peasants and townspeople of St Albans rose up in revolt for a charter of rights; the rising was suppressed by Richard II in person. John Ball, the rebel priest, was hanged, drawn and quartered; the others were pardoned.

The Earl of Essex lived at Cassiobury, and Queen Elizabeth often came there as his guest.

The Rye House Plot, an abortive plot to murder King Charles II, was planned at Rye House on the River Lea in 1683.

INDUSTRY PAST AND PRESENT

Present industry includes intensive agriculture, pharmaceuticals, printing, engineering, chemicals, electronics and light industry.

Hertfordshire was always an agricultural county. In Norman times the woollen trade flourished. A great corn market was held in Royston from the time of Elizabeth. The county was famous for its horses in the 17th century, and in the 18th century paper-making began, especially in Watford, and straw-plaiting and associated industries (bleaching, cleaning, bonnet-making) grew into thriving businesses. The county has

long been famous for watercress and roses.

LANDMARKS
Ashridge Estate
Northaw Great Wood
Whippendell Wood

TOPOGRAPHY INCLUDING RIVERS

Hertfordshire, in the south-east midlands, is bordered by Bedfordshire and Cambridgeshire in the north, Essex in the east, Middlesex in the south, and Buckinghamshire in the west. The west and north-western part of the county is hilly, forming part of the chalky range of the Chilterns (near the town of Dunstable these are called the Dunstable Downs). South of this range, the land is gently undulating, with some low hills along the border with Middlesex. The soil contains a good deal of flinty stones, used in local buildings. The highest point is near Hastoe village, 803 feet.
Rivers: Lea, Colne, Stort, Ivel, Rib, Mimram.

MONUMENTS

Hatfield House, built by Robert Cecil from 1607 to 1611, on an Elizabethan E-plan.
St Albans Abbey: The abbey church and gate house are all that remain of the original buildings for a 10th-century Benedictine community. The church is the second longest in England and became a cathedral in 1877.
Knebworth House was begun in 1492 by Sir Robert Lytton. The exterior was redecorated in Gothic style by Sir Edward Bulwer-Lytton in 1843.
Shaw's Corner, the Edwardian house in which George Bernard Shaw lived until his death in 1950, at the age of 94.

St Albans: The Roman theatre, and other remains, were part of one of the finest towns in Roman Britain, called Verulamium. Destroyed by Boadicea during the revolt of the Iceni, it was rebuilt almost immediately afterwards.

FAMOUS PEOPLE AND LOCAL CHARACTERS

St Alban was the first martyr for the Christian faith to die in Britain. The Roman Emperor proclaimed that all Christians should deny Christ or die, so they fled and hid themselves. One holy man took refuge with a Roman soldier called Alban, who was a pagan. By this man's goodness and gentleness, Alban was converted to Christianity. He disguised himself as the holy man and allowed himself to be captured. He confessed to being a Christian, was tortured, condemned to death, and executed.

Nicholas Breakspear, the only English Pope (Adrian IV, 1154-59), was born in Bedmond, near Abbots Langley.

Sir Francis Bacon, the philosopher. lived at Gorhambury House in St Albans.

The Cecils of Hatfield House were ministers of state to Queen Elizabeth I and King James I.

William Cowper, the poet, spent 18 months in a private madhouse in St Albans, after attempting suicide in London.

Cecil Rhodes, the British Empire builder, was born at Bishops Stortford in 1853.

Charles Lamb, the essayist, owned a cottage in Westmill. He fell in love with Ann Simmons, whom he met at Widford; two of his sonnets refer to her.

William Lamb, Lord Melbourne, lived at Brocket Hall near Welwyn. He was Prime Minister to Queen Victoria, and husband of the notorious Lady Caroline Lamb.

George Bernard Shaw lived in Ayot St Lawrence.

Queen Elizabeth, The Queen Mother was born at St Paul's Waldenbury near Hitchin.

Local Characters

Lady Catherine Ferrers lived at Markyate in the 18th century, and is believed to have led a secret double life as a highwayman. She would steal out of the house at night, dressed in men's clothes and wearing a mask, riding a distinctive black horse with white legs. She terrorized travellers on the Holyhead road for years, until she was eventually shot one night at a place known as No Man's Land. She managed to reach her home, but shortly afterwards, died of her wounds.

ART AND LITERATURE

'But yet his horse was not a whit
Inclined to tarry there;
For why? – his owner had a house
Full ten miles off, at Ware.'
William Cowper
The Diverting History of John Gilpin

'Slow journeying on
To the green plains of pleasant Hertfordshire.'
Charles Lamb,
The Lord of Light Shakes Off

'And now I see these fields once more
Clothed, thank the Lord, in summer green,
Pale corn waves rippling to a shore
The shadowy cliffs of elm between,

Colour-washed cottages reed-thatched
And weather-boarded water mills,
Flint churches, brick and plaster patched,
On mildly undistinguished hills.'
John Betjeman
Hertfordshire (1954)

LOCAL FOLKLORE

The Wicked Lady
Lady Ferrers, known as the 'Wicked Lady', is said to ride abroad in Hertfordshire still, revisiting the scene of her crimes.

The Legend of Piers Shonks
A great dragon had its lair under the roots of a yew tree in the parish of Brent Pelham, and terrorized the surrounding countryside.
Piers Shonks, the Lord of the Manor, determined to destroy this dragon. He set out one day in full suit of armour, carrying his sword and spear, and soon arrived at the dragon's lair.
A fierce battle ensued, as the two fought back and forth, until finally Shonks thrust his spear down the dragon's throat and killed it. But the devil then rose up, seeking revenge for the death of his servant. He vowed that he would have Shonks, body and soul, whether he was buried inside the church or outside. However, Piers Shonks was as crafty as he was brave, and he outwitted the devil: as he lay dying, he took his bow and shot an arrow which struck the north wall of the nave of St Mary's Church. He requested that he be buried there, in a tomb in the wall, which was therefore neither inside the church, nor outside.

Jack O'Legs, the Weston Giant
Jack O'Legs, a giant of a man, lived in a wood near Weston, and, not unlike Robin Hood, used to rob the rich to feed the poor. He also

WYLLYOT'S MANOR, POTTERS BAR

fed himself by regularly stealing bread from the bakers in Baldock. It was these bakers who put an end to his exploits, by taking their revenge on him for the constant thefts of their wares. They put out his eyes, and hanged him in Baldock Field. Jack O'Legs's last request was that someone should put his bow and arrow in his hands, and that, wherever his arrow landed, there he should be buried. The arrow landed just inside Weston Churchyard, and to this day, just inside the gate, lie two large stones, 14 feet apart, which are said to mark his grave.

DISTINCTIVE FLAVOUR

A common nickname for Hertfordshire people is '**Hertfordshire Hedgehogs**', referring to their slow-moving country ways. Londoners are said to call those lacking in world-wise ways '**Hertfordshire thickheads**'. In earlier days, doctors used to recommend Hertfordshire to people in poor health, as the climate is mild, dry, and generally healthy. The county became so popular amongst the noble and wealthy that a common saying developed: *'He who buys a home in Hertfordshire pays two years' purchase for the air.'*

Elstree Studios, home of one of Britain's most successful film companies is in Hertfordshire.

COUNTY DIARY

April:	East Herts Festival, Stevenage
May:	Hertfordshire Show, Redbourn
July:	(Biennial) International Organ Festival, St Albans
July:	British Rose Festival, St Albans

HUNTINGDONSHIRE

COUNTY FACTS

Derivation of name: Huntingdonshire comes from the Old English, Huntersdune, meaning 'a good base wherefrom to mount a hunting expedition', 'Huntsman's Hill'.

First Recorded: 1011 as Huntadunscir

Motto: Labore Omnia Florent (All Things Prosper by Industry)

County Town: Huntingdon

Towns: Alwalton, Brampton, Buckden, Godmanchester, Hemingford Grey, Huntingdon, Kimbolton, Old Fletton, Ramsey, St Ives, St Neots, Sawtry, Stilton, Warboys, Yaxley.

The growth of Peterborough has expanded to many Huntingdonshire villages drawing them in to form suburbs of this ancient city: Old Fletton, Orton Longueville, Orton Waterville, Water Newton, Woodston and Stanground to name but a few.

Local Government

Cambridgeshire County Council and one District Council. The Everton and Gibraltar detached part of Huntingdonshire is administered by Bedfordshire County Council.

HISTORY

The region was part of the country inhabited by the Iceni Tribe.

The Danes, who invaded in AD 870, were driven out in 921 by Edward the Elder. Huntingdonshire was born. Oswald, Archbishop of York, and Bishop of Worcester, began building Ramsey Abbey in 967. It was dedicated in 974.

Whilst ploughing one day in the village of Slepe, a ploughman discovered the body of a man. It was revealed to him in a dream that this was the body of St Ivo, a Persian Archbishop, who had preached the Gospel in England for many years. The relics were conveyed to Ramsey Abbey, and many miracles were wrought at the shrine dedicated to him. Slepe was thought to be too common a name for the scene of such a miracle, so its name was changed to St Ives. Through inheritance, the Earldom of Huntingdon fell to Scottish kings, and Stuart monarchs often visited the shire.

The community of Little Gidding was founded by Nicholas Ferrar in 1626, as a seminary of religious worship, piety and virtue, learning and study.

The last fight of the Civil War took place at St Neots on July 10 1648. The Cavaliers, under the Earl of Holland, were defeated by Cromwell's troops, under Colonel Scroop,

TOPOGRAPHY INCLUDING RIVERS

Huntingdonshire, in the south-east midlands, is bordered by Northamptonshire in the north and west, Cambridge in the east, and Bedfordshire in the south. The land bordering the Ouse in the south is predominantly fertile meadow. The centre and west of the county is a mixture of woodland and farming country, and in the north-east are the Fens, well drained, to form good grazing land. The highest point is near Covington, 256 feet.

Rivers: Nene, Ouse, Kym.

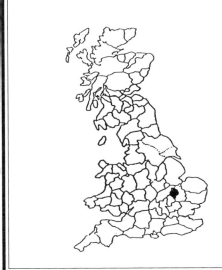

and were forced to flee.

At the beginning of the 19th century, a large number of French prisoners were confined at Norman Cross, taken during the prolonged war with France.

The county was noted in the great days of the coaching age: all traffic bound for the north from London passed through the shire, and the two main roads from London to York met at the Wheatsheaf Inn at Alconbury.

INDUSTRY PAST AND PRESENT

Present industry includes agriculture, sugar-beet processing and engineering.

Huntingdonshire has always been mainly an agricultural county. Prior to the draining of the fens in the 17th century, the industries of turf-cutting, reed-cutting for thatch, and the making of horse-collars from rushes, were carried out in Ramsey and the environs. Saltpetre was manufactured in the 17th century. Pillow-lace making, and straw-plaiting flourished in the 18th century. The manufacture of paper and parchment was carried on at the beginning of this century, and lime-burning was common throughout the county.

LANDMARKS

Portholme Meadow

MONUMENTS

Kimbolton Castle, the last home of Katherine of Aragon, and now a public school, was originally a medieval mansion. Later remodelled, it partially collapsed in 1707, and was rebuilt by Sir John Vanbrugh. **Ramsey Abbey Gatehouse** is all that remains of one of England's richest abbeys. Its other buildings were razed to the ground at the Reformation.

FAMOUS PEOPLE AND LOCAL CHARACTERS

William Sawtry, priest and follower of Wycliffe, was born in Sawtry in the 13th century. He was unfrocked because of his attitude to faith, and burnt in chains at Smithfield in 1401. He was the first Christian martyr to be burnt in England after the conquest.

Sir Robert Cotton, the antiquary, came from Conington. He founded the Cottonian Library.

Oliver Cromwell was born in Huntingdon in 1599. He represented Huntingdon in Parliament, and became Protector of the Commonwealth of England, Scotland and Ireland after the execution of Charles I.

Samuel Pepys went to school in Huntingdon. His family lived in Brampton. In 1667, Dutch ships came sailing up the Medway. In the general panic by the English, Pepys ordered his wife and father to bury his money in the garden to keep it from falling into foreign hands. Having done so, they forgot exactly where they had buried it, and Pepys spent a trying time digging up the garden in search of it.

William Cowper stayed in Huntingdon in 1765-1767, after being released from a mental asylum in St Albans.

H Royce, of Rolls Royce fame, was born in Alwalton.

ART AND LITERATURE

William Cobbett thought the countryside between Huntingdon and Godmanchester *'The most beautiful scene and by far the most beautiful meadows that I ever saw in my life'*.

'the flat plains of Huntingdon'
William Wordsworth
The Prelude

'Ah! if you had been with me at St Neots! The delicious silence of the fields! No sound but the larks singing! And the sense that no hateful city was anywhere near!'
George Gissing,
in a letter to Gabrielle Fleury, 1900

'Huntingdon is a faire and ancient Towne, a sweet river running by it, and the Country about it so abounding in Wheate, that when any King of England passe thro it, they have a Costome to meet his Majestie with an hundred plows...'
John Evelyn (1654)

LOCAL FOLKLORE
Robin Hood
Legend has it that Robin Hood was really the Earl of Huntingdon, who had renounced his riches for a life of poverty and adventure in the forest.

The Trial of the Witches of Warboys
An old lady named Samuel, who was in her eighties, went to visit a neighbour's sick child. She was wearing a black cap on her head, and the frightened child cried out that she was a witch. The child's condition deteriorated, and the doctor declared that witchcraft was afoot. When the child's sisters also fell ill, Mother Samuel's reputation as a witch grew. Eventually she, her husband, and her own daughter were all tried for witchcraft, found guilty and executed.

The Grey Goose Feathers
Long ages ago, the Fenmen formed themselves into a secret brotherhood known as 'The Brotherhood of the Grey Goose Feathers'. Any member of the brotherhood, who had in his possession a grey goose feather by way of recognition, was ensured of immediate help from all the Fenmen if he found himself in trouble.

King Charles I, after his escape from Oxford, took refuge in Norfolk for a while, but then wished to rejoin his troops. He was advised that the safest route was through the desolate wastes of the Fens. An innkeeper named Porter was sent for, as he was known as a guide to travellers across the trackless wastes. Some of the King's friends thought it unwise for him to make the journey alone with only this unknown man as guide. Porter said, to put their minds at rest, he would initiate his charge into the Brotherhood of the Grey Goose Feathers. He divided a goose feather in two, giving one half to the king and keeping the other half himself, saying as he did so, "Whilst fishes have scales, and birds have feathers, I will do all I can for you, and so will every other man who belongs to the Brotherhood of the Grey Goose Feathers."

So the King and Porter set off alone. At St Ives they had to cross a ford, which was guarded by two of Cromwell's soldiers. Porter showed them his grey goose feather, and they replied, "Pass, all is well".

When the King arrived in safety, he rewarded Porter for his help, but he kept his half of the feather.

One of Cromwell's officers heard how the sentries had let the King pass at the ford, and he marched them straight to Cromwell for retribution. But Cromwell was a Fenman too. He told the officer, "It is better for a king to escape than for the Fenman to go back on a man who carries a split goose feather."

Not long after this, King Charles was captured, tried, and sentenced to death. The night before the execution, a messenger came to Cromwell, from the King. The message he gave was this: "His Majesty does not beg for mercy, but he demands as a right the help you are sworn to give to every man who carries this token."

He flung down a grey goose feather on the table in front of Cromwell. Cromwell ordered everyone out of the room, and sat looking at the feather. When the servants came in the next morning, he was still there, looking at it. The King was duly executed, but Cromwell was never the same again. The remorse he felt at the breaking of his vow to the Brotherhood ate into him. And he received from all the Fenmen, who had previously served him well, a broken feather as a sign that his ties with the Brotherhood were broken. They told him that they were returning to the Fens, where men kept their word, and neither he nor any of his family would share in the fellowship of the Brotherhood from henceforward.

DISTINCTIVE FLAVOUR

Huntingdon Pudding, a local dish, is a steamed suet pudding flavoured with gooseberries.

Stilton Cheese used to be sold at Stilton; it was not made there, however, but at Wymondham, near Melton Mowbray.

Barnack village was famous for its stone; quarries were worked from Roman times until the 18th century, when they were exhausted. The site of the quarrying is marked by large mounds and hollows known as the Hills and Holes.

COUNTY DIARY

March:	National Shire Horse Show, Alwalton
July:	East of England Show, Alwalton

K<u>EN</u>T

HISTORY

The Jutes were the creators of the Kingdom of Kent: they are believed to have landed in AD 449, with Hengist and Horsa as their leaders. St Augustine arrived in Thanet circa 600, and converted the people of Kent to Christianity.

In the 8th century, the Anglo-Saxon Kingdom of Mercia conquered the Kingdom of Kent.

On December 29th, 1170, Thomas Becket, Archbishop of Canterbury, was murdered in the cathedral by four of Henry II's knights.

In 1381, during the peasants' rising, the Archbishop's palace was plundered; 100,000 Kentish men gathered round Watt Tyler of Essex. Kentish men also took a leading part in Jack Cade's rebellion of 1450. Then in 1554, the men of Kent, under Sir Thomas Wyatt, rose up to challenge Queen Mary's choice of Philip of Spain as husband. This rebellion lasted only two or three days.

The county was subdued by the Parliamentarians during the Civil War. In 1648, a widespread insurrection was organized on behalf of the Kind, which was crushed by Fairfax.

In 1667 a Dutch fleet led by De Ruyter came up the Medway, levelling the fort at Sheerness, and burning ships at Chatham.

Tunbridge Wells developed into a spa town in the 17th and 18th centuries.

INDUSTRY PAST AND PRESENT

Iron was worked in the Weald from Roman times. In the 10th century the salt industry flourished along the coast. The wool-trade also flourished and in the reign of Edward III, Flemish weavers settled in the Weald, from which time weaving was a flourishing industry. Fruit culture and hop-growing, for which the county is still famous, began in Tudor times. The first paper mill in England was set up in Dartford. The export of wool was forbidden in 1630, which led to a thriving wool smuggling trade.

Intensive agriculture, market gardening – hops, and fruit growing: Kent has half the orchards, and produces half the hops, and over one-fifth of the soft fruit grown in England and Wales. Fishing, ship-building, chemical works, engineering. Sheep-farming, dairy cattle. Dockyards on Thames and the Channel.

TOPOGRAPHY INCLUDING RIVERS

Kent, in the south-east of the country, is bordered by the Thames Estuary in the north, the English Channel in the east and south, Sussex in the south and Surrey in the west. The county is roughly triangular in shape. Running across the centre of the county from west to east is the chalk ridge of the North Downs, reaching over 800 feet in places in the west of the county. South of the Downs runs a parallel ridge called the Ragstone Ridge. The Vale of Kent, rich lowland south of the Downs, is part of the Kent Weald. In the north, along the banks of the Thames, the coast is generally low-lying and marshy. There are several low, marshy islands in the Medway Estuary, although the cliffs of the Isle of Sheppey rise to some 90 feet. There are high, chalky cliffs around the east coast of the Isle of Thanet (which actually used to be an island, cut off from the mainland by a channel called the Wantsume), and further south from Deal to Folkestone; the latter are known as the White Cliffs of Dover. Romney Marsh is a wide expanse of low-lying marsh in the south of the county, with the shingly promontory of Dungeness extending southwards into the English Channel. The rivers of Kent include the Darent, the Medway, the Great Stour, and the Little Stour.

THE DARK ENTRY.

LANDMARKS

The Downs
The White Cliffs of Dover
Romney Marsh
Brands Hatch motor racing track

MONUMENTS

Allington Castle: This Norman moated castle is now a Carmelite Friary.

Canterbury Cathedral was founded in AD 597. William de Sens designed the choir and apse after a fire in 1174. The nave was designed by Henry Yevele in 1374. The Norman crypt is the largest in the world.

Aylesford Priory: Built in the 13th century, the priory fell into decay at the Reformation, but was reoccupied by Carmelites in 1949. Chartwell, the country home of Sir Winston Churchill from 1924 to 1965.

Deal Castle, the finest and best preserved of the line of forts built along the coast by Henry VIII circa 1540. Its shape resembles that of the Tudor rose.

Dover Castle: Begun in the 12th century by Henry II, on a site which has been occupied or fortified from prehistoric times, it is the earliest castle in England in which the fortifications are arranged concentrically.

Hever Castle: This late 13th-century moated castle, altered in the 15th century, was the girlhood home of Anne Boleyn.

Knole: One of the largest private houses in England, it was built in 1454 by the then Archbishop of Canterbury, Thomas Bourchier.

Leeds Castle: A wooden castle was built on the site in Saxon times; in 1119 it was rebuilt in stone. Leeds was the favourite country retreat of medieval queens for 300 years.

Rochester Cathedral: Founded in AD 604 by St Augustine, the cathedral was rebuilt by Bishop Gundulph circa 1080.

Sissinghurst Castle: A tall Tudor gate-tower is the entrance to one of the finest gardens in Britain, a series of outdoor 'rooms' of different colours and styles created by Harold Nicholson and his wife, Vita Sackville-West, in the 1930s.

Walmer Castle: One of the series of coastal defence castles built by Henry VIII, the castle is now the official residence of the Warden of the Cinque Ports.

FAMOUS PEOPLE AND LOCAL CHARACTERS

Geoffrey Chaucer, most famous for his *Canterbury Tales*, lived in Kent from 1386 until his death in 1400.

William Caxton, the first English printer and publisher, is believed to have been born in Hadlow in 1422.

Sir Philip Sydney was born on November 30th, 1554, at Penshust Place, north-west of Tunbridge Wells. He spent his childhood and youth there.

Christopher Marlowe was born in Canterbury in February 1564. The son of a shoemaker, he was educated at The King's School, Canterbury.

William Pitt, the Whig statesman and orator, was the first Earl of Chatham.

Charles Dickens spent his childhood in Chatham, and the last 14 years of his life in Rochester. He also spent his summers in Broadstairs, in a house owned by Miss Mary Strong, the model for Betsey Trotwood in *David Copperfield*.

Ellen Terry, the actress, lived in Smallhythe. Her home, Smallhythe Place, is now a museum to her memory.

H.G. Wells was born in Bromley on the 21st September, 1866.

Sir Winston Churchill lived at Chartwell for more than 40 years.

Harold Nicholson, the diplomat, and his wife, the poet **Vita Sackville-West**, lived at Sissinghurst and created the garden there.

Local Characters

Benjamin Beale, a Quaker of Margate, invented the bathing machine.

Elizabeth Barton was known as the Holy Maid of Kent. She lived in Bonnington, and had visions and made prophecies. Having been miraculously cured of a disease, she retired to a Convent in Canterbury. She spoke out against Henry VIII's proposed divorce in 1527, warning him that he would be damned for it. After this, she was manipulated to speak out by various members of the clergy who were also against the divorce, and she was finally hanged at the order of Henry VIII in 1533.

In Lenham Church is a memorial tribute to **Mary Honeywood**, who died at the age of 92, leaving 367 living descendants: she had 16 children, 114 grandchildren, 228 great-grandchildren, and 9 great-great grandchildren!

Nicholas Wood of Hollinbourne suffered from the condition known as bulimia, to the extent that he 'would devour at one meal what was provided for twenty men, eat a whole hog at a sitting, and at another time thirty dozen of pigeons...'.

Castleton's Oak, an inn near Biddenden, is named after a local parishioner. At the age of 70, he made his own coffin, expecting to be needing it in the near future. It remained empty for another 30 years, till he died at the age of 100!

ART AND LITERATURE

'In 1422 I was born and learned my English in Kent, in the Weald, where English is spoken broad and rude.'
  William Caxton

'the ten miles between Maidstone and Tunbridge (which the Kentish folk call the Garden of Eden) … there, there are, on rising grounds … not only hop-gardens and beautiful woods, but immense orchards of apples, pears, plums, cherries and filberts … and, all taken together, the vale is really worthy of the appellation which it bears.'
  William Cobbett
  Rural Rides (1830)

'Kent, sir – everybody knows Kent – apples, cherries, hops and women.'
  (Anon)

'There is lay in the early sunshine of Spring. It looked a town rather than a house, but a town built, not hither and thither, as this man wished or that, but circumspectly, by a single architect with one idea in his head. Courts and buildings, grey, red, plum colour, lay orderly and symmetrical; the courts were some of them oblong and some square; in this was a fountain; in that a statue; the buildings were some of them low, some pointed …'
  Virginia Woolf,
  describing Knole, in Orlando (1928)

'the gallant squires of Kent.'
  Macaulay
  The Armada

'On Margate sands, I can connect nothing with nothing.'
  T.S. Eliot

LOCAL FOLKLORE

The townspeople of Strood sided with Henry II in his quarrel with Thomas Becket, and cut off the tail of Becket's mule as he went through the town, at which the angry saint declared that all their descendants would be born with tails. According to Polydore Vergil, 'afterward

DANDELION GATEWAY.

WALMER CASTLE.

(by the will of God), it so happened that everyone which came of that kindred of men which played that naughty prank were born with tails, even as brute beasts be.' The inhabitants of Strood and the surroundings are still jestingly referred to as 'Kentish long-tails'.

Sir Robert Shurland, once Lord Warden of the Cinque Ports, was warned that his horse would be the death of him. To avoid this he therefore had it killed. Years later, walking on the beach, he struck his foot against what he at first took to be a rock – but on closer investigation he found it was the skull of his dead horse. A piece of the bone pierced his foot, and he later died from blood poisoning. He is buried in the Church at Minster, and on his monument, just by his right leg, is the head of a horse.

Sir Henry Wyatt was a prisoner in the tower in the reign of Richard III, and was kept alive by a cat, who used to bring a pigeon to his windowledge every day. After his release, Wyatt took up residence in Allington Castle; he was devoted to cats for the rest of his life.

Bloody Baker
Legend tells that Sir John Baker had had to flee the country after fighting a duel, but he returned in the reign of Queen Mary, as he was a Catholic. He lived in his old house at Cranbrook, alone except for one foreign servant. Soon, strange tales began to be told in the neighbourhood, of people mysteriously

disappearing, and dreadful screams issuing from the house at dead of night. Baker began to buy back the property he had previously forfeited, although he still lived the life of a recluse. After a while, however, he began to pay court to a rich young lady in the neighbourhood, often urging her to come and visit him in his house. She decided to pay him a surprise visit one day, and accompanied by an older lady, she went to the house and knocked on the door. There was no reply, but, the door being unlocked, she decided to go straight in. At the top of the stairs they saw a parrot in a cage, who uttered the following warning:
'Peep O! pretty lady! be not too bold,
Or your red blood will soon run cold!'
The two then looked into one of the rooms, and found it was full of the bodies of murdered women. Hearing a noise, they rushed to hide under the stairs. Just then, in came Baker and his servant, dragging another dead body with them. As they passed the staircase, one of the dead woman's hands caught in the bannisters. Baker swore, and hacked the hand off with a knife; it fell straight into the lap of the hiding woman. As soon as the men had disappeared, the two ladies made good their escape, carrying the hand with them. Once back home, they told their neighbours the story, and showed them the hand, which bore a beautiful ring, to prove it. They planned to confront 'Bloody Baker' with his crimes. They invited him to a party, and there the young lady recounted the story of Baker's house, pretending it had been a dream. Baker laughingly cried that dreams were pure fabrication. She then

confronted him with the hand, still bearing the ring: 'Is this a fabrication too?', she demanded. Baker turned pale, and was seized by the law officers who had been hiding in the room. It is said that he was burnt alive for his bloody crimes.

DISTINCTIVE FLAVOUR
Kent is known as the **Garden of England**.

In the county, the natives who live west of the river Medway are known as **Kentish men**; those who live east of the river Medway are known as **Men of Kent**. It is believed that Kentish men are of Anglo-Saxon origin, and Men of Kent are of Jutish origin.

Kentish Well Pudding is a local fish with a crust and topping of suet and currants, filled with butter and sugar.

The county is famous for its **oast-houses**, which have tall conical or pyramidal roofs; inside are the kilns for drying the hops which are grown throughout the county.

Kent County Cricket Club was founded in 1859. Their main ground is St Lawrence, at Canterbury. Their crest is a white horse.

COUNTY DIARY

February:
    International Show Jumping Festival, Gillingham
June: International Balloon Festival, Leeds Castle
June: International Folklore Festival, Folkestone
July: County Show, Maidstone
July: Kent Cricket Week, Canterbury
July: Chaucer Festival, Canterbury
September:
    Heavy Horse Show, Dunton Green

LANCASHIRE

COUNTY FACTS

Derivation of name: From the Brittonic/Anglo Saxon meaning the Roman fort on the River Lune. The local English population frequently called any Roman settlement 'ceaster' – hence Lune-ceaster, which became Lancaster.

First Recorded: During the 12th century.

Motto: In Concilio Consilium (In Counsel is Wisdom)

County Town: Lancaster

Towns: Accrington, Ashton-under-Lyme, Barrow-in-Furness, Blackburn, Blackpool, Bootle, Bolton, Burnley, Bury, Crosby, Fleetwood, Formby, Kirkby, Lancaster, Liverpool, Lytham St Annes, Manchester, Morecambe, Oldham, Preston, Rochdale, St Helens, Salford, Southport, Warrington, Widnes, Wigan.

Local Government

Lancashire County Council, Cheshire County Council and Cumbria County Council. Twelve Metropolitan Boroughs and eighteen District Councils.

HISTORY

In the 7th century, Lancashire was part of the Kingdom of Northumbria, ruled by the Angles.

Following the Norman Conquest, the county grew in prosperity, with many boroughs being granted charters for fairs and markets.

In 1353 Henry, Duke of Lancaster, was empowered to enjoy all the liberties and regalities of a sovereign of a County Palatine. The Reformation was not generally accepted in Lancashire; many of the local clergy remained loyal to the 'old religion', and many of the leading county families suffered for recusancy.

Lancashire was famous for its witches, especially in the region of Pendle Hill. In 1612, the witch-finder, Thomas Potts, was sent north. The most celebrated witches, the Demdikes and the Chattoxes, confessed and were condemned to death.

In 1648, at the Battle of Preston, the Lancashire Royalists were defeated; the second Civil War came to an end.

In 1715 a large contingent of Lancastrians joined the Scots army to proclaim the Pretender King at Lancaster. However, the rebellion was soon quelled.

Lancashire was the heart of the Industrial Revolution. Inventions such as Kay's Fly Shuttle, Hargreave's Spinning Jenny, and Crompton's Mule, all accelerated the expansion of the cotton industry.

The Cotton Famine hit the county in the 1860s, when the cotton mills were cut off from their traditional source of raw materials by the American Civil War, causing real hardship to the cotton workers.

The Lancashire coast developed as a recreation and pleasure resort in the 18th century, with Southport, Morecambe and Blackpool being the favourite attractions.

The first railway in England, from Manchester to Liverpool, opened in 1830.

INDUSTRY PAST AND PRESENT

Lancashire is a centre of cotton and man-made fibre industries; other activities involve chemicals; petroleum; engineering and pharmaceuticals. Tate and Lyle's sugar refining concern is based in Liverpool. Though much reduced, Liverpool's docks still have a part to play in Lancashire's economy. In the 14th century, Edward III married the daughter of the Earl of Hainault, and was impressed by the skill of the cloth weavers in her country. He invited the Flemish clothiers to settle in England to teach his people. Many of them came to Bolton. Later, in the 17th century, Protestants fled from

TOPOGRAPHY INCLUDING RIVERS

Lancashire, in the north-west of England, is bordered by Westmorland to the north, the West Riding of Yorkshire to the east, Cheshire to the south, and the Irish Sea to the west. Furness, a separate part of Lancashire, in the north-west, is bordered by Westmorland and Cumberland in the north and west.

The land from the west coast is low-lying and flat, but rises towards the east to moorland, and the heights of the Pennines (the 'Backbone of England'), which form the eastern boundary of the county. Pendle Hill rises among these moors. Further north, Morecambe Bay stretches inland and separates the main part of Lancashire from Furness in the north-west. This is mountainous country, with a low coastline, off which lies the long strip of Walney Island. The highest point is The Old Man of Coniston, 2633 feet.

Rivers: Ribble, Calder, Hodder, Mersey, Wyre, Lune.

persecution in France and settled in Lancashire; they too were skilled spinners and weavers. Under these influences, the Lancashire cotton and associated industries expanded and flourished. Everything contributed to speed the rapid growth of the cotton trade: iron ore was produced in Furness, to make the mill engines; the Lancashire coalfield provided the fuel to work them; raw cotton was shipped to the booming port of Liverpool, and the finished cotton stuffs were shipped abroad from the same port. Manchester, Bolton, Bury, Rochdale and Staleybridge were among the main cotton working towns, where spinning, weaving, and bleaching were carried out. The streams of the county supplied the necessary water for the bleaching and dyeing processes.

The woollen industry flourished from the 13th century, based on the sheep farming of the northern uplands and Furness.

The prosperity of Liverpool was closely bound up with the slave trade; in the 18th century, roughly a quarter of its ships were engaged in the business.

LANDMARKS

Pendle Hill
Pennines
Coniston Water
The Manchester Ship Canal

MONUMENTS

Manchester Cathedral, built in the 15th century, is a fine example of Perpendicular Gothic church building. It was given cathedral status in 1848.

Liverpool's two cathedrals were both built in the 20th century. The Anglican Cathedral is built in medieval style, the Roman Catholic one is modernistic: circular in shape, it is 193 feet in diameter.

Speke Hall, one of the finest half-timbered Elizabethan houses in the country, was built between 1530 and 1598.

Holker Hall, built in the 17th century, was the former residence of the Dukes of Devonshire.

Gawthorpe Hall, a late 16th century Palladian manor house, was built around a 14th century peel tower.

Hoghton Tower, rebuilt in 1565, the house was the scene of a visit by James I during which he was so delighted with a loin of beef that he knighted it and dubbed it 'sirloin'.

Rufford Old Tower, a medieval timber-framed manor house, with the brick-built

east wing added in 1662.

Lancaster Castle; begun in 1102, the castle, built on top of a steep hill above the city, was extended by John of Gaunt. In its long history, the castle has been a fortress, a prison, and a crown court. The beacon tower on top of the keep is known as 'John of Gaunt's Chair'.

Hall i'th'' Wood: A black and white timbered manor house dating from 1483. It was here that Samuel Crompton invented the Spinning Mule in 1779.

Blackpool Tower, built in the 19th century, is 518 feet high. It was modelled on the Eiffel Tower in Paris.

Furness Abbey, Lancashire's largest monastic ruin is a pleasing pink sandstone structure. It is more celebrated for the monk's varied buildings than for the church itself.

FAMOUS PEOPLE AND LOCAL CHARACTERS

A mysterious young lady rented Frinsthwaite House in the 18th century. She died young, and her grave is referred to as the 'Princess's Grave'. She was the daughter of Prince Charles Edward Stuart and Clementina Walkinshaw – Princess Clementina Johannes Sobieski Douglas.

John Barrow, born in 1764 near Ulverston, was founder of the Royal Geographical Society, and secretary to the Admiralty from 1804-1839.

William Wordsworth lodged at Hawkshead whilst at school.

Thomas de Quincey was born in Manchester in 1785, and educated at Manchester Grammar School.

Harrison Ainsworth was born in Manchester on February 4th, 1805.

Mrs Gaskell came to live in Manchester after her marriage to the minister of Cross Street Unitarian Chapel. Charlotte Brontë used to visit Mrs Gaskell there, and began Jane Eyre whilst staying in the city.

Charlotte and Emily Brontë went to school in Cowan Bridge.

John Ruskin bought a house in Coniston in 1871 and retired there in 1884. He died on 20 January 1900, and is buried in the churchyard at Coniston.

Frances Hodgson Burnett was born in Manchester in 1849, and spent her childhood in Salford.

Alcock and Brown, Manchester men, made the first non-stop crossing of the Atlantic by air in 1919.

Beatrix Potter lived at Hill Top Farm in Near

Sawrey until her death in 1943.

The county has produced several well-known show-business personalities, including **Al Read**, **George Formby**, **Gracie Fields**, **Ken Dodd**, **Gerry and The Pacemakers**, **Frankie Goes To Hollywood**, **Cilla Black** and **The Beatles**.

Local Characters
Ralph Rooney of Hawkshaw used to cover 40 miles a day, walking, playing his concertina, with children following him, pied-Piper-like, wherever he went. He travelled to Land's End and John O'Groats, playing for his supper, bed, and breakfast.

ART AND LITERATURE

'Dreary was the prospect on all sides, black moor, bleak fell, straggling forest, intersected with sullen streams as black as ink, with here and there a small tarn, or moss-pool, with waters of the same hue … The whole district was barren and thinly populated.'
(round Pendle Hill)
Harrison Ainsworth
The Lancashire Witches

'Oh, all you true worth men of Manchester True bred bloods of county Lancaster When I forget what you have to me done Then let me headlong into confusion run.'
John Taylor, 1618

In 1538 Manchester was *'the fairest, best builded, quickliest and most populous town of all Lancashire.'*

In the 1950s, **Sir Hugh Casson** referred to industrial Lancashire as *'a vast ocean of ugliness, hopelessly, helplessly depressing … backyards, dustbins of industry – in a smoke-stained, unloved wasteland.'*

'As far as the eye can reach, one sees nothing but chimneys, blazing furnaces, many deserted but not pulled down, with wretched cottages around them.'
(Manchester)
Queen Victoria, in her diary, 1852

'The air of Lancaster is salubrious, the environs pleasant, the inhabitants wealthy, courteous, hospitable and polite.'

'No other town in the UK has so many royal visits.'
(Barrow-in-Furness)

'Earth, sweet earth, sweet landscape, with leaves throng.'

Gerard Manley Hopkins,
of the Ribble Valley

LOCAL FOLKLORE

*'If Pendle Hill do wear a hood,
Be sure the day will ne'er do good.'*

The Old Hall boggart at Clitheroe was a fearsome creature who used to roam the streets at midnight uttering hideous howls, and clanking chains.

Horse Shoe Corner in Lancaster is so named as being the place where John O'Gaunt's horse is said to have cast a shoe.

The Sale of a Wife

A cobbler at Blackburn used to ill-treat his wife shockingly, though she was a very decent woman. One day he put a halter round her, and said he was going to sell her; she was ready enough. He put her up to auction and people began to bid in fun, but there was one decent old man who liked the look of her very much. He had no money, but borrowed 2s from a shopkeeper and, when that was not enough 2s 6d.

He got the wife, and she said she was glad to go to him, and said, 'You've got me and everything about me, I expect.' He said he did not care for that, as long as he had got her. But she put her hand in her bosom, and pulled out a bag with £200 in it. The old man bought a little business with it, and she was set up for life.

The people used to sing at the cobbler:

'Oh Mister Duckworth
You are a cure.
You sold your wife for beer,
And live at (Cuckold's) Moor.'

The Dragon of Wantley

This dragon was the terror of all the countryside. He had forty-four iron teeth, and a long sting in his tail, besides his strong rough hide and fearful wings.

He ate trees and cattle, and once he ate three young children at one meal. Fire breathed from his nostrils, and for long no man dared come near him.

Near to the dragon's den lived a strange knight named More of More Hall, of whom it

FURNESS ABBEY

was said that so great was his strength that he had once seized a horse by its mane and tail, and swung it round and round till it was dead, because it had angered him.

Then, said the tale, he had eaten the horse, all except its head. At last the people of the place came to More Hall in a body, and with tears implored the knight to free them from the fearful monster, which was devouring all their food, and making them go in terror of their lives. They offered him all their remaining goods if he would do them this service. But the knight said he wanted nothing except one black-haired maid of sixteen, to anoint him for the battle at night, and array him in his armour in the morning. When this was promised, he went to Sheffield, and found a smith who made him a suit of armour set all over with iron spikes, each five or six inches in length.

Then he hid in a well, where the dragon used to drink, and as it stooped to the water, he knight put up his head with a shout and struck it a great blow full in the face. But the dragon was upon him, hardly checked by the blow, and for two days and a night they fought without either inflicting a wound upon the other. At last, as the dragon flung himself at More with the intention of tossing him high into the air, More succeeded in planting a kick in the middle of its back. This was the vital spot: the iron spike drove into the monster's flesh so far, that it spun round and round in agony groaning and roaring fearfully,

but in a few minutes all was over, it collapsed into a helpless heap, and died.

The Captured Fairies

In the village of Hoghton, where all industrious people were weavers, there were two idle fellows, who did no work, but spent their days at dominoes, and their nights in poaching. Each of them owned a lurcher, but the dogs grew so clever that they would often go off alone, and both of them were at last shot by keepers, who were waiting for a chance to rid the neighbourhood of them. Soon afterward the two men themselves narrowly escaped being caught, and as a result they lost their nets, and being too poor to buy new ones, they were compelled to use sacks for their poaching instead. One night they entered a warren, put a ferret down a hole, and fixed their sacks at the mouths of the burrows. Almost at once there was a frantic struggling in the sacks, so the men seized them firmly, recovered their ferret, and made for home. What was their horror when they suddenly heard a voice from one of the sacks, 'Dick, where art thou?' A voice from the other sack replied,

'In a sack
On a back,
Riding up Hoghton Brow.'

The men dropped their loads in terror, and fled home, leaving their sacks full of fairies. Next morning, when they ventured back, they found the sacks neatly folded at the roadside, but no trace of their occupants. They picked up the sacks with care, crept home, and entirely gave up poaching as a means to a living. Their conversion into industrious weavers aroused suspicion in the village, and at last they were driven to confess what had happened. The tale made them the butt of the village youngsters, who would often in mischief, cry out in their hearing, 'Dick, where art thou?'

The Unbidden Guest

'Owd Jeremy' lived in a wretched hovel in a lane leading from the town of Clitheroe. He had the reputation of being a wizard, and claimed to be on familiar terms with the Evil One, and to be able to foretell men's destinies by his help. This cottage was furnished with all the apparatus of a wizard, and would strike awe into those who came to consult Jeremy; but in fact he was a charlatan, and had no faith in the powers he so often invoked.

For all his strange and solitary existence, Jeremy loved the world outside his home, and one day, when an inquirer had just left the cottage, he stood gazing out of the window towards Pendle, and thinking of its ancient beauty, so much more powerful and enduring than the life of a man, and as he turned back to the darkness of the cottage, he saw a stranger sitting in the clients' seat, who said to him, 'Devildom first, and poetizing afterwards.'

'What do you want?' said Jeremy.

'Security,' said the stranger. 'For five and twenty years you have been duping fools in my name, and amassing wealth for yourself, and now I want my share.'

Jeremy pointed to his poverty-stricken abode, for, in spite of his reputed lore, he remained

MANCHESTER CATHEDRAL

very poor, but already he suspected who his dreadful visitor was, and, rising in his agitation, he saw from the window that darkness had suddenly fallen, and a terrible clap of thunder broke over the cottage at the same moment. In panic Jeremy murmured, 'What security do you seek?'

The stranger produced a written bond, and demanded Jeremy's signature, but the sturdy old man refused to sign. Then the Devil threatened that by the next day he should have a rival who would take the bread out of his mouth, and expose all his pretences and sham wisdom. But if he signed the bond, he was to have twenty-two years of life and success such as he had never dreamed of.

But still Jeremy, after deep thought, stoutly refused to sign. The visitor departed, the storm abated, and the sun shone again.

But for five days no one came to Jeremy's house, and when at last he crept out to buy food, the people he passed, instead of shrinking from him in terror, called out jeering remarks, and children went on with their games, as though they had never feared him in their lives.

Next day a shower of stones broke old Jeremy's window, but no one else came to the house, and at last he cried aloud in his misery, 'I wish I had another chance!'

Immediately there was a loud burst of thunder, and there sat his visitor as before, with the parchment on the table in front of him.

'Are you ready to sign?' he demanded.

'I cannot write.'

The devil seized him by one finger, which he used as a pen, and made a neat X writing beside it, 'Jeremiah Parsons, his mark.'

He disappeared as mysteriously as he had come, and almost at once a man knocked at the door, wishing to have his future declared to him. He told Jeremy that he had first tried the new wizard's house in Clitheroe, but found it completely deserted. All fell out as the Devil had foretold. For twenty-two years Jeremy's fame continued to soar, till after one wild night, his cottage was discovered in ruins, and no trace of him remained.

DISTINCTIVE FLAVOUR

Lancastrians are friendly, straightforward, sometimes blunt, 'nosy'; tough and hardy; they use colourful speech, with lively imagery, and have a robust humour; they are taletellers; comic tales are told with dead-pan faces. 'Lancashire grit' pulls them through hard times. There is a distinction between Scousers (Liverpudlians) and Lancastrians.

ENTRANCE TO LANCASTER CASTLE

Scousers are said to be the natural comics of Britain.

'Tha gaumless fooil' = you clumsy creature
'stop skriking' = stop screaming
'sithee?' = do you see?
Other common local phrases: 'Theer's nowt so queer as fooak', 'Reet poorly'; 'gradely'; 'nobbut and summat'; 'owt?'; 'Nowt.'

Well known **local specialities** are Lancashire hotpot, black pudding, tripe, and the original fish and chips.

Preston North End football club play at Deepdale Road – they were the first champions of the football league.

Everton play at Goodison Park; **Liverpool** at Anfield Road; **Manchester United** at Old Trafford; **Manchester City** at Maine Road.

The Grand National is held at Aintree, Liverpool.

COUNTY DIARY

April:
    Grand National, Aintree
June:
    Vintage and Veteran Car Run, Manchester to Blackpool
July:
    Hallé Proms, Free Trade Hall, Manchester
    St Helens Show
August:
    Blackpool Illuminations
September:
    Bowling Festival, Morecambe
    Lancashire County Show

LEICESTERSHIRE

COUNTY FACTS

Derivation of name: Leicestershire is an English corruption of the Latin meaning 'a fort on the river Leire'. The 12th-century writer William of Malmesbury referred to the Leire as the Legra.

First Recorded: 1087 as Laegreceastrescir

Motto: For'ard, For'ard

County Town: Leicester

Towns: Ashby de la Zouch, Barrow upon Soar, Barwell, Birstall, Braunstone, Blaby, Castle Donington, Coalville, Earl Shilton, Enderby, Glenfield, Glen Parva, Hinckley, Kegworth, Leicester, Loughborough, Lutterworth, Market Bosworth, Market Harborough, Melton Mowbray, Mountsorrel, Oadby, Quorndon, Shepshed, Syston, Thurmaston, Whitwick, Wigston.

Local Government
Leicestershire County Council and eight District Councils.

HISTORY

The region was part of the ancient Kingdom of Mercia.

Invasion by Danes began circa AD 850, when they followed the course of the River Trent. In 877 they formed the confederation known as the five boroughs, or the Danelaw, which included Leicester, Derby, Nottingham, Stamford and Lincoln. Leicester was then under uninterrupted Danish rule for 40 years. William the Conqueror captured Leicester in 1068, and Hugh de Crentemesnil was appointed Governor.

Simon de Montfort, known as 'Simon the Righteous', was Earl of Leicester in 1239. The inheritance later fell to Blanche, wife of John of Gaunt, who became Earl of Lancaster, Derby, Lincoln and Leicester.

The county became a centre for Lollardism under John Wyclif, the translator of the Bible. After his death, followers of Lollardism were persecuted, and Wyclif's bones were exhumed, burnt, and the ashes thrown into a stream at Lutterworth.

A Parliament was held in Leicester Castle Hall, aimed at making peace between the uncles of Henry VI. The members came armed with bats or bludgeons, which led to the nickname of 'Parliament of Bats' being attached to the proceedings.

The town of Leicester fought for the Yorkists in the Wars of the Roses, under Sir William Hastings.

The famous Battle of Bosworth took place on August 22nd 1485, between Richard III and the usurper Henry of Richmond. During the battle King Richard was told that Henry was nearby with only a slender guard; taking with him his personal household of knights and friends he valiantly charged and succeeded in slaying Sir William Brandon and Sir John Cheyne and came close to engaging Henry in personal combat. However, Richard was eventually surrounded by the troops of the treacherous Sir William Stanley and killed. Henry Tudor was proclaimed King. King Richard's body was then shamefully exposed to public view for two days and interred without any monument in the house of the Franciscan friars in Leicester. His bones were eventually thrown into the waters of the River Soar.

Historically, the death of this, the last Plantagenet king, marked the end of the Middle Ages, and established Henry VII as the first Tudor monarch.

During the Civil War, the county was almost wholly in support of Parliament. Leicester was besieged and taken by Royalists and was extensively sacked and robbed by the victorious troops.

George Fox, son of a Leicestershire weaver, preached Quakerism widely in the county.

TOPOGRAPHY INCLUDING RIVERS

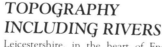

Leicestershire, in the heart of England, is bordered by Nottinghamshire in the north, Lincolnshire and Rutland in the east, Northamptonshire in the south, Warwickshire in the south and west, and Derbyshire in the north-west.

Although the county is fairly flat, it is not low-lying like the Fens. From Leicester, in the centre, the land rises to the east, and in the west towards the craggy and untamed Charnwood Forest, where Bardon Hill, the highest point in the county, rises to 912 feet. The countryside is dotted with small coppices of trees, or even little woods, which were strategically planted as fox coverts, providing the finest fox-hunting country in the land.
Rivers: Soar, Wreake.

INDUSTRY PAST AND PRESENT

Present industries include hosiery and footwear, mixed agriculture, a small coalfield and light engineering.

The woollen industry flourished in Norman times, and in 1343 Leicestershire wool was rated at a higher value than that of most other counties. Blue slate was quarried in Swithland from ancient times, and the limestone quarry at Barrow-on-Soar is of similar antiquity.

Coal was worked from the 15th century. The stocking industry, for which the county is famous, originated in the 17th century.

LANDMARKS

Charnwood Forest
Vale of Belvoir
Bosworth Battlefield

MONUMENTS

Ashby de la Zouch Castle; the ruins date from the 12th to the 15th centuries. The walls of the tower are 8 feet 7 inches thick.
Belvoir Castle, originally a fortress, it was rebuilt in the 17th century, and circa 1800 was converted into a mock medieval castle.
Foxton Staircase; these ten canal locks, grouped in two sets of five, enable barges to rise 75 feet in the space of 300 yards.
Kirby Muxloe Castle is a fortified house built in the 15th century. The owner, Lord Hastings, was beheaded before the castle could be completed.
Leicester Guildhall is a medieval building, consisting of a hall, mayor's parlour, library and cells.
Stanford Hall has been the home of the Cave family since 1430. The present mansion dates from 1697.
East Midlands Airport is more use than ornament.

FAMOUS PEOPLE AND LOCAL CHARACTERS

John Wyclif, the founder of Lollardism, was rector of Lutterworth.
Cardinal Wolsey fell ill on his journey to London and imprisonment, and he died in the county and was buried in Leicester Abbey. His famous dying words were, 'If I had served my God as well as I have served my king, He would not have deserted me in my grey hairs.'
John Cleveland, the poet, was born in Loughborough in 1613.
Dr Johnson's first job was as an usher at the grammar school in Market Bosworth. He described this life of drudgery as 'unvaried as the note of the cuckoo'.
William Wordsworth stayed for a time at Hall Farm in the grounds of Coleorton Hall, owned by his patron Sir George Beaumont. When Beaumont died in 1827, he left Wordsworth £100 a year, for an annual holiday.
Thomas Macaulay, historian and poet, was born at Rothley Temple, north of Leicester, in 1800.

Local Characters

Daniel Lambert was born near Leicester on 13 March 1770. He followed in his father's footsteps and became keeper of the jail in 1791. At the age of 23 he weighed 32 stone, despite leading an active, healthy life. Profiting by his growing notoriety, he went to London to exhibit himself as the fattest man in the world. He died at the age of 39, when he measured 5 feet 11 inches in height and weighed nearly 53 stone. His waistcoat measured 102 inches round the waist. 'Daniel Lambert' became synonymous with immensity: George Meredith referred to London as the 'Daniel Lambert of cities', and Herbert Spencer spoke of 'a Daniel Lambert of learning'.

ART AND LITERATURE

'Beneath yon eastern ridge, the craggy bound,
Rugged and high, of Charnwood's forest ground,
Stand yet, but, stranger! hidden from thy view,
The ivied Ruins of forlorn Grace Dieu.'
William Wordsworth (1811)

'The shady walks of Belvoir'
Francis Thompson (1881)

'O Charnwood, be thou called the choicest of thy kind,
The like in any place, what flood hath happed to find?
No tract in all this isle, the proudest let her be,
Can show a sylvan nymph for beauty like to thee.'
Michael Drayton
Charnwood Forest

William Burton described Leicestershire thus:
'...it hath the proportion of a hart, broad at the top, and narrower towards the bottom, which shape it truly beareth, for that it lieth almost in the hart and centre of the whole continent of the kingdom. The ayre is generally good, pure, and healthful, by reason whereof many sweet and pleasant seats and dwellings are here found, healthfull by nature and much beautified by Art and industry.'

'[Belvoir Castle and countryside]
Thy walks are ever pleasant; every scene
Is rich in beauty, lively, or serene;
Rich – is that varied view with woods around
Seen from the seat, within the shrubb'ry bound
Where shines the distant lake..'
George Crabbe
The Borough (1810)

LOCAL FOLKLORE

Sir Ambrose Cave

One night, whilst Queen Elizabeth I was dancing, her garter slipped from her leg. Sir Ambrose Cave, of Stanford Hall, noticed it, picked it up and offered it to the Queen. She told him he could keep it. Sir Ambrose immediately tied it to his left arm, vowing that he would wear it as long as he lived. A portrait of him in Stanford Hall shows him wearing it.

Hidden Treasure

Richard III stayed a night at the White Boar Inn just before the Battle of Bosworth, and he hid £300 in the false bottom of the bed. As he was unable to return to claim it himself, it stayed there undiscovered until the reign of Elizabeth I. The then landlord discovered the money, and he became rich. After his death, his widow was murdered on account of her wealth.

Bell the Giant

The legendary leaps of Bell the Giant explain the origins of certain place names in the county.
At Mount Sorrel, he mounted his sorrel horse: he then took one huge leap of a mile and landed at a place called Oneleap (now Wanlip); then he took another great leap to Birstall, which exertion caused him and his horse to burst; a third and final mighty leap killed him, and he was buried where he fell, at Belgrave. A rhyme from 1852 commemorates the legend:

'Mountsorrel he mounted at
Rodely he rode by
Onelep he leaped o'er
At Birstall he burst his gall,
At Belgrave he was buried at.'

BELVOIR CASTLE.

Leicestershire is the land of **fox-hunting**, the home of the Cottesmore, The Quorn, and the Belvoir hounds.

A characteristic of Leicestershire folk is said to be unfriendliness.

Whetstone Cakes are traditionally made in the county. These biscuits are flavoured with caraway seeds and rose water.

Melton Mowbray is famous for its pork pies.

The **Leicestershire** county cricket team play at Grace Road in Leicester. Their badge is a gold running fox on a green background. The club was founded in 1879.

There is a motor racing circuit at **Donington Park**.

FINGER PILLORY, ASHBY-DE-LA-ZOUCH.

Black Annis's Bower

The Dane Hills, now part of the city of Leicester, were once wasteland. A cave cut in the side of one of the hills was known as Black Annis's Bower, and here was said to lurk Black Annis, a fearful hag, with long nails and sharp teeth, who fed on human flesh. It was said that she had scooped out the cave herself, with her claws; these same claws were used to scratch children to death. She would then suck their blood, and hang out their skins to dry.

Ashby Folville Church

Two old ladies, coming home late one night, lost their way in the darkness, and despaired of ever finding the right path. Then they heard the bells of Ashby Folville Church ringing out, and they followed the direction of the sound, till they came to familiar paths, and arrived home in safety.

One of the ladies dropped a handkerchief on the spot at which they first heard the bells, and on retracing their steps and finding it the next day, they resolved to donate the produce from that piece of land to the church every year, in gratitude for their safe return home. Until the early 19th century, the floor of the church was strewn for six months of the year with hay or rushes taken from the piece of land the ladies marked out.

COUNTY DIARY

April:	National Folk Music Festival, Loughborough
May Day:	County Show, Leicestershire
August:	Air display, East Midlands Airport
August:	Medieval Jousting Tournament, Belvoir Castle

LINCOLNSHIRE

COUNTY FACTS

Derivation of name: Its Brittonic name was Lindon, meaning a lake (llyn), a widening of the River Witham. The Romans named the place colonia, that is, a colony or settlement for retired soldiers. The local English condensed the name Lindum colonia to make Lincoln.

First Recorded: 1016 as Lincolnescire

Motto: Perseverantia vincit (Perseverance succeeds) – the motto of Kesteven. Service Links All – the motto of Lindsey.

County Town: Lincoln

Towns: Barton-on-Humber, Boston, Bourne, Bracebridge Heath, Brigg, Broughton, Cleethorpes, Crowle, Epworth, Gainsborough, Grantham, Grimsby, Holbeach, Horncastle, Humberston, Immingham, Lincoln, Louth, Mablethorpe, Market Deeping, North Hykeham, Scunthorpe, Skegness, Sleaford, Spalding, Stamford, Sutton Bridge, Waddington.

Lincoln is a county of a city unto itself.

Local Government

Lincolnshire County Council and Humberside County Council and twelve District Councils.

The three ancient Divisions of Lincolnshire are Holland, Kesteven, and Lindsey. Between 1889 and 1974 they had their own separate County Councils, although Lincolnshire as a whole had never had a County Council of its own until 1974, when these three separate County Councils administering Lincolnshire were abolished. The government of the real county was handed over to Lincolnshire and Humberside County Councils.

HISTORY

Before the Roman Conquest, the region was inhabited by the ancient British tribe of Coritani.

In the 9th century Lincolnshire was invaded by the Danes; eventually nearly half the population of Lincolnshire were Danish. Lincoln and Stamford were two of the five towns included in the Danelaw.

From ancient times, the region has been divided into three parts; the Parts of Lindsey in the north, were practically an island, bounded by the swamps of the Trent and the Witham in the west and south, and by the North Sea in the east; the Parts of Kesteven, in the south-west, were a forest region; and the Parts of Holland in the south-east were fenland.

During the Wars of the Roses, the county was mainly Lancastrian, although Grantham and Stamford were Yorkist strongholds. The Lincolnshire rising of 1470 was crushed at the Battle of Losecoat Field near Stamford.

A protest movement against the dissolution of the monasteries began in Louth in 1536, led by 'Captain Cobbler' (a shoemaker) and various members of the clergy. Nearly 100,000 men gathered and marched on Lincoln, but the gentry gradually started pulling out, and the protest lost momentum and died after less than two weeks.

In the Civil War, Lindsey declared for the King, although the rest of the county was generally on the side of Parliament: it was a training ground for Cromwell's 'Invincible Ironsides'.

INDUSTRY PAST AND PRESENT

Present industry includes intensive agriculture, market gardening and bulb growing: tulips, daffodils, narcissi. Other activities are tourism, engineering and the manufacture of diverse machinery.

The main industry of the county was wool from very early times. In the 13th century Lincoln was noted for its scarlet cloth and for the famous Lincoln green. The same century saw the growth of the fishing industry

TOPOGRAPHY INCLUDING RIVERS

Lincolnshire, in the east of England, is bordered by the Humber Estuary in the north, the North Sea and the Wash in the east, Norfolk, and Cambridgeshire and Rutland in the south, and Nottinghamshire and Yorkshire in the west.

The land in Holland in the south-east is low-lying, flat Fen country. Further north, is the undulating, chalky country of the Lincolnshire wolds making up Lindsey. In the west, a long, narrow ridge of high ground begins near Grantham and runs north through Lincoln, towards the Humber Estuary. The highest point is near Normanby-le-Wold, 584 feet.

Rivers include the Trent, the Welland, the Ancholme, the Witham, the Brant, the Glen, the Bain, and the Steeping.

THE LINCOLN IMP

particularly in Boston (famous for its fish market), and Grimsby. Grimsby grew to be the largest fishing port in Europe. Prior to the great draining of the fens in the 17th century, a trade in goose feathers and in wild fowl had flourished there. Gooseherds used to build nests for their geese one above the other – high-rise nests – to enable larger numbers of geese to breed in the same area. In the 18th century, the agricultural revolution enabled more intensive use of the land and therefore increased production. New grazing areas also became available due to the drainage of the fens.

Smuggling was a flourishing trade: the smugglers took out wool and brought in gin and unmanufactured tobacco.

LANDMARKS

The Fens
Lincoln Edge
The Wolds
Gibraltar Point
The Marsh

MONUMENTS

Lincoln Castle, built by William the Conqueror in 1068.

Lincoln Cathedral, begun in 1072. Much of the present church dates from rebuilding after an earthquake in 1185. It was completed in 1280.

Alford Manor House; the original timbered building, dating from circa 1540, was encased in red brick in the early 18th century.

Belton House is a magnificent example of Restoration country house architecture. Built in 1688, it was the home of the Brownlow family for nearly 300 years.

Crowland Abbey: an Abbey was founded in 716, on the site of St Guthlac's cell; it suffered much destruction. The oldest parts of the present Abbey date from the 13th century. Hereward the Wake is said to be buried here.

Doddington Old Hall, an Elizabethan manor house built between 1593 and 1600.

Gainsborough Old Hall, built circa 1500, was the meeting place of the Pilgrim Fathers.

Grimsthorpe Castle; originally a medieval castle, it was transformed into a stone Tudor house in 1540. The north front was added in 1722 by Sir John Vanbrugh.

Harrington Hall, a 17th century Caroline mansion, whose terrace was the 'High Hall Garden' of Tennyson's '*Maud*'.

Tattershall Castle: The medieval brick tower keep rises 110 feet above the flat countryside.

Boston Stump is the name given to the 272 foot high tower of St Botolph's Church.

FAMOUS PEOPLE AND LOCAL CHARACTERS

Nicholas Breakspear, the only English Pope (Adrian IV, 1154-1159), was rector at Tydd St Mary.

Aaron the Jew was a money-lender in Lincoln. His loans financed the building of Lincoln Cathedral, Peterborough Cathedral, Kirkstead Abbey, Louth Park Abbey and Revesby Abbey. His loans to Henry II accounted for half the monarch's income.

John of Gaunt lived at Bolingbroke; his son, Henry IV, was born there.

Richard Fox was born in Ropsley. He became one of Henry VII's most trusted statesmen. He was Bishop of Exeter, then Wells, then Durham, then Winchester. He was Chancellor of Cambridge University, Master of Pembroke College, and founded Corpus Christi College, Oxford.

Cardinal Wolsey was Bishop of Lincoln in 1514-1515.

William Byrd, the composer, a Lincoln man, was appointed organist at Lincoln Cathedral at the age of 20.

Sir Harry Vane lived at Belleau Manor; in 1635 he sailed to Massachusetts in the 'Abigail', and became Governor there. He was executed for treason by Charles II.

Sir Isaac Newton, born in 1642 at Woolsthorpe Manor, went to school in Grantham. He propounded theories of gravity and laws of motion, and invented calculus.

Bonnie Prince Charlie came to Saltfleet in 1744 as part of a reconnaissance prior to his attempt to restore the Stuart dynasty.

Sir Joseph Banks lived at Revesby. A

naturalist explorer, he accompanied Captain Cook on his voyage to the Pacific. He became known as the Father of Australia.

Dick Turpin, the highwayman, is said to have been a butcher at Long Sutton in the Fens, before turning to crime.

Alfred Lord Tennyson was born in 1809 at Somersby Rectory, near Horncastle. He spent childhood holidays at Mablethorpe.

Charles Hobart-Hampden, the third son of the Earl of Buckinghamshire, went to Louth Grammar School. As a sailor, he fought Brazilian slavers. He commanded a ship in the American Civil War, several times breaking the Northern blockade of the Confederate States. Later, he took command of the Turkish fleet in the Black Sea.

Captain John Smith was born in 1580 in Willoughby. He went out with the Colonists to Jamestown, and was captured by Red Indians. He was saved from execution by the Princess Pocahontas.

Paul Verlaine, the French poet, came to Friskney as a teacher in the 1870s, having just come out of prison for shooting and wounding his friend, the poet Rimbaud.

Sir Malcolm Sargent and **Sir Michael Tippet** both came from Stamford.

Mrs Margaret Thatcher was born in Grantham.

Local Characters

Henry Alington, born in 1799, took the name of Pye. He was a solicitor and local dignitary of Louth, and County Treasurer for Lindsey. In 1868 his partner was declared bankrupt, and Pye, who had been using the County Treasurer's fund to meet private debts, had a choice between suicide or flight. He rode off just as the police were at his door. He tried to row across the Humber, although he was 68, and had only one leg; after 3 days on the water, he was picked up and managed to get to London. He and his daughter escaped to Belgium, where he lived as an undeclared outlaw until his death in 1882.

Wreckers used to work on the Lincolnshire coast. A Mablethorpe man last century is reported as saying, 'Times are bad. But maybe the good Lord will send us a wreck!'

Henry Chaplin was born in 1841 near Stamford. He was MP for mid-Lincs for 38 years. Chaplin was engaged to marry Lady Florence Paget, known as the 'pocket Venus', who had previously encouraged the attentions of Chaplin's rival, Hastings. The wedding dress was chosen, and the couple had received congratulations from the Prince of Wales, when, on 16 July 1864, Lady Florence left Chaplin at the door of Marshall & Snelgrove's in London, walked through the store, met Lord Hastings at the other side and went straight to St George's Hanover Square with him, where they were married.

ART AND LITERATURE

'Sleaford for sleep
Boston for business
Horncastle for horses
Louth for learning.'
    Lincolnshire folk saying

'I have always held and am prepared against all evidence to maintain that the cathedral at Lincoln is out and out the most precious piece of architecture in the British Isles and roughly speaking worth any two other cathedrals we have.'
    John Ruskin

Lincolnshire - *'the sink of 13 counties'.*
    Daniel Defoe

'How often, when a child I lay reclined,
I took delight in this locality!

Here stood the infant Ilion of the mind
And here the Grecian ships did seem to be.
And here again I come and only find
The drain-cut levels of the marshy Lea
Gray sand banks and pale sunsets – dreary wind,
Dim shores, dense rains, and heavy-clouded sea!'
    Tennyson,
    Mablethorpe

'The waters are out in Lincolnshire. The arch of the bridge in the park has been sapped and sopped away. The adjacent low-lying ground, for half a mile in breadth, is a stagnant river, with melancholy trees for islands in it, and a surface punctured all over, all day long, with falling rain…'
    Charles Dickens
    Bleak House (1852-3)

'A very paradise and a heaven for the beauty and delight thereof.'
(The Fens)
    William of Malmesbury

'Gosberton Church is very high
Surfleet Church is all awry
Pinchbeck Church is in a hole
And Spalding Church is fit to foal.'
    Local rhyme

'By this to Lincoln come, upon whose lofty scite
Whilst wistly Witham looks with wonderful delight
Enamour'd of the state, and beauty of the place,
That her of all the rest especially doth grace…'
    M. Drayton
    Poly-Olbion (1622)

'Clear Ban, the pretty brook'
'The crystal Trent, for fords and fish renown'd.'
    M. Drayton

Lincolnshire - *'all flats, fogs and fens.'*
    George III

'Kirkby with Mucky-cum-Sparrowby-cum-Spinx
Is down a long lane in the county of Lincs
And often on Wednesdays, well-harnessed and spruce,
I would drive into Wiss over Winderby Sluice.

A whacking great sunset bathed level and drain
From Kirkby with Muckby to Beckby-on-Bain,
And I saw, as I journeyed, my marketing done
Old Caistorby tower take the last of the sun.'
    John Betjeman
    A Lincolnshire Tale (1945)

LOCAL FOLKLORE

Tom Thumb
Legend has it that Tom Thumb is buried in Tattershall Church.

The Lincoln Imp
The Angel Choir of Lincoln Cathedral was built between 1256 and 1280. A malicious little imp kept hindering the progress of the work, and would not stop until the angel threw a stone, hitting him on the leg. The Lincoln Imp is portrayed on a corbel; 12 inches high, and nursing his leg.

The Relics of St Oswald
The relics of St Oswald were carried to the monastery of Bardney, where it was hoped they would be buried. However, the inhabitants of the monastery refused to admit the relics, as Oswald had reigned over them as a foreign King, and they would have nothing to do with foreigners. So that night, the relics of St Oswald were left outside in the open air, covered only by a makeshift tent. But all through the night, a pillar of light could be seen shining upwards from the relics to Heaven. In the morning, the monks opened the doors of the monastery, and begged that the relics, which were so obviously beloved of God, be placed within the monastery. The relics being duly placed within a shrine, the monks of Bardney vowed that the doors of the monastery would never be closed again, by night or by day. From this comes the local saying that anyone who leaves a door open must have been 'Born at Bardney'.

The Ungrateful Sons
'They have a tradition at Winterton that there was formerly one Mr Lacy, that lived there and was a very rich man, who, being grown very aged, gave all that he had away unto his three sons, upon condition that one should keep him one week, and another another. But it happened within a little while that they were all weary of him, after they had got what they wanted, and regarded him no more than a dog. The old man perceiving how he was slighted, went to an attorney to see if his skill could not afford him any help in his troubles. The attorney told

GRANTHAM CHURCH

him that no law in the land could help him nor yield him any comfort, but there was one thing only which would certainly do, which, if he would perform, he would reveal to him. At which the poor old man was exceeding glad, and desired him for God's sake to reveal the same, for he was almost pined and starved to dead, and he would willingly do it rather than live as he did. 'Well,' says the lawyer, 'you have been a great friend of mine in my need, and I will now be one to you in your need. I will lend you a strong box with a strong lock on it, in which shall be contained £1,000; you shall on such a day pretend to have fetched it out of such a close, where it shall be supposed that you hid, and carry it into one of your sons' houses, and make it your business every week, while you are sojourning with such or such a son, to be always counting of the money, and rattling it about, and you shall see that, for love of it,

they'll soon love you again, and make very much of you, and maintain you joyfully, willingly and plentifully, unto your dying day.' The old man having thanked the lawyer for this good advice, and kind offer, received within a few days the aforesaid box full of money, and having so managed it as above, his graceless sons soon fell in love with him again, and made mighty much of him, and perceiving that their love to him continued steadfast and firm, he one day took it out of the house and carried it to the lawyer, thanking him exceedingly for the lent thereof.

But when he got to his sons he made them believe that (he) had hidden it again, and that he would give it to him of them whom he loved best when he dyed. This made them all so observant of him that he lived the rest of his days in great peace, plenty and happiness amongst them, and dyed full of years. But a while before he dyed he upbraded them for their former ingratitude, told them the whole history of the box, and forgave them.'

Bayard's Leap

A witch called Old Meg was terrorising the countryside near Cranwell, blighting crops and bewitching cattle. At last a man dared to do away with her: riding his horse Bayard, and armed with a sword, he called out to her in her hut. When she came out, he struck at her, wounding her, but she leaped up behind him on Bayard, and drove her nails deep into the horse's flank. Bayard gave three mighty leaps, and then the man turned and killed Old Meg with a sword-stroke so powerful that it also killed Bayard. Today, enormous metal horseshoes mark the spot of Bayard's leap.

The Escaping Soul

Two travellers laid down by the roadside to rest, and one fell asleep. The other, seeing a bee settle on a neighbouring wall, and go into a little hole, put the end of his staff into the hole, and so imprisoned the bee.

Wishing to pursue his journey, he endeavoured to awaken his companion, but was unable to so do, till, resuming his stick, the bee flew out to the sleeping man, and went into his ear. His companion then woke him, remarking how soundly he had been sleeping, and asked what he had been dreaming of.

'Oh', said he, 'I dreamed that you shut me up in a dark cave, and I could not awake till you let me out.'

It is believed that the man's soul was in the bee.

DISTINCTIVE FLAVOUR

The **Lincolnshire Red Shorthorn** cow is a local breed.

At **Gibraltar Point**, birds such as redshanks, shelduck and the short-eared owl are to be found as well as flowers such as glasswort, spring beauty, and dewberries.

Tetney is famous for its willow trees, from which cricket bats are made.

Woodhall was the base of the RAF squadron the Dam Busters, during the Second World War.

Stamford cloth was famous throughout Europe for centuries: it is said to have been used on the Field of the cloth of Gold in the reign of Henry VIII.

The Stamford Mercury, started in 1695, is claimed to be the oldest English newspaper to have been published continuously under the same title.

Lincolnshire is famous for its windmills, many of which were used to drive the pumps which drained the Fens. **Heckington** windmill has eight sails; the windmill at **Burgh Le Marsh**, is left-handed.

The nickname of an inhabitant of Lincolnshire is '**Yellowbelly**'.

Horse racing is held at **Market Rasen**.

COUNTY DIARY

March:
　　Lincolnshire Horse Trials, Lincoln
June: Lincolnshire County Show, Lincoln
July: Medieval Joust and Fayre, Lincoln Castle
August:
　　Lincolnshire Sheepdog Trials, Skendleby

MIDDLESEX

COUNTY FACTS

Derivation of name: From the Old English, meaning the territory of the Middle Saxons, (between Essex, Wessex and Sussex)

First Recorded: 704 as Middleseaxan

County Towns: Clerkenwell, Brentford and Westminster. Clerkenwell was the centre for the Justices of the Peace in Middlesex. Brentford was never a seat of administration but the centre of polling in the county, whilst the Middlesex Guildhall in Westminster opposite the House of Commons was the centre of administration until 1965.

Towns: Acton, Ashford, Barnet (partly in Herts), Brentford, Chelsea, Chiswick, Ealing, Edgware, Enfield, Edmonton, Feltham, Finchley, Friern Barnet, Fulham, Hackney, Hammersmith, Hampstead, Hampton, Harrow, Hayes, Hendon, Hornsey, Hounslow, Isleworth, Islington, Kensington, Kingsbury, Mill Hill, Monken Hadley, Northwood, Paddington, Poplar, Potters Bar, Ruislip, St Marylebone, St Pancras, Shoreditch, Southall, Southgate, Staines, Stepney, Stoke Newington, Sunbury-on-Thames, Teddington, Tottenham, Twickenham, Uxbridge, Wembley, West Drayton, Westminster, Willesden, Wood Green, Yiewsley.

London is a county of a city unto itself.

Local Government

Middlesex County Council operated from 1889 until 1965 when it was abolished and local government was handed over to seventeen London Boroughs (two shared with Herts and Surrey towns), the remaining areas of the County were placed under the control of Herts and Surrey County Councils, plus one and a half District Councils. The ancient corporation of London, administers the great City of London. Tower Hamlets had its own Lord Lieutenant, whilst the City of London appointed the Sheriff for the County of Middlesex. The City of Westminster had its own custos rotulorum.

HISTORY

Before the Roman Conquest, the region was occupied by the tribe of the Trinobantes.

A fierce battle was fought at Battle Bridge, near Kings Cross, between Boadicea and the Romans.

In the 6th century the region was colonised by an offshoot of the tribe of the East Saxons. The name of the county derived from its position between the kingdoms of the East and the West Saxons.

In the 9th century Middlesex formed part of the Danelaw. In 866 a treaty between Alfred and Gunthrum made the River Lea the boundary between the Saxons and the Danes. For the first time, Middlesex was formally separated from Essex and obtained its own distinctive name.

At the Battle of Hastings the men of Middlesex were commanded by the Sheriff or Portreeve of London, described by Edward the Confessor's Great Charter to Westminster Abbey as 'Edgar the Minister'.

Much of the north and eastern part of the county was forest; it was known as the Great Forest of Middlesex, and covered more than one third of the county at the end of the Saxon period. Large-scale disafforestation began in the 13th century.

When William the Conqueror marched on London, his armies laid waste the surrounding countryside, resulting in much improverishment.

In 1215, Middlesex was ravaged by William, Earl of Salisbury, and Falkes de Bréauté.

On April 14th, 1471, the Middlesex side of Barnet in South Mimms Parish was the site of a hard fought contest between Warwick the Kingmaker and Edward IV. Having swung over to the Lancastrian side in search of greater prominence, power and prestige, Warwick paid the ultimate penalty for his treachery at the Battle of Barnet in the Wars of the Roses, where he and his forces were soundly defeated by the Yorkist army under Edward.

Henry VIII hunted in Bushey Park, which he enclosed behind a brick wall.

The Hampton Court Conference was an ecclesiastical council which resulted in a revision of the Prayerbook and the authorised translation of the English Bible.

During the Civil War, Middlesex supported Parliament. The county joined with Hertfordshire and Essex in 1642 in a petition that the votes of the bishops and Catholic lords should be disallowed in the House of Lords.

A fruitless treaty was signed at Uxbridge between Charles I and the Parliamentarians in 1645.

Twickenham is said to be the birthplace of Middlesex, as it was in conjunction with this

TOPOGRAPHY INCLUDING RIVERS

Middlesex, in the south-east of England, is bordered by Hertfordshire in the north, Essex in the east, Surrey and Essex in the south, and Buckinghamshire in the west. Roughly in the shape of a parallelogram, the county is an undulating plain, falling gently from a broken range of low hills in the north, southward to the Thames, which forms the sinuous southern boundary. Here and there isolated hills rise from this plain, at Harrow, Highgate, and Hampstead. The highest point is Bushey Heath, 504 feet.

Rivers: Thames, Brent, Crane, Lea and Colne.

town that Middlesex was first recorded. 'Twickenhem in the province of Middleseaxan.'

INDUSTRY PAST AND PRESENT

Middlesex is the centre of high finance and is home to the headquarters of many national institutions and commercial enterprises. It also displays light industry, photographic and camera services, general manufacturing and quarrying.

The woollen and leather industries flourished in Norman times. Animals were taken to London for slaughter, and hides were tanned in Enfield. The manufacture of paper developed in the 17th century. Middlesex also became known for its orchards and market gardens. In early times, Fulham was a haunt of wild fowl. China works at Chelsea produced excellent porcelain in the 18th century. Brickmaking was one of the major industries: Hampton Court Palace was built of Middlesex brick. Gravel has also been dug from the 17th century.

LANDMARKS

River Thames
Hampstead Heath
Heathrow Airport, the busiest international airport in the world
London Parks: Hyde Park, St James's, Green Park
Wembley Sports Stadium, one of the few remaining buildings from the British Empire Exhibition of 1924, and now the national stadium for soccer and many other sports.
Grimsdyke, a Saxon earthwork, at Harrow.

MONUMENTS

Buckingham Palace, built as a house for the Duke of Buckingham in 1703, it became a royal residence when George III bought it in 1762. Now the principal residence of the British Monarch.
St Paul's Cathedral: a wooden church was built on the site in AD 604, and endowed by King Ethelbert. A 13th-century church was destroyed by the Great Fire of London in 1666. In 1675 the building of the present cathedral began, to a design by Sir Christopher Wren.
Tower of London, begun by William the Conqueror, and completed by Henry I's Bishop of Durham, the tower has housed many eminent prisoners: Kings of Scotland, England and France; Sir Thomas More; the Duke of Monmouth.
Mansion House; the Palladian-style house built between 1739 and 1753 is the residence of the Lord Mayor of London.
Houses of Parliament, technically the Palace of Westminster. The neo-gothic new House was built in 1840 after fire had destroyed most of the previous building.
Westminster Abbey, founded by Edward the Confessor in 1050 and rebuilt in 1245 by Henry III. The Abbey is an excellent example of early English architecture.
Forty Hall, a magnificent hall in Enfield built circa 1630 by Sir Nicholas Raynton.
Kenwood House; this Georgian country mansion was enlarged in 1767 by Robert Adam for its owner, Lord Mansfield.
Wrotham Park, built in 1754 for Admiral Byng.
Grimsdyke, built by Norman Shaw in 1872, was the home of W.S. Gilbert from 1890.
Gunnersbury Park Mansion, the home of Lord Nathan Rothschild from 1836, and now a museum of local history, industry and crafts.
Syon House was once a Bridgettine monastery. After the Dissolution, the abbey and park were granted to the Duke of Somerset, the Protector. He built a house here circa 1547, the shell of which is the core of the present building. It was here that John Dudley, Earl of Northumberland, persuaded Lady Jane Grey to accept the English Crown. Katherine Howard, the 5th wife of Henry VIII, was kept here to await her execution.
Chiswick House, a Palladian-style villa created between 1720 and 1725 by the 3rd Earl of Burlington.
Hampton Court; although Cardinal Wolsey planned and built the palace for himself, he nevertheless handed it over to Henry VIII in 1520.
Osterley Park; the original house was built in the late 16th century by Sir Thomas Gresham, founder of the Royal Exchange. The present Classical mansion was built between 1761 and 1780.
Harrow School; one of England's most famous public schools, founded in 1571 by John Lyon.

Boston Manor, known to many merely as a tube station, is an exceptional early 17th-century house with elaborate plasterwork ceilings.

FAMOUS PEOPLE AND LOCAL CHARACTERS

Francis Bacon was born in the Strand, in London, in 1561. He died in Highgate in 1626.
Charles Lamb was born in London in 1775, and lived in Islington, Enfield, and Edmonton.
John Keats lived in Hampstead; he went to school in Enfield.
Famous ex-pupils of Harrow include **Lord Byron**, **Sir Winston Churchill**, **Robert Peel**, **Sheridan**, **Lord Palmerston**, and **John Galsworthy**.
W.S. Gilbert, the lyricist and collaborator with Sullivan on operettas, lived in Grimsdyke, Harrow Weald. He was Deputy Lieutenant of Middlesex.
Harrison Ainsworth lived in Kensal Green from 1834 to 1853, and wrote some of his best novels here.
David Garrick, the actor, was Lord of the Manor of Hendon in 1756.
Lord William Russell lived at Highwood House. On hearing that he was to be arrested for his part in the Rye House Plot of 1684, he escaped from the house by jumping from a second storey window.
Samuel Taylor Coleridge lived at No.3 The Grove, Highgate, from 1816 until his death in 1834.

Local Characters

Dawley Court, Harlington, now demolished, was the home of the well known Middlesex de Salis family. A **Peter de Salis** came to England from Switzerland in 1709; the family have produced several well known military men. **Sir Cecil Fane de Salis** was Chairman of Middlesex County Council from 1920 to 1925.
Dr William Dodd was a schoolmaster in Ealing. He was also the last man in England to be executed for forgery.

ART AND LITERATURE

'An acre in Middlesex is better than a principality in Utopia.'
  Macaulay
  Literary Essays, (1825)

'Gaily into Ruislip Gardens
Runs the red electric train,
With a thousand Ta's and Pardon's
Daintily alights Elaine;
Hurries down the concrete station
With a frown of concentration,
Out into the outskirt's edges
Where a few surviving hedges
Keep alive our lost Elysium – rural Middlesex
again.

We'll cut Windsmoor flapping lightly,
Jacqmar scarf of mauve and green
Hiding hair which, Friday nightly,
Delicately drowns in Drene;
Fair Elaine the bobby-soxer,
Fresh-complexioned with Innoxa,
Gains the garden – father's hobby –
Hangs her Windsmoor in the lobby,
Settles down to sandwich supper and the television
screen.

Gentle Brent, I used to know you
Wandering Wembley-wards at will,
Now what change your waters show you
In the meadowlands you fill!
Recollect the elm-trees misty
And the footpaths climbing twisty
Under cedar-shaded palings,
Low laburnum-lean-on railings,
Out of Northolt on and upward to the heights of
Harrow hill.

Parish of enormous hayfields
Perivale stood all alone,
And from Greenford scent of mayfields
Most enticingly was blown
Over market gardens tidy,
Taverns for the bona fide,
Cockney anglers, cockney shooters,
Murray Poshes, Lupin Pooters,
Long in Kensal Green and Highgate silent under
soot and stone.'

John Betjeman
Middlesex

'No, Sir, when a man is tired of London, he is
tired of life; for there is in London all that life can
afford.'

Samuel Johnson
Letter to Boswell, (1777)

'Hell is a city much like London – A populous and
smoky city.'

Shelley
Peter Bell the Third

'Hounslow Heath is a sample of all that is bad in
soil, and villanous in look.'

Cobbett
Rural Rides

'Middlesex for sin'   (Tradit.)

'If one thing is more certain than another in the
formation of Saxon England, it is the utter
insignificance of Middlesex.'

Sir Mortimer Wheeler
London and the Saxons (1938)

'There is no place in the world which has the same
interest for an Englishman as the county of
Middlesex.'

W.J. Loftie
History of London

'It is very beautiful.'

Doctor Arnold
at Laleham

LOCAL FOLKLORE

Earl Holland

Earl Holland was first a Royalist, then a
Parliamentarian, and then turned Royalist
again. He was condemned to death by
Cromwell, and his ghost is said to haunt
Holland House still.

The Two Pickpockets

A skilful pickpocket was working in Oxford
Street one day, when he discovered that
someone had picked his own pocket. He
turned and saw a beautiful girl walking rapidly
away. He caught up with her, and it transpired
that she had picked his pocket. Rather than
compete on the same patch, the two teamed
up, and became so successful that they decided
to get married, and breed a race of the best
pickpockets in the world. When their first
son was born, however, he was deformed: his
fist was clenched tight, and his arm bent to
his chest. Realising that this would impede
his skill in picking pockets, the distressed
parents took him to a series of doctors, to see
if he could be cured. A specialist had a
beautiful gold watch, by which he was
checking the baby's pulse, and he remarked
how alert the child was, as his eye followed
the watch swinging to and fro. Suddenly the
baby straightened out his bent arm, and
opened his clenched fist to make a grab for
the gold watch – and out fell a gold ring
belonging to the midwife....

The Holy Well

There was once a holy well at Muswell Hill,
whose water was believed to have curative
powers. King Malcolm IV of Scotland is said
to have visited it.

DISTINCTIVE FLAVOUR

In many of the manors around London, the
custom of **Borough-English**, or junior right,
was prevalent: this meant that if a man died
intestate, the inheritance passed to the
younger son. In other manors, the custom of
Gavelkind held: this meant that if the man
died intestate, the inheritance was divided
amongst the sons and daughters, with the
widow having half the estate for her lifetime.

During the **First World War**, a German
Zeppelin was shot down over Potters Bar, and
another over Cuffley (Herts), in 1916. The
crew of both are buried in Potters Bar
churchyard.

The fair at **Pinner** has been an annual event
since 1386.

The Ealing Film Studios opened in 1931. It
was the most productive unit in the country
for 25 years, being most famous for the series
known as the Ealing Comedies, such as Hue
and Cry, Passport to Pimlico, and Kind Hearts
and Coronets. Famous actors at the studios
include Stanley Holloway, Jack Warner, and
Margaret Rutherford.

Northolt Airfield was the base of Fighter
Command in the Second World War.
Uxbridge RAF Depot was the HQ of Fighter
Command during the Battle of Britain.

Cricklewood and **South Acton** were famous
for their laundries: South Acton was known
as 'Soapsud Island'.

The pupils of **Harrow school** are known as
Old Harrovians.

The Metropolitan Police College is in
Hendon.

Colindale is the home of the **British Museum
Newspaper Repository**.

The publishers **Penguin Books** are based in
Harmondsworth.

Willesden is famous as the home of the
Guinness Brewery.

The Middlesex (57th) Regiment fought with
the Spanish in the Peninsula War and held
back the might of Napoleon at Albuhera on
the 16th May 1811. When their leader,
Colonel Inglis was dying he called out to his
weary troops, "Die hard, 57th". They held

HARROW SCHOOL: THE OLD BUILDING

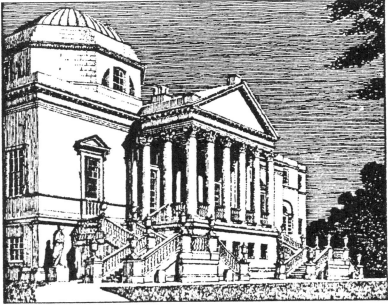

CHISWICK HOUSE

COUNTY DIARY

January:
    International Boat Show, Earls Court

February:
    Crufts Dog Show, Earls Court

May:
    Flower Show, Chelsea
    FA Cup Final, Wembley
    Rugby League Cup Final, Wembley

May 16:
    Middlesex or Albuhera Day

June: Test Match, Lord's
    Trooping the Colour, the Mall
    Middlesex County Show, Uxbridge

July: Proms Concerts, Royal Albert Hall
    Royal International Horse Show, Wembley
    Brentford Show and Carnival

September:
    Middlesex County Awards

October:
    Quit Rent Ceremony – the Queen's Remembrancer receives the Quit-rent of a bill-hook, a hatchet, six horse shoes and 61 nails, two holding for the comptroller of and the city solicitor. The tradition dates from 1234.
    Horse of the Year Show, Wembley

November:
    State Opening of Parliament

the centre of the battle against the advancing French army where the fire was the fiercest, the loss the heaviest and therefore the glory of dying hard the greatest. From that day onwards they were a junior regiment no longer, and were nicknamed 'The Diehards' for their bravery and gallantry.

Lord's cricket ground is the property of the Marylebone County Cricket Club, although Middlesex County Cricket Club play there, and also have their HQ there. The ground was named after a groundsman, Thomas Lord. Middlesex County Cricket Club was founded in 1863.

Wembley Stadium is the national stadium for soccer and many other sports.

Twickenham is the HQ for Rugby Union.

Lancaster Gate is the HQ of the Football Association.

In the famous Oxford versus Cambridge **University Boat Race**, the teams can choose either the Middlesex or the Surrey side, should they win the toss, before rowing the course from Putney to Mortlake.

In 1988 many Boroughs re-erected **boundary signs for Middlesex**, on learning that it was *not* the County of Middlesex that was abolished, but merely the County Council. This goes some way towards eradicating the erroneous belief that Middlesex is only a 'Postal' county.

NORFOLK

COUNTY FACTS

Derivation of name: Anglo-Saxon origin - 'the place of the North folk'.
First Recorded: 1043
County Town: Norwich
Towns: Attleborough, Aylsham, Caister, Cromer, Diss, Downham Market, East Dereham, Fakenham, Great Yarmouth, Heacham, Hunstanton, Kings Lynn, North Walsham, Norwich, Sheringham, Sprowston, Swaffham, Terrington St Clement, Thetford, Thorpe St Andrew, Wells-next-the-Sea, Wymondham. Norwich is a county of a city unto itself.

Local Government
Norfolk County Council and seven district councils.

HISTORY

In early days Norfolk was dominated by the tribe of the Iceni, their most famous leader being Queen Boadicea, who led her people against the Romans in AD 61.

Circa 400, a tribe known as the Angulus, or Angles, from Holstein, began to settle in the area, which became known as East Anglia. Thetford was the seat of the King of the East Angles.

Christianity was introduced into East Anglia by AD 617 by St Felix.

1065 – Domesday Book records Norfolk as being the most populous place in England.

King John, whilst travelling from King's Lynn to Newark, shortly before his death in 1216, lost his baggage, containing most of his treasure, in the Wash.

1549 Kett's Rebellion: 20,000 rebels, led by Robert Kett, a tanner, and his brother William, a butcher, of Wymondham, because of economic grievances. The rebellion was defeated and the ringleaders executed.

The county mainly supported parliament during the Civil War, and became one of the six counties of the Eastern Association. King's Lynn remained staunchly Royalist, however, and Norwich was one of the first cities to welcome the return of Charles II.

In the 17th and 18th centuries, Norwich was the second city in the country, after London. The influx of Flemish weavers in the 14th, and in particular in the 16th century, stimulated the already thriving wool trade to the height of its prosperity, and the ports of King's Lynn and Great Yarmouth were among the most important in the land.

The 'Norwich school' of painting flourished during the early 19th century.

INDUSTRY PAST AND PRESENT

Present industries include agriculture (wheat, barley, sugar-beet), poultry farming, thatching, fishing, tourism, sweet making and the manufacture of footwear. Famous concerns include Colman's mustard, Norwich Union Insurance, and the largest Christmas cracker making factory in the world.

Wool was a flourishing industry in the Middle Ages.

LANDMARKS
The Fens
The Broads
Blakeney Point
Thetford Chase – the largest man-made forest in Europe.
Grimes Graves – a large number of depressions, which are the partly filled in shafts of mines dug by neolithic man nearly 4000 years ago.

MONUMENTS
Blickling Hall, a red-brick Jacobean house built between 1616 and 1628.
Felbrigg Hall; this Jacobean hall, set in a huge park, was the home of the Windham family for 300 years.
Holkham Hall, a Palladian mansion built between 1734 and 1759 for Thomas Coke, Earl of Leicester, to a design by William Kent.
Oxburgh Hall, begun in 1482, the gatehouse and the north front are the only parts of the 15th-century brick building to survive. The rest dates from early 19th century.
Sandringham House is the private country residence of the Queen, with an estate of

TOPOGRAPHY INCLUDING RIVERS

Norfolk is the largest county in East Anglia, bordered by the Wash and the North Sea to the north and east, Suffolk in the south, and Cambridgeshire and Lincolnshire to the west. The coastline stretches for 100 miles. The land rises steadily from the east to the west, with a sudden fall to the Fens, bordering Cambridgeshire and Lincolnshire. In the east is the area known as the Broads, 200 miles of intercommunicating waterways, which resulted from extensive digging for peat in the Middle Ages. The highest point is near Roman Camp, Sheringham, 336 feet.
Rivers: Bure, Yare, Tas, Thet, Waveney, Little Ouse, Wissey, Nar, Ouse, Wensum, Burn, Stiffkey, Chet, Ant.

20,000 acres.

Norwich Cathedral was begun in 1094, and finished in 1145. The tower is the highest Norman tower in Britain.

Wymondham Abbey was founded in 1107. The monks built the octagonal tower circa 1400, and the parishioners built their own, square, tower in 1448.

Caister Castle, the remains of a moated castle begun in 1432 by Sir John Fastolfe.

Castle Acre Castle and Priory; the 13th-century gateway, with two round towers, is still standing. Of the remains of the Cluniac priory, the 12th-century arcaded west front is most impressive.

Castle Rising, a 12th-century castle built on spectacular earthworks of uncertain origin, although part date back to the Roman occupation.

FAMOUS PEOPLE AND LOCAL CHARACTERS

Sir Thomas Gresham founded Gresham's School, in Elizabethan times; pupils include **W H Auden** and **Benjamin Britten**.

John Rolfe, a member of the family who lived at Heacham Hall, married the Red Indian Princess **Pocahontas** in 1614.

Viscount 'Turnip' Townshend, in the 17th century, devised the 4-course system of husbandry to improve the quality of the soil – wheat, turnips, barley, clover.

Oliver Goldsmith immortalised the village of Houghton in his poem *The Deserted Village*.

Parson Woodforde, author of *Diary of a Country Parson*, was rector of Weston Longeville until his death in 1803.

Fanny Burney, the first great English woman novelist, was born in King's Lynn in 1752.

Admiral Lord Nelson was born in Burnham Thorpe in 1758.

Elizabeth Fry was born in 1780 in Norwich.

Baron Lytton, a member of the Bulwer family of Heydon Hall, was born in 1803. His best known novel is *The Last Days of Pompeii*.

Anna Sewell, author of *Black Beauty*, was born in Yarmouth in 1820, and lived in Norwich.

Sir Rider Haggard, was born in West Bradenham in 1856; he settled in Ditchingham after his return from Africa.

Nurse Edith Cavell was brought up in the vicarage at Swardeston.

R H Mottram, author of *The Spanish Farm*, was Lord Mayor of Norwich.

Dorothy L Sayers described villages in the Fens region in her *The Nine Tailors*.

ART AND LITERATURE

'Very flat, Norfolk.'
Nöel Coward
Private Lives

'Scarce a tree to be seen for miles, or a house, except here and there a warren house or eminence. I observed many barrows, and now and then some ancient boundary ditches.'
Rev. Dr Stakeley,
on Breckland

'A fine city, truly, is that, view from whatever side you will: but it shows best from the east, where ground, bold and elevated, overlooks the fair and fertile valley in which it stands…At the foot of the heights flows a narrow and deep river…flanked on either side by rich meadows of the brightest green, beyond which spreads the city; the fine old city, perhaps the most curious specimen at present extant of the genuine old English town.'
George Borrow,
on Norwich, 1851

*'There after supper lit by lantern light
Warm in the cabin I could lie secure
And hear against the polished sides at night
The lap lap lapping of the weedy Bure,
A whispering and watery Norfolk sound
Telling of all the moonlit reeds around.'*
John Betjeman
Norfolk

*'Bitter, bitter of to behould the grasse to growe,
Where the walls of Walsingham so stately did show
Levell, levell with the ground the towres do lye
Which with their golden glittering tops pearsed once to the skye.
Where were gates, no gates are nowe; the waies are unknown…'*
Anon,
on the destruction of the holy shrine at Walsingham

*'…I was quite tired, and very glad, when we saw Yarmouth. It looked rather spongy and soppy, I thought, as I carried my eye over the great dull waste that lay across the river; and I could not help wondering, if the world were really as round as my geography-book said, how any part of it came to be so flat. But I reflected that Yarmouth might be situated at one of the poles; which would account for it.
As we drew nearer, and saw the whole adjacent prospect lying a straight low line under the sky, I hinted to Peggotty that if the land had been a little more separated from the sea, and the town and the tide had not been quite so much mixed up, like toast and water, it would have been nicer. But Peggotty said, with greater emphasis than usual,*

that we must take things as we found them, and that, for her part, she was proud to call herself a Yarmouth Bloater.'
Charles Dickens
David Copperfield

LOCAL FOLKLORE

Blickling Hall
Blickling Hall was the childhood home of Anne Boleyn. On the anniversary of her execution, she is said to drive up to the hall in a coach drawn by headless horses, driven by a headless coachman, while she herself sits with her head on her lap.

Stowe Hall
Stowe Hall was the home of the Hare family for over 400 years. In the Chapel is a lifesize wax effigy of Sarah Hare, who died in 1744, allegedly as a result of pricking her finger while doing needlework on the Sabbath.

The Norfolk Labourer
There is a tale of the Norfolk labourer who, at 85, after 75 years of service, was bidden by his master to enjoy his well-earned rest. The old man retorted, 'There, now, if I'd ha' known that won't a goin' to be a parmanency, I wouldn't never ha' taken the blasted job!'

The Pedlar of Swaffham
There once was a pedlar who had a dream that if he went to London Bridge and stood there, he would soon hear some joyful news. He ignored the dream at first, but when it recurred, he decided to resolve his mounting curiosity, and accordingly went to London, and stood on the bridge there for two or three days – but heard nothing that might yield him any comfort. Finally, a shopkeeper nearby, who had seen the pedlar standing there all that time, came up and asked him why he was standing there. The pedlar explained his dream to the shopkeeper, who laughed heartily, saying he shouldn't take so much notice of dreams. He added that he himself had had a dream the night before, in which he was in a place called Swaffham, which he had no knowledge of, and he had dreamt that behind a pedlar's house, under an oak tree in a certain orchard, if he were to dig he would find a vast treasure! The shopkeeper

said that he wouldn't be such a fool as to undertake such a long journey on the strength of a dream like that. At which news, the pedlar hurried back home, and dug under an oak tree in the orchard behind his house, and found a vast horde of treasure, with which he became exceedingly rich. He paid for the rebuilding of Swaffham Church, which was almost in ruins, and there is a statue to him there to this day.

Black Shuck

Black Shuck was a calf-sized dog that haunted the county, and was a portent of death and disaster. Sometimes he was invisible, only his hot breath, his footsteps, his fearful howls, or the clanking of his chain giving warning of his presence. Sometimes he appeared without his head, but always with his eyes glowing in the middle of where his head should be.

At Garveston, 'They du speak of a dog that walks regular. They call him Skeff and his eyes are as big as saucers and blaze wi' fire. He is fair as big as a small wee pony, and his coat is all skeffy-like, a shaggy coat across, like an old sheep. He has a lane, and a place out of which he come, and he vanish when he hev gone far enough.'

The Silver Chalice

In the village of Lyng a river channel was reputed to run from the River Wensum to and under St Edmund's Chapel in the east of the parish. Once, two watermen picked up a silver chalice in this channel, and at once began to quarrel over who should keep it.

'I found it first so it should belong to me,' said one of the pair.

'I picked it up first, so I reckon it's mine,' said the other.

The dispute grew more and more bitter until, at last, one of the men lost his temper and swore at his companion. The chalice immediately jumped into the air, fell into the water and was never found again.

A NORFOLK WHERRY

DISTINCTIVE FLAVOUR

Caution is the dominant characteristic of Norfolk people, especially where strangers are concerned. 'We'll summer and winter 'em fust,' – until they have their measure and accept them.

Norfolk people are **averse to change**: 'If the world like to change, we 'on't'. They are also self-reliant, and self-supporting, due to their long-standing geographical isolation.

Pheasants are so common in Norfolk that they are sometimes referred to as '**Norfolk sparrows**'.

Norfolk turkeys are also famous – well known as being 'bootiful', according to Bernard Mathews.

Cromer crabs and **Yarmouth bloaters** are local specialities.

Norwich City Football Club play at Carrow Road; they are known as the 'Canaries'.

COUNTY DIARY

June: Royal Norfolk Show, New Costessey
August: Raft Races, Great Yarmouth
September:
Battle of Britain Motor Boat Championships, Oulton Broad

NORTHAMPTONSHIRE

COUNTY FACTS

Derivation of name: Northamptonshire comes from the Old English North Hamtune, meaning northern home farm or town.
First Recorded: 1011 as Hamtunscir
Motto: Rosa Concordiae Signum (A Rose, the Emblem of Harmony)
County Town: Northampton
Towns: Bozeat, Brackley, Brigstock, Brixworth, Broughton, Bugbrooke, Burton Latimer, Corby, Daventry, Desborough, Duston, Earls Barton, Eye, Finedon, Higham Ferrers, Irthlingborough, Kettering, Kings Cliffe, Long Buckby, Middleton Cheney, Moulton, Northampton, Oundle, Peterborough, Raunds, Roade, Rothwell, Rushden, Thrapston, Towcester, Wellingborough, Wittering, Woodford.
The Soke of Peterborough: A Liberty within Northamptonshire, which was important enough to become an administrative county council in 1889, and which throughout history has had unique privileges due to its exclusive ecclesiastical position. Soke comes from the Norman word soc or sac meaning a liberty. Peterborough is one of the few names in Britain derived entirely from a Christian saint, as the city was recorded in the Domesday Book as Burg or Borough and after it was rebuilt it was renowned for its strong defences. Eventually Peter, the saint to which the great cathedral (then only an abbey) was dedicated, was prefixed onto the existing name and is quite literally akin to its great Russian namesake St Petersburg.

Local Government
Northamptonshire County Council, Cambridgeshire County Council and eight District Councils.

HISTORY

After the Norman Conquest, Northampton rose in importance, lying as it did halfway between the national capital of Winchester and the capital of the north, York, and halfway between the Welsh marches and the east coast.

In 1095, William Rufus called the Council of Rockingham at Rockingham Castle, to discuss the question of royal supremacy in ecclesiastical matters.

Henry I called the barons to swear loyalty to his daughter Matilda, at Northampton. Here too, Stephen called his first council to receive the allegiance of those who had previously sworn to his cousin.

Many councils and parliaments were held at Northampton from the 12th century onwards, and the county saw the inauguration of several of the crusades.

The county was also a favourite royal hunting ground.

Lollardism was favourably received in the county.

In 1460, the king's standard was set up in Northampton, and the first decisive battle in the Wars of the Roses was fought.

In February, 1586, Mary Queen of Scots was executed at Fotheringhay Castle, and was buried in Peterborough Cathedral.

A local man, Robert Catesby, was the instigator of the Gunpowder Plot.

The county was divided in allegiance during the Civil War. In June 1645 the Battle of Naseby began a long series of victories for the Parliamentarians.

The last blows were struck for the Commonwealth regime at Staverton Field, near Daventry, by Lambert, one of Cromwell's generals. They were defeated, and the monarchy was restored.

1768 saw the scandal of the so-called 'Spendthrift Elections', in which there was a triangular fight between Lord Northampton, Lord Halifax, and Lord Spencer for the honour of being nominated MP for Northampton. The poll lasted 14 days, and although there were only 930 eligible voters, 1,149 votes were recorded.

INDUSTRY PAST AND PRESENT
Agriculture, footwear manufacturing, engineering, leather processing and paper making are current activities.

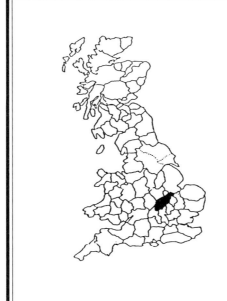

TOPOGRAPHY INCLUDING RIVERS

Northamptonshire, in the east midlands, is bordered by Leicestershire and Rutland in the north, Huntingdonshire and Bedfordshire in the east, Buckinghamshire and Oxfordshire in the south, and Warwickshire in the west.

The land around Towcester in the south, is fairly hilly, and in the west of the county the limestone hills are a continuation of the Cotswolds. In the north-east corner is a level stretch of land known as Peterborough Fen. The highest point is Arbury Hill, 734 feet.

Rivers: Nene, Welland, Avon, Swift.

Iron-mines and stone-quarries were worked in Roman times. Wool and leather industries flourished in Norman times. Other early industries included charcoal-burning, brick and tile manufacture, and brewing. The 17th and 18th centuries saw the introduction of pipe-making, whip-making, silk-weaving and paper-making.

MONUMENTS

Brixworth and **Earls Barton** possess two of the most important Saxon churches in Europe.
Fotheringhay displays a large collegiate church.
Rockingham Castle, a royal fortress built for William the Conqueror. It was granted by Queen Elizabeth I to Edward Watson, whose descendants have lived there ever since.
Boughton House; the 17th-century house was transformed from a 15th-century monastery. It is a treasure house of fine art.
Althorp; this mansion, of medieval origin, has been the home of the Spencer family since 1508.
Holdenby House was built in 1580. Charles I was held prisoner here before his execution.
Sulgrave Manor was the ancestral home of George Washington, the first President of the USA. Built in 1560 by Lawrence Washington, it is one of the few English country homes to fly the American flag.

FAMOUS PEOPLE AND LOCAL CHARACTERS

Thomas Fuller, the antiquarian and divine, was born in Aldwinkle in June 1608.
John Dryden, the poet and dramatist, was born on August 9, 1631, in Aldwinkle All Saints. He lived in Titchmarsh.
John Clare, the 'Northamptonshire poet', was born on July 13, 1793, in Helpston. He started writing poetry whilst employed at a lime kiln. In 1820, he published *Poems Descriptive of Rural Life and Scenery*, by John Clare, a Northamptonshire Peasant. After brief success in London, he returned to Northamptonshire, disillusioned with the worldly life of the capital, and he finally died in the county asylum.
Jerome K Jerome, the author, died in Northampton General Hospital on June 14, 1927, having fallen ill suddenly whilst on a motoring tour of England.

Local Characters
Sir Thomas Tresham, a Catholic, became obsessed with the Roman Catholic religion

and with the Holy Trinity. He built Rushton Triangular Lodge in 1593. The lodge has three sides, three triangular gables on each side, and a three-sided chimney. Biblical quotations in Latin are sculpted in a frieze, consisting of 33 letters. Each side of the building is 33 feet long.
This lodge was used by the keeper of the rabbits on Sir Thomas's estate.

ART AND LITERATURE

'No shire within this Realme can answere the like Number of Noblemen as are seated in these parts; nor is any other so plentifully stored with gentry, in regard whereof it may seem worth to be termed the Herald's Garden.'
Norden,
writing about Northamptonshire in the 17th century

'Here he lives in state and bounty
Lord of Burleigh, fair and free
Not a lord in all the county
Is so great a lord as he.'
Alfred Lord Tennyson
The Lord of Burleigh

Daniel Defoe considered Northampton, *'The handsomest and best built town in all this part of England.'*

'I've left my own old home of homes
Green fields and every pleasant place

I miss the hazel's happy green
The bluebell's quite hanging blooms
Where envy's snear was never seen
Where staring malice never comes

I miss the heath, its yellow furze,
Molehills and rabbit tracks that lead
Through besom, ling, and teazel burrs
That spread a wilderness indeed;
The woodland oaks and all below
That their white powdered branches shield
The mossy paths: the very crow
Croaked music in my native fields.'
John Clare
The Flitting

LOCAL FOLKLORE
The Wild Geese
St Werburg, daughter of King Welfhere of Mercia, was Abbess of Weedon in the 7th century. One day, she saw a skein of wild geese hovering around the fields. She bade them begone, but they refused to leave, until St Werburg, by a miracle, restored to life one of their number who had been killed, and

eaten. The geese then flew off, and no wild geese have since been seen in Weedon.

There was once a well in Oundle, from which could clearly be heard a drumming noise, although only at certain times; the beating of the drum was said to portend some great event. It was heard before the deaths of Charles II, and James II. The well has now vanished, although it is commemorated in the name Drumming Well Lane.

Stowe-Nine-Churches
Church Stowe used to be known as Stowe-Nine-Churches. Tradition holds that the Lord of the Manor wished to build a church in Stowe, and set his craftsmen to work on the site he had chosen, on the top of a hill. They laid the foundations, but next morning, all the stones had disappeared – including their tools, and building materials. After a search, they discovered them, neatly laid on a different site. Nine times they started building the church, and nine times the foundations were mysteriously moved to the other site.
They abandoned the attempt to build on the hill, and the church was erected instead on the place to which the foundations had persistently been moved. A church stands there to this day.

DISTINCTIVE FLAVOUR
Northamptonshire County Cricket Club was founded in 1820. Their badge is the Tudor Rose.

There are many **Scots accents** around Corby as the celebrated steelworks there drew many employees from north of the border.

COUNTY DIARY

July:	International Organ Week, Oundle
	World Conker Championships, Kettering

NORTHUMBERLAND

COUNTY FACTS

Derivation of name: Northumberland comes from the Anglo Saxon meaning 'the place of those north of the Humber'.
First Recorded: 895 as Norohymbraland
County Town: Newcastle-upon-Tyne
Towns: Alnwick, Ashington, Blythe, Berwick-upon-Tweed, Cramlington, Gosforth, Haltwhistle, Hartley, Hexham, Longbenton, Morpeth, Newbiggin-by-the-Sea, Newburn, Newcastle-upon-Tyne, North Shields, Ponteland, Prudhoe, Tynemouth, Seaton Delaval, Wallsend, Westerhope, Whitley Bay, Wide Open.

Newcastle-upon-Tyne is a city of a county unto itself. Berwick-upon-Tweed was a bone of contention between England and Scotland, changing hands 13 times between 1300 and 1482, when the present county and national border was settled in favour of the English. In 1551, Berwick-upon-Tweed was declared a free town independent of both countries, and a county unto itself in the reign of William IV. In 1836 Berwick, on the basis of past charters, was decreed to be 'not in Northumberland' and was made 'a county to all intents and purposes but for parliamentary elections and assizes'. An Act of Parliament placed it in England as opposed to Scotland. Nonetheless its geographical position north of the River Tweed, the historic England/Scotland border, indicates it is more at home in the county that bears its name, Berwickshire.

Two large chunks of Co Durham are detached within Northumberland – it will come as a surprise to many to learn that the town of Bedlington (or Bedlingtonshire as it was up until Henry VIII's reign, with its own courts and justices of the peace), is anciently within Co Durham. There is also a large area of Durham within Northumberland along the banks of the Tweed, stretching from Cornhill-on-Tweed in the west right over to Holy Island in the east, the island containing Lindisfarne and sacred to the Christian church. This area (known as Islandshire) contains the Berwick suburbs south of the River Tweed, Tweedmouth and Spittal, and the villages of Cornhill-on-Tweed, Norham, Ancroft, Kyloe, and Elwick at its most southern tip.

Local Government

Northumberland County Council, six District Councils and two Metropolitan Boroughs.

TOPOGRAPHY INCLUDING RIVERS

Northumberland, the most northerly English county, is bordered by Berwickshire and Roxburghshire in the north, the North Sea in the east, County Durham in the south, and Cumberland in the west.

Behind the eastern coast, which is low lying and sandy, is a coastal plain. To the north is rich grazing land, and further west, bare, upland country leads to the Cheviot Hills. The Pennine moors and dales lie in the south-west of the county, and are richly wooded towards the Tyne valley. The River Tyne runs along part of the southern border of the county. The highest point is in the Cheviots, 2676 feet.
Rivers: Tyne, Coquet, Rede, Aln.

HISTORY

Before the Roman Conquest, the region was occupied by the Celtic tribes of Maiatai and Coroniatotai.

In AD 121 the Emperor Hadrian visited Britain and ordered the construction of the great wall, 80 miles in length, from Bowness to Wallsend, to mark the extent of Roman occupation.

In AD 407, the Romans left and a series of invasions and battles followed which characterize the county's history, until that part of the Kingdom of Northumbria known as Bernicia, stretching from the Tees to the Forth, was formed under King Ida.

In the 7th century, Oswald led the people against the invading Welsh at the Battle of Heavenfield, and after their victory, the people of Northumberland agreed to become Christian.

The 7th and 8th centuries saw the Golden Age of Northumbrian Christianity, with men whose names were famous throughout Europe – St Cuthbert, the Venerable Bede, and Wilfrid the Builder of Churches.

There followed raids by Scots and Vikings, who defiled the holy shrines. Northumbria ceased to be a kingdom, and became subjugated to Wessex.

Northumberland fell to the Scots, but Henry II claimed it back for England. Many castles were built to protect it from attack by the Scots: Wark, Harbottle, Newcastle, Alnwick, Bamburgh, Morpeth, and Warkworth. Peel towers were built for the refuge of the lesser gentry.

The Battle of Otterburn was fought in August 1388 between the English and the Scots. The victory was undecided. The battle is commemorated in the Ballad of Chevy Chase. In 1496, the shire was laid waste by James IV of Scotland, in support of the rebellion by Perkin Warbeck.

During the Civil War, the county was Royalist, and was attacked by the Scots.

On 9 September 1513, the fierce and historic battle of Flodden Field was fought between the armies of Scotland and England. Although it settled nothing, the Scots were defeated, and the losses were enormous – estimated at between 9,000 and 16,000 dead. James IV of Scotland was killed in the battle and his body was taken to Berwick where it was embalmed, encased in lead and then taken on to London. The scene of the battle is in the village of Branxton, and a granite cross is supposed to mark the spot on which King James fell.

In the Jacobite Rising of 1715, many Northumbrian squires joined the Scots against the Elector of Hanover, and proclaimed King James III at Warkworth.

Northumberland was the birthplace of the railways, the invention of local man George Stephenson.

INDUSTRY PAST AND PRESENT

Nowadays one finds agriculture, tourism, dock-related industry and heavy industry.

The salt industry flourished around the mouth of the river Blyth in the 13th century, and was the main trade of North Shields in the 15th century. Coal was worked in Roman times, and later, in the 14th and 15th centuries. Lead mines around Hexham were very prosperous in the 16th and 17th centuries. In the 20th century, the county has suffered greatly from the decline in ship-building, coal-mining, and heavy industry.

LANDMARKS

Hadrian's Wall

Holy Island, or Lindisfarne, on which St Aidan, Bishop of Iona, founded a priory, AD 635.

The Cheviot Hills

Cheviot Hill, which is 2,676 feet high

Kielder Forest

Kielder Water, one of the largest artificial lakes in Europe

The Farne Islands, a bird sanctuary

MONUMENTS

The five bridges over the Tyne at Newcastle combine to make a memorable townscape.

Alnwick Castle; this border castle was the home of the Percy family from 1309.

Bamburgh Castle; the keep was erected in the 12th century. It was the first English castle to fall to gunfire during the Wars of the Roses. It was restored in the 19th century.

Dunstanburgh Castle, the remains of a large castle begun in 1313 by the Earl of Lancaster.

Belsay Castle was built in the 14th century to guard the main route from Newcastle to Jedburgh.

Corbridge is the site of the Roman fort of Corstopitum, with a sunken strongroom and elaborate water supply system.

Hexham Abbey; behind the 19th-century façade is the 12th-century church, a masterpiece of Early English Gothic architecture.

Seaton Delaval Hall; this splendid baroque house, built between 1718 and 1728, is held to be Sir John Vanbrugh's masterpiece.

Warkworth Castle, built in the 12th century. This was one of the most important castles in the north of England for four centuries. It was here that the owner, Henry Percy, plotted the overthrow of Henry IV with his son Harry Hotspur.

FAMOUS PEOPLE AND LOCAL CHARACTERS

St Cuthbert is believed to be of Northumbrian birth. He was led to take his monastic vows by a vision on the death of Bishop Aidan, and in 651 he entered the monastery at Melrose, where he later became Prior. In 676 he became an anchorite on Farne Island, and is said to have performed miracles there. In 684 he was persuaded to become Bishop of Hexham, but retired three years later to Farne,

The Cloisters, Chillingham Castle.

where he had built a cell of stone and turf open to the sky. He died on the island on March 20th, 687.

Mark Akenside, the poet, was born in Newcastle Upon Tyne in 1721, the son of a butcher. The local community raised the money to send him to Edinburgh University to train for the ministry. He later changed his mind and took up medicine – and returned the money raised.

George Stephenson was born in 1781 in Wylam near Newcastle-Upon-Tyne. He was the son of a colliery foreman. He became an engine-wright at Killingworth colliery, and made his first locomotive in 1814, to haul coal from the pits. He designed the Rocket, which travelled at an amazing speed of 30 miles per hour, for which he won a prize of £500 from the Liverpool and Manchester Railway. Stephenson became the first President of the Institute of Mechanical Engineers.

Grace Darling was born in Bamburgh in 1815. She was the daughter of the lighthouse keeper. On 7 September 1838, the 'Forfarshire' was wrecked off the coast in a gale. Despite the danger, Grace insisted that she ride out in the storm; her father reluctantly came with her, and they rescued nine survivors from the wreck.

Swinburne, the poet and critic, spent his holidays at Capheaton Hall, which was owned by his grandfather.

Local Characters

Lord Armstrong of Cragside was an inventor. His was the first house in England to be completely fitted out with electric light, in 1880.

Sir Bertram, a 14th-century knight, accidentally killed his lover, Isabel Widdington. He lived the rest of his life in expiation as a hermit, and was known as the Hermit of Warkworth.

ART AND LITERATURE

'And they hae burnt the dales o' Tyne
And part of Bamburghshire,
And three good towers on Redeswire fells
They left them all on fire.'
The Battle of Otterburn,
Ancient Ballad

Alnwick:
'On a little hill on [the river's] *margin are seen….the fine remains of Hulne Abbey: more to the left are little swellings, the hollows of which are fringed with a chain of small, rough thickets…Over these* [the plains beyond] *the eye gradually rises to where the vast mountains of*

Cheviot erect their huge conic heads…'
Bishop Thommas Percy
(18th century)

'Hae ye ivver been at Elsdon? –
The world's unfinished neuk;
It stands amang the hungry hills
An' wears a frozen leuk.
The Elsdon folks like diein' stegs
At ivvery stranger stare,
An' hather broth an' curlew eggs
Ye'll get for supper there.'
George Chatt
At Elsdon

Swinburne considered Northumberland 'The crowning county of England – yes the best!'

'Thy tower proud Bamburgh, mark'd they there
King Ida's castle, huge and square
From its tall rock look grimly down
And on the swelling ocean frown…'
Sir Walter Scott
Marmion

LOCAL FOLKLORE

The Hedley Kow
The village of Hedley on the Hill used to be plagued by a mischievous sprite or goblin known as the Hedley Kow. He was continually playing tricks on the villagers, changing himself into a cow, or a bale of straw, or a donkey, upsetting the milk, and unravelling knitting. When a baby was to be born, and a man was in haste to fetch the midwife, the Hedley Kow would so torment the horse that the horse and rider would time and again fall to the ground. After each prank, the folk would hear the Kow laughing in glee as he vanished out of sight.

Long Lonkin
The Nafferton Tower in Horsley was known as 'Lonkin's Hall', and said to be the lair of Long Lonkin, who had murdered a woman and her child and thrown their bodies into a stream. Up until the last century, his ghost was supposed to haunt the place, and children were warned to be sure and be home before dark, or Lonkin would get them…

The Massingham Affair
In 1879, a burglary at the vicarage of Edlingham brought the village notoriety. Two men were wrongly convicted, and served ten years in prison before the real culprits were brought to justice. The case inspired the novel *The Massingham Affair*, by John Grierson.

The Legend of the Long Pack
A pedlar called at Lee Hall in Bellingham one night, asking for lodging. The owner of the hall was out, and the maid, Alice, refused the man lodging, but said he could leave his heavy pack in the kitchen over night. Later that night, she suddenly noticed that the pack was starting to move. She called out for help. A ploughboy fired a shot into the bag, and blood poured from the hole. Inside, they found the body of a young man. The servants realized that a raid on the hall was imminent, and that the dead man was one of a pack of thieves. They mustered help, and then blew the silver horn that they found on the body. Summoned by the horn, the robbers arrived, but were met with unexpected force, and fled. The man in the pack was buried in the churchyard.

DISTINCTIVE FLAVOUR

A traditional Northumberland dish is **Pan Haggerty**, a layered pie of potato, onion, and grated cheese, fried on both sides, or with the top browned 'before the fire' (or under the grill!).

Berwick Cockles is the name given to a local old-fashioned peppermint sweet.

Dog shows were first established at Newcastle-on-Tyne in 1859. The **Bedlington terrier** takes its name from the town, where it was originally bred for badger baiting.

Cheviots are a distinctive breed of sheep, with white faces.

Chilingham Park is known for the small herd of white cattle, which are descended from prehistoric wild oxen. They are believed to have been trapped in the park when it was walled in 1220. The small, creamy-white cattle have crescent-shaped, black-tipped horns and black muzzles.

A pagan New Year's Eve celebration is held in the town of **Allendale**. Twenty-four masked men march into the town behind a band, carrying barrels of blazing tar on their heads.

COUNTY DIARY

May 1:	Riding the Bounds, Berwick-upon-Tweed
May:	County Show, Corbridge
June:	Northumberland miners' picnic, Bedlington
December 31:	New Year's Eve Celebrations, Allendale

NOTTINGHAMSHIRE

COUNTY FACTS

Derivation of name: The place of Snot's people.
First Recorded: 1016 as Snotinghamscir
Motto: Sapienter Proficiens (Advancing Wisely)
County Town: Nottingham
Towns: Arnold, Balderton, Beeston, Blidworth, Carlton, Clifton, East Retford, Eastwood, Edwinstowe, Hucknall, Ilkeston, Keyworth, Kimberley, Kirkby in Ashfield, Langold, Mansfield, Mansfield Woodhouse, Newark, New Clipstone, Nottingham, Nuthall, Radcliffe-on-Trent, Ravenshead, Ruddington, Selston, Southwell, Stapleford, Sutton-in-Ashfield, Warsop, West Bridgford, Worksop.
Nottingham is a county of a city unto itself.

Local Government
Nottinghamshire County Council and eight District Councils.

HISTORY

Christianity was introduced into the valley of the Trent circa 630 by St Paulinus.

In the 9th century, Nottingham was part of the confederacy of five Boroughs known as the Dane Law.

In 1174, Henry II gave Nottingham Castle to his son John, and it became his favourite residence. After Runnymede, John prepared to make his last stand at Nottingham Castle. He died at Newark.

Sherwood Forest was made a royal hunting ground by King Richard.

East Stoke was the site of a bloody battle in 1487 between the forces of Henry VII and those of Lambert Simnel. The Pretender's forces were completely routed.

On 20 August 1642, King Charles I raised his standard at Nottingham in a formal declaration of war. The Civil War began.

INDUSTRY PAST AND PRESENT

Present industries include hosiery, coal mining, engineering, agriculture and rose growing.

The Nottinghamshire coalfield was worked from the 13th century: in 1259, Queen Eleanor was unable to stay in the county because of the smoke from the sea coal. Hops were grown extensively, and Worksop was famous for its liquorice.

In 1589, Reverend William Lee, of Calverton, invented the stocking frame, from which developed the great hosiery and lace trades, which were the staple industries of the county in the 18th and 19th centuries. In the 18th century there were also many cotton mills in the county, and silk mills in Nottingham.

LANDMARKS

Sherwood Forest
Clumber Park

MONUMENTS

Welbeck Abbey has a tunnel 1¼ miles long leading from it, big enough for a horse and carriage to pass through, to enable the reclusive 5th Duke of Portland to leave and enter his estate unseen.

Thoresby Hall; the present neo-Tudor mansion is the third to be erected in Thoresby Park.

Newstead Abbey was converted into a house in the 1540s. It was the ancestral home of Lord Byron, who was forced to sell it in 1818 to pay his debts.

Southwell Cathedral is celebrated for 'The Leaves of Southwell' – exquisite, life-like foliage carvings in its chapter house.

TOPOGRAPHY INCLUDING RIVERS

Nottinghamshire, in the north midlands, is bordered by Yorkshire in the north, Lincolnshire in the east, Leicestershire in the south, and Derbyshire in the west. From its eastern border with Lincolnshire, the county is mainly flat, although there are some rolling hills in the western part, which includes the coal mining belt. The broken wooded district of Sherwood Forest begins in the west and centre of the county. The highest point is Strawberry Bank, Huthwaite, 650 feet.
Rivers: Trent, Idle, Maun, Devon.

FAMOUS PEOPLE AND LOCAL CHARACTERS

Thomas Cranmer, the first protestant Archbishop, was born in Aslockton and lived there for 14 years.

Henry Ireton was born in 1611 in Attenborough. He married Cromwell's daughter Bridget, and became Cromwell's right-hand man. He signed the death-warrant of Charles I. He died of overwork and the plague, and was buried in Westminster Abbey. On the Restoration of the monarchy, his body was taken from his grave and hanged for a day from Tyburn Tree. He was then re-buried, under what is now Marble Arch.

William Brewster was born in Scrooby, and became one of the leaders of the Pilgrim Fathers.

Robert Dodsley was born in 1704 in Mansfield. He ran away to London and became a footman. He wrote poems, produced a play with the help of Alexander Pope, and opened a bookshop. He published 'London' by Samuel Johnson, and the two became great friends. It was Dodsley who suggested the idea of the English Dictionary to Johnson. He became one of the great 18th-century publishers.

Lord Byron inherited Newstead Abbey from a great uncle at the age of 10, and lived there intermittently for several years after leaving Cambridge. When he died, his body was brought from Greece to be buried at Hucknall Torkard, where his mother and daughter are also buried.

Samuel Butler, the novelist and satirist, was born in 1835 at Langar, the son of a rector.

Jesse Boot, the 1st Lord Trent, was born in 1850 in Nottingham, and opened his first shop in Beeston in 1877. He built up one of the largest pharmaceutical retail businesses in the world.

David Herbert Lawrence was born at Eastwood on September 11, 1885, the son of a coalminer. He was unable to follow in his father's footsteps as he was prone to consumption. He won a scholarship to Nottingham High School, and got a teaching certificate from the university. His frank and outspoken novels shocked the Establishment, particularly *Lady Chatterley's Lover*, which he printed privately in Florence in 1928, but which was not officially published in England and the USA for another 30 years.

Local Characters

Ann Harrison lived in Bingham for 99 years. She worked as a fish-seller, and, all her life, put every other half-crown she earned into the collection at Bingham Church.

ART AND LITERATURE
The smug and silver Trent'

Hills of Annesley, bleak and barren
Where my thoughtless childhood strayed,
How the northern tempests, warring,
Howl, above thy tufted shade.'
Byron

[The dwellings looked like]...*'black, poisonous herbage, in thick rows and crowded beds, stretching right away, broken now and then by taller plants, right to where the river glistened in a hieroglyph across the country. The steep scarp cliffs across the river looked puny. Great stretches of country darkened with trees and faintly brightened with cornland, spread towards the haze, where the hills rose blue beyond grey.'*
D H Lawrence
Sons and Lovers (1913)

'Little I thought, when I was a lad
and turned my modest penny
over on Boot's Cash Chemist's counter
That Jesse, by turning many
millions of similar honest pence
over, would make a pile
that would rise at last and blossom out
in grand and cakey style
into a university…'
D H Lawrence

LOCAL FOLKLORE
'Tis commonly reported that before an Heir of the Cliftons, of Clifton in Nottinghamshire, dies, that a sturgeon is taken in the River Trent by that place.'
– Aubrey,
in Miscellanies (1696)

The Legend of Robin Hood
Lythe and Listin, gentilmen
That he of frebore blode:
I shall you tel of a gode yeman
His name was Robyn Hode.

Robin Hood was captain of a band of outlaws who lived in Sherwood Forest, and would lie in wait for and rob rich travellers, to distribute their wealth to the poor.

He is said to have been born at Locksley (some tales claim that he was really the Earl of Huntingdon), and was forced to become an outlaw through having squandered his inheritance. Others say that he gave up the life of luxury of his own free will.

Robin Hood was a merry man, but courteous; always ready to engage in a fight, and challenge anyone whom he thought a suitable candidate for his band of outlaws. He was also a very fair man, and would mete out his own brand of justice in an unjust world.

His companions were Little John, his second-in-command, Much the Miller's son, Will Scadlock, or Scarlet, and Friar Tuck. He also had a lady-love named Maid Marion.

One of his main foes was the Sheriff of Nottingham, whom he managed to outwit and humiliate on numerous occasions.

Whether or not Robin Hood was an historical person, he remains one of the most famous folk-heroes in England.

Robin Hood and the Potter
One day, Robin Hood met a potter in the forest, who was reputed to be a champion fighter. They fought, and the potter won; after this they became friends. Robin borrowed the potter's clothes, and, thus disguised, journeyed to Nottingham, where he did a roaring trade in pots. He made a gift of some of his pots to the Sheriff's wife, and as a result was invited to dine. At an archery contest, he excelled himself, and admitted that he knew the infamous Robin Hood. The Sheriff asked him to lead him to the outlaw, and Robin agreed and took him into the forest. When he sounded his horn, the merry band appeared, and surrounded the Sheriff. They deprived him of his horse, and Robin declared that worse would have befallen him, had it not been for the hospitality shown to Robin by the Sheriff's wife. The Sheriff was forced to make his way back to the castle on foot, and the band of outlaws celebrated yet another successful trick on the Sheriff of Nottingham.

Tales of the Mad Men of Gotham
Tales abound of the quirky doings of the mad men of Gotham – the men who built a hedge round a cuckoo so that it would stay and sing for them all year; who tried to drown an eel in a pond; who burnt a forge down to get rid of a wasps' nest; and who dragged a cart to the top of a barn to shade the roof from the sun. But history suggests they weren't as mad as they made out. King John one day attempted to pass through fields belonging to the village on his way to Nottingham. The villagers, worried that his doing so might establish a permanent right of way, stopped him by force. When he subsequently sent his soldiers to

SHERWOOD FOREST

punish them, the villagers decided to pretend that they were mad, and therefore not responsible for their actions. Whatever the truth of the matter, the right of way was never established...

DISTINCTIVE FLAVOUR

Nottingham city is renowned for its pretty girls and for its beautiful lace.

An area in the north east of the county is known as the '**Dukeries**', because of the large number of rich estates that used to be there.

Mansfield Pudding is a brandy-flavoured suet sponge pudding, served sprinkled with caster sugar.

Hemlock Stone, in Bramcote, stands 30 feet high, and is around 70 feet in circumference; it is believed to weigh over 200 tons. It is popularly connected with Druidical rituals.

Nottinghamshire County Cricket Club, founded in 1841, play at Trent Bridge, in Nottingham. Their crest is the county badge of Nottinghamshire.

The village of **Laxton** preserves the old agricultural system of strip or open-field farming. The system is registered as an Ancient Monument.

COUNTY DIARY

May:	Nottinghamshire Show, Winthorpe, Newark
July:	National Rowing Championships, Holme Pierrepont
September:	Powerboat Grand Prix, Holme Pierrepont

OXFORDSHIRE

COUNTY FACTS

Derivation of name: Oxford comes either from the Old English 'Oxenford', meaning a place where there was a ford over the Isis for the passage of cattle, or 'Ousenford', meaning a ford over the River Ouse, a possible alternative name for the River Isis. Either way it means the place for oxen to cross - ford for oxen.

First Recorded: 1010 as Oxenfordscir

Motto: Sapere Aude (Dare to be Wise)

County Town: Oxford

Towns: Bampton, Banbury, Benson, Bicester, Bloxham, Burford, Carterton, Caversham, Chinnor, Chipping Norton, Cowley, Dorchester, Eynsham, Goring-on-Thames, Headington, Henley-on-Thames, Horspath, Kidlington, Littlemore, Marston, Oxford, Thame, Wheatley, Witney, Woodstock
The City of Oxford was in a unique position of having its own Sheriff.

Ackhamstead, Borycot and Lillingstone Lovell are three detached parts of Oxfordshire in Buckinghamshire, administered by Buckinghamshire County Council. Lenhill is a detached part of Oxfordshire under Gloucestershire County Council control.

Local Government
Oxfordshire County Council and four District Councils.

HISTORY

Before the Roman Conquest, the region was occupied by the tribes of the Dobuni and the Catuvellani. The ancient Icknield Way runs through the county and it was made into a Roman street.

After the Roman occupation, the region became part of the Kingdom of Wessex.

In the 7th century, the county was converted to Christianity by St Birin. In the 10th century, the county became known as Oxfordshire.

On St Brice's Day, 1002, there was a great massacre of the plundering Danes, at the order of Ethelred the Unready.

Great national councils were held at Oxford during the civil war in 1135, and 1139.

The Empress Matilda was besieged at Oxford, and she escaped across the Thames, which was conveniently frozen over. The war was ended by the council of Oxford in 1153.

It was at Woodstock that Thomas Becket was forced to assent to the Constitutions of Clarendon.

The 12th and 13th centuries saw the rise of the University at Oxford.

The Battle of Danesmoor was fought near Banbury, between an army led by Robert of Redesdale, and the royal forces led by the Earl of Pembroke. The insurgents won the day. An attempt to assassinate Henry VIII was made at Woodstock by William Morisco.

During the reign of Queen Mary, the Protestant martyrs Ridley, Latimer and Cranmer were burnt at the stake in the county. Oxford was the headquarters of the Royalists, and the residence of the King during the greater part of the Civil War, and the Battles of Chalgrove and Copredy Bridge took place in the county.

When plague broke out in London, Charles II took refuge in Oxford. Parliament was held there in 1681.

Most of Oxfordshire was staunchly Jacobite during the 1740s, and attachment to the cause lingered into the 19th century.

The Oxford Movement, which began in 1833, was a Catholic revival movement, which sought to expose what the leaders saw as the dangers of secular authority within the Church.

INDUSTRY PAST AND PRESENT

Nowadays, one can find agriculture (large arable farms), motor manufacturing, engineering, glove making, lingerie making and printing in Oxfordshire. In Oxford itself, publishing is a major activity. Witney Blankets come from the town of the same name.

Up until the 14th century, Oxfordshire was the second most prosperous county in the kingdom, due to its abundance of well-watered pastures, which bred sheep whose wool was famous throughout the country. Other smaller industries later grew up, such as plush-making in Banbury, leather in Bampton and Burford, gloves in Woodstock, and malt in Henley. Banbury was famous for its cheese. In the 15th century, 14 Banbury cheeses were among the provisions sent to France for the Duke of Bedford.

LANDMARKS
The Cotswolds
Wychwood Forest
Otmoor
Rollright Stones

MONUMENTS
Blenheim Palace, a baroque mansion built

TOPOGRAPHY INCLUDING RIVERS

Oxfordshire, in the central southern part of England, is bordered by Warwickshire and Northamptonshire in the north, Buckinghamshire in the east, Berkshire in the south, and Gloucestershire in the west.

The county is mainly flat, or quietly rolling, rising in the west to the Cotswold Hills. The central part of the county is rich meadowland, leading towards the hills and vales of the Chilterns in the south. The highest point is Portobello in the Chiltern Hills, 836 feet.

Rivers: Thames, Evenlode, Cherwell, Windrush.

between 1705 and 1722 as a gift to the 1st Duke of Marlborough from Queen Anne. It was the birthplace of Winston Churchill.

Oxford University, the oldest English university. University College was founded in 1249.

Dorchester Abbey, founded circa 1140. The interior is a mixture of Norman and Gothic architecture.

Stonor Park: this Tudor mansion house, set in a magnificent park, was the home of the Roman Catholic Stonor family for at least 800 years.

Broughton Castle, a moated manor house, dating back to the early 14th century.

Chaseton House; the Jacobean manor house, built in 1603, was once the home of Robert Catesby, a conspirator in the Gunpowder Plot.

Greys Court, a manor house dating mainly from the 16th century.

Minster Lovell, the ruins of a 15th-century manor house, which was the home of the Lovell family for generations.

Rousham House; the castellated house built in 1635 was much embellished by William Kent circa 1730. Shooting holes used by the Royalist owners in the Civil War can still be seen in the doors.

FAMOUS PEOPLE AND LOCAL CHARACTERS

John Wyclif, the founder of Lollardism, was Master of Balliol College, Oxford, in the 14th century.

Geoffrey Chaucer was a frequent visitor at Woodstock, where lived his son, Thomas, who was Speaker of the House of Commons.

John Skelton is said to have been created poet laureate at Oxford.

John Wilmot, 2nd Earl of Rochester, was born at Ditchley on April 10th, 1647. He went to school in Burford.

Alexander Pope stayed at Stanton Harcourt, where he completed the 5th volume of his translation of the *Iliad*.

R D Blackmore was born at Longworth on June 7th, 1825.

Charles Dodgson, alias **Lewis Carroll**, was lecturer in Mathematics at Christ Church College, Oxford. His book, *Alice in Wonderland*, originated during a river trip at Oxford, from a story told to Alice Liddell, daughter of the Dean of the college.

William Morris lived at Kelmscott for 25 years, and did much of his writing there.

Robert Bridges, the poet, lived at Chilswell from 1907 until his death in 1930.

Sir Winston Churchill was born at Blenheim Palace in 1874. He visited it frequently. He is quoted as saying, 'At Blenheim I took two very important decisions: to be born and to marry.'

Flora Thompson was born at Juniper Hill near Brackley in 1876.

William Morris, Viscount Nuffield, the motor manufacturer, was born in the county in 1877. The chairman of Morris Motors until 1952, he established the Nuffield Foundation, endowing it with £10 million.

Eric Arthur Blair, alias George Orwell, lived in Henley-on-Thames and Shiplake as a boy.

ART AND LITERATURE

'To the University of Oxford I acknowledge no obligation, and she will as cheerfully renounce me for a son as I am willing to disclaim her for a mother. I spent fourteen months at Magdalen College; they proved the fourteen months the most idle and unprofitable of my whole life.'

Edward Gibbon, author of
The Decline and Fall of the Roman Empire

Henry James described Oxfordshire as *'the sweetest, flattest, reediest streamside landscape that the heart need demand.'*

'I never saw so great a thing with so much littleness in it.'

Alexander Pope,
on Blenheim Palace

'For some minutes Alice stood without speaking looking out in all directions over the country – and a most curious country it was. There were a number of little brooks running from side to side, and the ground was divided up into squares by a number of hedges, that reached from brook to brook.

"I declare it's marked out just like a large chess-board!" Alice said at last. "There ought to be some men moving about somewhere…"'

Lewis Carroll
Alice Through the Looking Glass
(describing the view from Beckley over the northern part of Otmoor)

'Perhaps in no county of England is the love of beer among the labouring poor so general or so extravagant as in Oxfordshire.'

Clare Sewell Read

'Towery city and branchy between towers;
Cuckoo-echoing, bell-swarmed, lark charmed,
rook racked, river-rounded,
The dapple-eared lily below thee; that country and town did
Once encounter in, here coped and posed powers.'

Gerard Manley Hopkins
Duns Scotus's Oxford

'Shines, billowing cold and gold from Cumnor Hurst,
A winter sunset on wet cobbles, where
By Canterbury Gate the fishtails flare.
Someone in Corpus reading for a first
Pulls down red blinds and flounders on, immers'd
In Hegel, heedless of the yellow glare
On porch and pinnacle and window square,
The brown stone crumbling where the skin has burst.

A late, last luncheon staggers out of Peck
And hires a hansom: from half-flooded grass
Returning athletes bark at what they see.
But we will mount the horse-tram's upper deck
And wave salute to Buols', as we pass
Bound for the Banbury Road in time for tea.'

John Betjeman
On an Old-Fashioned Water-Colour of Oxford
(1945)

LOCAL FOLKLORE

The Legend of the Rollright Stones
The Rollright stones stand on a hill overlooking Long Compton. There are about 60 of them - the 'King stone', a single large stone; the 'Whispering Knights', a group of five stones; and the remaining stones in a large circle. They date from the neolithic period.

The legend attached to them is as follows: A king was marching at the head of his army, intending to conquer England. Five of his knights stood apart, whispering together, plotting the king's downfall. As he neared the ridge of the hill, a witch suddenly appeared in front of him, and declared:
"Seven long strides shalt thou take,
And if Long Compton thou canst see,
King of England thou shalt be."
The King replied,
"Stick, stock, stone,
As King of England I shall be known!"
Then he took the seven long strides, but suddenly a mound of earth rose up in front of him, and the witch cackled,
"As Long Compton thou canst not see,
King of England thou shalt not be;
Rise up, stick, and stand still, stone,
For King of England thou shalt be none;
Thou and thy men hoar stones shall be,
And I myself an elder-tree."
And the King, all his soldiers, and the five treacherous knights, were instantly turned to stone. The witch turned into an elder tree. It was believed that if a knife was stuck into any of the elder trees which grew round about, it would draw human blood.

A farmer once tried to take one of the

BROUGHTON CASTLE

Whispering Knights and use it to build part of his barn. He found the stone impossibly heavy, and the three oxen who dragged the cart it was in fell down dead with the exertion. However, the farmer persevered and built the stone into his barn. No sooner was it in place, however, than ill-fortune befell the farmer, until he realized that the stone was the cause of his troubles. In desperation he levered it out of the wall and placed it in his cart, with no trouble at all. His old, tired horse, trotted up the hill with it and, once it was replaced in its rightful position, the farmer once more prospered. No-one has ever dared to remove the Rollright Stones since.

Minster Lovell

The Lovell family lived at Minster Lovell from the 12th century.

In the 15th century, Francis Lovell the last Lord, supported King Richard at the Battle of Bosworth Field, and had to flee to France after the defeat of the King's army. In 1487 he returned in support of Lambert Simnel's claim to the throne. Again Francis was on the losing side, and he fled from the field of battle. It is said that he made his way home to Minster Lovell, where he hid in a secret room in the house. A faithful servant had the key, and promised to keep him supplied with food until his master was able to escape. However, something went wrong with the plan, Francis Lovell was never seen again. Years later, in 1708, some workmen at the house discovered an underground vault. They broke into it, and for a few seconds were confronted by the skeleton of a man, sitting at a table, with pen and papers in front of him, and a decaying cap lying on the floor. Then, the fresh air turned the dreadful sight to dust as the workmen watched.

It is assumed that the skeleton was that of Francis Lovell, but whether his servant deliberately left him to starve to death, or whether some misfortune befell the servant which prevented him fulfilling his promise, no-one can say.

It is claimed that the ghost of Francis Lovell still haunts the ruins of the hall.

The Oxford Student

There was once an Oxford student, who made love to the daughter of a brewer in the town, and got her with child. She pressed him to marry her, and he always put her off, but at last he said that if she would meet him at Divinity Walk the next moonlight night, he would arrange it. So early on the night of the next full moon, she set out for the open orchard land that bordered Divinity Walk in those days. She was very early, so for safety she climbed one of the apple trees and hid there. Presently she heard a heavy step, and saw her lover plodding up the hill with a spade across his shoulders. He came up to the very tree where she was hiding, and began to dig – a long, narrow, deep hole: a grave. Then he stood and waited with his dagger in his hand. But the girl, lying along the branch above him, never stirred, and at length he went away, and she ran, as fast as her feet could carry her, back to her father's house. Next day, as she was going down Brewer's Lane, the student saw her, and greeted her lovingly.

But the girl said:

'One moonshiny night, as I sat high,
Waiting for one to come by,
The boughs did bend; my heart did break,
To see what hole the fox did make.'

As she spoke, the student whipped out his dagger, and stabbed her to the heart. Then there was the greatest fight between Town and Gown that ever was known, and Brewer's Lane ran with blood. The cruel student was killed, but nothing would bring the poor girl back to life, and they say she was buried in the very grave that was dug for her by her false lover.

DISTINCTIVE FLAVOUR

Banbury Cakes are small sponge cakes flavoured with currants, spice, and honey, and wrapped in a puff pastry case.

Oxford Bags were trousers with very wide, baggy legs, popular in the 1920s.

'Oxford English' is supposed to be a form of pronunciation typical of the University, which is somewhat affected or pretentious.

Oxford Down sheep have short wool, and a brown face and legs.

There are several dishes named after Oxford colleges, but the most celebrated is **New College Pudding**, a rich fruit concoction with an appropriate amount of alcohol in it.

THE ENTRANCE GATE, MAGDALEN COLLEGE

COUNTY DIARY

February:	Torpids (College Rowing Races), Oxford
May:	Eights Week (College Rowing Races), Oxford
July:	Royal Regatta, Henley

RUTLAND

COUNTY FACTS

Derivation of name: It means Rota's land, a personal possession of Queen Edith, wife of Edward the Confessor. It was an endowment/dowry for Norman Queens until it became a county. Who was Rota? Unknown except he lived before Queen Edith and was sufficiently important enough to own or rule his own kingdom. Although small as a county, for one man it was a very big territory.

First Recorded: 863 as Roteland

Motto: Multum In Parvo (Much In Little)

County Town: Oakham

Towns: Barrowden, Cottesmore, Edith Weston, Empingham, Ketton, Langham, Oakham, Ryhall, Uppingham, Whissendine.

Local Government
Leicestershire County Council and one District Council.

HISTORY

Before the Roman conquest, the region was inhabited by the British Coritani tribe, The Roman Ermin Street passes through the region.

In the 8th century it became part of the Kingdom of Mercia.

Rutland is marvellous hunting country, and it was designated a forest, subject to forest laws, and preserved for the chasing of deer and wild boar.

The Saxon King Ethelred gave Rutland to Emma, his Queen, who later married King Canute. It became the custom for monarchs to bestow Rutland on their Queens and court favourites. One of these was the notorious courtier, Piers Gaveston, favourite of Edward II.

The title of Lord of the Manor of Oakham was granted to his blacksmith by William the Conqueror. It was decreed that all royalty and peers of the realm passing through Oakham should present a horseshoe to the Lord of the Manor, and the custom survived for centuries. The oldest surviving horseshoe dates from 1470. (The blacksmith took his surname from his occupation – de Ferrers. Oakham Castle was built by his descendant, Walkelin de Ferrers, in 1191.)

During the Wars of the Roses, the Battle of Losecoat Field was fought in the county in 1470: the Lancastrians threw off their coats as they fled, pursued by the Yorkists.

In the 15th century, Oakham became a noted place for trade. Its merchants were of the Staple of Calais.

Rutland was staunchly puritan, and supported the Parliamentary cause during the Civil War.

INDUSTRY PAST AND PRESENT

Present industry includes agriculture, cement making and iron-ore quarrying.

Rutland has always been a mainly agricultural county. Wool was exported in the 14th century. Stilton cheese has been made for many years in Leyfield Forest and the Vale of Catmoss.

LANDMARKS

Rutland Water is a huge man-made lake, with a surface area of 3,100 acres.

MONUMENTS

Oakham Castle; all that survives of the medieval fortified manor house is the Great Hall, one of the finest examples of Norman domestic architecture in England.

Burley-on-the-Hill, a Palladian house built between 1694 and 1708 for Daniel Finch, the 2nd Earl of Nottingham.

Wing Maze, believed to date from medieval times, is 40 feet in diameter.

FAMOUS PEOPLE AND LOCAL CHARACTERS

Archdeacon Robert Johnson founded both Oakham and Uppingham schools in 1584.

Sir Everard Digby of Stoke Dry, financed **Guy Fawkes** and the Gunpowder Plot. He was hanged for his part in the conspiracy.

Sir Isaac Newton lived in Market Overton with his grandmother as a child.

Titus Oates was born in Oakham in 1649. He was the originator of the so-called 'Popish Plot' of the late 16th century. By his lies, he doomed many innocent people to death. The

TOPOGRAPHY INCLUDING RIVERS

Rutland, the smallest county in England, situated in the east midlands, is bordered by Lincolnshire in the north and east, Northamptonshire in the south and Leicestershire in the west.

The county is characterized by ridges of low, undulating hills and valleys running roughly east-west, the highest point being near Manton, towards the centre of the county. The River Welland runs along most of the south-eastern boundary. The highest point is Ranksborough Hill, 625 feet.

Rivers: Welland, Eye, Wash, Chater.

panic he caused earned him the dubious title of 'Biggest liar in Christendom'.

John Clare, the poet, lived for a while in Pickworth.

Local Characters

Jeffrey Hudson was a dwarf, born in Oakham in 1619. At the age of 9, he was 18 inches tall, and he was served up in a pie to Queen Henrietta, wife of Charles I, during a visit to Burley-on-the-Hill. She was so delighted with him that she took him back to court with her as a page. He later fought bravely in the Civil War.

Amelia Woodcock lived in Wing during the 19th century, and was known as the Wise Woman of Wing. By her vast knowledge of herbs, and her skill, she was able to cure many kinds of ailments, and her fame spread to such an extent that the number of people flocking to be cured by her could not be accommodated within the village. The Wise Woman died in 1867.

ART AND LITERATURE

'There are some beautiful spots on its banks towards the little village of Tickencote southward, where the bank on the field side rises very stunt in some places from the edge of the river, and may, by a fancy used to a flat country, be easily imagined into mountains. The whole prospect is diversified into gently-swelling slopes and easy-swimming valleys.'

    John Clare (1817)

'Back, back through long vistas of years I am wafted,
But the glow at my heart's undiminished in force;
Deep, deep in that heart has fond memory engrafted
Those quick thirty minutes from Ranksborough Gorse.

He's away! I can hear that identical holloa!
I can feel my young thoroughbred strain down the ride,

I can hear the dull thunder of hundreds that follow,
I can see my old comrades in life by my side.'

    W Davenport Bromley
    The Dream of an Old Meltonian

(Ranksborough Gorse is a famous fox covert not far from Langham)

LOCAL FOLKLORE
Wing Turf Maze
Legend has it that the turf maze at Wing was used by penitents, possibly blindfolded, who would crawl round it on their knees, reciting prayers, to gain spiritual benefit and increase their powers of meditation.

DISTINCTIVE FLAVOUR
Rutland is proud of being the **smallest county in England**.

Ruddles beer originates from the county, and the motto attached to it refers to the size of the county: 'Much out of little.'

Rutland is the home of the oldest and most famous hunt in the kingdom – the Cottesmore. **The Cottesmore hounds** were established in 1732. In the season the Cottesmore meets four times a week, on Mondays, Tuesdays, Thursdays and Saturdays.

The village of **Ketton** is famous for its stone, a honey-coloured limestone used in the building of most of the houses.

MARKET PLACE, OAKHAM.

SHROPSHIRE

COUNTY FACTS

Derivation of name: Comes from 'the scrub' and the county could easily have followed in the footsteps of Dorset and Somerset and be known as Shropset, but due to the power and influence of Shrewsbury the county name took its form from the town which is pronounced 'Shro'sbury' leading the district to be called Shrewsburyshire which was inevitably shortened to Shropshire. Norman clerks found the Shrewsburyshire intolerable to write or pronounce and abbreviated it all to Salop, which became the name of the County Council for a while until local opposition brought the administrative county back under the name of Shropshire. Latin: Civitas Scrobbensis 'the city around the scrub folk'.

Motto: Floreat Salopia (Let Salop Flourish)

County Town: Shrewsbury

Towns: Albrighton, Bishop's Castle, Bridgnorth, Broseley, Cleobury Mortimer, Church Stretton, Coalbrookdale, Craven Arms, Dawley, Donnington, Edgmond, Ellesmere, Hadley, Ironbridge, Littleshall, Ludlow, Madeley, Market Drayton, Much Wenlock, Newport, Oakengates, Oswestry, Pontesbury, Shawbury, Shifnal, Shrewsbury, Telford, Wellington, Wem, Whitchurch.

The towns of Halesowen and Oldbury are Shropshire detached surrounded by Staffordshire, Warwickshire and Worcestershire. Halesowen itself is actually partly in Worcestershire and partly in Shropshire detached.

Local Government

Shropshire County Council and six District Councils. Shropshire detached, Halesowen and Oldbury, are administered by two Metropolitan Boroughs.

HISTORY

Before the Roman conquest, the region was occupied by three principal tribes – the Cornavii, the Ordovices, and the Silures. In the 1st century, Caractacus, the leader of the Silures, was finally defeated by the Romans under Scapula.

In the 8th century, King Offa of Mercia built the dyke which served as the western boundary of his territory, which passes through the county.

Many castles were built in the county by nobles who for the most part supported the cause of Matilda in her war with Stephen.

At the Shrewsbury Parliament in the 13th century, representatives of the commons took part in the deliberations by legal authority for the first time.

The many raids into the county by the Welsh were finally crushed in the reign of Edward I, who built a large number of border castles along the Welsh Marches, to keep the peace. In 1403 there was a battle near Shrewsbury between Henry IV and Harry Hotspur, son of the Earl of Northumberland, which ended in victory for the King.

In the 15th century, the court of the Marches was set up to curb the power of the Lord Marchers, and to secure justice for the Welsh.

Shropshire was mainly Royalist during the Civil War.

After his defeat at Worcester, Charles II fled through the county, and hid overnight at Boscobel. He also took refuge in an oak tree in the grounds whilst Cromwell's men searched the house; the soldiers passed right underneath the tree, and never spotted him. The 'Royal Oak' gave its name to many pubs, and became a tourist attraction – to its fatal detriment, as it was ultimately hacked to pieces by souvenir hunters. The present 'Royal Oak' is said to be grown from one of its acorns. In the 18th century, Shrewsbury and Ludlow had their own 'season', when county families were in residence.

INDUSTRY PAST AND PRESENT

Agriculture, dairy and beef farming, farming equipment manufacture, heavy ironwork, engineering, china making, bricks and tiles and electrical goods are important components of the economy.

Lead was worked by the Romans in the Stiperstones and Shelve, and coal was dug in the Clee Hills in the 13th century. The wool

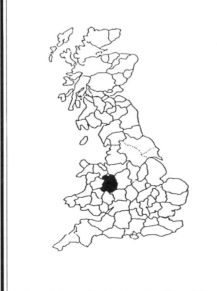

TOPOGRAPHY INCLUDING RIVERS

Shropshire, in the west midlands, is bordered by Cheshire in the north, Staffordshire in the east, Herefordshire and Worcestershire in the south, and Wales in the west.

Mountainous and rugged in the south west, the highest point here being the Stiperstones, the county is more level in the east, although still hilly, with the River Severn winding through lush valleys. North of the Severn are the meres for which the county is famous. The Salop plain stretches from Whitchurch in the north to Church Stretton in the south west, and the Wrekin rises from this plain to around 1,200 feet. In the south are the Clee Hills, with Brown Clee, the highest point in the county, rising to 1,772 feet.

Rivers: Severn, Perry, Roden, Tern, Clun, Onny, Corve, Rea.

trade flourished in the 13th and 14th centuries, and in the 16th century, Oswestry was famous for its Welsh cottons. The county rose to great importance during the industrial revolution; Coalbrookdale was the site of the ironworks where iron was first successfully smelted with coke.

LANDMARKS

The Wrekin, a hill topped by a large fort
The Stiperstones, and the Devil's Chair
The meres – Shropshire's Lake District
Clee Hills
Brown Clee, the highest point, at 1,772 feet
Wenlock Edge
Severn Gorge – the birthplace of the industrial revolution
Offa's Dyke

MONUMENTS

The Iron Bridge at Ironbridge, the first iron bridge constructed in England, between 1777 and 1779.
Lord Hill's Column, the highest Doric column in the country.
Attingham Hall, a classical-style mansion built in 1785 for the 1st Lord Berwick.
Bridgnorth Castle, a Norman castle, of which the keep, which leans at 17° from the perpendicular, was built in a great hurry!
Buildwas Abbey; extensive ruins still exist of this abbey, founded in the 12th century.
Haughmond Abbey; ruins of an abbey founded at the beginning of the 12th century by the Augustinians.
Bentnall Hall is a late Elizabethan stone house near the Severn Gorge.
Shrewsbury Castle; the red sandstone castle begun in circa 1080 was rebuilt in the 13th century. It now houses the Shropshire regimental museum.
Shrewsbury Abbey was at one point a candidate for the seat of a bishop, until Henry VIII decided that this would be too costly. Only the west tower and nave survive today.
Lilleshall Abbey, the ruins of a house founded circa 1148 for Arroasian canons.
Ludlow Castle, built by Roger de Lacy, a Norman knight, circa 1090, was the principal defensive castle on the Welsh Marches.
Boscobel House, originally a timber-framed farmhouse, it was converted to a hunting

THE KEEP, LUDLOW CASTLE

lodge in the 17th century. Charles II hid from the Parliamentary soldiers in an oak tree in the grounds.
Stokesay Castle, a fortified manor house dating from the 12th century, surrounded by a moat.
Wroxeter Roman City; these are the remains of Viroconium, the fourth largest city of Roman Britain.

FAMOUS PEOPLE AND LOCAL CHARACTERS

William Langland, author of the 14th-century *Piers Plowman,* is claimed to have been born at Cleobury Mortimer. A window in the church of St Mary is dedicated to him.
Sir Philip Sidney lived at Ludlow Castle as a boy, and attended school in Shrewsbury.
Samuel Butler, the satirist, lived for a while in Ludlow Castle from 1660, as secretary to the Lord President of Wales. Part of his *Hudibras* was written there.
Robert Clive (Clive of India) was Mayor of Shrewsbury in 1762, and MP for Shrewsbury from 1761 to 1774.
William Hazlitt, the essayist and critic, lived for most of his life in Wem.
Charles Darwin was born in Shrewsbury in 1809, and lived there until the age of 16.

A E Housman, poet, and author of *A Shropshire Lad* is buried in the Church of St Lawrence, in Ludlow.
Mary Webb was born at Leighton-Under-the-Wrekin on 25 March 1881. 'Sarn Mere' in her *Precious Bane* is Bosmere Pool.
Wilfred Owen was born in Oswestry in 1893, and attended Shrewsbury Technical College.

ART AND LITERATURE

'Cluntun and Clunbury
Clungunford and Clun
Are the quietest places
Under the sun.'
          A E Housman

'On Wenlock Edge the wood's in trouble
His forest fleece the Wrekin heaves
The gale, it plies the saplings double
And thick on Severn snow the leaves.'
          A E Housman
          Bredon Hill

'Into my heart an air that kills
From yon far country blows
What are those blue remembered hills,
What spires, what farms are those?'
          A E Housman

'The grove I mentioned is the finest I ever saw,

there are six walks through it and just in the middle you look twelve ways which discovers as many several prospects either to the house or entrance or fountaines or gardens and fields; the Grove itself is peculiar, being composed of all sorts of greens that hold their verdure and beauty all the yeare…'

Celia Fiennes, on Patshull Park, in
My Great Journey to Newcastle and Cornwall (1698)

LOCAL FOLKLORE

Wild Edric

Edric, a bold and dashing man, was Lord of the Manor of Ledbury North. Once, returning home late at night, he came across a gathering of noble fairy ladies. Seized with passion for the fairest of the ladies, he carried her off to his home. She spoke not a word to him for three days and nights, after which she acknowledged him as her husband. She told him he would have good fortune from then on, unless he reproached her 'either with the sisters from whom you snatched me, or the place or wood or anything thereabout, from which I came'. From then on, she warned, he would have no joy, and when she was gone, he would fail... He swore to be faithful to her and they lived happily for many years.

However, one night, Edric returned late from hunting, and she was nowhere to be seen. He summoned her to him, and she took a long time to appear. Angrily he said, "Was it your sisters that kept you so long?" – and immediately his wife vanished.

Edric searched far and wide for her, but she never returned; shortly afterwards he died of grief.

The Origin of the Wrekin

There was once a wicked giant living in Wales, who had a grudge against the Mayor of Shrewsbury and all the townsfolk. He determined to dam up the River Severn and cause it to flood and swamp the town.

So one day he set off from his lair, carrying a huge spadeful of earth with which to dam the river, and headed for Shrewsbury. After much trudging, he arrived near the town of Wellington, completely worn out. There he met a cobbler, carrying a sack full of old boots and shoes. The giant, quite out of breath, asked the cobbler how far it was to Shrewsbury. The cobbler asked him why he wanted to know, and the giant explained his wicked intention of damming up the river and drowning the people of Shrewsbury. The cobbler was most distressed at the thought of losing so much custom at one fell swoop, so he replied, 'Shrewsbury! You'll never get there! It's too far! I've just come from there, and in the time it's taken me to walk to here, I've worn out all these boots and shoes! That's how long it'll take you to get there.' The giant was dismayed at the thought of having to walk so far, so he decided to give up his plans and just turn back for home. Rather than carry the load of earth any further, he dropped it on the ground where he was standing, scraped his boots on his spade, and tramped off home to Wales. The pile of earth that he dumped there became known as the Wrekin, and the earth that he scraped off his boots next to it is the little Ercall.

Crawls

Many hundred years ago there was a young lady, her father's only daughter and heiress, whom a gallant knight wooed and sought for his bride. And she loved him well, and gave him her promise. But when her father came to hear of it, he would by no means give his consent, for the knight was a younger son and landless. The young lady, though, was firm, and held to her word. One day she came and told her father that she and her true love would be married the next morning at Bromfield Church. The father was angry, as he might well be. He upbraided her for a headstrong lass, who must e'en take her own way, but of all his broad lands he vowed she would have none but what she could crawl round by morning light. She said not a word, but went quietly away. An old servant brought her a pair of leathern breeches to guard her poor knees ('else they would ha' wore out'), and thus strangely equipped she crawled round the fields all through that dark cold winter's night, and came in covered with mud to her father at his breakfast, saying that she had taken him at his word, and crawled round so much fair meadow land as reached nearly to Downton. The old man was so much delighted at his girl's brave spirit that he forgave her obstinacy, and took her back into favour. He made her heiress of all his estates, which continued to belong to her descendants for many generations, and the land she crept round during that long dreary night still bears the name of 'Crawls'.

The Devil at the Card Party

A party of clergy were assembled one Sunday night at Plaish playing cards. All the doors were locked, when suddenly they burst open without any apparent cause. The men locked them again, but presently they burst open a second time, and again a third. Then the devil appeared in the midst of the company, and they all rose up and fled, excepting the host, whom the others basely left face to face with the Enemy. None ever saw that wretched man again, either alive or dead.

Only a great stain of blood, shaped like a human form, was found on the floor of the room and, despite all efforts, the mark could never be washed out. Ever since then a ghostly troop of horse rides through the house at midnight, with such a noise that none can sleep.

DISTINCTIVE FLAVOUR

Shropshire Pie is made from rabbit, with artichoke hearts and 'dumplings' made of rabbit livers, bacon and oysters.

Telford is a new city begun in 1963. It is named after Thomas Telford, the stone mason whose bridges, viaducts and canals can be seen all over the county. Telford is attracting modern industries from other parts of Britain and from abroad.

The meres of Shropshire are a haven for birdlife.

In the tiny village of **Aston-on-Clun**, a huge oak tree is decorated each year with flags from all nations; the custom dates from 29 May 1786, when the tree was decorated to celebrate the marriage of local landowner John Marston with Mary Carter.

COUNTY DIARY

April:	National Hill Climb Meeting of the Severn Valley Motor Club, Alberbury
May:	Shropshire and West Midlands Agricultural Show, Shrewsbury
July:	International Music Festival, Shrewsbury
July:	Powys Eisteddfod, Oswestry

S OMERSE T

COUNTY FACTS

Derivation of name: Somerset comes from the Old English, meaning 'dwellers round Somerton', a farmstead tended during the summer but not occupied in winter.

First Recorded: 1015 as Sumaersaeton

Motto: Defendamur (We Defend)

County Town: Taunton

Towns: Bath, Bedminster, Bishopsworth, Bridgwater, Brislington, Burnham-on-Sea, Chard, Clevedon, Crewkerne, Frome, Glastonbury, Highbridge, Ilminster, Keynsham, Knowle, Long Ashton, Midsomer Norton, Minehead, Nailsea, Paulton, Porlock, Portishead, Radstock, Shepton Mallet, Somerton, Street, Taunton, Watchet, Wellington, Wells, Weston-Super-Mare, Wincanton, Yeovil.

All of Bristol south of the River Avon is geographically in Somerset although Bristol was declared by Edward III in 1373 'a city and county unto itself forever'.

Local Government

Somerset County Council, Avon County Council. The parish of Holwell is under Dorset County Council; Kilmington is administered by Wiltshire County Council. There are nine District Councils.

HISTORY

Bath was known as Aqua Sulis in Roman times.

In AD 577 Ceawin captured Bath, and the region between the Axe and Avon was incorporated into the Kingdom of Wessex.

Alfred the Great raised a fort on the Isle of Athelney, to hold his Danish adversaries at bay in 878. He was victorious over the Danes, and his act of thanksgiving for this victory was the founding of Althelney Abbey.

Kilmington, the most easterly parish in Somerset under Wiltshire County Council administration, was the scene for a battle between the Danes and Alfred the Great.

Somerset played a considerable part in the Civil War, and was staunchly Royalist. Taunton was a Parliamentary stronghold, isolated in this Royalist territory. The Royalists won a notable victory at the Battle of Lansdown, near Bath. Robert Blake then led a Parliamentary force in the county with great success.

The Duke of Monmouth, Charles II's illegitimate son, led a rebellion to overthrow James II. In 1685, his army fought the Battle of Sedgemoor, which disastrous engagement was over in $1^{1}/_{2}$ hours, leaving 300 rebels dead. The 'Bloody Assize' held by Judge Jeffreys followed the rebellion in the autumn of the same year.

INDUSTRY PAST AND PRESENT

The Somerset economy features dairying, tourism in the coastal resorts, footwear (Clark's shoe factory is based in Street), apple growing for cider, fishing and the production of Cheddar cheese.

Somerset has always been an agricultural county. Grain was grown and exported from the 11th to the 18th century, and cider-making has flourished for centuries. Coal mining and stone quarrying have been carried on from early times, and lead and slate were worked from the early 19th century. The wool trade flourished from the 14th to the 19th centuries. Glove-making developed in the 18th century in Stoke and Yeovil and in many of the surrounding districts.

LANDMARKS

Mendip Hills
Quantock Hills
Exmoor National Park
Blackdown Hills
Brendon Hills
Cheddar Gorge and Caves
Wookey Hole Caves
Porlock Hill – one of the steepest roads in Britain

TOPOGRAPHY INCLUDING RIVERS

Somerset, in the south-west of the country, is bordered by the Severn Estuary and Gloucestershire in the north, Wiltshire in the east, Dorset in the south, and Devon in the west.

The central plain of the county resembles the Fens, in being flat and prone to flooding, although it is broken mid-way by the ridge of the Polden Hills. The dykes which drain the plain are known as 'rhines'.

The plain is bounded by the Mendip Hills in the north-east, which are cut by numerous gorges, including the Cheddar Gorge, the largest and most well known. North of the Mendips, Dundry Beacon rises to 1,668 feet. The steep Quantock Hills form the western border of the plain, and further west lies the moorland mass of Exmoor, with the Brendon Hills projecting eastward. South of the Quantocks is the fertile Vale of Taunton Dean, and the bare ridges of the Blackdown Hills trace the southern border with Devon. The highest point is Dunkery Beacon, Exmoor, 1706 feet.

Rivers: Barle, Yeo, Avon, Exe, Tone, Parrett, Brue, Cary and Frome.

MONUMENTS

Wells Cathedral, dating from the 12th and 13th centuries, is England's most wholly Gothic Cathedral: it contains the most extensive example of medieval sculpture still surviving in the British Isles.

Dunster Castle; this crenellated castle set on a hill dates from 1070. It was the home of the Luttrell family for 600 years.

Cadbury Castle; this fort, standing on a hill, is believed to be the site of King Arthur's Camelot.

Taunton Castle, a 13th-century Bishop's fortress. The Great Hall was a law court for centuries, and was the scene of Judge Jeffreys's 'Bloody Assize' in 1685.

Glastonbury Abbey, the ruins of the abbey date from the 12th century. The body of King Arthur is said to lie here.

Farleigh Hungerford, the ruins of a castle built circa 1380 for Sir Thomas Hungerford.

Nunney Castle, the ruins of a rectangular moated castle begun in 1373. The four towers rise 50 feet out of the moat.

Montacute House, an Elizabethan house built between 1588 and 1601 for Sir Edward Philips, later Speaker of the House of Commons.

Cleeve Abbey, the remains of a Cistercian Abbey founded in 1198.

Clevedon Court was once a fortified manor house, built in the 12th century, and much altered since then. It has been the home of the Elton family since 1709.

Bath has three main attractions: its Roman Baths; its late Perpendicular Abbey church and the crescents and squares of its Georgian heyday.

FAMOUS PEOPLE AND LOCAL CHARACTERS

Roger Bacon, the founder of English philosophy, was born in the county in 1219. He became a Franciscan friar in 1257.

Sir Thomas Hungerford, the first speaker of the House of Commons, in the 14th century, was a Somerset man.

Robert Blake was born in Bridgwater in 1599. He was an MP, the defender of Taunton in the Civil War, and the Commonwealth's 'General at Sea' against the Netherlands and Spain.

John Locke, liberal philosopher, and founder of Empiricism, was born at Wrington in 1632.

William Dampier, the explorer and buccaneer, was born in the county in 1652. He was one of the first Englishmen to set eyes on Australia.

Beau Nash was Master of Ceremonies at Bath for 50 years. He established the Assembly Rooms there.

Richard Sheridan met **Elizabeth Lindley** in Bath, and escorted her to France in 1772, where she was intending to enter a convent. However, they fell in love en route, and were married shortly afterwards.

Sir Samuel Hood, Admiral in command of the Mediterranean fleet in 1793, was a Somerset man.

Thomas de Quincey, the essayist and critic, attended Bath Grammar School from 1796 to 1799, until he was removed because of an accident.

Samuel Taylor Coleridge, the poet, lived at Nether Stowey for two years, and wrote the *Rhyme of the Ancient Mariner* whilst there.

William Wordsworth and his sister **Dorothy** came to live nearby, and the three took to rambling together in the Quantock Hills.

Arthur Hallam, close friend of the poet Tennyson, is buried at Clevedon. Tennyson's long poem *In Memoriam* commemorates him.

John Stuart Mill, the philosopher, spent much of his childhood at Forde Abbey, near Chard.

Walter Bagehot, the economist, and author of *The English Constitution*, was born in Langport in 1826.

Sir Henry Irving, the actor, was born in the county in 1838.

Ernest Bevin, TUC leader, and Foreign Secretary in 1945-51, was born in the county in 1881.

T S Eliot, the poet, was buried in East Coker in 1965, the village from which his ancestors had left for New England in the 17th century.

ART AND LITERATURE

'"And the people of Bath", continued Cain, *"never need to light their fires except as a luxury, for the water springs up out of the earth ready boiled for use."'*

Thomas Hardy
Far From the Madding Crowd

Her, Somerset receives, with all the counties blest
That nature can produce in that Bathonian Spring
Which from the Sulphury mines her med'cinall force doth bring;

Michael Drayton
Poly-Olbion

'There twice a day the Severn fills
The salt sea-water passes by,
And hushes half the babbling Wye,
And makes a silence in the hills.'

Alfred Lord Tennyson
In Memoriam

'In my beginning is my end. Now the light falls
Across the open field, leaving the deep lane
Shuttered with branches, dark in the afternoon,
Where you lean against a bank while a van passes,
And the deep lane insists on the direction
Into the village, in the electric heat
Hypnotised.'

T S Eliot
East Coker

'When Lady Russell, not long afterwards, was entering Bath on a wet afternoon, and driving through the long course of streets from the Old Bridge, to Camden-place, amidst the dash of other carriages, the heavy rumble of carts and drays, the bawling of newsmen, muffin-men and milk-men, and the ceaseless clink of pattens, she made no complaint. No, these were noises which belonged to the winter pleasures; her spirits rose under their influence; and, like Mrs Musgrove, she was feeling, though not saying, that, after being long in the country, nothing could be so good for her as a little quiet cheerfulness.'

Jane Austen
Persuasion

LOCAL FOLKLORE

Legend of Glastonbury

Joseph of Aramathea is said to have buried the chalice used at the Last Supper under the waters of a spring on the slopes of Glastonbury Tor. He thrust his thorn staff into the ground and it took root, to produce the winter-flowering thorn tree peculiar to Glastonbury.

Legend of Bath

Bladud, a British Prince, suffered from leprosy. He was driven out of his father's palace to herd pigs, who were suffering from the same disease. One day he noticed the pigs rolling in the warm mud around some freshwater springs, and realized that they were being healed. He did the same, and he too was cured of his leprosy. When he became King, he built a city around these healing springs, which became the city of Bath.

Alfred and the Cakes

In 865, the Danes descended on Wessex and conquered the people, who all submitted to them save King Alfred.

Over that winter, he lived like an outlaw in the region of the Isle of Athelney, taking shelter when and where he could.

One day, he had taken shelter in a herdsman's

cottage, and was sitting by the fire mending his weapons, while the herdsman's wife was baking on the hearth. She suddenly realized that the cakes were burning, and scolded King Alfred roundly for his negligence:

'Ca'sn thee mind the ke'aks, man, and doozzen zee'em burn?
I'm boun' thee's eat 'em vast enough az zoon az 'tiz the turn.'

The Fiddlers and the Maids

At the village of Stanton Drew there are four groups of stones which, when they were complete, formed three stones and a triangle. They are known as the fiddlers and the maids. Legend has it that a bridal pair held their marriage revels here one Saturday night, and they danced and feasted until midnight, when the piper, who was a religious man, declared that he would not play on the Sabbath. The bride was angry at this, and vowed that she would find someone else to play for them, if she had to go down to hell to fetch him. All of a sudden, an old man with a long beard appeared and offered to play for them. They were delighted, but when he started with a slow and stately tune, they shouted that they wanted something more lively. So the new piper started playing more briskly, and the revellers danced on, and gradually realized that he was getting faster and faster, and that they were getting worn out. However, to their horror, they saw the piper change into his real guise of the Devil, and try as they might, they could not stop their feet from whirling them round ever faster and faster as the music grew wilder and wilder.

Next morning, the villagers found no sign of the revellers, but the meadow was strewn with large stones, that had not been there the day before; hiding under a hedge, almost crazed with fear, was the original piper, who had seen the devil appear, and witnessed the revellers being turned into stone.

King's Sedgemoor

Late one night, a local farmer heard a man shouting from the other side of a rhine: 'Come over and fight!' Thinking it was some drunkard, the farmer took no notice. It was later remembered that 'Come over and fight!' was the last cry of Monmouth's army at the Battle of Sedgemoor, as they were massacred by the King's guns.

The Legend of Wooky Hole

Two of the stalagmites at Wooky Hole are believed to be the petrified remains of a witch and her dog, turned to stone by a monk who doused them with holy water.

DISTINCTIVE FLAVOUR

Somerset is known as England's premier dairy county. It is the home of **Cheddar Cheese**.

Miss Sally Lunn was born and lived in Bath, and was the original maker of the sponge cakes which take her name. These cakes, well risen with yeast, would be cut in slices, toasted and buttered, and sent out to all the elegant tea parties of the neighbourhood, in the early 19th century.

Many Somerset buildings are made from the distinctive **Ham Hill stone**, a yellow stone quarried from Hamdon Hill south of Stoke-cum-Hamdon.

On the last Thursday in October, the children of Hinton St George celebrate **Punkie Night**, when they parade through the streets with lanterns made from turnips and mangolds.

On May Day, a **Hobby Horse festival** is held in Minehead.

Somerset Cricket Club was founded in 1875. Their main ground is Taunton, although matches are sometimes held in Bath, Glastonbury, or Weston-Super-Mare. Their badge is the Wessex Wyvern.

THE MARKET CROSS, SHEPTON MALLET

THE BISHOP'S EYE, WELLS

COUNTY DIARY

May:	North Somerset Show, Ashton Court
June:	Royal Bath and West Show, Shepton Mallet
June:	Arts Festival, Bath
August:	The Mid-Somerset Show, Shepton Mallet
August:	Air Day, RNAS Yeovilton
Summer:	County Amateur Dramatics Festival, Burnham on Sea
October:	Fair, at which the ponies of Exmoor are rounded up for sale, Bampton
October:	Punkie Night, Hinton St George
October:	South Western Dairy Show, Shepton Mallet

STAFFORDSHIRE

COUNTY FACTS

Derivation of name: Stafford comes from the Old English, 'ford by the landing place', staeth being landing place.
First Recorded: 1016 as Staeffordscir
Motto: The Knot Unites
County Town: Stafford
Towns: Aldridge, Biddulph, Bilston, Brierley Hill, Brownhills, Burslem, Burton upon Trent, Cannock, Coseley, Darlaston, Fenton, Great Barr, Hanley, Harborne, Kidsgrove, Leek, Lichfield, Longton, Newcastle-under-Lyme, Rowley Regis, Rugeley, Sedgeley, Smethwick, Stafford, Stoke-on-Trent, Stone, Streetly, Tamworth, Tipton, Tunstall, Uttoxeter, Walsall, Wednesbury, Wednesfield, West Bromwich, Willenhall, Wolverhampton.
The city of Lichfield is a city of a county and declared 'not part of the body of the county at large' which gives the city a special status that was increasingly eroded by repeated Acts of Parliament.

Local Government
Staffordshire County Council, four Metropolitan Boroughs, and nine District Councils. That part of Staffordshire detached in Worcestershire, Clent and Broome, is administered by Hereford and Worcester County Council.

HISTORY

Before the Roman conquest, the region was inhabited by the tribes of the Cornavii in the east and the Ordovices in the west.
In the 7th and 8th century, Staffordshire was part of the Saxon kingdom of Mercia, under Penda, and later Offa.
A cathedral was built at Lichfield in 669, and the see became second only in importance to Canterbury.
Richard II was held prisoner at Lichfield, and escaped at night by jumping into the castle moat, only to be later recaptured and carried to his death.
In 1459, during the Wars of the Roses, the Battle of Blore Heath ended in defeat for the Lancastrians, despite the Yorkists numbering only half as many men.
In 1487 the Battle of Stoke saw the end of the Pretender Lambert Simnel's ill-fated attempt to wrest the crown from Henry VII. Claiming to be the eldest son of Edward IV and one of the mysterious 'Princes in the Tower', his adherents raised support from Ireland and also gathered a small group of loyal Yorkists. However, he was defeated by the Tudor forces at Stoke and on his capture set to work in the royal kitchens to turn the spit by the fire.
In the Civil War, the towns declared for the king, and the country places for Parliament. After his defeat at Worcester, King Charles fled, and, disguised as a servant, rode out of the county with a Miss Lane of Bentley Hall, on his way to the coast and escape.
In the 17th and 18th centuries, the coal and iron industries of the south of the county brought great prosperity and earned for the region the name of Black Country.

INDUSTRY PAST AND PRESENT

The Potteries in the north are famous for their china production (Wedgwood, Minton Spode); Burton on Trent is the home of Bass beer; there is a leather works at Walsall. The 'Black Country' in the south produced coal iron ore and limestone.
Coal and iron were worked from the 13th century. The moorlands of the north were prime sheep pasture-land, and the wool trade flourished in Wolverhampton in the 14th century. The clothing trade prospered in Tamworth, Burton, and Newcastle-under-Lyme. Pottery was an ancient craft, but developed rapidly in the 17th and 18th centuries as new methods of glazing were introduced.

LANDMARKS

Cannock Chase, an 'area of outstanding natural beauty'

TOPOGRAPHY INCLUDING RIVERS

Staffordshire, in the north midlands, is bordered by Cheshire in the north, Derbyshire and Leicestershire in the east, Warwickshire and Worcestershire in the south, and Shropshire in the west.
The hills in the north are a continuation of the moors of Derbyshire and rise in places to 1,500 feet above the River Trent. They are broken by several wooded valleys – the Manifold, Milldale and Dovedale. The northern part of the county is known as the Potteries. The centre and south of the county are generally level, with a few low valleys intersected by the Trent, Blithe, and Tame rivers. In the centre of the county is a wide tract of heather and forest known as Cannock Chase. The southern part of the county is known as the 'Black Country', from the iron and coal and associated industries which are carried on there. The highest point is the Ordnance Station on Roaches, 1657 feet.
Rivers: Trent, Penk, Sow, Blithe, Tean, Dove, Churnet, and Tame.

Kinver Edge
Manifold Valley, and Thor's Cave

MONUMENTS

Lichfield Cathedral, England's only medieval three-spired cathedral, dedicated to St Chad.

Tutbury Castle; built on a steep rock, the castle remains date from the 12th century. Mary Queen of Scots was twice imprisoned here.

Tamworth Castle, a Norman castle built on a mound raised in 913 by Ethelfleda, daughter of Alfred the Great.

Moseley Old Hall, an Elizabethan house, in which Charles II was sheltered after his defeat at the Battle of Worcester in 1651.

Chillington Hall has been the seat of the Giffard family since the 12th century. The hall was rebuilt in the 18th century in Georgian style.

Eccleshall Castle; the remains of this 13th-century castle include a nine-sided tower.

Wightwick Manor, a half-timbered manor house, built between 1887 and 1893. It houses a collection of watercolours by Ruskin, drawings by Burne-Jones, and wallpapers and fabrics by William Morris.

Alton Towers. When completed in the 19th century, this neo-Gothic mansion, home of the Earls of Shrewsbury, was the largest private house in Europe. It is now better known for its leisure park, attracting more than 2 million visitors every year.

FAMOUS PEOPLE AND LOCAL CHARACTERS

Mary, Queen of Scots was imprisoned at Tutbury Castle, where she complained of her proximity to the privies.

Izaak Walton, author of *The Compleat Angler*, was born on August 9 1593, in Stafford. He fished the streams of Staffordshire.

Elias Ashmole was born in Lichfield in 1617. He amassed a large collection of rarities, which he gave to Oxford, thus laying the groundwork for the Ashmolean Museum.

Jane Lane was sister of Colonel Lane of Bentley Hall. Charles II rode disguised as her manservant in order to escape from the midlands and reach the coast, from where he sailed for France.

Samuel Johnson was born in Lichfield on 18th September, 1709. The son of a bookseller, he was the compiler of the first dictionary of the English Language.

David Garrick, the actor, was born in 1717, and lived in Lichfield until the age of 20.

Josiah Wedgwood was born in Burslem in 1730. He founded the Wedgwood pottery, and invented the Pyrometer, for measuring extreme heat.

Josiah Spode, founder of the Spode pottery works, was born in the county in 1733.

Anna Seward, a poetess who lived in Lichfield in the 18th century, was known as the 'Swan of Lichfield'.

Richard Sheridan, the dramatist, was MP for Stafford from 1780 to 1806.

Jerome K(lapka) Jerome, the writer, was born in Walsall on 2 May 1859.

Commander Edward John Smith came from Hanley; he was master of the ill-fated 'Titanic'.

Arnold Bennett was born in Hanley on May 27 1867. His novels are set in the Potteries.

Local Characters

On 16th December 1292, a boy named **William Bond**, working with a carpenter on the roof of the Parish Church in Burton, fell through the roof to his death in front of the altar during vespers.

Dr William Palmer lived in Rugeley in the 19th century. He became known as the 'Prince of Poisoners'. He was tried for the murder by poison of a young lawyer named Cook, and at this trial, his other evil doings came to light. It was discovered that he had poisoned his wife, whom he had previously insured for £13,000; his brother Walter, also insured for £13,000; his wealthy mother-in-law; two racing friends; four of his five children; an illegitimate daughter; and some pigs belonging to a neighbour. His trial at the Old Bailey in May 1856 lasted 12 days. He was hanged on 14 June 1856, before a crowd of around 30,000 people.

Wily Will Willett claimed to have danced for 12 days and nights from September 2 to September 14, 1752. Although he did indeed dance non-stop between those dates, it was actually only one day, as those were the famous '11 days' which were missed out when Britain adopted the new-style Calendar.

ART AND LITERATURE

'Say for what were hopyards meant,
Or why was Burton built on Trent?'
A E Housman
A Shropshire Lad

'We came down to the Potteries yesterday afternoon...Untidiness; things left at a loose end. Broken walls, deserted entrances to what had been spacious gardens. Everything very misty...Men in bright neckties sallying forth, rather suspicious, defiant, meanly-shrewd look. Mean stunted boy crouching along smoking a pipe which he hid in his hand while holding it in his mouth...deserted goal posts in gloomy mist. Mild wind, cold, chilling, clammy...'
Arnold Bennett
Diary, 1907

'One insult that no Black countryman will tolerate is to be mistaken for a Brummie.'
Phil Drabble
Black Country

Arnold Bennett referred to the Trent as, 'The calm and characteristic stream of middle England.'

LOCAL FOLKLORE

The origins of white pottery

A potter named Astbury was travelling to London when he realized that his horse seemed to be losing its sight. He stopped for aid in Dunstable, where an ostler burned a flint-stone until it was quite white, ground it to a powder, and then blew a little of this powder into the horse's eyes, causing them to run and then become clear again. Astbury was most grateful to the ostler for restoring the horse's sight, and he was also interested in the fact that the burnt flint turned white, and became clay-like when mixed with the moisture from the horse's eyes. He had been looking for something which would make his dark pottery white. On returning home, he mixed powdered flints with his clay, and sure enough, the resultant pottery was white. This method has been used ever since in the manufacture of pottery.

Giffard's Cross

Sir John Giffard had a collection of wild animals at his home, Chillington Hall, among which his favourite was a fierce panther.
One day this animal escaped from its cage in the park. Sir John and his eldest son searched for the animal till they came upon a young woman and a child walking along the road. Just at that moment, they spotted the panther, crouched ready to spring on his prey. Although still a long way off, Sir John prepared to fire his cross-bow. His son, seeing how exhausted his father was from the exertion of the chase, and fearing that he might miss, called out, 'Prenez haleine, tirez fort!' (Take breath, pull strong!). Just as the panther sprang, Sir John loosed the bolt, which struck the panther in the head, and killed it instantly, thus saving the woman and child.
Sir John erected a cross on the spot where his

prized animal fell, and from then on, he adopted his son's words of counsel as the family motto.

The heir of Broughton Hall

Broughton Hall was Royalist in the Civil War. One day a band of Roundheads rode up the drive. The young heir unwisely taunted them from an upstairs window, shouting "I'm for the King!" The Roundheads shot him dead. The boy was wearing red stockings when he died, and his ghost, recognizable from these stockings, has been seen in the long gallery where he was shot, and elsewhere in the hall. Centuries later, a guest arrived at a party at the hall, apologizing for not wearing fancy dress. The host was puzzled at this, as he had not intended a fancy dress party anyway. The guest assumed he was merely being polite, and explained that it was not until he saw a young man in Cavalier costume and red stockings that he realized that it was supposed to be a fancy dress party...

The ghost of Charnes Hall

Mrs Yonge, of Charnes Hall, was believed to be mortally ill. She asked for the servants to be brought to her bedside that she might bid them farewell, and one of the coachmen noticed that she was wearing a valuable ring. He bribed the sexton of the chapel to leave the vault open after the funeral, and that night, he opened the coffin, and tried to take the ring from the dead woman's finger. It would not come, so he decided to cut off the whole finger with his knife. As he was cutting, blood suddenly started to spurt from the finger, and the 'corpse' sat up in the coffin. Mrs Yonge had been prematurely pronounced dead! The coachman fled, and Mrs Yonge stumbled back to the Hall, where she lived on for many years. However, her ghost is said to haunt the Hall, searching for the ring she lost during her day in the tomb.

Blake Mere

Blake Mere, on the moors in the north of the county, is also known as Mermaid Pool. Many years ago, a young girl was drowned there as a witch. Not long afterwards, the man who had been her chief tormentor was also found drowned in the pool, with his face covered in talon scratches.

DISTINCTIVE FLAVOUR

The village of Longnor shot to fame in 1972 when it was chosen by a TV company for a programme on tobacco smoking habits. All the smokers in the village gave up for a week, and pubs and shops stopped selling tobacco and cigarettes. The pubs made up in beer sales what they lost in tobacco, as so many journalists and TV crews descended on the village.

Flash claims to be the highest village in England, at 1,158 feet above sea-level.

Tamworth is famous for its pigs, which are a sandy red colour.

The traditional **Horn Dance** is held every September at Abbots Bromley. The dance dates from Norman times, and is believed to have religious origins. There are twelve people who take part: a man on a hobby horse, a maid, a jester, a boy carrying a bow and arrow, two musicians, playing an accordion and a triangle, and six men wearing great reindeer antlers on their shoulders.

Cannock Chase is a haven for foxes, wild deer, badgers, red squirrels, grouse, and green woodpeckers.

The racecourse at Uttoxeter is held to be the finest National Hunt Steeplechase course in the Midlands.

The famous '**Five Towns**' that make up The Potteries are Burslem; Hanley; Longton; Stoke and Tunstall.

ALTON TOWERS – 'A HUGE IMITATION OF STONEHENGE.'

COUNTY DIARY

May:	Staffordshire County Show, Stafford
June:	National Craft Fair, Stoke-on-Trent
September:	Dr Johnson Commemoration, Lichfield
September:	Horn Dance, Abbots Bromley

SUFFOLK

COUNTY FACTS

Derivation of name: Of Anglo-Saxon origin.
First recorded: 895 as Suth Folchi
Motto: Opus Nostrum Dirige (Direct Our Work)
County Town: Bury St Edmunds
Towns: Aldeburgh, Beccles, Bury St Edmunds, Bungay, Felixstowe, Framlingham, Gorleston-on-Sea, Hadleigh, Halesworth, Haverhill, Ipswich, Lakenheath, Lavenham, Leiston, Little Yarmouth (or Southtown), Long Melford, Lowestoft, Melton, Newmarket, Stowmarket, Sudbury, Woodbridge.

Local Government
Suffolk County Council and seven district councils. With a small part of the extreme north-east corner of the county around Gorleston and Little Yarmouth under the control of Norfolk County Council, and synonymous with Great Yarmouth for parliamentary purposes.

HISTORY

After the Romans left, the Angles from Holstein established themselves in East Anglia – known as the South folk (Suffolk) and the North folk (Norfolk).

King Edmund was killed by the Danes in 870, and later became St Edmund the Martyr. A wooden church was built to house the body of St Edmund. From the 11th century, the town in which it was situated was renamed St Edmundsbury.

On St Edmund's day, November 20, 1214, 25 disaffected barons swore at the high altar of the Abbey of Bury St Edmunds that they would force from King John a charter of rights: this was Magna Carta.

The county in the main supported parliament during the Civil War, although there were many squires, and wool merchants, who sided with the King. Many of these families left the country to settle in America, and as a direct result the prosperity of the county dwindled, and once more came to rely mainly on its agriculture.

INDUSTRY PAST AND PRESENT

Lowestoft is one of the most important fishing ports in England. The port of Felixstowe handles an ever-increasing amount of traffic.

TOPOGRAPHY INCLUDING RIVERS

The most eastern county of England, bordered by Norfolk to the north, the North Sea to the east, Essex to the south, and Cambridgeshire to the west. In the west and south-west of the county, there are low, undulating hills. The north-west corner is part of the fen country. The coast is low-lying, and is gradually being encroached on by the sea. North of Lowestoft, which is the most easterly point in England, is a small part of the Broads country. The highest point is Rede, 420 feet.
Rivers: Deben, Stour, Waveney, Lark, Little Ouse.

Past industries included wool (the village of Lindsey gave its name to Lindsey Woolsey); smuggling; and chalk mining. (Subsidence starting in 1967, in Bury, was found to be caused by old chalk mine workings underground). In the 13th and 14th centuries, Ipswich was a leading commercial town and flourishing port for trade with many countries.

LANDMARKS

Minsmere Nature Reserve
Orford Ness

MONUMENTS

Bury St Edmunds Abbey was once larger than Ely Cathedral, but all that remains are two gatehouses and fragmentary ruins.
Framlingham Castle appears to be one of the most complete in Britain, retaining a full complement of towers.
Orford Castle, by contrast, is represented solely by its keep.
Ickworth, a vast classical Rotonda built to display one man's collection of art, is more curious than beautiful.
Heveningham Hall is a first-rate example of a late 18th-century, Classical country seat.
Snape Maltings are home to some of the most adventurous musical events in the cultural calendar.
Sizewell Nuclear Power Station is monumental, but hardly a monument.

FAMOUS PEOPLE AND LOCAL CHARACTERS

Cardinal Wolsey was born in Ipswich in 1475.
John Daye, born in Dunwich 1522, was the first printer to cut and use Anglo-Saxon type in England.
Thomas Nashe, the poet, was born in Lowestoft in 1567.
In 1589 **Richard Hakluyt** published his *Principall Navigations, Voiages and Discoveries of the English Nation* – a scientific study of the problems and perils facing sea captains on still uncharted oceans. He learned several foreign languages, to be able to listen and talk to sailors from all over the world, to help in

compiling the work. He was offered various high positions in Westminster, Lincolnshire, and even America, but chose instead to become rector of Wetheringsett, where he spent the last 16 years of his life. He is buried in Westminster Abbey.

Dr Thomas Young, Milton's tutor, lived in Stowmarket.

Thomas Cavendish, the second Englishman to sail round the world, lived at Grimston Hall, above Trimley Marshes.

William Dowsing was born in Laxfield. The 'Puritan zealot' was appointed Parliamentary visitor to the churches of Suffolk in 1643, with the task of destroying superstitious pictures, ornaments, and 'all such trumperies'. He was responsible for much destruction.

David Garrick, actor and theatre manager, began his career in Ipswich.

George Crabbe, the poet, was born in Aldeburgh in 1754. He went to school in Bungay, and hated it. Echoes of his misery there are to be found in his poem *The Borough*, about Aldeburgh, where he became curate.

Robert Bloomingfield, the poet, was born in Honington in 1766.

Chateaubriand, the French writer and diplomat, lived in Bungay for some years after escaping from the Terror in France.

John Constable, artist (*Flatford Mill*, *The Haywain*), was born at East Bergholt in 1776.

Edward Fitzgerald, poet, translator of *Omar Khayyam*, lived for many years at Woodbridge. Orwell Park was the home of **Admiral Vernon**, known as 'Old Grog', from an old grogram cloak which he always wore.

Elizabeth Garrett Anderson, the first woman Doctor in England, and in 1908 the first lady mayor, is buried in Aldeburgh churchyard.

Randolph Churchill lived in East Bergholt.

Joseph Conrad referred to Lowestoft as his 'spiritual Birthplace'.

Havelock Ellis spent the last years of his life in Hintlesham.

Eric Blair lived for a while in Southwold, and included a Suffolk river in his pseudonym – **George Orwell**.

Benjamin Britten, son of a Lowestoft dentist, was born in 1913. Before the war, he had bought and restored a mill at Snape where he established the Aldeburgh Festival, with Peter Pears.

Scott and Black took off from Mildenhall in 1934 for their famous win in the air race to Australia.

Angus Wilson had a cottage near Bury St Edmunds.

Local Characters

A Polstead girl, **Maria Marten**, fell in love with **William Corder**, the local ne'er-do-well. Believing they were running away to be married, she met him one night in the Red Barn, and was murdered. Her body was not discovered until her mother, who had had the same hideous recurring dream, insisted on having the barn floor dug up: her corpse was found buried there. Corder was tried and hanged for the murder.

In the 18th century, **Margaret Catchpole**, a servant, and tomboy, fell in love with **William Lauder**, a ferryman and a smuggler. The pair went smuggling round Ipswich, Bawdsey, and Levington. In 1797 Margaret stole a coach horse from her employer and went to London, dressed as a man. She tried to sell the horse, but was arrested and sent to Ipswich Gaol. She escaped, and she and Lauder were attempting to get away to Holland, when a local man informed on them and Lauder was shot. Margaret was sentenced to transportation to Australia.

Willy Lott lived in his cottage in East Bergholt for 80 years, and never left it for more than 4 days in succession.

ART AND LITERATURE

'…that undulating, yet hardly hill country which I most love.'
> **Angus Wilson**
> on the countryside near Bury

'The sound of water escaping from mill-dams, willows, slimy posts and brickwork – I love such things.'
> **John Constable**

'I take Bury to be the most attractive town in Suffolk.'
> **M R James**

'To alight in Bury is to feel you have arrived.'
> **William Addison**

'…it is crowded with nobility and gentry and all sort of the most agreeable company…'
> **Daniel Defoe,**
> on Bury St Edmunds

A BENCH END, IXWORTH THORPE CHURCH

WEST STOW HALL

Since 1948, the annual **Aldeburgh Festival** of Music and the Arts had been held in the county. Most of the events take place at Snape Maltings.

'**The Foggy Foggy Dew**' is a well-known Suffolk song.

'**Silly Suffolk**' – probably means 'happy', when referring to the inhabitants...

Dunwich was once a thriving town, and in the 13th century, the population was so great that there were nine churches in the town. Fishing was the main industry. However, the sea was already eating away at the town; a storm in 1326 washed away three of the churches. Continuous storms and erosion have destroyed Dunwich, which now consists of a mere handful of cottages, a pub and a general store.

William Cobbett called Bury 'The nicest town in the world'.

'My chief Amusement in life is Boating on River and Sea. The Country about here is the Cemetery of so many of my oldest Friends: and the petty race of Squires who have succeeded only use the Earth for an Investment: cut down every old Tree: level every Violet Bank: and make the old Country of my Youth Hideous to me in my Decline. There are fewer Birds to be heard as fewer Trees for them to resort to. So I get to the Water: where Friends are not buried nor Pathways stopt up: but all is, as the Poets say, as Creation's Dawn Beheld. I am happiest going in my little boat round the coast to Aldbro', with some Bottled Porter and some Bread and Cheese, and some good rough Soul who works the Boat and chews his Tobacco in peace.'
Edward Fitzgerald

LOCAL FOLKLORE
King Edmund
King Edmund fled from the Danes after the defeat of his army, and took refuge under a bridge. He was betrayed by a wedding party crossing the bridge. One version of the story

has it that the Danes stood back to allow the party to cross, and saw the King's spurs reflected in the water. The other had it that the bride saw him, pointed him out to the Danes, and added the reward money to her dowry. When he was dragged out, Edmund laid a curse on the bridge and on every bride and groom who should cross it on their wedding day. To this day, no girl will go to her wedding over Goldbrook Bridge.

The Haunting of High House
Similarly, there are two versions of the haunting of High House at Oulton: the one tells of the squire who murdered his wife in a room by the front door, and was thereafter condemned to ride repeatedly up to and into the house on a black horse, with ravening hounds at his heels. The other tells of the wife who poisoned her husband the squire, and is condemned to walk very night at midnight, holding the poison cup before her as she goes. Whichever is the correct tale, rumours of ghosts were useful for keeping locals away from any smuggling activities that might be going on.

DISTINCTIVE FLAVOUR
Horseracing at Newmarket
The HQ of the Jockey Club is based at Newmarket.

LITTLE SAXHAM CHURCH

COUNTY DIARY

May:	Suffolk County Show, Ipswich
June:	Music Festival, Aldeburgh
June:	East Coast Boat Show, Ipswich

SURREY

COUNTY FACTS

Derivation of name: It has been suggested that the Suthinge were a Germanic tribe that settled in this area. A different suggestion is that Surrey derives from the Old English 'Suthrige', meaning the kingdom south of the Thames.

First Recorded: 722

County Town: Guildford

Towns: Banstead, Barnes, Battersea, Camberley, Camberwell, Carshalton, Caterham, Chertsey, Clapham, Croydon, Dorking, Dulwich, Egham, Epsom, Esher, Ewell, Farnham, Godalming, Guildford, Haslemere, Horley, Kingston-upon-Thames, Lambeth, Leatherhead, Mitcham, Purley, Putney, Redhill, Reigate, Richmond, Southwark, Streatham, Sutton, Tooting, Walton-on-Thames, Wandsworth, Wimbledon, Woking.

Local Government

Surrey County Council, seven London Boroughs and ten District Councils.

HISTORY

Much of the county was given to William's nobles after the Norman Conquest. The medieval castles of Surrey – Warrenne, Farnham, Guildford, Thunderfield, Clare – were planned to watch the routes to London from the south, and from the Kentish ports to Winchester and the West.

The county was a favourite Royal hunting ground.

On 15 June, 1215, the struggle for power between King John and the barons reached its conclusion in the field of Runnymede (near Egham). After several days of negotiations, King John reluctantly agreed to set his seal to Magna Carta, a charter of rights by which the king and his barons alike were bound.

By the time of the Stuarts, Royal houses in the county included Nonsuch, Richmond, Oatlands, Byfleet, Woking, and Guildford. Many leading men also settled in the county in Tudor times, such as Sir Francis Walsingham, Lord Howard of Effingham, and the Earl of Lincoln.

TOPOGRAPHY INCLUDING RIVERS

Surrey, in the south-east of England, is bordered by Berkshire, Buckinghamshire, and Middlesex in the north, Kent in the east, Sussex in the south, and Hampshire in the west.

The Thames forms the northern boundary of the county. Crossing the centre of the county from east to west are the North Downs, a line of chalk downs, with gentle slopes on their north side, and steeper, more sheer drops on the south. Box Hill lies within this range. Beyond these is another range of sandy hills, from which rises Leith Hill, the highest point in the county, at 965 feet. These hills give way to the Surrey Weald.

Rivers: Mole, Wey, Thames, Eden.

INDUSTRY PAST AND PRESENT

Present industry includes market gardening, dairying, light industry and all the services one expects in London's premier commuter county.

Guildford was an important centre of the cloth trade. Glass and iron were produced in the Weald, using charcoal from the forests for smelting. Chiddingfold was one of the chief glass-producing districts in late Tudor times. The county was strongly agricultural, with prime sheep pasture-land.

LANDMARKS

North Downs
Box Hill, 400 feet high
Hindhead Common
Kew Gardens
Runnymede
The Silent Pool
Virginia Water Lake, covering some 160 acres
Richmond Park

MONUMENTS

Guildford Cathedral; this red-brick cathedral, designed in 1932, was consecrated in 1961.

Clandon Park, a classical mansion built in the 18th century for the 2nd Lord Onslow.

Farnham Castle, begun by the Bishop of Winchester, Henri de Blois, the present building dates from the late 12th and early 13th centuries, although it has been much repaired and altered since.

Hatchlands, a classical mansion built circa 1756 by Admiral Boscawen. The interior is the earliest known work in England by Robert Adam.

Chessington Zoo, founded in 1931 by Reginald Stuart Goddard.

Loseley House; the Elizabethan mansion is home to the descendants of the builder, Sir William More, relative of Sir Thomas More.

Polesden Lacey; this Edwardian house was adapted from the original Regency one built in 1824.

Wisley, the garden of the Royal Horticultural Society.

Gatwick Airport, the world's second busiest international airport.

FAMOUS PEOPLE AND LOCAL CHARACTERS

Lord Howard of Effingham, who lived in Surrey, was commander of the fleet which defeated the Spanish Armada in 1588.

Fanny Burney, the novelist, met the French refugee General Alexandre D'Arblay at Mickleham. They were married in 1793 and lived at Bookham.

William Cobbett, author of *Rural Rides*, was born in Farnham on 9th March 1762. He spent his days as a labourer in the fields.

John Keats and **Robert Louis Stevenson** both stayed at the Burford Bridge Hotel, at the foot of Box Hill. Keats finished *Endymion* whilst staying there.

George Meredith, the writer, lived in Flint Cottage on Box Hill for 40 years. He is buried in Dorking cemetery.

Lewis Carroll often came to stay with his sister at Guildford. He died there on January 14th, 1898.

Thomas Robert Malthus, the economist and demographer, was born near Dorking in 1766.

ART AND LITERATURE

Matthew Arnold styled himself *'the hermit of the Mole'*.

'Pear and apple in Croydon gardens
Bud and blossom and fall,
But your Uncle Dick has left his Croydon
Once for all.'

> **John Betjeman**
> Croydon (1932)

'Mole, that like a nousling mole doth make
His way still underground, till Thames he overtake.'

> **Edmund Spenser**
> Faerie Queene (1590)

'He decided to commence with the Botanical Gardens, where he had already made so many studies, and chose the little artificial pond, sprinkled now with an autumn shower of red and yellow leaves, for though the gardeners longed to sweep them off, they could not reach them with their brooms. The rest of the gardens they swept bare enough, removing every morning Nature's rain of leaves; piling them in heaps, whence from slow fires rose the sweet, acrid smoke that, like the cuckoo's note for spring, the scent of lime trees for the summer, is the true emblem of the fall. The gardeners' tidy souls could not abide the gold and green and russet pattern on the grass. The gravel paths must lie unstained, ordered, methodical, without knowledge of the realities of

STOKE D'ABERNON

life, nor of that slow and beautiful decay that flings crowns underfoot to star the earth with fallen glories, whence, as the cycle rolls, will leap again wild spring. Thus each leaf that fell was marked from the moment when it fluttered a good-bye, and dropped, slow turning, from its twig.

But on that little pond the leaves floated in peace, and praised heaven with their hues, the sunlight haunting over them.'

> **J Galsworthy**
> The Forsyte Saga (1922)

LOCAL FOLKLORE

The Legend of the Silent Pool

A village maiden named Emma, bathing naked in the pool, was disturbed by Prince (later King) John. She retreated further and further into the pool, until she lost her footing and, unable to swim, sank under the water. Her brother, who was nearby and heard her cries, plunged in to try to save her, but he too was unable to swim, so brother and sister drowned together.

Mother Ludlum's Cauldron

Mother Ludlum was a kindly witch, who lived in a cave in the grounds of Moor Park, which came to be known as Mother Ludlum's Hole. She would lend the villagers anything they asked for: when they got back from visiting her at her cave, there would be the article waiting on their doorstep. Her only stipulation was that whatever was borrowed had to be returned within two days.

One day, a man borrowed her cauldron, and he failed to return it within the stated time. When he did take it back to her, she refused to accept it, and immediately afterwards, she vanished from the neighbourhood. The cauldron is to be seen in Frensham Church to this day.

DISTINCTIVE FLAVOUR

Surrey County Cricket Club was founded in 1845. Its ground is the Oval; Its badge the Prince of Wales's feathers.

Surrey is favourite **London commuter land**, being variously referred to as the 'Stockbroker belt' and 'Gin and Jaguar belt'. Guildford has been called the 'buckle in the Stockbroker's belt'.

The RAC Country Club is at Woodcote Park near Epsom.

Epsom Downs is the setting for two of the most famous horse races, the Derby and the Oaks.

Racing also takes place at **Lingfield**.

COUNTY DIARY

May:	Bach Festival, Tilford County Show, Guildford
June:	All-England Championships, Wimbledon
June:	Derby Day, Epsom Downs
July:	Swan Upping, River Thames

S~USSE~X

COUNTY FACTS

Derivation of name: From the Old English, the territory of the South Saxons.
First Recorded: 722 as Suth Seaxe
County Town: Chichester
Towns: Arundel, Battle, Bexhill, Billingshurst, Bognor Regis, Brighton, Burgess Hill, Chichester, Crawley, Crowborough, Eastbourne, East Grinstead, Goring-by-Sea, Hailsham, Hastings (one of the Cinque Ports), Haywards Heath, Horsham, Lancing (North & South), Lewes, Littlehampton, Newhaven, Peacehaven, Portslade, Rustington, Rye (Cinque Port), St. Leonards, Seaford, Selsey, Shoreham-by-Sea, Southwick, Steyning, Storrington, Worthing.
Chichester is a county of a city unto itself.

Local Government
East Sussex County Council and West Sussex County Council and fourteen District Councils.

HISTORY

In the 5th and 6th centuries, the region was invaded and settled by a Germanic tribe from that part of the continent known as Saxony – hence their name, Saxons.

In the 7th century the people of Sussex were converted to Christianity by (later Saint) Wilfrid.

It was at Chichester/Bosham harbour that King Canute (1016-1035) proved to his fawning subjects that he could not rule the waves. (His daughter is reputed to be buried in Bosham churchyard).

1066 – Battle of Hastings. William the Conqueror defeated Harold II.

1264 – Defeat of Henry III by the barons, led by Simon de Montfort, at Lewes.

INDUSTRY PAST AND PRESENT

Arable farming on the chalk uplands has always been important. The proximity of the coast has always meant that Sussex plays an essential part both in defence and in communications. Both light industry and computer trades are prevalent. Tourism, both coastal and enticed by the heritage, adds to the county's coffers.

TOPOGRAPHY INCLUDING RIVERS

Sussex is bordered by Hampshire to the west, Surrey to the north, Kent to the east, and the English Channel to the south. In the south, from the coastal plain the land slopes gradually up to the ridge of the South Downs, a range of chalky hills running east-west, which rise in places to between 800 and 900 feet high. The steep, sheer slopes of the north side fall down to the weald, an irregular plain broken by long, deep valleys. Further north is the forest ridge, rising east of Horsham and reaching a peak in the centre of St Leonard's forest. Pine, birch and larch trees are characteristic of this ridge, which includes Ashdown Forest. The highest point is Blackdown Hill, 918 feet.
Rivers: Arun, Adur, Cuckmere, Ouse, Rother.

LANDMARKS

South Downs Way – bridleway which runs for 80 miles between Eastbourne and the Hampshire border.
The Long Man – a white chalk figure, believed to have been cut by the Saxons, lying stretched out on the north face of Windover Hill above Wilmington, 226 feet high
Devil's Dyke, north of Hove
Seven Sisters cliffs
Beachy Head
Hammer Ponds – dating back to 17th century iron-smelting days

MONUMENTS

Bodiam Castle was built in the late 14th century. Surrounded by a copious moat, it is almost *too* photogenic.
Battle Abbey was built by William the Conqueror, who had vowed to build a church on the site if God gave him victory. God could not however protect the foundation from Henry VIII, and not a stone of its church remains.
Goodwood House is a sprawling Georgian structure, whose name means more to devotees of the turf than of taste.
Pevensey Castle retains large sections of a late Roman defensive fort constructed to repel the Saxons.
Petworth House now administered by the National Trust exhibits, on a smaller scale those qualities which one either loves or loathes at Versailles.
Herstmonceux – now the home of the Royal Greenwich Observatory – is a late 15th-century brick castle.
Royal Pavilion, Brighton began life as a self-effacing villa. As such it was entirely out of keeping with the Prince Regent's enthusiasm for architectural fireworks, and was therefore re-vamped in an oriental mode.
Windmills – now very few of the many that used to be a particular feature of Sussex mainly sited on the downs. Famous pair of windmills on Blayton Hill, called Jack and Jill: Jill was built in 1821 but had to wait many years for her mate – Jack was built in 1876.
Chichester Cathedral is a major work of English Romanesque. It provided the

Victorians with an unexpected excitement when its central spire collapsed neatly into itself.

FAMOUS PEOPLE AND LOCAL CHARACTERS

The poet **Shelley** was born at Field Place near Horsham, 1792.

Charles Dickens gave readings of his works to audiences in the Town Hall at Brighton. He wrote *Dombey and Son* and most of *Bleak House* while staying in hotels in Brighton.

Aubrey Beardsley, the artist, lived in Brighton.

The Prince Regent patronised Brighton and as a result it was frequented by the cream of society in the latter half of the eighteenth century. He was widely acclaimed when he completed the 55 miles from London to Brighton in a coach and four in the record time of 4^1/$_2$ hours.

Ellen Terry 'retreated' to Winchelsea.

Virginia Woolf wrote her later novels at Rodmell, near Lewes. She drowned herself in the Ouse.

George Orwell spent five miserable years at school in Eastbourne. *Animal Farm* and *1984* are said in part to reflect the loneliness and misery that he claimed to have experienced there.

Anna Sewell, Henry James, Rudyard Kipling and **Hilaire Belloc**, all lived in the county.

Local characters

Phoebe Hessel, born 1713. When 15, she fell in love with a soldier called Samuel Golding. In order to follow him, she enlisted in a regiment bound for the then West Indies. She served for 5 years, without being recognised as a woman. She fought at the Battle of Hontenay, and was at the Siege of Gibraltar. When she was finally found out, she was discharged from the army. She then married Golding and they settled in Sussex. In 1814, at the age of 99, she became Brighton's oldest inhabitant. She died aged 108.

Jack Fuller, who lived in the early 19th century, weighed over 20 stone, and was nicknamed 'Hippo'. At the age of 50 he started building follies in weird and wonderful shapes – a cone, a pyramid, a tomb, an obelisk, an observatory, and a hermit's tower.

ART AND LITERATURE

*'When I am lying in the Midlands
That are sodden and unkind
The great hills of the South Country
come back into my mind.'*
Hilaire Belloc
The South Country

*'If I ever become a rich man,
Of if I ever grow to be old,
I will build a house with deep thatch
To shelter me from the cold,*

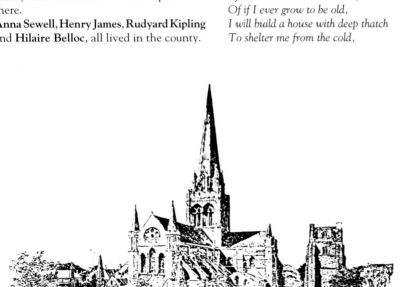

CHICHESTER CATHEDRAL

*and there shall the Sussex songs be sung
And the story of Sussex be told.'*
Ibid

*'I never get between the pines
But I smell the Sussex air.'*
Ibid

*'Each to his choice, and I rejoice,
The lot has fallen to me
In a fair ground, a fair ground
Yea, Sussex by the sea!'*
Rudyard Kipling,
Sussex

Horace Walpole dismissed Sussex as Saxon, and *'an area of England that dampens curiosity'.*

*'The Sussex men are noted fools
And weak in their brain-pan.'*
William Blake,
On Friends and Foes

'This wild walk…It is England at her quietest and most beautiful…Everywhere there are poplars and willows, beeches and oaks, with tiny church spires and towers peeping out from between the clustering trees, and ancient grey bridges at every bend.'
B Mais,
describing the course of the western
Rother between the Hampshire border and Midhurst

'A sacred and feudal skulk-away…(a place of) feudal peace.'
Eric Blight,
on Petworth House

'No breeze so fresh and invigorating as that of the Sussex Downs; no turf so springy to the feet as the soft greensward.'
Ainsworth

'In this country, not far from Battle Abbey, in the place where so great a slaughter of Englishmen was made, after any shower presently sweateth forth very fresh blood from out of the earth.'
William of Newbury (1136-1208)
(The earth of Sussex used to be very rich in iron ore…)

In the sixteenth century the roads of Sussex were reputed to be the worst in England. The historian, Leland, referred to *'Sowsexe full of dyrt and myre'.*

Sir Noel Coward found Sussex *'terribly piece full'.*

'Our blunt, bow-headed, whale-backed Downs.'
Rudyard Kipling

Gilbert White described the Downs as 'Majestic Mountains.'

'Its lovely breadths delight us when the white clouds and the flocks move over them together; when the waves break into cliffs they are the characteristics of our shores and through its thin coat of whitish mould go the thirsty roots of our three trees, the beech, the holly and the yew.'

Hilaire Belloc,
on the chalk of Sussex

'Then came William, eorl of Normandy, into Pevensey on Michaelmas Even, and as soon as they were prepared, they built a stronghold at the town of Hastings. This was made known to King Harold; he gathered a great army and came against them at the ancient apple tree. William came upon them unawares, before they had gathered; the king, nevertheless, fought very hard against them with those men who would stay with him, and there were many killed on both sides.'

Anglo-Saxon Chronicles: 1066

'Bugger Bognor!'
King George V

LOCAL FOLKLORE

The Bosham Bell
During a raid by the Danes, the famous tenor bell was carried off from the church at Bosham, despite the pleadings of the monks. They rang a peal of thanksgiving on the remaining bells, that their lives had been spared – and heard an answering peal from the stolen tenor bell. The violent vibration of this sound caused the raiders' ship to rock, and the tenor bell slid off into the deep water. Despite all their efforts, the bell could not be recovered. Villagers claim that they often hear the tenor bell joining in with the ringing of the others. The local couplet runs:

'Ye bells of Bosham, ring for me,
For as ye ring, I ring wi' ye.'

St Wilfrid came to Sussex in 680, during a famine and drought. He prayed to God for rain – and the rain came. His miracle laid the foundation for his conversion of the people of Sussex to Christianity.

The Famous Curse of Battle Abbey
On the dissolution of the monasteries in the reign of Henry VIII, Battle Abbey was handed over to Sir Anthony Brown, owner of Cowdray Hall. Sir Anthony celebrated with a huge banquet in the Abbot's Hall. During this feast, a hooded monk approached him and delivered the following curse:

'By fire and water thy line shall come to an end, thus shall it perish out of the land!'

Two centuries later, in 1793, Cowdray Hall was gutted by fire. At the same time, its owner was drowned in the River Rhine. In 1815, the two sons of his only sister were drowned on the beach at Bognor. The Cowdray Estate passed out of the Brown family in 1843...

Smuggling
From the 17th to the 19th centuries, smuggling was a flourishing industry in the county. People from all walks of life were involved in one way or another. One Sunday, the vicar of Hove Parish Church arrived to take the service, and was surprised to hear the bells being rung. The Sexton told him, "It's no use, Sir, you can't preach today". "Why not?" exclaimed the vicar. "Because the church is full of tubs and the pulpits full of tea", came the reply.

The Grey Lady of Patcham Church
Many locals have seen the Grey Lady of Patcham Church, sitting in one of the pews. The next time they look, she has gone - but no-one has ever seen her walking out of the door...

Miscellany
It is said that the **Sun Oak**, near Coolhurst, on midsummer day will lay its shade across an acre of ground.

Every Sussex man knows that where **rosemary** flourishes, the 'missus' is the master.

DISTINCTIVE FLAVOUR

In the 18th and 19th centuries, **bird catching** was a way of life for many, especially in the Brighton area. Wheatears in particular were considered a delicacy.

Gingerbread was a speciality of Horsham. There were three main types – 'hared', 'rich' and 'dark brown', which contained treacle. A wide variety of different moulds were used.

Being a coastal county, fish is naturally very popular. The following are well-known local specialities: **Selsey cockle**, **Pulborough eel**, **Chichester lobster**, **Arundel mullet**, **Amberley trout**, and **Rye herring**. **Sussex smokery** is a dish of haddock, lemon juice and garlic.

Sussex pudding is famous.

Stoolball is a local game, very popular until the 18th century, although it is still played in some parts of Sussex today. Its rules are similar to cricket: there are 11 players in each team, using a bat something like a table tennis bat. The wicket is a 12-inch square stool, raised on a stake over 4 feet high.

In 1637, **Henry Brand of Selsey** was whacked on the head by a cricket bat wielded by Thomas Hatter, and he later died murmuring 'Who won?'

Sussex County Cricket Club was formed in 1839. Maurice Tate made his debut for Sussex at the age of 17. C B Fry and Ranjitsinhji were Sussex batsmen. Fry created a record in 1901 for a run of centuries and total runs of 3,000. David Sheppard captained Sussex in 1953. He later abandoned the game to enter Holy Orders.

A Sussex Toast
"'Ere's from we an' our'n to you an' your'n, for sure there never was folk, since folk was folk, ever loved folk 'arf as well as we an' our'n love you an' your'n."

COUNTY DIARY

January: Chess Congress, Hastings
Good Friday: Marbles Championships, Tinsley Green
Shrove Tuesday: Pancake race, Bodiam – women only
April: Clown Convention, Bognor Regis
May: Ceremony of Blessing the Sea, Hastings
Easter Monday: Polo meeting, Cowdray Park
May-August: Glyndebourne Festival Opera
June: South of England Show, Ardingly
June: Women's International Tennis Tournament, Eastbourne
July: The Gold Cup, Goodwood
August: National Town Criers' Championships, St Leonards
November: Annual International Sea Angling Festival, Hastings
November: Veteran Car Rally from London to Brighton

WARWICKSHIRE

COUNTY FACTS

Derivation of name: From the Anglo Saxon, meaning 'the dairy farm by a river dam'. War means an offshoot from a larger farm; Wic is a weir or dam, constructed for catching fish.

First Recorded: 1016 as Waeinewiscscr

Motto: Non Sanz Droict (Not Without Right)

County Town: Warwick

Towns: Atherstone, Aston, Bedworth, Birmingham, Castle Bromwich, Coleshill, Coventry, Edgbaston, Kenilworth, Leamington Spa, Nuneaton, Rugby, Selly Oak, Small Heath, Solihull, Stratford-upon-Avon, Sutton Coldfield, Warwick.

Coventry is a county of a city unto itself. Because Birmingham is squashed into the far north western corner of Warwickshire, many of its suberbs have pushed into surrounding counties, whilst the Yardley arm of Worcestershire acts like a pincer thrust from the south east up to Castle Bromwich almost cutting Birmingham off from the rest of the county.

Local Government

Warwickshire County Council and three Metropolitan Boroughs. There are five District Councils.

HISTORY

The region was part of the Kingdom of Mercia in the 7th and 8th centuries.

The Roman roads Watling Street, Fosse Way, and Icknield Street pass through or touch the county.

The impregnable castles of Warwick and Kenilworth were built in Norman times.

It was at Kenilworth Castle that Edward II signed the renunciation of his crown in 1327. After the failure of the Peasants' Revolt, John Ball fled to Coventry, where he was captured. Lollardy was rife in Coventry and many persecutions took place in 1485 and 1519. In 1519, seven craftsmen were burned, mainly for teaching their children the Lord's Prayer and the Ten Commandments in English.

Robert Catesby, a Warwickshire man, was a prime mover in the Gunpowder Plot, and there was a whole network of conspirators' houses in the county. When the plot failed, the conspirators rode madly off, stealing some of the King's horses from Warwick Castle. They were surrounded and defeated at Holbeche.

The first battle of the Civil War, the Battle of Edge Hill, was fought on October 23, 1642. It was an inconclusive battle, with many casualties on both sides.

INDUSTRY PAST AND PRESENT

Present industry includes vehicle manufacture, chocolate making, brewing, engineering and most kinds of light industry. In Norman times the county was almost wholly agricultural, with fine sheep pasturage. The woollen industry flourished, and Coventry in particular was famed for its wool and cloth.

Coalfields in the north grew in importance from the 17th century. The 18th century saw the silk industry flourishing at Coventry and Kenilworth, and the needle industry round Alcester. Birmingham became famous for its pens, pins, toys, and brooches.

LANDMARKS

Forest of Arden
Guy's Cliff

MONUMENTS

Kenilworth Castle, founded circa 1122 by Geoffrey de Clinton, the castle was turned into a palace by John of Gaunt in the 14th century. It later became the home of Robert Dudley, favourite of Elizabeth I.

Warwick Castle; this romantic medieval fortress was the home of the Earls of Warwick.

Baddesley Clinton, one of the finest examples of a medieval moated house in England.

Coventry Cathedral; the old cathedral was bombed during the Second World War. The present Cathedral, designed by Sir Basil Spence, was completed in 1962.

Arbury Hall; the Hall has an Elizabethan exterior, but the interior is in 'gothic revival' style. George Eliot was born on the estate.

Compton Wynyates, one of the finest Tudor houses in Britain, was begun in 1480 by Sir Edmund Compton. It is surmounted by twisted chimneys.

Packwood House is a timber-framed Tudor house built circa 1550.

Ragley Hall; this magnificent Palladian-style country mansion was begun in 1680, and decorated by Gibbs and Wyatt.

Stoneleigh Abbey is an Italianate mansion, built in the early 18th century, around the remains of an abbey. The 14th-century monastery gatehouse still survives.

TOPOGRAPHY INCLUDING RIVERS

Warwickshire, in the Midlands, is bordered by Staffordshire in the north, Leicestershire and Northamptonshire in the east, Oxfordshire and Gloucestershire in the south, and Worcestershire in the west.

It is a gently undulating county; a range of limestone hills rises on the south-eastern boundary, which includes Edgehill. The north of the county is the site of the ancient Forest of Arden, of which relatively little remains. The highest point is Ilmington Downs, 854 feet.

Rivers: Avon, Tame, Anker.

Royal Shakespeare Theatre, built in 1932 to replace the theatre destroyed by fire in 1926.

Anne Hathaway's Cottage; this timber-framed thatched cottage was the birthplace of the wife of William Shakespeare.

Charlecote Park, an Elizabethan mansion, much altered, but with the interior reconstructed in Elizabethan style in the 19th century.

Rugby School; the Public School, founded in 1567, and made more famous by Thomas Hughes' *Tom Brown's Schooldays*.

FAMOUS PEOPLE AND LOCAL CHARACTERS

Richard Neville was Earl of Warwick in the 15th century. He was known as 'Warwick the Kingmaker': during the Wars of the Roses, he first proclaimed the Yorkist Edward IV King, and later changed sides and restored the Lancastrian Henry VI.

Sir Thomas Malory, author of the *Morte d'Arthur*, is believed to have been the Lord of Newbold Revel. He represented Warwickshire in Parliament.

Michael Drayton, the poet, was born at Hatshill, near Nuneaton, in 1563.

William Shakespeare, the most celebrated playwright in the English language, was born on 23 April 1564 in Henley Street in Stratford-on-Avon. He was the son of a glover. He divided his time between London and Stratford, settling finally at New Place in Stratford in 1610. He died on 23 April 1616.

Dr Samuel Johnson lived for a while in Birmingham, during which time he had his first work published, and met and married his wife.

Walter Savage Landor, the writer, was born on January 30, 1775, in Warwick. He was educated at Knowle and Rugby.

Thomas Arnold became headmaster of Rugby School in 1828.

Mrs Gaskell went to Avonbank School in Stratford between 1824 and 1827.

George Eliot (Mary Ann Evans) was born on 22 November 1819 at South Farm on the Arbury Hall Estate, where her father was agent to the Newdigate family. She went to schools at Attleborough, Nuneaton, and Coventry.

Lewis Carroll attended Rugby School in 1846.

G M Trevelyan, the historian, was born in Stratford on February 16th 1876.

Rupert Brooke, the poet, was born on August 3rd, 1887, in Rugby.

THE GUILD HALL, ASTON CANTLOW

ART AND LITERATURE

Henry James described Warwickshire as '*The core and centre of the English world; midmost England, unmitigated England...the genius of pastoral Britain.*'

'*The road very wide and smooth; rows of fine trees on the sides of it. Beautiful whitethorn hedges, and rows of ash and elm dividing the fields; the fields so neatly kept, the soil so rich; the herds and flocks of fine cattle and sheep on every side...Here is wealth! Here are all the means of national power, and of individual plenty and happiness!*'

Cobbett,
on Warwickshire, in The Political Register (1817)

'*What, would you make me mad? Am not I Christopher Sly, old Sly's son of Burton-heath; by birth a pedlar, by education a card-maker, by Transmutation a bear-herd, and now by present profession a tinker?*'

William Shakespeare
Christopher Sly in The Taming of the Shrew

George Eliot describes Arbury Hall as Cheverel Manor in *Scenes of Clerical Life* (1858):

'*A charming picture Cheverel Manor would have made that evening, if some English Watteau had been there to paint it: the castellated house of grey-tinted stone, with the flickering sunbeams sending dashes of golden light across the many-shaped panes in the mullioned windows, and a great beech leaning athwart one of the flanking towers, and breaking, with its dark flattened boughs, the too formal symmetry of the front; the broad gravel-walk winding to the right, by a row of tall pines, alongside the pool — on the left branching out among swelling grassy mounds, surmounted by clumps of trees, where the red trunk of the Scotch fir glows in the descending sunlight against the bright green of limes and acacias...*'

LOCAL FOLKLORE

Guy's Cliffe

Guy was a poor boy, who proved his worth through prodigious feats of arms, and married Phyllis, daughter of the Earl of Warwick. He went on a crusade to the Holy Land, and later returned, to fight the Danes outside Winchester. Single-handed, he fought the Danish giant Colbrand, and slew him. Amongst other celebrated feats, he strangled a wild boar; he rid Dunsmore Heath of the terrifying Dun Cow; and he vanquished many dragons. He then retired to live as a hermit in a cave in the Forest of Arden. Each day he went to beg for food at Warwick Castle, and was fed by his wife, Phyllis, although she was unaware of who he was. Just before his death, however, he revealed his identity to her. She died two weeks after him, and they were buried together in the same grave. The cave in which Guy lived as a hermit is known as Guy's Cliffe.

The Legend of Edgehill

Legend has it that for several nights after the famous Battle of Edgehill, two phantom armies could be seen, and heard, fighting the battle all over again. Each night, after the King's soldiers had been defeated and fled the scene of battle, the Parliamentary soldiers would remain for a time in triumph, and then they too would vanish.

Lady Godiva

Lady Godiva was the wife of Earl Leofric of Mercia. The town of Coventry was oppressed by heavy tolls imposed by Leofric, and Lady Godiva begged him to relieve the townspeople from the heavy burden. Leofric refused to listen to her, but she continued to petition him on their behalf, until in exasperation he promised to grant her wish if she would consent to ride naked through the town, from one end to the other. Leofric assumed that she would not assent to this suggestion, but Lady Godiva unexpectedly agreed. She let down her long hair, which covered her body like a veil, and, attended by two knights, she rode on horseback through Coventry and returned triumphantly to the castle. Leofric in his astonishment freed the townsfolk from their tolls, and granted them a charter to confirm his action.

One version of the legend has it that, on realizing his wife's determination, Leofric ordered the people of Coventry to remain indoors, and not look out of their windows during his wife's ride, on pain of death. Everyone naturally obeyed, with the exception of a Taylor named Tom. As Lady Godiva passed his house, he peeped out of a window - and was immediately struck blind by an act of God. He was thereafter known as 'Peeping Tom'.

DISTINCTIVE FLAVOUR

Warwickshire has variously been described as 'Shakespeare Country', and 'the Country of the Bard'.

Warwickshire County Cricket Club was founded in 1884. Their main ground is at Edgbaston in Birmingham. Their badge is a bear and ragged staff.

The game of Rugby originated in Rugby: a tablet on Doctor's Wall at the school tells that it was 'the exploit of William Webb Ellis, who with a fine disregard for the rules of football as played in his time, first took the ball in his arms and ran with it, thus originating the distinctive feature of this Rugby game AD 1823.'

BADDESLEY CLINTON

WARWICK

COUNTY DIARY

April:	Shakespeare's Birthday Procession, Stratford-on-Avon
April:	International Antiques Fair, NEC, Birmingham
May:	National Classic Motor Show, NEC, Birmingham
June:	Royal International Horse Show, NEC, Birmingham
July:	Royal International Agricultural Show, Stoneleigh
October:	International Motor Show, NEC, Birmingham

WESTMORLAND

COUNTY FACTS

Derivation of name: Westmorland comes from the Old English 'Westmoringaland', meaning 'land of the people west of the moors'.
First Recorded: 966 as Westmoringaland
County Town: Appleby
Towns: Ambleside, Appleby-in-Westmorland, Grasmere, Kendal, Kirkby Lonsdale, Kirkby Stephen, Milnthorpe, Shap, Windermere.
To promote recognition of the continuing existence of Westmorland as a county, despite no longer having a County Council, the County Town of Appleby officially added Westmorland to its name, hence: Appleby-in-Westmorland.

Local Government
Cumbria County Council and one District Council.

HISTORY

In early times, the region was part of the kingdom of the Strathclyde Britons.
St Cuthbert brought Christianity to the region in the 7th century.
Henry I constituted the county of Westmorland, which was composed of two baronies – that of Appleby and that of Kendal. Hugh de Morvill, Baron of Appleby, was one of the assassins of Thomas Becket.
In 1584, in the Border wars with the Scots, the county sent 4,152 horsemen, 1,400 archers, and 1,300 bill-men.
Westmorland was Royalist during the Civil War.

INDUSTRY PAST AND PRESENT

The most prominent industry remains sheep farming and its attendant services, though tourism is an essential part of the economy. Sheep farming has been carried on in the moorland districts for centuries. The clothing industry was introduced to Kendal by John Kempe of Flanders during the reign of Edward III, and spread to the surrounding districts. The distinctive Kendal cloth was known from the 15th century.

TOPOGRAPHY INCLUDING RIVERS

Westmorland, in the north-west of England, is bordered by Cumberland in the north, Durham and Yorkshire in the east, Yorkshire and Lancashire in the south, and Lancashire in the west.
The Pennine hills rise in the east of the county, and further west, the beautiful Eden valley runs from the south-east north through Kirkby Stephen and Appleby. Further west rise the mountains and hills (known as 'Fells') of the Lake District, including Helvellyn on the western border. Further south is the Kendal valley. The lakes include Windermere, Ullswater, Haweswater, and Grasmere, and there are many smaller lakes, or tarns, higher up in the fells. The highest point is Helvellyn, on the Cumberland border, 3118 feet
Rivers: Eden and Rothay.

The clothing industry began to decline in the early 18th century; about this time, comb manufacture, and the boot and shoe trade began in Kendall.

LANDMARKS
The Lake District
Lake Windermere, the largest natural lake in England
Helvellyn
Kirkstone Pass
Loughrigg Fell
Langdale Pikes
Grisedale

MONUMENTS
Levens Hall; originally a medieval refuge tower against the Scots, Levens Hall was converted into a mansion circa 1586. The gardens were laid out between 1689 and 1700.
Sizergh Castle; the peel tower was built circa 1350; the medieval house was added later. Sizergh Castle has been owned by the Strickland family for 700 years.
Dove Cottage; the home of William and Dorothy Wordsworth from 1799 to 1808.

FAMOUS PEOPLE AND LOCAL CHARACTERS
Catherine Parr, the sixth wife of Henry VIII, is believed to have been born at Kendal Castle.
Cardinal Christopher Bainbrigg, Archbishop of York from 1508 to 1514, was born near Appleby.
Bernard Gilpin, the 'Apostle of the North', was born in Kentmore in 1517.
George Romney, the artist, lived and died in Kendal.
John Robinson, an 18th-century politician from Appleby, is said to have been the original 'Jack Robinson'.
Richard Watson, Bishop of Llandaff from 1782 to 1816, and Professor of chemistry at Cambridge, was born in Heversham, and lived at Calgarth on Windermere.
William Wordsworth and his sister **Dorothy** settled in Grasmere in 1798. Wordsworth

HELVELLYN

married in 1802. The family moved to Rydal Mount above Rydal Water in 1813, and he spent the rest of his life there. He became poet laureate in 1843. He died on April 23, 1850, and is buried in Grasmere Churchyard. It was at Gowbarrow Park that he saw the celebrated 'host of golden daffodils'.

Thomas de Quincey took over Dove Cottage from the Wordsworths, moving in with over 5,000 books. He was editor of the *Westmorland Gazette* for a year.

Michael Faraday, the scientist and founder of the science of electromagnetism, was born in Kirkby Stephen in 1791.

Thomas Arnold, the headmaster of Rugby School, moved to Fox House, just outside Ambleside, in 1832. His son, Matthew Arnold, the poet, spent much of his childhood and youth there.

ART AND LITERATURE

'If from the public way you turn your steps
Up the tumultuous brook of Greenhead Ghyll,
You will suppose that with an upright path
Your feet must struggle; in such bold ascent
The pastoral mountains front you, face to face.
But, courage! for around that boisterous brook
The mountains have all opened out themselves,
And made a hidden valley of their own,
No habitation can be seen; but they
Who journey thither find themselves alone
With a few sheep, with rocks and stones, and kites
That overhead are sailing in the sky.'
William Wordsworth
Michael. A Pastoral Poem (1800)

'The left hand wind with all his rout
The lusty Lord Dacre did lead

With him the bows of Kendal stout
With milk-white coats and crosses red.'
The Battle of Flodden Field

'We entered Westmorland, a County eminent only for being the wildest, most barren and frightful of any that I have passed over in England...'
Daniel Defoe
Tour Through the Whole Island of Great Britain (1724-6)

'We walked...along the border of Windermere all beautiful with wooded shores and islands - our road was a winding lane, wooded on each side, and green overhead, full of Foxgloves – every now and then a glimpse of the lake, and all the while Kirkstone and other large hills nestled together in a sort of grey black mist.'
John Keats, 1818

LOCAL FOLKLORE

Robin the Devil

Major Robert Philipson, a Royalist, was besieged on Belle Isle by Colonel Briggs, a Roundhead. Philipson, who became known as 'Robin the Devil', is said to have ridden his horse into Kendal Church in a vain attempt to have his revenge on Briggs, who was attending a service at the time.

Legend has it that the ruins in Mallerstang known as **Pendragon Castle** are the remains of a castle built by Uther Pendragon, the father of King Arthur.

Devil's Bridge, Kirkby Lonsdale

A cow belonging to an old woman wandered across the River Lune, and when she went to fetch it back, she found the river in full spate, far too deep and swiftly flowing for her to cross.

As she stood wondering how to retrieve her cow, the devil suddenly appeared, and offered to build her a bridge over the river. All he asked in return was the first living thing to go across it. The old woman agreed to the bargain.

When she came back the next day, she found the bridge built, and the devil awaiting his payment. The devil was expecting her to come across the bridge to fetch the cow, but she, being a wily old woman, had seen through his plan. She set down a little dog which she had hidden under her cloak, and threw a bun onto the bridge. The dog ran after it, and thereby fulfilled the old lady's part of the contract. But according to legend, a dog has no soul, so the devil gained nothing. With a howl of rage, he vanished.

DISTINCTIVE FLAVOUR

The people of Westmorland are typically said to be: tall, wiry, long-armed, big-handed, dark-grey-eyed; cautious, reserved, staid, matter-of-fact, sober-minded, unemotional, and thrifty.

Kendal is known as 'the Auld Grey Town', because of its many grey limestone buildings.

'Kendal Green' was the distinctive green woollen cloth made in the town.

Westmorland Three Decker. This county speciality consists of three layers of fruit sandwiched between four layers of pastry, baked in the oven for an hour. Sometimes two different fruits are used.

The motto of the town of Kendal is 'Pannus mihi panis', meaning 'Wool is my bread'.

COUNTY DIARY

August: Grasmere Sports, Grasmere
September: Westmorland County Show, Kendal

WILTSHIRE

COUNTY FACTS

Derivation of name: Anglo-Saxon, derived from West Saxon settlers known as the Wilsaetan who lived along the Wylye valley. Saetan means settlers. Their main village, Wilton, 'farmstead on the banks of the Wylye', became the first centre of Wiltshire.
First Recorded: 878 as Wiltunschir
County Town: Trowbridge
Towns: Aldbourne, Amesbury, Avebury, Bradford on Avon, Calne, Chippenham, Chiseldon, Corsham, Cricklade, Devizes, Durrington, Hawthorn, Highworth, Holt, Lacock, Lyneham, Malmesbury, Marlborough, Melksham, Mere, Pewsey, Ramsbury, Salisbury, Stratton St Margaret, Swindon, Tisbury, Trowbridge, Warminster, Westbury, Westbury Leigh, Wilton, Wootton Bassett, Wroughton.

Government
Local: Wiltshire County Council and five district councils. With three distant detached parts of the county around Wokingham, Twyford and Swallowfield under Berkshire County Council control and two small detached parts under Gloucestershire County Council. There are also small straggling areas in the south-west under the administration of Hampshire County Council.

HISTORY

Wiltshire was the heartland of the kingdom of Wessex in Anglo-Saxon times. Wilton was the capital of Wessex.

Purton village is thought to have been the site of the Battle of Ellandune between Wessex and Mercia in 823, when 'the brook of Ellandune ran red with gore, stood dammed with battle-wreck, grew foul with mouldering corpses.'

878 - the Danes were defeated at the Battle of Ethandun by Alfred the Great; they were forced to surrender, and left Wessex for good.

1086 – William the Conqueror held a great council at Old Sarum, at which he made arrangements for the Domesday Book to be compiled.

During the Civil War between King Stephen and Empress Matilda, Marlborough Castle is supposed to have been the stronghold of Baron FitzGilbert, 'the worst robber-baron of them all'.

The Protestant martyrs, John Maundrell and his companions, were burned at the stake at Salisbury in 1556.

1643 – Siege of Wardour Castle, in which Lady Blanche Arundell held out for 5 days and nights with 50 retainers, against a parliamentary army of 1,300 men.

1645 – The steeple of Calne parish church collapsed. John Aubrey remarked, 'One of the pillars was faulty, and the churchwardens were dilatory, as is usual in such cases'. The disaster was caused, according to Aubrey, by 'the throwing of a stone by a boy'.

Three disastrous town fires hit Marlborough in 1653, 1679 and 1690; after the last one the town passed a byelaw prohibiting the use of thatch within its boundaries.

In 1666 a group of young aristocrats took refuge from the Great Plague of London at Carlton House. Among them was John Dryden. It was here that he wrote his *Annus Mirabilis*, which describes the events of that year.

INDUSTRY PAST AND PRESENT

Some present day industries are: Dairying, barley, wheat, pigs, Swindon railway works, bacon-curing.

In the Middle Ages, Wiltshire had a thriving weaving industry, based on the sheep that grazed the hills around the Vale of Avon.

Dew pond making is an old Wiltshire craft. Dew ponds are shallow artificial ponds which rarely if ever dry up, even during prolonged drought. The dew pond at Oxenmere is reputed to be the oldest in England.

In the 18th century, Wiltshire was producing more than 5,000 tons of cheese a year.

LANDMARKS

Salisbury Plain

Avebury – one of the largest prehistoric stone circles in the world, mostly demolished

Silbury Hill – the largest artificial mound in Europe

Savernake Forest – over 4,000 acres, 16 miles round

The Forest of Clarendon – a favourite hunting ground of Norman and Medieval kings

White horses: Two in Pewsey Vale; one on Hackpen Hill; one on the downs above Broadtown; one on hill above Cherhill; one the oldest, on the north-west scarp of Salisbury Plain; and one near Marlborough.

West Kennet Long Barrow, dating from circa 2000 BC, it was used for burials for about 300 years.

TOPOGRAPHY INCLUDING RIVERS

Wiltshire is bordered by Gloucestershire to the north, Berkshire and Hampshire to the east, Dorset to the south, and Somerset to the west. Two-thirds of the country, in the south and east, are rolling chalk downs; the north-west lowlands are meadow dairy land – land of milk and cheese: hence the saying 'As different as chalk from cheese.' – adding, 'And chalk is church, while cheese is chapel'. The highest point is Milk Hill, near Alton Barnes, 964 feet.
Rivers: Avon, Wylye, Kennet, Nadder, Bourne.

MONUMENTS

Stonehenge – dating from circa 2000 BC is probably Britain's best known National monument.

Longleat House is an Elizabethan house without; a 19th-century re-creation within.

Wilton House boasts the exquisite Double Cube Room, whose decorations and proportions have never ceased to seduce the visitor.

Salisbury Cathedral is so obviously impressive that even in the 17th-century, when Gothic was considered vulgar, it won the heartfelt praise of Sir Christopher Wren. Its spire is perhaps the most painted of all subjects for watercolourists.

Lacock Abbey like Woburn Abbey is a secular building, pirated from the wreckage of a major monastery. At Lacock, the monk's cloister has been adapted to make a courtyard house of subtle charm.

Stourhead's magnificent landscape gardens are too popular for their own good – it is impossible for the visitor to appreciate their intended effect of artful solitude.

Malmesbury Abbey, though distressingly reduced, can nonetheless reward the visitor with Romanesque carvings of the first rank, and 14th-century vaults of unexpected grace.

RAF Lyneham – base of RAF Transport Command.

FAMOUS PEOPLE AND LOCAL CHARACTERS

Thomas à Becket, later Archbishop of Canterbury, lived at Ford, as parish priest of Winterbourne.

William Ayscough, Bishop of Salisbury, took refuge in Edington Church during Jack Cade's Rebellion, a peasant revolt, in 1449. The mob dragged him out and up the hill, where they stoned him to death.

King Henry VIII met **Jane Seymour** at Wulfhall.

Lord Chief Justice Popham, who presided at the trials of Sir Walter Raleigh and Guy Fawkes, lived in Wiltshire.

Sir Stephen Fox, Paymaster General to the Forces under Charles II, was born at Farley.

Sir Christopher Wren was born in East Knoyle in 1631.

John Aubrey, 17th century naturalist and antiquarian, was born at Easton Piers.

George Crabbe (1754-1832) was rector of Trowbridge for 18 years.

Dr John Priestley, tutor to the Marquis of Shelbourne's sons, discovered oxygen gas in the 'laboratory' at Bowood House, in 1774.

William Fox Talbot, pioneer of photography, lived in Lacock Abbey. He took his first successful photograph in 1835, from the oriel window of the Abbey.

Great Somerford was the home of **Captain Mark Phillips**, husband of the Princess Royal.

Local Characters

The wife of **Sir Thomas Bonham**, of Wishford, presented him with twins. He, alarmed at this increase in his family, his fortune being very low, set off on a Crusade to the Holy Land. He was gone 7 years. Just before his wife was due to remarry, he returned, although he was so unkempt and unshaven that she didn't recognize him until he had had a bath. She duly called off her impending marriage. Within a year, she presented Sir Thomas with another addition to the family – septuplets. They were carried to the church in a seive to be baptised. The seive hung in the church for centuries, and a seive with 7 dolls in it used to be carried every year in the Wishford Oak Apple Day Procession.

Lyddie Shears, the celebrated witch, lived in Winterslow.

The thresher-poet **Stephen Duck** was born at Charlton St Peter in 1705. He was taken to London, where his poetry was much admired for a short while, until he fell from favour and became a figure of fun at court. Unable to return to Wiltshire, nor to put up with the persecution, he drowned himself. Each year, he is supposedly commemorated by the 'Duck Feast' at Charlton, when a toast is drunk to his memory by 13 'Duck' men.

Richard Jefferies and **Alfred Williams**, poets and naturalists, came from Swindon.

In the 11th century, a monk from Malmesbury, one **Elmer**, fastened fabricated wings to his hands and feet, and tried to fly from the tower, like Daedalus. According to the historian, William of Malmesbury, he flew 'more than the distance of a furlong; but, agitated by the violence of the wind and the current of air, as well as by the consciousness of his rash attempt, he fell and broke his legs and was lame ever after.'

A **Thomas Gawain of Broadchalke**, in return for certain services, was entitled to 'Christmas day dinner at the Abbey of Wilton and afterwards he could go on drinking as long as he could see without candles'.

ART AND LITERATURE

'The view was over a broad plain, beautiful with wheat, and enclosed by a perfect amphitheatre of green hills. Through these hills there was one narrow groove, or pass, southwards, where the white clouds seemed to close on the horizon. Woods hid the scattered hamlets and farmhouses.'
Richard Jefferies
The Story of My Heart

'Alderbury without a Prewitt Is like figgetty pudden without suet.'
Local saying

'The turfe is of short sweet grasse, good for the sheep, and delightfull to the eye, for its amoothness like a bowling green, and pleasant to the traveller, who wants here only a variety of objects to make his journey lesse tedious, for here is…not a tree, or rarely a bush to shelter one from a shower.'
John Aubrey OE

Charles I did *'love Wilton above all places'*; he went there every summer.

LOCAL FOLKLORE

Stonehenge

Stonehenge was erected by the Devil in a single night. As he flew through the air, he boasted that no-one would ever know how the stones got there. A friar, hiding in a ditch, retorted, 'Ah, that's more than thee canst tell!' The startled Devil dropped the stone he was carrying into the brook at Bruford, where it remains. In a rage, he seized one of the great stones and hurled it at the friar, whom it hit on the heel. Hence the name of the heel stone, which stood 100ft outside the great circle.

The Gipsy's Curse, Odstock

Joshua Scamp was an honest gipsy who lived in the 19th century. His son-in-law, having borrowed his coat, stole a horse in South Newton, leaving Joshua's coat to incriminate him. For his daughter's sake, Scamp refused to plead his innocence, and so was hanged. The gipsy tribe in the region came to regard Scamp as a martyr, and assembled at Odstock on the anniversary of his death; the celebrations gradually became more uproarious as the years went by. Eventually a church meeting resolved to stop it. The briar rose planted on Joshua's grave was pulled, and the church door was locked.

The gipsies were furious. The gipsy queen cursed the parson, the sexton, the churchwardens, a couple of renegade gipsies who had enrolled as special constables, and lastly, anyone who in future should lock the church door. The parson's curse was that within a year his voice would no longer be

SALISBURY

heard from the pulpit; he had a stroke which affected his speech. The sexton's curse was that death would come swiftly and suddenly; he was found dead by the roadside one morning. The valuable herd of cattle belonging to the chief warden was destroyed by anthrax, and his curse, that no son of his would inherit his farm, proved true, when all his male children were born dead. The renegade gipsies mysteriously disappeared.

In this century, two people who have both locked the church door have met an untimely death soon afterwards. After the second death, the church key was thrown into the river...

The Vicar of Chute

During the plague, the Vicar of Chute persuaded the victims to go to a camp prepared for them on the causeway, a section of the Roman Road, where he said he would see that those that survived were fed until the epidemic passed. He then went away, and left them all to starve. His penitent ghost is said to haunt the Chute causeway to this day.

THE TOMB OF WILLIAM LONGESPÉE

Devizes Cross

There is an inscription on Devizes market cross which reads: 'On Thursday the 25th January 1753, Ruth Pierce, of Pottern in this county, agreed with 3 other women to buy a sack of wheat in the market, each paying her due proportion towards the same. One of these women, in collecting the several quota of the money, discovered a deficiency and demanded of Ruth Pierce the sum which was wanting to make good the amount. Ruth Pierce protested that she had paid her share, and said that she wished that she might drop down dead if she had not. She rashly repeated this wish; when to the consternation and terror of the surrounding multitude, she instantly fell down and expired, having the money concealed in her hand.'

The Bishop's Canning Men

Two Bishop's Canning men were found one moonlit night raking the surface of a local pond with hayrakes. On being challenged, they pointed to the reflection of the moon in the pond, and said they were trying to retrieve 'thik gurt yaller cheese'. The men who had challenged them rode off and quickly spread the word about these 'dunner-haided soons, a-raking atter the shadder of the moon'. They made verses up about it – and any Wiltshire man is known as a Moonraker. The twist to the story is that the challengers were excisemen, searching for smugglers, which is just what the Bishop's Canning men were. At the bottom of the pond were kegs of brandy, left there earlier for safety. The mime of half-wits raking the moon was the best ruse the smugglers could think of on the spur of the moment – and it worked!

'Ah, we were too vly war they! There bain't no vlies on we!'

DISTINCTIVE FLAVOUR

Wiltshire words:

To snark	= to snore
To pussyvanter	= to waste time, dither
A diggles	= an abundance
To lollop	= to lounge about

Wessex people are known for their slowness of movement.

Oak Apple Day is held at Wishford on 29 May. All the villagers go up the hill to cut green wood with which to decorate their houses and the church. Prizes are given for the best decorated, and for the branches with the most oak-apples on.

Downton Cuckoo Fair used to be held on April 12, because cuckoos arrive in Southern England about then. On April 12 they used to open the forest gate at Downton to let the cuckoo through!

One of the last strongholds of the **Snakeshead Fritillary** in England is to be found in North Wiltshire.

There is a nature reserve specifically for the protection of the **Purple Emperor** butterfly at Blackmoor Copse, near Farley.

The **Great Bustard** appears on the Wiltshire coat of arms. Attempts are being made to rehabilitate a few bustards in an enclosure of several acres near Porton.

The rare **Hobby Falcon** has its main preserve on Salisbury Plain.

Wiltshire is the chief habitat of the **Cirl Bunting.**

COUNTY DIARY

Good Friday:	International Canoe Race, Devizes to Westminster
May:	Grovely Forest Rights – Oak Apple Day, Wishford
June 21:	Druids' Dawn Ceremony, Stonehenge

WORCESTERSHIRE

COUNTY FACTS

Derivation of name: Worcester comes from the Anglicized Latin, meaning 'fort of the Wigoran'.

First Recorded: c. 1040 as Wirceastrescir

County Town: Worcester

Towns: Alvechurch, Bewdley, Broadway, Bromsgrove, Droitwich, Dudley, Evesham, Great Malvern, Hagley, Halesowen, Kempsey, Kidderminster, Malvern Wells, Pershore, Redditch, Rednal, Rubery, Stourbridge, Stourport-on-Severn, Tenbury Wells, Upton-upon-Severn, Worcester. Worcester is a county of a city unto itself.

Local Government

Hereford and Worcester County Council, and three Metropolitan Boroughs. There are six District Councils.

The parishes of Yardley, Moseley and Kings Norton thrust themselves into Warwickshire as far as Birmingham. The parishes of Oldberrow, Alderminster, Tredington, Shipston-on-Stour and Tidmington are detached parishes under Warwickshire County Council. One of the most important parts of detached Worcestershire is Dudley, an island of the county in Staffordshire. Other instances of such detachment are legion.

HISTORY

The region was converted to Christianity in the 7th century by missionaries from Lindisfarne and Whitby. The Abbey of Evesham was founded at the beginning of the 8th century. The region then grew in prosperity.

In 1041, Worcester was razed to the ground by Hardicanute in revenge for a revolt by the townsfolk against taxes.

The county suffered from raids by the Danish and the Welsh; Benedictine monasteries, such as at Worcester and Evesham, were fortified for the defence of the county.

In the 16th and 17th centuries, the manufacture of cloth grew into a thriving trade in the county, and the clothiers became the ruling body, until the Civil War.

In the Civil War, the landed gentry mostly sided with the King, and the clothiers for Parliament. Worcester was the first city to declare for the king, and the last to surrender in 1646. The county saw much fighting during the Civil War, and was considerably impoverished as a result.

In 1651, Charles II marched into Worcester with his Scottish army, and received a warm welcome from the citizens. Cromwell and his army took up their positions outside the city gates, and Charles and his army attacked their camp. At first they were successful, but then reinforcements, led by Lambert, came to Cromwell's aid, and the King's army was completely routed. Charles had to flee for his life.

After the war, non-conformism was rife in the county, and Quakerism abounded.

INDUSTRY PAST AND PRESENT

Worcester industries include: potteries (Royal Worcester), fruit growing, ironworks, electrical manufactures, engineering and agriculture with much fruit growing in evidence.

The salt-beds in Droitwich were worked from early times. The Romans paid their soldiers partly with Droitwich salt, from which comes the word salary (sal = salt). Pershore got its name in Saxon times from the pear orchards around it; fruit-growing and the making of cider and perry flourished particularly in the 16th century. The clothing industry also thrived at this time. The silk trade was carried on in Kidderminster and Blockley in the 17th and 18th centuries. In 1751, Dr Wall of Worcester, who had been working on a substitute for china clay, opened the first porcelain factory. Worcester also saw the development of the glove trade.

LANDMARKS

Malvern Hills
Vale of Evesham
Clent Hills
Wyre Forest

MONUMENTS

Hanbury Hall is a red-brick house built in 1701.

Worcester Cathedral; much of the cathedral dates from the 14th century, although the earliest part was built by Bishop Wulfstan in the 11th century.

Bretforton Manor; this 16th-century gabled mansion was built on the site of a ruined monastery.

Hartlebury Castle, the residence of the bishops of Worcester for more than 1,000 years. The present mansion was built in 1675.

Pershore Abbey; King Ethelred endowed a monastery on this site in AD 689. Most of

TOPOGRAPHY INCLUDING RIVERS

Worcestershire, in the Midlands, is bordered by Shropshire and Staffordshire in the north, Warwickshire in the east, Gloucestershire in the south, and Herefordshire in the west.

The hilly, wooded region in the north west is all that remains of the once mighty Wyre Forest. The central plain of Worcestershire is bordered in the west by the sharp ridge of the Malvern Hills, which rise to 1,395 feet at Worcestershire Beacon, and form the boundary with Herefordshire. To the north of the plain, towards Birmingham, are the Clent and Lickey Hills. The fertile vale of Severn runs north to south through the centre of the county, and in the south, the Avon winds through the wooded Vale of Evesham. Bredon Hill, 991 feet high, is close to the southern border.

Rivers: Stour, Severn, Teme, Avon.

what survives today dates from the 13th century.

FAMOUS PEOPLE AND LOCAL CHARACTERS

Samuel Butler, the author of *Hudibras*, was born at Strensham in 1612, the son of a farmer. He went to school at Worcester, and worked as secretary to Thomas Jeffery, a Justice, at Earl's Cross.

Samuel Johnson went to school for a time in Stourbridge.

William Shenstone, the poet, was born on November 13th, 1714, in Halesowen.

Lucien Bonaparte, brother of Napoleon, lived in exile in Thorngrove for a short time.

Sir Rowland Hill was born in Kidderminster in 1795. He established the penny post.

William Huskisson, MP for the county, was the first victim of a railway accident: he was knocked down and killed at the opening of the route between Manchester and Liverpool.

Mrs Henry Wood (author of *East Lynne*) grew up in Sidbury.

Jenny Lind, known as the 'Swedish Nightingale', lived at Wynd's Point in Malvern. She was the founder of musical scholarships.

Edward Elgar, the composer, was born in Upper Broadheath in 1857.

A E Housman was born on 26 March 1859 in Fockbury, the son of a solicitor. He was educated at Bromsgrove School, and taught there for a short while.

Stanley Baldwin, three times Prime Minister, was born at Astley Hall in Bewdley in 1867.

Mrs Woodhul-Martin, the only woman to contend for the Presidency of the USA, came to live at Norton Park.

ART AND LITERATURE

'The dark, rich flats of hedgy Worcestershire'
Henry James
A Passionate Pilgrim (1875)

'[Hagley Park] is a hill of three miles, but broke into all manner of beauty; such lawns, such woods, rills, cascades, and a thickness of verdure quite to the summit of the hill, and commanding such a vale of towns, and meadows, and woods extending quite to the Black Mountains in Wales, that I quite forgot my favourite Thames…'
Horace Walpole

'In summertime on Bredon
*   The bells they sound so clear;*
Round both the shires they ring them

In steeples far and near
A happy noise to hear.'
A E Housman
Bredon Hill

'Meantime you gain the Height, from whose fair Brow
The bursting prospect spreads immense around;
And snatch'd o'er Hill and Dale, the Wood and Lawn,
And verdant Field, and darkening Heath between,
And villages embosom'd soft in Trees,
And spiry Towns by dusky columns mark'd
Of rising Smoke, your Eye excursive roams…
To where the broken Landskip by degrees,
Ascending, roughens into ridgy Hills;
O'er which the Cambrian mountains, like far Clouds
That skirt the blue horizon, doubtful, rise.'
James Thomson,
on Hagley Park, in The Seasons (1726-30)

LOCAL FOLKLORE

Osebury Rock

A man and a boy were ploughing one day in the field when they heard the sound of crying coming from Osebury Rock. They went to investigate, and there found a fairy crying that he had lost his pick. The ploughman found it for him, and the fairy in gratitude told them that if they looked in a corner of the field where they had been ploughing, they would find their reward. When they went to look, they found bread, cheese, and cider laid out for them.

Inkberrow's Ting-Tang

Many years ago, the church at Inkberrow was pulled down, and building started on a new site. Now this site chanced to be very near where some fairies lived, and they were not happy that the church should be built so close to them. For a long while, the building work was obstructed, and the workmen would arrive each morning to find the stones they had laid the day before removed to the site of the previous church. However, they persevered, and eventually the church was rebuilt. For many years afterwards, a voice could be heard lamenting from time to time:
Neither sleep, neither lie,
For Inkbro's ting-tang hangs so high.

DISTINCTIVE FLAVOUR

Worcestershire Sauce is made in Worcester, from the recipe of Sir Marcus Sandys, once Governor of Bengal. The ingredients are brown vinegar, walnut ketchup, anchovy essence, soy sauce, cayenne, and shallots. Traditionally, this mixture is bottled, and

THE EDGAR TOWER, LEADING TO THE PRECINCTS OF WORCESTER CATHEDRAL

shaken two or three times a day for a fortnight.

Worcestershire County Cricket Club was founded in 1865. Their main ground is at Worcester. Their badge is a shield argent bearing fesse between three pears sable.

Great Malvern is known for its waters, whose medicinal properties have been celebrated for over 300 years.

Worcestershire was once **described by a cartographer** as giving the impression that a bomb had blown it up, with all its bits strewn into other counties. This is on account of the very large number of detached portions away from the main body of the county. They can be found in Warwickshire; Gloucestershire; Herefordshire; Staffordshire and in the case of Daylesford and Icomb, locked between Gloucestershire and Oxfordshire.

COUNTY DIARY

June:	Three Counties Show, Great Malvern
August:	Three Choirs Festival, held alternately at Worcester, Hereford, and Gloucester
June:	Jazz Festival, Upton-on-Severn

YORKSHIRE

COUNTY FACTS

Derivation of name: York comes originally from the Latinized Celtic Eboracum, meaning the estate of Eburos; to this was added the wic (dwelling) termination by the Angles, producing Eoforwic. This was rendered as Jörvic by the Danes, which then became York.

First Recorded: 1050 as Eoferwicucir

Motto: Audi Consilium (Heed Counsel)

County Town: York

Major Towns:

North Riding: Guisborough, Marske, Middlesbrough, Northallerton, Pickering, Richmond, Scarborough, Thirsk, Whitby.

East Riding: Beverley, Bridlington, Filey, Hedon, Kingston-upon-Hull, Pocklington. Kingston-upon-Hull is a county of a city unto itself.

West Riding: Barnsley, Bingley, Bradford, Castleford, Dewsbury, Doncaster, Goole, Halifax, Harrowgate, Huddersfield, Leeds, Pontefract, Rotherham, Saddleworth, Selby, Skipton, Todmorden, Wakefield. Todmorden is shared between Lancashire and Yorkshire, with the boundary running down the middle of the High Street.

Local Government

North Riding: Cleveland County Council and North Yorkshire County Council, and seven District Councils.

East Riding: Humberside County Council and North Yorkshire County Council, and seven District Councils.

West Riding: Humberside County Council (around Goole), North Yorkshire County Council, nine Metropolitan Boroughs and five District Councils.

York is a county of a city unto itself.

HISTORY

Before the Roman Conquest, the region was occupied by a fierce tribe known as the Brigantes.

During the Roman Occupation, Eboracum (York) became the chief seat of government for the whole island of Britain. Constantine the Great was proclaimed Roman Emperor at York in AD 306.

After the departure of the Romans, the region was invaded by the English, who founded the Kingdom of Deira on the chalk downs east of York and in the fens of Holderness. The inhabitants were converted to Christianity by Paulinus, who became Bishop of York.

In 664, at the Council of Whitby, it was decided that the Christian customs of Rome should be adopted, rather than those of the Celts.

Caedmon, the father of English song, lived as a servant in Whitby. He knew nothing about singing, or verse-making, and used to avoid it, until he was commanded to sing in a dream. He later became a monk.

Religion, literature and learning flourished in the region in the 7th and 8th centuries.

In 867 the region was attacked by the Danes, who made it their chief stronghold. They divided York into three parts or 'tredings', from which came the three Ridings of the

TOPOGRAPHY INCLUDING RIVERS

Yorkshire, in the north-east of England, is the largest English county. Roughly square in shape, with the lower left-hand corner pulled down a bit, the county is bordered by Durham in the north, the North Sea in the east, the Humber Estuary, Lincolnshire, Nottinghamshire, and Derbyshire in the south, and Lancashire and Westmorland in the west.

The Backbone of England, the Pennine Chain, forms the western boundary of the county. These are of limestone in the north-west, and hard millstone grit further south. Several rivers rise in the Pennines and flow south-east through the beautiful Yorkshire Dales. East of Thirsk, in the North Riding, the steep ascent of Sutton Bank rises to the Hambleton Hills, which lead on to the North Yorkshire Moors and the Cleveland Hills.

South of the moors the land flattens into the Vale of Pickering, and rises again in the East Riding to the chalk downs, known as the Yorkshire Wolds. The flat land along the Humber Estuary ends in the narrow, shingly promontory of Spurn Head. The City of York is situated at the junction of the three Ridings, in the Vale of York, which is the widest plain in England. The highest point is Mickle Fell, 2591 feet.

The rivers of the Yorkshire Dales are, north to south, the Swale, the Ure, the Nidd, the Wharfe, the Aire and the Calder. Other rivers in the county are the Tees, the Ouse, the Ribble, the Derwent, the Don, and the Humber.

county.

Harold, King of England, had banished his brother Tostig for his ill-treatment of the northern kingdom. Tostig sought help from Hardrada of Norway, and they invaded Yorkshire. King Harold marched against them, and after a brief battle, defeated and killed them both. It was whilst celebrating this victory that he heard that William of Normandy had invaded Sussex.

The Normal earls built many castles, at Richmond, Pontefract, Conisbrough, Knaresboro, Tickhill, and Skipton.

In 1138, at the Battle of the Standard, Yorkshiremen fought gallantly against the invading Scots.

During the reign of Edward III, York became the military and civil capital of the whole country. Hull grew in importance, and was made the sole port for the exportation of Yorkshire wool. It thus became one of the first ports in the kingdom.

The shire was staunchly behind the House of Lancaster in the Wars of the Roses. In 1460, at the Battle of Wakefield, the Duke of York was killed, and the Lancastrians were victorious.

Cardinal Wolsey was Archbishop of York. He was arrested at Cawood Castle one evening during dinner, from where he set off on his journey to the tower. He never arrived there, as he died en route.

In 1536, Yorkshiremen rallied in the Pilgrimage of Grace, under Robert Aske. The uprising ended with the leaders, Aske, Hussey, and the Percys, and the Abbots of Fountains and Jervaulx, and others, being hanged.

Mary Queen of Scots was imprisoned for a time in Sheffield Castle, and then Sheffield Manor.

An abortive revolt against the new religion grew up in Doncaster in 1569, but the conspiracy failed.

During the Civil War, the county was divided: the towns of the West Riding, and Hull, were for Puritanism and Parliament; the rich, central plain of York was for the Church of England and King Charles. On 2 July 1644, the Battle of Marston Moor marked a turning point in the Civil War, when the Parliamentary forces under Cromwell and the Yorkshire Fairfaxes won a clear victory over the forces of the King.

Many of the county's castles were beseiged. Knaresboro was one of these: a youth whose father was in the garrison climbed up each night and delivered provisions through a hole in the wall to his waiting father. He was eventually seen, and fired on, but he was released after the capture of the castle.

INDUSTRY PAST AND PRESENT

Present Industry

North Riding: Mixed agriculture, tourism at coastal resorts, fishing.

East Riding: Docks, fishing, tourism at coastal resorts.

West Riding: Textiles, clothing, steel, cutlery, tools, engineering, coal, tourism in Yorkshire Dales National Park.

Past Industry

North Riding: Sheep-farming was widespread in the region from earliest times. Whitby was famous for its jet, and for alum, which was also dug at Guisborough. Fishing was the main industry in the coastal towns and villages, and Whitby was known for its whaling, and Staithes for its cod, haddock, and mackerel. Iron-ore was worked from the middle of the 19th century.

East Riding: The rich agricultural soil produced large quantities of oats, barley and wheat, plus turnips and swedes. Hull and Bridlington flourished as fishing ports.

West Riding: The great woollen trade developed shortly after the Norman Conquest, and the region grew to become the chief seat of woollen manufacture in the kingdom. The wide availability of water-power, and later the introduction of coal, contributed to the flourishing of the industry. Woollen and worsted cloth were produced in Leeds, yarn in Bradford, fancy goods in Huddersfield, and carpets, and cotton, in Halifax.

Coal was dug in Leeds in the 13th century, and the rich seams in the West Riding were worked over many centuries.

Sheffield was famous for its cutlery and iron trade from early times: a line in Chaucer's Canterbury Tales runs: 'a Sheffield whitel bore he in his hose!' Pontefract was famous for its liquorice in the 16th century.

LANDMARKS

North Riding
Clevedon Hills
Hambleton Hills
Sutton Bank
Yorkshire Moors
Farndale Daffodils
Early Warning Station, Fylingdales
East Riding
Flamborough Head

Bempton Cliffs
Yorkshire Wolds
Spurn Head
West Riding
Yorkshire Dales
Pennines
Malham Cove
Ingleborough
Whernside
Pen-y-Ghent
Ilkley Moor
Brimham Rocks

MONUMENTS

York Minster, the largest Gothic church in England.

North Riding

Knaresboro Castle; the keep, whose walls are 15 feet thick, is almost all that remains of this medieval fortress.

Richmond Castle; begun in 1071, the castle was mostly in ruins by the 16th century. Most of the remains date from the 11th and 12th centuries.

Whitby Abbey, the remains of an 11th-century monastery in a spectacular position overlooking the sea.

Jervaulx Abbey; the ruins of the Cistercian abbey date from the 12th century.

Rievaulx Abbey; this Cistercian abbey, founded in 1131, was the earliest large Cistercian church building in England.

Castle Howard, built between 1700 and 1714, is one of the largest and most spectacular houses in the country.

Beningborough Hall, a large house of stone and brick, was built in 1716.

East Riding

Beverley Minster; the original Saxon Church, founded in the 7th century by St John of Beverley, was badly damaged by fire in 1188. It was rebuilt in the 13th century.

Burton Agnes Hall; this mansion, built between 1598 and 1610, is famous for its bow windows, which were unknown elsewhere at this period.

Burton Constable is an Elizabethan mansion built in 1570.

West Riding

Conisbrough Castle, a medieval fortress, is believed to have been built by Hamelin Plantagenet, half brother of Henry II.

East Riddesden Hall is a Jacobean manor house built by a rich Halifax clothier in 1640.

Harewood House; the interior of this country mansion, dating from 1759, was decorated by

Robert Adam.

Lotherton Hall is a rambling Edwardian mansion housing paintings, ceramics and silver.

Selby Abbey; founded in the 11th century, the abbey was restored after a disastrous fire in 1906.

Shibden Hall; this 15th-century half-timbered house, much altered in the 19th century, now houses the Folk Museum of West Yorkshire.

Temple Newsam, a Tudor and Jacobean mansion, was rebuilt circa 1630. It was the birthplace of Lord Darnley, the second husband of Mary Queen of Scots.

Oakwell Hall; this moated Elizabethan manor house was the original of 'Fieldhead' in Charlotte Brontë's *Shirley*.

Ripon Cathedral; a monastery was founded on the site in AD 669 by Bishop Wilfrid of York, parts of which still remain, making the Cathedral one of Britain's oldest buildings.

Roche Abbey, the ruins of a Cistercian Abbey founded in 1147, in a river valley.

Fountains Abbey, founded in 1132, became the richest Cistercian house in England. It is one of the most complete sets of Cistercian buildings to survive the Dissolution.

Bolton Abbey was founded in the 12th century by Augustinian canons.

FAMOUS PEOPLE AND LOCAL CHARACTERS

North Riding

Caedmon, the poet, known as the father of English song, was a monk at Whitby Abbey. His work is said to mark the beginnings of English literature.

Byron spent his honeymoon (which he called his 'treaclemoon') at Halnaby Hall, south of Darlington.

Anne Brontë died in Scarborough on May 28th, 1849.

Lewis Carroll (Charles Lutwidge Dodgson) lived at Croft as a boy, and went to school at Richmond.

East Riding

Andrew Marvell was born on 31 March 1621 in Winestead, south-east of Hull. He was MP for Hull from 1659 until his death.

William Wilberforce was born in Hull in 1759. He was the parliamentary leader of the campaign against the slave trade, which was abolished in 1807.

West Riding

Miles Coverdale, who produced the translation known as the *Great Bible for the Common People*, in 1538, was born in Coverdale.

Samuel Daniel, the poet, was tutor to Lady Anne Clifford, daughter of the 3rd Earl of Cumberland, at Skipton Castle, in the 1590s.

William Bradford, one of the Pilgrim Fathers, was born in Austerfield.

William Congreve, the dramatist, was born in February 1670 in Bardsey.

The Brontë children were born in Thornton: Charlotte in 1816, Bramwell in 1817, Emily in 1818, and Anne in 1829. The family later moved to Haworth, where their father was the Rector. The three girls went to school at Roe Head, near Heckmondwike, and Charlotte taught there for a while. The three girls published their novels and poems under the pseudonyms of Currer, Ellis, and Acton Bell.

Charles Kingsley visited Malham Tarn and Wharfedale in 1858; the setting of the first few chapters of *The Water Babies* is said to derive from the scenery there.

George Gissing, the novelist, was born on November 22nd, 1857, in Wakefield.

Benjamin Waugh, the founder of the NSPCC, was born in Settle.

York

Sir John Vanbrugh, the architect, was married in York at the age of 54.

Laurence Sterne preached at Sutton-in-the-Forest and Stillington. He joined the Demoniacs Club in Skelton. He published the first two volumes of *Tristram Shandy* at his own expense in York. He then moved to Coxwold, to a cottage he named 'Shandy Hall'.

Sydney Smith was rector of Foxton-le-Clay in 1806. He became a farmer, a magistrate, and the village doctor.

Local Characters

Sir Tatton Sykes, of Sledmere, in the East Riding, would go for daily walks, swaddled in waistcoats, and followed by a footman. As the day progressed, he would peel off each successive waistcoat, which were duly collected up and carried by the footman.

Robert Thompson of Kilburn was a craftsman who became known as the 'Mouseman'. He

left his own distinctive mark on his work by carving a mouse on all his hand-made oak furniture.

Blind Jack Metcalf of Knaresborough was born in 1717. He lived to the age of 93, and amongst his many occupations he was a violinist, a soldier, a forest guide, and a major road builder.

ART AND LITERATURE

Until the mid 17th century, in Halifax, the theft of cloth valued at $13^{1}/2$d or more was punishable by beheading. A famous Beggar's or Vagrant's Litany ran thus:

> 'From Hull, Hell and Halifax
> Good Lord deliver us!'

'*Wide around*
Hillock and valley, farm and village, smile:
And ruddy roofs and chimney-tops appear,
Of busy Leeds, up-wafting to the clouds
The incense of thanksgiving: all is joy,
And trade and business guide the living scene,
Roll the full cars adown the winding Aire
Load the slow-sailing barges, pile the pack
On the long tinkling train of slow paced steeds.'

John Dyer
The Fleece (1757)

In 1132 Archbishop Thurston of York allocated to a group of dissenting monks '...*a place remote and uninhabited, set with thorns, amongst the hollows of the mountains and rocks, more fit, it seemed, for the lair of wild beasts than for human use.*'

Serlo, a monk,
on the setting for Fountains Abbey

'...*no language can describe the effect of the deep, clear azure of the sky and ocean, the bright morning sunshine on the semi-circular barrier of craggy cliffs surmounted by green swelling hills, and on the smooth, wide sands, and the low rocks out at sea - looking, with their clothing of weeds and moss, like little grass-grown islands - and above all, on the brilliant, sparkling waves. And then the unspeakable purity and freshness of the air!*'

Anne Brontë,
of Scarborough, in Agnes Grey (1847)

*'Where, behind Keighley, the road,
Up to the heart of the moors
Between heath-clad showery hills
Runs, and colliers' carts
Poach the deep ways coming down,
And a rough, grimed race have their homes –
There on its slope is built
The moorland town…'*

Matthew Arnold
Haworth Churchyard

*'Here domes and statues, spires and cranes cluster
Beside grain-scattered streets, barge-crowded
water,
And residents from raw estates, brought down
The dead straight miles by stealing flat-faced
trolleys
Push through plate-glass swing doors to their
desires…'*

Philip Larkin,
on Hull - Here

*'[The West Riding of Yorkshire is] a charming
region, a beautiful green hill county…The houses
of rough grey stone look so neat and clean in
comparison with the blackened brick buildings of
Lancashire, that it is a pleasure to look at them.'*

Engels
The Condition of the Working Class in England
(1845)

*'In winter nothing more dreary, in summer nothing
more divine, than those glens shut in by hills, and
those bluff, bold swells of heath.'*

Emily Brontë
Wuthering Heights

*'There be such a company of wilful gentlemen
within Yorkshire as there be not in all England
besides.'*

The Abbot of York to Henry VIII

In the time of Elizabeth I, the men of Halifax
were spoken of as behaving *'after the rude and
arrogant manner of their wilde country.'*

LOCAL FOLKLORE

St Oswald's Well
The following traditional belief attached to
St Oswald's Well in Roseberry Topping: the
prognosis for a sick man could be discovered
by throwing his shirt into the well. If it
floated, he would recover. If it sank, the
patient would die.

Arthur's Oven
Legend has it that King Arthur and all his
men lie sleeping in a large cave near Richmond
Castle, known as Arthur's Oven. One day
potter Thompson met a stranger near the
castle, who led him into this cave, and thence

to a vast underground vault, where he saw
many knights sleeping on the ground. The
stranger showed Thompson a horn and a
sheathed sword. He told him that if he blew
the horn and took the sword out of its sheath,
the knights and their king would be freed
from the enchantment that bound them.
Thompson started to unsheath the sword,
but as he did so he saw the knights begin to
stir as though waking up. In panic, he let the
sword fall back into the sheath, and the
sleeping knights sank back down onto the
ground. As Thompson fled from the cave, he
heard a sad voice crying:

*'Potter Thompson, Potter Thompson,
If thou hadst either drawn
The sword or blown the horn
Thou'd been the luckiest man
That ever yet was born.'*

The Legend of Semerwater
Many years ago there was a village called
Simmerdale, in the North Riding of Yorkshire.
One day a witch came to the village and
began begging for food. She asked at each
house, and everyone refused her, until she
came to the very last house in the village,
which belonged to a Quaker woman. The
Quaker woman gave her meat, bread, and
beer. When the witch had finished her meal,
she rose, and waving an ash twig over the
village, she cried:

*'Simmerdale, Simmerdale,
Simmerdale, sink
        Save the house of the woman who
gave me to drink.'*

As she spoke, water poured into the valley
and covered the whole village, except for the
Quaker woman's house. Even today, people
around Semer Water claim they can
sometimes see the ruins of a village, and a
church, under the peaceful waters of the lake.

The Waff
Not very many years have gone by since a
man of Guisborough entering a shop in
Whitby saw his own wraith standing there
unoccupied. He called it a 'waff'. Now it is
unlucky in the highest degree to meet one's
own double; in fact, it is commonly regarded
as a sign of early death. There is but one path
of safety; you must address it boldly.

The Guisborough man was well aware of this
and went up without hesitation to the waff.
'What's thou doing here?' he said roughly.
'What's thou doing here? Thou's after no
good, I'll go to bail. Get thy ways yom, wi'
thee, get thy ways yom.' Whereupon the waff
slunk off abashed and the evil design with
which it came there was brought happily to
nought.

Wade and his Wife
Wade and his wife and son possessed the
powers of the ancient Titans, whose mighty
grasp could lift the hills and toss the ponderous
rocks. To their gigantic operations are
ascribed the castles of Mulgrave and Pickering,
the Roman road supposed to communicate
between them, several Druidical stones in
the vicinity, and other works equally
stupendous. In the building of Mulgrave and
Pickering castles, Wade and his wife, whose
name was Bell, divided their labours, a single
giant being sufficient for rearing each castle;
but, having only one hammer between them,
it was necessary to toss it backward and
forward, giving a shout every time it was
thrown, that when the one threw it to
Mulgrave or to Pickering the other might be
ready to catch it! The Roman road which is
called Wade's causey, or Wade's wife's causey,
was formed by them in a trice, Wade paving,
and Bell bringing him stones; once or twice
her apron strings gave way, leaving a large
heap of stones on the spot!

Young Wade, even when an infant, could
throw a rock several tons weight to a vast
distance; for one day, when his mother was
milking her cow near Swarthouse, the child,
whom she had left on Sleights Moor, became
impatient for the breast, and, seizing a stone
of vast size, heaved it across the valley in
wrath, and hit his mother with such violence
that, though she was not materially hurt, her
body made an impression on the stone which
remained indelible, till the stone itself was
broken up, a few years ago, to mend the
highways!

The Bishopsthorpe Ghost
Robert Johnson, a slaughterer, accompanied
by a boy who was apprenticed to a Jubbergate
butcher, was sent one night to a farm beyond
Bishopsthorpe to fetch some sheep. As they
returned in the darkness, nearing the hauling
lane, each suddenly saw a coffin suspended in
the air, and moving slowly along in the
direction of York. It tilted occasionally, as if
borne on the shoulders of men who were
thrown out of step by the rugged character of

the roadway. The coffin was covered with a heavy black pall of velvet, fringed with white silk, and was in size and appearance the resting-place of a full-grown man. Behind it, with measured tread, walked a Bishop in lawn, bearing on his hands a large open book, over which his head bent, but from his lips no sound came. On went the procession, with the steady precision observed in bearing the dead to the grave, whilst the sheep kept pace, and would not be driven past the strange sight. Nobody could be mistaken in the apparition. The night, though dark, was too light to admit of mistake...The spectre procession moved at a leisured pace for some considerable distance till it came to the field where Archbishop Scrope was beheaded. Then it disappeared as hastily as it had come, and returned to its rest. But not so with the man and boy...Having arrived at their destination...after very few particulars, spoken amid much fear, they were taken off to bed, where they remained for many days, wrung in mind and body by the terrible shock...When sufficiently recovered, their story was repeated with particular detail, and gained universal credence, from the fact many villagers and many citizens had experienced like sight and sensations. The boy forsook his business and took to the sea, lest he should ever again be compelled to take a similar journey, and be subject to like experience, whilst the man ever after avoided that road at nightfall, but never swerved from declaring his story true... More than once after this, men who had sat late at their cups were frightened into sobriety by the reappearance of the strange funeral procession.

Mother Shipton

Mother Shipton was born at Knaresborough, and baptized by the name of Ursula Southell. Her stature was larger than common, her body crooked, her face frightful, but her understanding extraordinary.

Her mother died in childbirth, so she was put out to nurse with a poor woman outside the town, but strange manifestations made the nurse's life well-nigh impossible. Once, when the child was about six months old, the woman left the house for a short time, and on returning found the door open and an uproar in progress. She called some neighbours to her help, but as soon as the foremost of them entered the house large yokes, in the form of a cross, were put round their necks, to detain them, and when, after a hard struggle, they cast these off, a staff was laid across their shoulders, from which an old woman clung by heels or toes.

The men of the company made their escape somehow, but the women forced their way in, and were at once compelled to take hold of the four ends of a cross, and dance round, each of them goaded by an imp like a monkey, until they were utterly exhausted. At last the priest with a band of followers, succeeded in crossing the threshold, and searching the house - the child was nowhere to be seen; but was at length discovered hanging with its cradle, both unsupported, halfway up the chimney.

As the child grew, the work of the foster-mother was invariably interfered with in mysterious ways. Chairs and tables would march upstairs, the meat would be spirited away from the table, and the child Ursula would grin and say, 'Be contented. There is nothing here that will hurt you.'

At school she was a prodigy: she needed no teaching of alphabet or reading; at first sight she read whatever book was shown to her. At twenty-four she was married to Toby Shipton; but little is known of their life together.

Long before her death in 1561, she foretold its day and hour. As the time drew near, she took a solemn farewell of her friends, and when it arrived she lay quietly down on her bed to await her end.

She made many prophecies during her lifetime: she foretold that Cardinal Wolsey should never come to York with the King; in fact, he arrived within eight miles of it, but was summoned to return to the King, and died on his way to London. She is also said to have foretold the Great Fire of London and the plague, and other events of history.

The Boggart

In the house of an honest farmer in Yorkshire, named George Gilbertson, a Boggart had taken up his abode, He here caused a good deal of annoyance, especially by tormenting the children in various ways. Sometimes their bread-and-butter would be snatched away, or their porringers of bread-and-milk be capsized by an invisible hand; for the Boggart never let himself be seen; at other times, the curtains of their beds would be shaken backwards and forwards, or a heavy weight would press on and nearly suffocate them. The parents had often, on hearing their cries, to fly to their aid. There was a kind of closet, formed by a wooden partition on the kitchen-stairs, and a large knot having been driven out of one of the deal-boards of which it was made, there remained a hole. Into this one day the farmer's youngest boy stuck the shoe-horn, with which he was

THE CELLARIUM. FOUNTAINS ABBEY

KIRKSTALL ABBEY. WESTERN FAÇADE OF THE CHURCH

amusing himself, when immediately it was thrown out again, and struck the boy on the head. The agent was, of course, the Boggart, and it soon became their sport to put the shoe-horn into the hole and have it shot back at them.

The Boggart at length proved such a torment that the farmer and his wife resolved to quit the house and let him have it all to himself. This was put into execution, and the farmer and his family were following the last loads of furniture when a neighbour named John Marshall came up. 'Well, Georgey,' said he, 'and soa you're leaving t'ould house at last?' 'Heigh, Johnny, my lad, I'm forced tull it; for that damned Boggart torments us soa, we can neither rest neet or day for't. It seems loike to have such a malice again t'poor bairns, it onmost kills my poor dame here at thoughts on't, and soa, ye see, we're forced to flit loike.' He scarce had uttered the works when a voice from a deep upright churn cried out, 'Aye, aye, Georgey, we're flitting ye see.' 'Od damn thee,' cried the poor farmer, 'if I'd known thou'd been there, I wadn't ha' stirred a peg. Nay, nay, it's no use, Mally,' turning to his wife, 'we may as weel turn back again to t'ould hoose as be tormented in another that's not so convenient.'

DISTINCTIVE FLAVOUR

Yorkshire folk are known for being robust, efficient, vigorous, cautious with strangers, blunt in their speech, and extremely independent.

The white rose is the symbol of Yorkshire. Historically, it was the emblem of the House of York.

Yorkshire Pudding, traditionally eaten before the main meat course, this batter pudding is baked in a hot oven, and served with onions and gravy poured in a well in the centre.

Pontefract Cakes, or Pomfrets, are small, round liquorice sweets.

In the 18th century, every house in **Robin Hood's Bay** had a hiding place for contraband. The bow-sprit of a stranded ship once went through the window of an inn at Robin Hood's Bay.

The first cat's eyes (reflecting studs in the road) were produced in Halifax by Percy Shaw in 1934.

The cliffs at **Bempton** are the largest mainland breeding ground for seabirds in England. They are also the home of the only mainland gannet colony in the British Isles.

The Yorkshire Cricket Club is the only club in the country whose membership is restricted to those actually born within the county. The club was founded in 1863. Its main ground is at Headingley, in Leeds. Its crest is the White Rose of Yorkshire.

In **Goathland** in the North Riding, men and boys perform the plough stots dance in January, when they drag a plough around collecting money for the Plough Monday celebration. 'Stots' is the name for bullocks.

Harrogate became a fashionable spa town in the 18th and 19th centuries, with people coming from all over the country to take the waters. It is now famous as a conference centre.

Horse racing takes place at **Catterick**, **Doncaster**, and **Wetherby**.

COUNTY DIARY

January: Plough Stots Dance, Goathland
July: Great Yorkshire Show, Harrogate
August: International Festival, Harrogate
September: Air Display, RAF Finingley
September: St Leger, Doncaster

The *Real* Counties of

Wales

and

Monmouthshire

ANGLESEY

SIR MÔN

HISTORY

In 1098 William Rufus sent two earls, Hugh the Fat of Chester and Hugh the Proud of Shrewsbury into Anglesey on a punitive expedition. They blinded, burnt, and mutilated with Norman panache, but the people received unexpected help when Olaf of Norway, who happened to be on a piratical expedition of his own, came down the coast and killed Hugh of Shrewsbury for poaching on his patch.

INDUSTRY PAST AND PRESENT

Holyhead is the major terminus for the ferry service to Ireland, having the closest connections to Dublin. Agriculture is mixed, with stock raising and grains predominating. There is also some fishing and quarrying. In the 19th century, copper was mined extensively at Amlwch, together with some lead and silver. There was also some coal-mining at Maltraeth. During the war Valley was a major RAF base.

LANDMARKS

Holyhead Island has an important nature reserve.
Off the coast there are many water-worn rock-stacks, and two of these to the north of Holyhead have lighthouses.

MONUMENTS

There are a number of **cromlechs** dating from druidical times, **a megalithic chambered cairn** at Trefignath and a well preserved **Roman-British village** at Din Lligwy.
Beaumaris Castle was begun by Edward I as a classic piece of contemporary military engineering, but never completed. Possibly it was realised that situated where it was, it was much more likely to be fortified against the English than by them.
The suspension bridge over the Menai Strait, nearly half a mile long, was built by Thomas Telford in 1818-26. Further up the strait is Robert Stephenson's tubular railway bridge of 1846-50, supported on five huge piers.

FAMOUS PEOPLE AND LOCAL CHARACTERS

Owen Tudor was born at about the beginning of the 15th century, son of Meredydd Tudor, escheator of Anglesey. His father was at that time under a cloud, possibly for murder, and his early life is obscure. However, he seems to have entered the service of Henry V at a young age. He remained at the court, and after the death of Henry took up with his widow. Whether they were legally married is uncertain, but they lived together as man and wife. There was an Act of 1427-8 which made it a serious offence to marry a queen-dowager without the consent of the king, which suggests that they were not, and that he was regarded as an unsuitable husband for such an illustrious bride.
In 1436 the couple suffered a reversal of fortune. Owen's children were taken from the Queen, and she was incarcerated in Bermondsey Abbey where she soon died. He himself was thrown into Newgate, but shortly escaped. He was subsequently called before Henry VI to explain himself, and the story is

TOPOGRAPHY INCLUDING RIVERS

The county consists of a major island separated from the mainland of Wales by the Menai Strait, and several smaller ones, Holyhead being the only one of any importance. The islet of Priestholm, or Puffin Island, is the only other large enough to be worth naming. The western coastline is heavily indented, but the surface is flat and largely treeless. The highest point above sea level is Mynydd Twr, 720 feet.
River: Cefui.

that he demanded a safe-conduct, and even so found it necessary to take sanctuary in Westminster Abbey. Various strategems were employed to persuade him to leave the Abbey, including an offer to make wassail in a tavern. However, he appeared before the council, which gave him safe-conduct back to Wales. This was promptly violated by Lord Beaumont and the Earl of Suffolk, who threw him back into Newgate. However, his skill in getting out of that prison had not deserted him, and he made it back to Wales.

Subsequently he became a good friend to Henry VI, who appointed him keeper of the Parks at Denbigh. In 1461 he met his end through that friendship. Being captured after the Battle of Mortimer's Cross, he was beheaded at Hereford and his head set on the market cross. A local woman, believed to be mad, washed his face and combed his hair, and set candles around it.

Local Characters

Lewis Morris was born in 1700. He received little formal education, and had to learn English as a second language. However, he qualified as a land surveyor, which allowed him both to pursue his interest in botany and to establish the first printing press in North Wales.

He was commissioned to survey the entire Welsh coast, and later became superintendent of goldmines, which brought him into frequent conflict with the owners of mineral rights. Despite the heavy burden of public service which he undertook, he compiled his Celtic Remains, an historical, typographical and etymological dictionary, though this was not published until 1878. Morris died in 1765.

ART AND LITERATURE

'I thought on the day when the bands of Suetonius crossed the Menai Straight on their broad-bottomed boats, fell upon the Druids and their followers, who with wild looks and brandished torches lined the shore, slew hundreds with merciless butchery upon the plains, and pursued the remainder to the remotest fastness of the isle. I figures to myself long-bearded men with white vestments toiling up the rocks, followed by fierce warriors with glittering helms and short, broad, two-edged swords; I thought I heard groans, cries of rage, and the full, awful sound of bodies precipitated down rocks. Then as I looked towards the sea I thought I saw the fleet of Gryffith the son of a fugitive king, born in Ireland in the Commot of Columbcille, Gryffith the frequently baffled,

the often victorious; once a manacled prisoner sweating in the sun, in the market-place of Chester, eventually King of North Wales; Gryffith, who, 'though he loved well the trumpet's clang loved the harp better'.'

George Borrow

LOCAL FOLKLORE
The White Wishing-Stick

The harpist Einon ap Gwalchmai lived near Trefdraeth. He married Angharad, daughter of Llewellyn the Great's steward, but a strange girl lured Einon away. The girl was a demon, who held him spellbound for many years, until a white-clad stranger on a white horse appeared. He gave Einon a white wishing-stick, and drove the demon girl away. As his first wish, Einon asked to see her again, but she appeared as a monstrous hag.

The demon then approached Angharad, disguised as a handsome gentleman. He gave her a letter, which said that Einon had died nine years since, and paid court to her. She agreed to marry him, but a few hours before the ceremony Einon wished himself back home. There he was not recognised until he began to play his harp, when Angharad knew him at once. He gave her the white wishing-stick, whereupon the demon reassumed his monstrous shape and vanished.

The Heir to Penhesgyn Manor

There was once a huge poisonous dragon that lived near Penhesgyn Manor. A wizard prophesied that it would one day kill the heir to the farm, so he was sent to England for safety. But a local youth tricked the dragon with a polished pan, which he held before the dragon so that it thought its reflection was a rival, and attacked it. It kept on fighting its reflection until it collapsed with exhaustion, and the youth was able to kill it.

The heir was accordingly brought home, and shown the body. But he unwisely expressed his triumph at his escape by kicking its head. One of the poison fangs went through his boot into his foot, and he died.

Dr Owen Thomas

Dr Owen Thomas, the famous preacher, recounted that as a young man in Anglesey

he had a friend who was courting a young woman living some miles away. Returning late from visiting her, he passed by a small mansion, where he met a woman, dressed rather oddly, who wished him good night, to which he replied.

"Don't be afraid," she added, "You know me." In fact he recognised her as the late wife of the owner of the mansion.

She carried on, "You know I am dead and my husband has married a second wife, and everything is not as it was?"

He admitted he knew, and she asked him, as a favour which was to tell her son, with whom he had played as a boy, that there were a number of banknotes hidden in the library for him. She gave details of the shelf and the book where they were to be found. He promised to tell her son when he returned from China, which would be shortly. The ghost then vanished.

He fell ill after that, and feared for his life. He had to confide the story, but he was reluctant to inflict it on his widowed mother and sister, so he asked them to send Owen Thomas to him and told him the story. It happened that Thomas had access to the library at the mansion, so he went at once to the shelf and book, and found the notes, which he gave to the Ghost's son on his return.

DISTINCTIVE FLAVOUR

With the Isle of Wight the only major island off the British Mainland Anglesey has a reputation for fine seafood.

The longest place name in Britain is Llanfairpwllgwyngyllgogerychchwym-drobwllandysiliogogogoch.

In fact the 'gogogoch' termination has no meaning, and is a 19th-century English commentary on the rest of the name. The local people went along with the joke, and attached it to their railway station (now closed by Beeching).

COUNTY DIARY

May-June:
    Beaumaris Festival

BRECONSHIRE
SIR FRYCHEINIOG

COUNTY FACTS

Derivation of name: After a 5th-century British chieftain, Brychan.
First Recorded: 916 as Brycheiniog
Motto: Undeb Hedd Llwyddiant (Unity, Peace, Prosperity)
County Town: Brecon (Aberhonddu)
Towns: Brecon, Bronllys, Brynmawr, Builth Wells, Cefn-coed-y-cymmer, Clydach, Coelbren, Crickhowell, Gilwern, Hay on Wye, Llanddewi'r Cwm, Llanfaes, Llangennech Wells, Llanwrtyd Wells, Lower Cwmtwrch, Penrhos, Sennybridge, Talgarth, Upper Cwmtwrch, Ystradgynlais.

Local Government
Powys County Council, Gwent County Council and Mid-Glamorgan County Council. Four District Councils. The county is also known as Brecknock.

HISTORY

In 1282 the Welsh made their last stand for independence at Cilmery, near Builth Wells, under Llewellyn ap Gruffudd, who died in the battle.

INDUSTRY PAST AND PRESENT

Agriculture consists largely of animal husbandry. There is no manufacturing of note.
A little copper was mined in the 19th century. Builth Wells and Llandrindod Wells (in Radnor) were both spa towns in the 18th century, but now attract tourists mainly by their convenience for the Brecon Beacons.

LANDMARKS

Brecon Beacons are justly famous, and a favourite site for the organisers of outward bound courses.
At Cefn Carn Cafall near Builth Wells is a cairn with the mark of a dog's paw embedded in the topmost stone. The story is that when King Arthur was hunting with his dog Cafall, the dog stamped on the stone, leaving his mark. It is said that if the stone is removed it will always return, but souvenir-hunting tourists are advised not to try the experiment.

MONUMENTS

Partrishaw Church dates from the 15th century, and because of its remote location has very largely escaped official vandalism of the succeeding centuries. The rood-screen especially admired.
Brecon Cathedral is a former monastic church and although small by English standards nevertheless a stately and imposing building.

FAMOUS PEOPLE AND LOCAL CHARACTERS

Sarah Siddons was born at Brecon in 1755 into a theatrical family, and first appeared on stage as an infant. Her career was in many ways a theatrical archetype, as she proceeded through a provincial repertory company in Cheltenham to a London debut, where she fell foul of Garrick. She returned to the provinces, playing successively better roles in bigger theatres, till she returned to Drury Lane in 1782, transferring to Covent Garden when she found Sheridan too dilatory in paying her salary.
She retired from the professional stage in 1812, though she performed for charities and benefits for many years thereafter. Her salon was famous for its wit and liveliness, and she was on easy terms with Dr Johnson, Joshua Reynolds, Charles James Fox, and Edmund Burke, all of whom paid tribute to her intellect as much as to her charm.

Local Characters
Henry Vaughan was born in 1622 and educated at Oxford and London. On the outbreak of Civil War he returned to Wales and fought in the Royalist army. In 1646 he published his first book of poems, in which the influence of Donne is apparent, and another, much more highly regarded and showing the influence of Herbert, in 1650. He practised medicine at Brecon and Newton-by-Usk, spending his final years at Tretower Court, which still stands and may be viewed by the public.

TOPOGRAPHY INCLUDING RIVERS

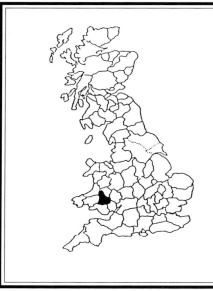

The county is bounded to the north by Cardiganshire and Radnorshire, to the west by Cardiganshire and Carmarthenshire, to the south by Glamorgan, and to the east by Monmouthshire and Herefordshire. The surface is very rugged, with two long ranges of mountains, the Epynt and the Beacons. The highest, Cader Arthur (Arthur's Chair) rises to 2,910 feet. Most of the rocks are Silurian and old red sandstone.
Rivers: Wye, Usk, Honddu, Irvon, Elan, Claerwen, Taff, Tawe.

LOCAL FOLKLORE

St Cadog

St Cadog returned from Ireland to the banks of the Usk, where he hoped to improve his Latin by studying under an Italian rhetorician who lived there. The Italian was willing to teach him and his disciples, but there was a famine in the land, so he wondered how they were all to be fed.

Cadog prayed to God, and was rewarded when a mouse ran out of its hole and placed a grain of corn on his tablet. It returned seven times, always with a grain. The saint therefore caught this mouse, and tied a long fine thread to its leg. Then he released it and followed the thread, which led to a tumulus. Under the tumulus was a beautiful house, stored with clean wheat, which the saint shared with all the poor people of the place.

On another occasion Ligessawc Longhand, a British general who had killed three of King Arthur's men sought refuge with Cadog. He stayed with him seven years until someone betrayed him to Arthur. Arthur came and demanded weregild. The case was tried on the banks of the Usk, the two parties bellowing their arguments across it, and eventually the price was set at 100 heifers all red before and white behind. No one knew where to get 100 cattle of such colouring, but Cadog called for heifers of any colour, and by miracle transformed them.

Then it was time to drive them across, and it was agreed that Cadog's men should drive them into the middle of the river, where Arthur's should take over. But as Arthur's men took charge of each beast, it was transformed into a bundle of hay.

Cadog certainly had a way with animals. His horses were white painted wood except when in use, but then they could make the round trip from Brecon to Llancarfan to Neath and back to Brecon in a single day.

The Lake Fairies

There is a small lake in the mountains near Brecon, and in the old days a door would open in a rock near this lake once a year on May Day. Those who had the courage to enter would be conducted down a passage which led to a small island in the centre of the lake. Here they would be entertained in an enchanted garden by the fairies, who with great courtesy provided the choicest fruit and flowers, though nothing could be seen by anyone from the lakeside, no matter how good his eyesight. Only one condition was made: nothing might be taken away.

But one sacrilegious wretch took a flower from his garland and put it in his pocket. The fairies pretended not to notice, and bade him and their other guests farewell with their usual courtesy, but as soon as he touched unhallowed ground on his return, the flower vanished and he lost his senses. Moreover, from that day to this the door has never opened again.

Subsequently the local people attempted to drain the lake to dig for fairy treasure, but a giant arose, and threatened to drown the whole countryside as far as the Wye if they persisted.

Llyn Safaddan

When Gryffud, son of Rhys ap Tudor, returned to Wales from the court of Henry I, accompanied by Earl Milo of Hereford, among others, they came to Llyn Safaddan, where Milo said, 'It is an ancient saying in Wales that if the natural prince of the country, coming to this lake, will order the birds to sing, they will immediately obey.'

Gryffud replied that as he had lordship over that part of the country, he should give the order. The birds paid no attention to him or to Payn FitzJohn, who was also of the company. Then Gryffud prayed to God that if he was truly of the line of the princes of Wales, to cause the birds to declare it. They all started singing immediately, to the great wonderment of all present, especially Milo, who had made the saying up on the spur of the moment.

Another legend of this lake is that it was at one time the site of a city, whose inhabitants were greatly given over to wickedness and riotous living. The King heard of this, and swore to destroy the place and all its inhabitants if it were true. He sent an inspector, who arrived, and found all the inhabitants engaged in dissolute activities of one kind or another, and no one prepared to give him hospitality or talk to him. The only open door gave onto a house where a baby had been deserted and was crying in its cradle. He spent some time rocking the cradle, and presently went to sleep.

Next day he set off back to report that the place was quite as bad as its reputation, regretting in passing that the baby would presumably be killed with the rest. As he set out there was a fearful thunderclap, and the sound of rushing waters. After a little while he noticed that one of his gloves was missing, and he must have dropped it in the cradle. As it was part of a good pair, he turned back, only to find that the whole city had been

TRETOWER CASTLE

overwhelmed, and was now a lake. Floating on the lake was the baby in the cradle with his glove. He took both back with him to the King, but ever since then people looking at the lake sometimes see the city, apparently floating on the surface.

DISTINCTIVE FLAVOUR

Until the mid 19th century it was the custom to 'carry the King of Summer and the King of Winter' at Defynnog. Two boys were dressed with birch branches, only their faces being visible. Summer was crowned with bright ribbons, Winter with holly. They were led in procession through the village and the surrounding farmhouses, preceded by a man with a drawn sword, collecting coins for beer, and finishing at the churchyard. There the boys were given a dole for their services, but Summer got more than Winter.

COUNTY DIARY

April:	Annual Antiques Fair, Brecon

CAERNARFONSHIRE

SIR GAERNARFON

COUNTY FACTS

Derivation of name: From Welsh = Fort in Arfon (Arfon being the district opposite Anglesey).
First Recorded: 1196 as Caer'n arfon
Motto: Cadernid Gwynedd (The strength of Gwynedd)
County Town: Caernarfon
Towns: Abersoch, Bangor, Bethesda, Betws-y-Coed, Caernarfon, Conwy, Criccieth, Deganwy, Deiniolen, Llanberis, Llandudno, Llandudno Junction, Llanfairfechan, Nefyn, Penrhyn Bay, Penygroes, Port Dinorwic, Porthmadog, Pwllheli, Tywyn.

Local Government
Gwynnedd County Council and three District Councils.

HISTORY

In 1283 Edward I finally subdued the last stronghold of the Welsh princes, though he had begun work on Caernarfon Castle the previous year.

In 1284 Edward II was born at Caernarfon Castle, and invested as Prince of Wales 'a prince who could speak neither Welsh nor English'. As every schoolboy knows, he came to an end of uncommon stickiness, very largely through his low sexual tastes.

In 1911 the future Edward VIII was invested as Prince of Wales in the castle.

In 1969 HRH Prince Charles, whose pronouncements on architectural matters express discrimination of the highest refinement, was invested Prince of Wales in the Castle.

INDUSTRY PAST AND PRESENT

Slate is still mined, but has suffered from the decline in favour of slate-fronted clocks, slate inkstands and similar fancy goods. Agriculture is mixed, with animal husbandry predominating.

Copper, lead and calamine were worked in the last century, mainly near Great Orme's Head. There was also a major brass foundry in Caernarfon in the last century, when the town had some importance as a port for the distribution of locally quarried slate. The importance of Caernarfon as a holiday resort has declined with the rise of Llandudno and Rhyl.

LANDMARKS

Great Orme's Head, near the mouth of the Conwy, is a very dramatic headland.

Snowdon is the highest mountain in Wales but not hard to climb. So many people have taken to availing themselves of this that the trails are in danger of being eroded by their feet.

MONUMENTS

Caernarfon Castle is constructed from masonry of different colours, and is very impressive. It took twelve years to complete and the entire income of the Archdiocese of York, which was kept vacant to liberate the money. Unlike most of the castles begun in the reign of Edward I, it was not wrecked during the Civil War. Tradition holds that the Emperor Constantine was born there in an earlier castle on the same site, though this is now doubted. It may derive from a resemblance between the walls and those of Constantinople.

The 'Ugly House', near Conwy, is supposed to have been built in a single day to avoid rates. The story is that no rates were chargeable on flimsy structures that were erected in less than a day, so a certain farmer gathered together his materials and then worked like fury from dawn, building his cottage. By sunset the roof was on, smoke was rising from the chimney, and the cottager was preparing for bed. The sheriffs had no option but to admit that it was a finished and habitable structure, but no one could call it graceful.

TOPOGRAPHY INCLUDING RIVERS

The county is bounded by Denbigh and Meirioneth in the east and south-east, elsewhere by the sea. It consists mainly of mountains, among the highest in Britain, and including Snowdon (3,560 feet). The geology is varied, including carboniferous limestone, old red sandstone, slate, quartz, porphyry, and many varieties of schist.
Rivers: Conwy, Cadnant, Glaslyn, Gwyrfai, Seiont, Ogwen.

Conwy Castle, together with its intact circuit of town walls, constitutes an almost perfect example of a new, fortified town created by Edward I to maintain his conquest of Wales. Its site, surrounded by mountains and complemented by a variety of bridges, is one of great drama. Few realize that the stern exterior protected lavish apartments within which have now entirely vanished.

Bangor Cathedral, though never of the first rank in architectural terms, nevertheless has a certain diminutive elegance.

FAMOUS PEOPLE AND LOCAL CHARACTERS

David Lloyd George was born at Caernarfon in 1863. He trained as a solicitor, but entered politics as Liberal MP for Caernarfon in 1890. He rose rapidly, becoming President of the Board of Trade in 1905, and Chancellor of the Exchequer in 1908, in which capacity he became embroiled in the Marconi Scandal of 1912, an early example of 'insider dealing' by a public official. But by that time he had introduced many features of 20th century Britain, including in his 1909 budget super-tax and land tax, which led directly to the 1911 Parliament Act limiting the powers of the House of Lords.

As Minister for Munitions in World War I he was responsible for English public houses being closed in the afternoon. This was so that the workers would be in a fit state to carry out their duties in the later shifts, and not suffer the accidents which were becoming endemic in the industry, often with tragic consequences. But there was a lighter side to his character – the exact number of his illegitimate children remains unknown to this day. In both Conservative and Labour party circles it was customary to twit Liberals when they rose to speak by singing,

> 'Lloyd-George knew my father,
> Father knew Lloyd-George.'

by way of suggesting that the Liberal might be more closely connected with the 'Welsh Wizard' than he knew. Conservatives sang it to the tune of 'Land of Hope and Glory', as one might expect; Labour supporters, to emphasise the Methodist strain in their tradition, sang it to 'Onward Christian Soldiers'.

Colonel T.E. Lawrence was born at Tremadog in 1888. He was educated at Oxford, and went to the Middle East in 1911 as an archeologist, becoming embroiled in World War I as an intelligence officer, and organised the revolt of the Arabs against the Turks. His experience led him to write The Seven Pillars of Wisdom, a book of rather doubtful scholarship and veracity, which nonetheless earned Lawrence considerable prestige. It cannot be said that the comment that the emblem of the Intelligence Corps represents 'a pansy resting on its laurels' has anything to do with him.

However, he found himself unsuited to the limelight, and twice sought obscurity as an aircraftman in the RAF, first under the name of Ross and later that of Shaw. He wrote no other original work of any merit, and his translation of the Odyssey is precious to a degree. Nonetheless, he was elected to a fellowship of All Souls, and gained the friendship of (among others) Bernard Shaw and Robert Graves. He died in a motorcycle accident in 1935.

A MEDIEVAL FLOOR TILE, BANGOR CATHEDRAL

Local Characters

Richard Robert Jones, also known as Dic Aberdaron, was born on an Aberdaron farm in 1780. He passed his life as a wandering minstrel, story-teller and magician throughout Wales, until his death in 1843. He was usually accompanied by a cat, and wore a hare-skin hat. He carried a ram's horn to announce his presence when he came to a farm or village. On one occasion at Mathlem Farm, Aberdaron, a field full of thistles was being reaped. To save the villagers from this chore, Dic summoned devils to do the reaping for them, which they achieved in minutes.

ART AND LITERATURE

'They beheld a scene which no other in this country can parallel, and which the admirers of the magnificence of nature will ever remember with regret ... the wild and stormy outline of the Snowdonian chain, with the giant Wyddfa towering in the midst. The mountain frame remains unchanged, unchangeable, but the liquid mirror it enclosed is gone.'

Thomas Love Peacock,
on the improvements at Tremadog.

LOCAL FOLKLORE

Bedd Gelert

Prince Llewellyn, great-grandfather of the last reigning prince, had a great hound named Gelert, a gift from his father-in-law, King John. One day he went hunting, leaving Gelert to watch over his baby son. While he was away a wolf came into the house, and would have killed and eaten the child, but Gelert fought with it, and after a bloody battle in which the cradle was overturned, killed it. When Llewellyn came home Gelert, covered in blood, greeted him. Llewellyn rushed in, and saw his child lying in a pool of blood. Too distracted to notice the corpse of the wolf, he thought Gelert must have gone mad and savaged the baby, so he stabbed him to death then and there.

Too late he realised his mistake: and though he built a costly memorial to the faithful hound, and Bedd Gelert is still named in his honour, Llewellyn never smiled again.

DISTINCTIVE FLAVOUR

Most of the people speak Welsh, which they maintain is of a purer form than that found in the south of the country.

Thomas Love Peacock chose **Llanberis** as the setting for *Headlong Hall*, one of the lightest and funniest of the 19th-century novels of ideas.

COUNTY DIARY

May:	Maelgwn Male Voice Choir Annual Celebrity Concert, Llandudno

CARDIGANSHIRE

SIR ABERTEIFI

COUNTY FACTS

Derivation of name: From the Welsh Ceredigion, meaning Territory of Ceredig, a dark-age prince. Ceredigion is now the name of the modern district council administering Cardiganshire.
First recorded: 991
Motto: Golud gwlud rhyddid (The wealth of the land is freedom)
County Town: Cardigan
Towns: Aberaeron, Aberporth, Aberystwyth, Borth, Cardigan, Lampeter, Llanarth, Llanbadarn, Llanddewi Brefi, Llandyfriog, Llandygwydd, Llanfihangel Ystrad, Llangoedmor, Llangranog, Llanon, Llanrhystud, Llanwenog, New Quay, Penparcau, Talybont, Tregaron.

Local Government
Dyfed County Council and Ceredigion District Council

HISTORY

The first ever Eisteddfod was held in Cardigan in 1176 under the sponsorship of Rhys ap Gwyffwd. There were two classes of event, those for bards and those for harpists and other musicians. Chairs were provided for the winners of both. It is recorded that one of Rhys's own harpists won, and one of Gwynedd's bards.

INDUSTRY PAST AND PRESENT

Agriculture is confined almost wholly to animal husbandry and some barley and rye. There are no manufactures of any importance, though this part of Wales has benefited greatly from tourism.
In the 19th century there was considerable lead-mining, with a high proportion of silver in the ore. There was also some zinc and copper working.

LANDMARKS

The coastline of Cardigan Bay is greatly enjoyed by yachtsmen.
Devil's Bridge is in fact a series of bridges at different levels crossing the River Menach as it plunges through a gorge with a complex of waterfalls. The earliest bridge was actuall built by monks from Strata Florida, but th story is that it was made by the Devil for a old woman whose cow had become strande across the gorge. His price was the first livin thing that should cross the bridge. Once was built, she tricked him by throwing a piec of bread over the bridge. Her dog went for th bread, and the dog was all the Devil got.

MONUMENTS

Aberystwyth Castle, though badly ruine still reminds the visitor that this mainly 19th century town had a stormy medieval past.
Cardigan Castle was built in 1160 by Gilbe de Clare.
Crosswood House is a very attractive examp of Queen Anne architecture, surrounded b a mature plantation.
Strata Florida is the remains of a mediev Cistercian abbey.

FAMOUS PEOPLE AND LOCAL CHARACTERS

Roderick the Great had his seat at Cardiga in the 10th century.

Local Characters
'Peter and Alistar' were two very over homosexuals who used to keep the King' Arms, a pub and small hotel, at Llandysu They ran the place extremely well, and th Welsh-speaking, chapel-attending loca packed it, as did the tourists. Someone onc ventured to ask one of them if he did no think it was rather strange to patronise place kept by such a couple. He replie nothing odd at all – "You see they're bot English. What else would you expect?"

ART AND LITERATURE

Lewis Morris, writing in 1760, describe harvest festival in Cardigan:

TOPOGRAPHY INCLUDING RIVERS

The county is bounded in the north by Merioneth and Montgomeryshire, in the east by Radnor and Brecon shires, in the south by Pembroke and Carmarthen shires, and in the west by the Irish Sea. Except in the south-west the surface is mountainous lower Silurian rock, and often very bleak. The highest point is Plinlimmon, 2468 feet.
Rivers: Teifi, Towy, Ystwith, Claerwen, Rhydol, Arth, Ayron, Wirrai, Lery.

'Here we have 45 persons, who have yesterday been reaping rye and some peas as well. A breakfast of bread and cheese, buttermilk and whey. A dinner of llymru and milk and bread and butter, but the supper, which is the great meal, is made up of the contents of a brewing pan of beef and mutton with arage and potatoes and pottage, and pudding of wheaten flour, about twenty gallons of light ale and over twenty gallons of beer. The red wooden fiddle must have strings, and a fiddler must play for them when they have eaten their belly-fuls, going into the barn and dancing on the wooden floor until they drip with sweat, there being a big can with beer at hand for them, and a piece of tobacco for each one.'

LOCAL FOLKLORE

Twm Shone Catti was a great thief in Tregaron, who ultimately married a rich woman, became a JP and mayor of Brecon. This is how a local man recalled him to George Borrow.

'One day in time of fair Twm Shone Catti goes into an ironmonger's shop in Llandovery. 'Master,' says he, 'I want to buy a good large iron porridge pot; please show me some.'
So the man brings out three or four big iron porridge pots, the very best he has. Twm takes up one and turns it round. 'This looks a very good porridge pot,' says he; 'I think it will suit me.' Then he turns it round and round again, and at last lifts it above his head and peeks into it. 'Ha, ha,' says he; 'this won't do; I see one hole here. What mean you by wanting to sell article like this to stranger?' Says the man, 'There be no hole in it.'
'But there is,' says Twm, holding it up and peeking into it again; 'I see the hole quite plain. Take it out and look into it yourself.'
So the man takes the pot, and having held it up and peeked in, 'As I hope to be saved,' says he, 'I can see no hole.'
Says Twm, 'Good man, if you put your head in, you will find that there is a hole.' So the man tries to put his head in, but having some difficulty, Twm lends him a helping hand by jamming the pot quite down over the man's face, then whisking up the other pots, Twm leaves the shop, saying as he goes, 'Friend, I suppose you now see that there is a hole in the pot, otherwise how could you have got your head inside?'

The Witch, Ceridwen

The witch Ceridwen boiled up a secret potion for a full year, three drops of which would endow the drinker with all knowledge and power. She intended it for her son Morfran, but it was stolen and drunk by a man called Gwion Bach.

Ceridwen chased after him, so he turned himself into a hare: she became a greyhound, so he turned into a fish; she became an otter, so he turned into a bird; she became a hawk, so he turned into a grain of wheat. She became a hen this time, and he was unable to change again before she ate him; but nine months later she bore him as her son. She put him in a leather wallet and threw him into the sea in a coracle, to be drowned or washed up as Fate would choose.

Somewhat later Prince Elphin came netting for salmon on the weir where he had the right just one day a year. On that occasion he found not a single fish, and as he was bewailing his lot he looked up, and saw the leather wallet hanging there. He opened it, and found therein a baby boy of such beauty that he named him Taliesin, which means ;radiant brow'. Taliesin grew up to be the greatest of Welsh bards, and is buried near Tre Taliesin.

The Mermaid

Near the beginning of the 19th century Pergrin, a fisherman from St Dogmael's, went to a recess in a rock near Pen Cemmaes, where a mermaid was combing her hair, and took her prisoner in his boat. She wept copiously as she begged him for her freedom, and at length said, "Pergrin, if you let me go I will give you three shouts when you need them most."

He released her, and on a fine calm afternoon some weeks later, when he was fishing, she suddenly put her head above the water and shouted three times, "Pergrin! Pergrin! Pergrin! take up your nets, take up your nets, take up your nets!" Pergrin and his companion did so immediately and rowed back, and by the time they reached Pwll Cam, a storm had broken. Eighteen other fishermen, who had not heard the mermaid's warning, were drowned.

Consurio

In Cardigan consurio (conjuration) is only practised by men, and there are three sorts who do it. The first sort have sold their souls to the Devil for the Art; the second have learnt it from books; and the third have it by hereditary gift. Only the third sort do good. Evan Isaac of Llandeilo related that as late as 1920 a woman from a village near Aberystwyth who had lost money consulted the local dewin, who told her that some local rascal, whose name he knew but could not reveal for fear of the law, had the money. However, she would have it back within a month. Nine days later she was dusting her mantleshelf, and found the money in an envelope behind an ornament.

'Knockers'

Cardigan miners maintain that 'knockers', little people similar to kobolds, share their labours. If work is going on and suddenly stops, you will hear the knockers knocking away for a little while until they stop too, presumably to find out why you have. They never do any harm, and experienced miners are quite happy to work alone, even when they are at their noisiest.

DISTINCTIVE FLAVOUR

Until the early part of this century it was the custom when people got married for the bride to ride off hell-for-leather behind her father on horseback. The rest of the wedding party would stream after them in hot pursuit, and the marriage was held when they were caught, in theory because their horse had foundered under its double load, but in practice, if the horse was of any value, because it was reined in.

The river Teifi is believed to have been the last resort of the British beaver.

COUNTY DIARY

August:	Talybont and North Cardiganshire Agricultural and Horticultural Show

CARMARTHENSHIRE

SIR GAERFYRDDIN

COUNTY FACTS

Derivation of name: From the Roman Morindun(um) fortress by the sea and Welsh Caer Mardin meaning Fort seafort. Mor also means sea in Welsh. The Welsh in the Middle Ages wrongly assumed Caer Mardin meant Merlin's Castle as the Welsh for Merlin is Myrddin. Another interpretation is stronghold of the sea fort.

First Recorded: 1109

Motto: Rhyddid Gwerin Ffyniant Gwlud (The freedom of the people is the prosperity of the country).

County Town: Carmarthen

Towns: Ammanford, Brynamman, Burry Port, Carmarthen, Glanamman, Hendy, Kidwelly, Laugharne, Llandeilo, Llandovery, Llandybie, Llanelli, Llangennach, Newcastle Emlyn, Pemberton, Penygroes, Pwll, St Clears, Tumble, Whitland.

Carmarthen is a county of a town unto itself.

Local Government

Dyfed County Council and three District Councils.

HISTORY

In 1843 the Rebecca Riots began in Carmarthen. Armed gangs of men, unconvincingly disguised as women, forgathered to attack toll-gates throughout Carmarthen, Cardigan, Pembroke and Brecon. Having destroyed the gates and appropriated the toll-money, they would spend it on liquor and indulge in riotous behaviour. Most of the toll-gates were legally abolished in the following year.

INDUSTRY PAST AND PRESENT

Agriculture is mainly devoted to cattle and fodder. There are woollen mills and milk-processing plants.

In 1353 Carmarthen was made the sole wool-mart for Wales.

LANDMARKS

Pumpsaint Gold Mines date back to Roman times. They were re-opened in 1935, but little gold has been obtained. In that year a Roman water wheel was found 160 feet down. The Brecon Beacons National Park is an important part of the county.

MONUMENTS

At **Meini Gwyr** there is a stone circle of unique design, with the stones set in a raised ring built to receive them.

Carmarthen Castle has always been the official residence of the Prince of Wales. it was garrisoned by Charles I in the Civil War, but taken by the Roundheads, who dismantled it.

The **Black Book of Carmarthen**, once held in the Augustinian Priory is the oldest extant Welsh manuscript.

Dynefor Castle – Norman ruins stand in the grounds of the modern castle, which in turn was built on the site of an older castle built by Roderick the Great.

Kidwelly Castle is one of the largest of Edward I's concentrically planned fortresses.

TOPOGRAPHY INCLUDING RIVERS

The county is bounded in the north by Cardiganshire, in the east by Breconshire, in the west by Pembrokeshire and in the south by Glamorgan and the sea. The country is rugged, and mainly of Silurian formation, but less mountainous than much of Wales. There is old red sandstone in the north, underlain with clay slate.

The highest point is Carmarthen Fau, 2525 feet.

Rivers: Towy, Taff, Gwendraeth Fawr, Gwendraeth Fechan, Lloughor.

FAMOUS PEOPLE AND LOCAL CHARACTERS

Twm Shone Catti worked for a while as a highwayman basing himself in a cave near Ystradd-ffin, but he had his ethics, and was greatly disgusted by the gratuitous cruelty of another highwayman who worked the same area. He therefore disguised himself as a poor farmer, with a poor old horse, but filled its saddle-bags with shells. Then he went by a place where his rival often lay in ambush. When the man sprang out and demanded 'Stand and deliver!' he threw the two saddlebags over the hedge. The highwayman without, curiously enough, shooting him in cold blood, went over the hedge after them. Thereupon Twm jumped onto his (far better horse and galloped away, to enjoy the far more valuable contents of its saddlebags.

Sir Richard Steele, the flamboyant essayis

Kidwelly Castle.

and founder of *The Spectator*, spent his declining years at Carmathen, and is buried there.

Local Characters

Vicar Pritchard of Llandovery was a drunken and dissolute man, with no noticeable vocation. His greatest friend was his nannygoat, which used to accompany him on his regular binges. One night he offered her beer, and she liked the taste, and drank more than was altogether wise for one so inexperienced. Drunken goat and drunken vicar staggered home, and next day both woke up with fearful hangovers. Pritchard called for 'hair of the dog', but the goat took one look at the beer, shuddered and refused. This superior wisdom on the part of the animal so impressed the vicar that thenceforth he turned over a new leaf, and never touched a drop.

ART AND LITERATURE

'[The Andes] stand together, and they are as Mountains piled upon Mountains, and as Hills upon Hills. Whereas we sometimes see these Mountains rising up at once from the lowest Valleys to the highest Summits, which makes the Height look horrid and frightful, **even worse** than those Mountains Abroad.'

Daniel Defoe,
of the Black Mountains

LOCAL FOLKLORE

Merlin

Merlinus Ambrosius, the mentor of King Arthur, was born in Carmarthen. His father was a demon, which is uncertain, though the finger has been pointed at Surcrag. Despite his disreputable origin, he was firmly on the side of the angels, but regrettably blood told in his case, and he was unable to resist the blandishments of ladies of doubtful character (and worse than doubtful motives), principally Nimuë, who imprisoned him in a rock, and Vivian, also known as 'The Lady of the Lake', who imprisoned him in a thornbush. Swinburne took a dim view of Vivian's character especially, and described her as more deserving the attentions of a police court than those of a sage. These imprisonments prevented Merlin from being on hand to furnish King Arthur with his invaluable advice at all times, the lack of which ultimately cost that impulsive monarch dear.

Siôn ap Siencyn

Siôn ap Siencyn of Pant Siôn went walking one afternoon in the woods. A bird began to sing in a tree, and Siôn sat down to listen. When the song was ended he stood up, and saw that the tree was withered, without leaf or bark. He went home, but found his house looking very old with a white-haired man standing at the door.

'What are you going here?' the white-haired man asked.

'May I not cross my own threshold?' Siôn responded.

'This is my house.'

'But I live here, with my father and mother. No more than ten minutes ago I went out to sit under a withered tree.'

'Then you must be Siôn ap Siencyn! I heard from my grandfather, who was your father, that you were lost long ago, and the Cadi Madog of Brechfa said that you were with the fairies, and would not return until the last drop of sap in that tree had dried up. Come in, uncle!'

With that he leaned forward to embrace him, but his arms met around empty air; where Siôn had stood there was nothing but a little heap of dust on the ground.

DISTINCTIVE FLAVOUR

Most of the people speak Welsh, which they maintain is of a purer form than that spoken in the north.

Carmarthen yeast cake is a kind of fruit loaf, enriched with golden syrup.

COUNTY DIARY

May-June:
  Eisteddfod Genedlaethol
  Urdd Gobaith Cymry
  Cwm Gwendraeth,
  Carmarthen

DENBIGHSHIRE

SIR DDINBYCH

COUNTY FACTS

Derivation of name: From the Welsh, din meaning little and bych meaning fort.
First Recorded: c.1350
County Town: Denbigh
Towns: Abergele, Brymbo, Bryn-teg, Cefn-y-bedd, Chirk, Coedpoeth, Colwyn Bay, Denbigh, Gresford, Holt, Kinmel Bay, Llangollen, Llanrwst, Llay, Old Colwyn, Rhos-on-Sea, Rhosllanerchrugog, Rhostyllen, Ruabon, Ruthin, Wrexham.

Local Government
Clwyd County Council and Gwynedd County Council. There are four District Councils.

HISTORY

In 1277 Denbigh was ceded to Edward I by Llewellyn, the last Prince of North Wales. He and his brother David rebelled in 1282, but without success; Llewellyn was killed in battle, and David executed as a traitor.

In 1402 Glendower besieged Denbigh castle, though without success. However, he razed the town.

INDUSTRY PAST AND PRESENT

Agriculture consists mainly of livestock farming. There is little manufacturing industry.

Lead, zinc and a little iron were worked in the last century, when Ruabon was a major iron and steel town. Denbigh was a tannery town.

LANDMARKS

The town and Vale of Llangollen provide the site for modern Eisteddfodau, which have taken place every year since 1947.

Parc-y-Meirch is a very fine double-ramparted iron-age fort, making use of natural escarpments. It was abandoned in Roman times, but re-fortified in the Dark Ages, by whom is uncertain.

TOPOGRAPHY INCLUDING RIVERS

The county is bounded in the west by Caernarfonshire, in the south and south-west by Merioneth and Montgomery-shire, in the east by Shropshire and Cheshire, in the north-east by Flintshire and in the north by the Irish Sea. The east of the county is mainly covered by the Clwydian Hills, and the west by the Hiraethog range. Most of the county is covered with new red sandstone. The highest points are Moel Sych and Cader Berwyn, 2713 feet.
Rivers: Conway, Clwyd, Dee.

MONUMENTS

Valle Crucis Abbey dates from 1201, and much of it is still standing. The cloister was rebuilt in the 14th century.
Ruthin has a number of major half-timbered buildings in a very good state of preservation.
Wrexham Church dates from the 14th century. The tower is exceptional, both for its height and the quality of its tracery.
Denbigh Castle still impresses visitors with the complexity of its 14th-century stonework.

FAMOUS PEOPLE AND LOCAL CHARACTERS

Sir Henry Morton Stanley was born at Denbigh in 1841. He was attracted to journalism from an early age, and was employed by the New York Tribune to go in search of David Livingstone, finding him in 1871. His manner of greeting him when he found him has since become well known. He found exploration agreeable, and confirmed Livingstone's discovery of the source of the Nile. He also traced the whole of the River Congo. He was instrumental in opening up the Belgian Congo, and identified the Ruwnzori Range as the 'Mountains of the Moon', beloved of 19th century fabulists. He died in 1904.

Local Characters
Thomas Edwards, whose portrait George Borrow noticed in Valle Crucis Abbey, was described as 'very clever and satirical'; so was his wife. He had two daughters, who were also satirical and clever (which may or may not have enhanced their prospects of marriage) – even the serving girl was clever and satirical to a remarkable degree, for it was impossible to live with Tom without becoming clever and satirical, if only in self-defence.

Tom made some of his living by playing interludes at social and artistic events, and used to walk up to fifteen miles to do so. He would then set to immediately, without pausing for refreshment, or even to get his breath back.

His autobiography, which Borrow read, betrayed a very powerful imagination, if less capacity for satire. It is a rags-to-riches-to-rags story, complete with a grasping and unscrupulous lawyer, superhuman feats of strength by the author, a duel with quarterstaves, and supernatural visitations. It is a great pity Edwards lived before the days of soap opera, for he had a fine eye for the telling detail: for instance, in his youth his parents were so poor that he could only get paper to practice writing on when a shop was burnt; his mother got some sheets charred at the edges in the ensuing fire sale, but even then, for his ink he had to squeeze elderberries.

The '**Ladies of Llangollen**' were two Irishwomen of wealth and culture, Miss Ponsonby and Lady Eleanor Butler, who retired to Plas Newydd, a handsome half-timbered house which they built below Dinas Bran. They became famous for their wit, hospitality and eccentric habits, so that their house, where they lived for fifty years, became the most inaccessible but one of the most brilliant salons of its time. There they entertained, among others, **Sheridan**, **Burke**, **Canning**, **Wellington**, **Scott** and **Wordsworth**.

ART AND LITERATURE

'At last one turns and looks westward. Everything is changed. Over the mouth of the Conway and its sands is the eternal softness and mild light of the west; the low line of mystic Anglesey, and the precipitous Penmaenmawr, and the great group of Carnedd Llewellyn and Carnedd David and their brethren fading away, hill behind hill, in an aerial haze, make the horizon; between the foot of Penmaenmawr and the bending coast of Anglesey, the sea, a silver stream disappears one knows not whither. On this side, Wales – Wales, where the past still lives, where every place has its tradition, every name its poetry, and where the people, the genuine people, still knows this past, this tradition, this poetry, and lives with it, and clings to it; while, alas, the prosperous Saxon on the other side, the invader from Liverpool and Birkenhead, has long ago forgotten his.'

    Matthew Arnold,
      on Llandudno

'With joy, my Duffryn Clwyd, I see thee bravely spread
Surveying every part; from foot up to thy head:
Thy full and youthful breasts, which in their meadowy pride
Are branched with rivery veins, meander-like that glide.'

    Michael Drayton

LOCAL FOLKLORE

The Ford of the Barking Dogs

At Llanferrys is the Ford of the Barking Dogs. In the old days all the dogs in Wales would gather there to bark, and no one ever dared to go and see what else they did there except Urien Rheged. He came to the ford at the time of barking, but found nothing but a woman washing herself. As he arrived the barking stopped, so Urien fell upon the woman and took advantage of her vulnerable condition.

When he had finished she said, very politely in the circumstances, 'The blessing of God be upon the feet that bore thee here.'

'Why?' Urien asked, since he knew he was good, but not that good.

'Because I am the daughter of the King of Annwn, and I am under a geas to come and wash here until I can have a son by a Christian. Come here in a year's time, and I will give you your son.'

In fact she gave him a son and a daughter, who were Owain and Morfudd.

The Fairy Bride

There was a farmer's son from Pentrevoelas who was minding his father's sheep when he saw a lovely young girl sitting by a stack of peat. She seemed to be in great distress, and was weeping piteously. He approached her, and tried to console her, and his efforts were rewarded, for she seemed happier. Thus encouraged he began to play court to her, which also seemed not to come amiss, but while this was going on an old man of formidable aspect suddenly appeared by her, and ordered her home. They both vanished. The young man returned to the spot many times hoping to meet her again, and at length did so, for she had managed to escape from her home in the land of allurement and illusion. But her father soon appeared again to interrupt their courtship. However, on this occasion she was able to persuade him that she truly did want to marry a mortal, and at length he gave his consent, together with a dowry of bright gold, on the single condition that he might never strike her with iron, or the marriage would be at an end.

They were married, and were happy together for several years, while she bore him three children. But one day they were on the hill trying to catch two ponies to take to a church festival. They had them cornered, and the farmer thought he could catch at least one of them, when it suddenly turned and bolted past him. In his anger he threw the bridle after it, but his aim was poor and it hit his wife. In a flash her father reappeared with a host of fairies, and took her back home, not even letting her bid her children farewell.

DISTINCTIVE FLAVOUR

The jaw-breaking expression 'Platycnemic men of Denbigh' in fact refers to some prehistoric graves found in the 19th century.

A reformed well-keeper tells the story that a farmer from Denbigh once went to Llenelian to preach. Seeing the well-keeper in the congregation, he attacked the whole practice of divination with great vigour. Sometime later he took a load of bark to Rhuddlan, where he quarrelled with the receiver about the weight. The receiver, who was a friend of the well-keeper, said that he would not forget the slur on his honour.

This preyed on the farmer's mind, so that he took to his bed where he lay on his back with his legs doubled up for some months. At last he sent for the well-keeper, and begged to be released from the spell. The well-keeper said he was not in the well, but the farmer refused to believe him, so that in the end the well-keeper had to promise to take him out of the well even though he was not in it. He then recovered, though he needed ointment for his legs.

DENBIGH CASTLE

COUNTY DIARY

August:	Denbighshire and Flintshire Show
July:	Llangollen International Music Eisteddfod

FLINTSHIRE

SIR FFLINT

COUNTY FACTS

Derivation of name: From the Old English, unspecialised meaning of the word = any hard rock, flint or stone.
First Recorded: 1277
Motto: Gorau Tarian Cifiawnder (The Best Shield is Justice)
County Town: Mold
Towns: Bagillt, Bodelwyddan, Broughton, Buckley, Caergwrle, Connah's Quay, Deeside, Dyserth, Ffynnongroyw, Flint, Greenfield, Hawarden, Holywell, Hope, Mancot, Meliden, Mold, Mostyn, Overton, Penley, Prestatyn, Queensferry, Rhyl, Rhuddlan, St Asaph, Sandycroft, Shotton.

Local Government
Clwyd County Council and four District Councils.

HISTORY

Flint Castle was built by Edward I, in 1277, though it was ruined in 1647 by Cromwell. Rhuddlan Castle was built by Edward I in 1277-82. From it he organised his administration, and promulgated the Statute of Rhuddlan in 1284. In 1646 it was besieged by the Roundheads, who ruined it, according to their custom.

INDUSTRY PAST AND PRESENT

The major industry is rayon manufacture, replacing the wool and cotton mills of the last century. Agriculture is mainly devoted to wheat. Rhyl is the most glittering jewel of Flintshire's necklace of coastal resorts.
Lead was worked in Roman times, and coal until the 19th century. In the 19th century Flint became the port of Chester, because of the silting of the Dee.

LANDMARKS

Gop Cairn is the largest prehistoric cairn in Wales, and over 60 feet high. It is built entirely of drystone.

MONUMENTS

Bachegraith House, near Tremeirchion, wa built by Sir Richard Clough. Its design s shocked the sensibilities of the local people that they maintained that the Devil had beer the architect, and supplied bricks baked in the fires of Hell.
Ewloe Castle is one of the very few in Wale that antedate Edward I. It also escaped Cromwell's attentions, and is consequently in a good state of preservation.
Flint Castle and **Rhuddlan** nearby are still exceptional monuments to Edward I' conquests, despite their damaged condition
St Asaph Cathedral, one of the smallest in Britain is a cruciform church with Perpendicular central tower.

FAMOUS PEOPLE AND LOCAL CHARACTERS

Nest, wife of **Maelgwyn Gwynedd**, lost precious ring from the regalia of North Wale while bathing in a pool. She turned for hel to St Asaph, for whom the cathedral was late named. He invited her and King Gwynedd t

TOPOGRAPHY INCLUDING RIVERS

There are three distinct parts of Flintshire. The major body of the county which is bounded in the south-west by Denbighshire, in the east by Cheshire, and in the north-east by the Dee estuary, and the north-west by the Irish Sea. The second part is known as Maelor and is separated from Denbighshire by the River Dee to the north-west and bounded by Cheshire on the north-east, and surrounded by Shropshire to the south and west. The third detached portion is small by comparison and is a tiny island in Denbighshire caught between Flint major and Flint Maelor centred upon the villages of Gresford, Marford and Rossett. The coastline is sandy. Most of the county is covered by new red sandstone, with some shale and old red sandstone underneath. The major underlying rock is limestone. The highest point is Moel Fammau (the Mother of Hills), 1820 feet.
Rivers: Elwy, Clwyd.

ST ASAPH CATHEDRAL

dinner with him. There he told the King how the ring had been lost. The King was angry, but Asaph prayed that it might be found, and ordered the first course, a fish from the Elwy, to be brought in. The King cut it open, and the ring fell out.

LOCAL FOLKLORE

St Winifred's Well

St Winifred's Well at Holywell is named after St Winifred, a virgin who refused the advances of King Caradoc, who, being unwilling either to take her by force or let her get away with such cheek, cut her head off. The well sprang from the point where her head touched the ground, and has healing powers. Moreover, her uncle Beuno was also a saint (it ran in the family) and he stuck her head back on and restored her to life, which she devoted to the metier of Abbess of Gwytherin (Denbigh). To remind them of his discreditable part in the story, all the descendants of Caradoc bark like dogs when they are born, and are only cured of it by being dipped in the well.

DISTINCTIVE FLAVOUR

At **Holywell** the method of cursing and lifting curses was as follows—

The name of the person or farm to be cursed is written on a piece of parchment, which is enclosed in a thin layer of lead, and attached to a piece of slate onto which the person's initials are cut. They are then thrown into the well, while the curse is repeated, and water is taken from the well and thrown back. Once the cursed person hears of this, he consults the well-keeper, who tells him his name is in the well. He reads two psalms, or has them read to him if he is unable, and walks three times round the well, while the psalms are read again. The well is dried, and he is given the lead and slate. Then he must go home, and read the psalm and the Book of Job for three consecutive Fridays.

Flintshire is the smallest county of Wales.

Flintshire was once included in the Earldom of Cheshire.

COUNTY DIARY

August: The Denbighshire and Flintshire Show

FLINT CASTLE – THE EASTERN TOWER VIEWED FROM INSIDE THE COURTYARD

GLAMORGAN
MORGANNWG

COUNTY FACTS

Derivation of name: From the Welsh Glanna Morgan meaning Morgan's shore. The area was ruled by several princes of the name of Morgan. Gwlad Morgan means the land of Morgan, after a 10th century Welsh prince.
First Recorded: 1242 as Gwlad Morgan
Motto: A ddioddetws a orfu (He that endureth, overcometh)
County Town: Cardiff.
Towns: Aberdare, Abercynon, Bargoed, Barry, Bridgend, Briton Ferry, Caerphilly, Cardiff, Clydach, Cowbridge, Hengoed, Llantrisant, Maesteg, Merthyr Tydfil, Morriston, Mountain Ash, Neath, Penarth, Pontypridd, Porthcawl, Port Talbot, Pontardawe, Pontycymer, Rhymney, Swansea, Tonyrefail, Treharris, Treorchy, Ystrad Rhondda.

Local Government
Mid-Glamorgan County Council, South Glamorgan County Council and West Glamorgan County Council and twelve District Councils.

HISTORY
In 1321 the barons revolted against the ravages of Earl Despenser, favourite of Edward II, and banished him. He was restored, with even greater estates shortly afterwards, but this was the beginning of a long, lawless period until Henry VIII took the place into his own hands. In 1346 some men from Llantrisant fought successfully under the Black Prince, distinguishing themselves at Crécy. This failed to impress their countrymen, who have referred to them as the 'Black Army' ever since.

INDUSTRY PAST AND PRESENT
Port Talbot is still a major centre of the steel industry, and the county contains much of the South Wales coalfield. There is also limestone, principally used for iron-smelting. Brickworks and brewing are important at Bridgend in the south of the county. Farming is mixed, and mainly for local consumption. Iron was heavily worked in the last century. At that time the county also imported tin and copper ores from Cornwall for local smelting, tin at Aberdare, copper at Swansea.

LANDMARKS
The Mumbles, a group of small offshore islets, are famous for their untouched beauty and wealth of birdlife.
The Gower Peninsula (from Welsh gwyr = crooked) is a place of pilgrimage for determined walkers.
Bury Holms Island can be reached on foot at low water. There are ruins of a pre-Norman village and an iron-age promontory fort.

MONUMENTS
Margam Abbey, to the south east of Neath, is ruined, but the walls of the polygonal chapter-house remain.
The keep of **Cardiff Castle** dates from 1150, and is one of the finest examples of its type surviving in Britain.
Caerphilly Castle was begun in 1271, but it has been heavily restored and improved over the centuries. It is an anthology of medieval defensive systems, including an elaborate water defence.
St Fagan's Castle is quite destroyed, but the wall houses the Welsh Folk Museum, with many characteristic buildings from different parts of Wales which have been dismantled and reconstructed.
Ewenny Priory is a major monastic survival.

FAMOUS PEOPLE AND LOCAL CHARACTERS
Dylan Thomas was born in Swansea in 1914. After school he went into journalism, but wrote poetry in his spare time. This caught the attention of Edith Sitwell, among others, and got him work with the BBC. During the war he is said once to have laid out Guy Burgess with a single blow at the Gargoyle Club, for not rising to his feet when 'God Save the King' was played.
His poetry gained in popularity, which led to a tour of the United States, where he allowed the adulation he received to go to his head, along with far more strong liquor than was good for him. He died of excess in 1953, not living to see the first production of what is certainly his finest work, the 'play for voices' *Under Milk Wood* (first produced in 1954 by the BBC). Later versions of that work have been marred by directorial self-indulgence, most notoriously the film starring Richard Burton with its gratuitous and jarring sex-scene. Were it not for this, Thomas's

TOPOGRAPHY INCLUDING RIVERS
The county is bounded in the north by Breconshire and Carmarthenshire, in the east by Monmouthshire, and in the south and west by the Bristol Channel. It includes the islands of Barry and Sully. The coastline marshy between the mouth of the Rumney and Penarth. Thereafter, except where it joins the cliffs that mark the boundary with Carmarthen, there are many shallow bays. Inland the terrain consists of hills, except in the vale of Glamorgan, a broad, level tract of sandstone marl over millstone grit. The highest point is Craig-y-Llyn, 1969 feet.
Rivers: Rumney, Taff, Daw, Ogmore.

reputation would doubtless stand higher today.

His readings of his own poems enjoyed a certain vogue in the United States after his death, with the result that a certain pop-person renounced his honourable name of Zimmermann in order to be known as Bob Dylan. The extent to which this bolstered Mr Dylan's subsequent career is uncertain, though it is not believed to have harmed Thomas's reputation to any significant degree.

Alun Lewis was born in 1915 in Aberdare, and educated at Aberystwyth University. He was killed in Burma in 1944, but his first books of short stories and poems had been published by that time. He acquired a posthumous reputation with further poetry, letters and short stories published after the war with the support of Robert Graves and A.L. Rowse.

Local Characters

Griffith Morgan was born in 1700 at Llanwyno. He was the greatest runner in Wales, and used to pace himself against hares. He also slept in a dunghill, because he thought it was good for his legs. In 1737 he completed a course of twelve miles in 53 minutes, upon which an enthusiastic admirer slapped him on the back. He thereupon died of heart failure.

Dr William Price was born at Llantrisant in 1800. He used to wear a fox skin on his head, and conducted druidical ceremonies of his own devising at the Rocking Stone on Pontypridd Common. He burdened his son with the name of Jesus Christ Price, and when he died in 1884, insisted on cremating the body in a nearby field, without religious rites. He was tried for this at Cardiff, but as it was impossible to say exactly what he was guilty of, the case had to be dismissed, thus paving the way for legal cremation in less flamboyant circumstances. Price died in 1893.

ART AND LITERATURE

'And after [King Arthur] had made his mind known to his nearest friends, they took counsel together, and decided to hold that feast in Caerleon-on-Usk in Glamorgan. For that was the fairest place in the isle of Britain, and richest in gold and silver and other treasurers, and the most worthy place to honour a festivity of so great renown.'

> **from the Dingestow Chronicle,**
> **D.M. Lloyd trans.**

LOCAL FOLKLORE

The 'Red Bandits of Mawddawy'

There was a young man who married with a lake maiden. Her father opposed the match, and offered the usual warning about never touching her with iron, but as always happens, he did so by accident, and she said she must go. He pleaded with her to stay, asking what might become of their children without a mother. She replied, 'Let them be red-haired and long-nosed!' and vanished, never to be seen again.

In fact the children prospered, becoming tall and athletic, and are still to be found on the banks of the Taff, red hair, long noses and all. However, in the lawless time between the death of Glendower and the accession of Henry VII their true nature emerged in habitual brigandry and cattle-rustling, so that they became known as the 'Red Bandits of Mawddawy'. Ultimately they were smoked out by John Wynn of Gwydir and Baron Owen, who condemned many of them to be hanged. An old woman pleaded for the life of her youngest son, but without avail. So she bared her withered and yellowed breasts before the sheriff, and proclaimed, 'These have given suck to those who will one day wash their hands in your life's blood!'

So it was that one day when the sheriff was returning past the scene of the hanging tree, a tree fell across the road in front of him, and brigands rushed out and murdered him. They fled at once, but then, remembering their mother's curse and not wishing her to be discredited, retraced their steps, to dabble their hands in his heart's blood before making good their escape.

Yarn Magic

A white witch who practised at Cilfynydd until her death in 1923 cured diseases by yarn magic. She would measure three spans of yarn, from her own elbow to the tip of her middle finger. Then she would measure again, and the yarn would be shorter – how much shorter depending on the severity of the attack. Then she would measure the yarn again, while she muttered a disease-breaking spell, and it would return to its original length. She then cut it off, tied it round her arm above the elbow, and left it there for three days. Then she measured it again, to see if the patient was cured. Once the cure was complete the yarn was burnt in the fireplace.

DISTINCTIVE FLAVOUR

Myrtle, the shrub used by Blake to symbolise matrimony, grows wild in Glamorgan, so

mild is the climate, especially in the Vale of Glamorgan.

Starting on Christmas Eve, and for three weeks to a month, they hold **Mari Lwyd** in Glamorgan. A man wrapped in a sheet, and carrying a horse's skull, heads the procession. He is accompanied by Punch and Judy, the Sergeant, the Corporal, the Merryman and various singers. They go to the door of a house and sing for admission. An inmate must sing a song of refusal, but after more singing they are let in. There they put on a mummer play, with Judy accusing Punch of having kissed all the women, and play pranks on the occupants. When they have exhausted their repertoire, food is laid out for them.

Glamorgan County Cricket Club is the object of intense local pride; indeed, it is treated almost as Wales' national side.

Male voice choirs are still a major aspect of Glamorgan life.

Glamorgan has supplied the nation with **memorable thespians**, including Richard Burton and Anthony Hopkins.

Caerphilly, the white, crumbly cheese is a celebrated export.

COUNTY DIARY

August: The Vale of Glamorgan Show, Penllyn.

MERIONETH

MEIRIONNYDD

HISTORY

In 1096 the Normans attempted to subdue the area, but were repulsed after the battle of Corwen. It was the first of many such battles in the area of the Bala Cleft over the next 300 years.

Harlech Castle, also known as the 'Castle of Lost Causes', was built by Edward I and taken by Glendower in 1401, who held it until 1409. Glendower is believed to have held his parliaments at Dolgellau. The castle also held out for eight years (1461-8) for the Lancastrians against Edward IV, a struggle which is commemorated in the song 'Men of Harlech'. It was finally the last castle in Wales to hold out for the Royalists in the Civil War.

INDUSTRY PAST AND PRESENT

Slate has been cut since the 16th century, and is still important in the county. Agriculture is mainly confined to sheep farming. Nuclear and hydro-electric power generation, tourism and forestry are other activities.

Lead and copper were worked in the last century, along with some gold, though now the only gold working is among the tailings from this industry. Flannel and woollens were important in the 18th century, with Welsh tweed being made at Dolgellau, stockings and caps at Bala. Lime-burning was once very important at Corwen.

LANDMARKS

Caer Idris has a summit consisting of huge columns of crystalline greenstone, resembling the columns of the Giant's Causeway.

MONUMENTS

Llanegryn Church has a 16th century rood screen, with exceptional carving.
Tywyn Narrow Gauge Railway Museum contains sections of track, rolling stock, fittings and ephemera relating to the history of such railways, as well as nine locomotives.

FAMOUS PEOPLE AND LOCAL CHARACTERS

Owen Glendower was born in Merioneth in 1349, and claimed descent from Llewellyn. He lived quietly until 1400, when Lord Grey of Ruthven repossessed himself by force of some land that Glendower had sued him for successfully in court. Grey then detained a writ of summons served on Glendower to assist Henry IV against the Scots, and put it about that Glendower had ignored it. He then seized all his lands in forfeit.

Glendower therefore laid claim to the Welsh throne, and the Welsh nobles rallied to him. There followed a war of sieges and skirmishes, culminating in 1402 with the Battle of Pilleth, where Glendower routed an English expeditionary force under Mortimer and took him prisoner. He set an extravagant ransom for Mortimer, which thrifty Henry refused to pay, as too much for a loser. This slight, together with Glendower's generous and courteous treatment of him, persuaded Mortimer to change sides.

In alliance with Percy they marched together on England, but were defeated at Shrewsbury in 1403. This was the point of decline for Glendower. He took more castles, but won no more pitched battles, and was forced into alliance with the unreliable French. However, he was never completely defeated, and outlived Henry. Henry V sent Sir Gilbert Talbot to negotiate terms with Glendower, who died before they could be finalized in 1415.

TOPOGRAPHY INCLUDING RIVERS

The county is bounded in the north by Caernarfonshire and Denbighshire, in the east and south by Montgomeryshire, in the south by Cardiganshire, and in the west by Cardigan Bay. Much of it is covered by the Snowdonia National Park. The county is almost wholly covered with slate. The highest point is Aran Fawddwy, 2972 feet.
Rivers: Dee, Mawr, Dovey.

ART AND LITERATURE

'Stand forward Seithenyn and behold the dwelling of heroes – the plain of Gwyddno the ocean covers!

Accursed be the sea guard, who after his carousal let loose the destroying fountain of the raging deep.

Accursed be the watcher, who after his drunken revelry, loose the fountain of the destroying sea.

A cry from the sea arises above the ramparts; even to heaven does it ascend – after the fierce excess comes the long cessation!

A cry from these ascends above the ramparts; even to heaven does the supplication come! – after the excess there ensues restraint!

A cry from the sea awaken me this night!

A cry from the sea arises above the winds!

A cry from the sea impels me from my place of rest this night!

After excess comes the far extending death!'

      Anon.
        Gwyddno.

'Snowdonia National Park shows how Wales looks if the English are put in charge; but they've left Ffestiniog-Blaenau right in the middle, to show how it would look if it were left to the Welsh.'

      N.C. Black

LOCAL FOLKLORE

King Bran of Harlech

King Bran of Harlech received an embassy from Matholwch, Lord of Ireland, paying suit to his sister Branwen, fairest of women. The suit was acceptable, and the engagement was therefore announced. But this angered Bran's younger brother, Evnisseyn, who felt that he should have been consulted. He therefore went to the place where the Irish kept their horses, and cut off all their tails and ears. Matholwch demanded Evnisseyn's life to atone for this insult and injury, which Bran refused. However, to pacify the Irish he gave them his magic cauldron. This was big enough to hold a man, and if a dead man was put into it, he was restored to life. The Irish seemed satisfied, and sailed away. But to a true Irishman, even such a remarkable gift is less than adequate compensation for ill-treatment of a horse. Matholwch therefore took it out on Branwen, by making her skivvy in the kitchens instead of treating her like a princess. He dressed her in sacking, and banished her from his bed, so that she had to sleep on a straw pallet. No one spoke to her, and her only friend in all the land of Ireland was a starling, which she tamed.

Meanwhile Bran had no knowledge of how his sister was being treated, as Matholwch imprisoned all Welshmen who came there, and permitted no boats to cross the sea. But Branwen wrote him a message which she tied to the starling's wing, and he carried her complaint to Bran. He roused the princes to rescue her. Soon the sea was black with their ships.

Matholwch was terrified when he saw the fleet approaching, so he brought Branwen forth, and clad her in rich clothing, and invited Bran and his followers to a great feast in his banqueting hall. There he swore fealty to Bran, and promised to hold the land of Ireland as his vassal. But along the hall he had left great bags, one against every pillar, and in each of the bags was an armed man, ready to fall upon his guests at the height of the revelry. But Evnisseyn was suspicious, so he went up to one of the bags and asked what was in it.

'Meal,' Matholwch replied.

'Then you won't mind my squeezing it,' Evnisseyn said, and he put his hands around the neck and throttled the man inside.

This was the signal for battle. It went on for many days, and the Welsh noticed that although they killed many Irish, there were always just as many the next day. Evnisseyn realised why this must be. 'I have brought all this trouble on my people, so I must atone,' he said.

That night he hid among a pile of Irish dead. The surviving Irish gathered them up as if for burial, but they put them in the cauldron, and they came out live men and as good as new, except for being unable to speak. When Evnisseyn was put in the cauldron he braced himself against the sides so that it broke asunder, and its power was lost; but the effort so cracked his heart that he died.

Next day the Welsh prevailed in battle, but Bran took a mortal wound. He lived long enough to carry Branwen back home, but she died of a broken heart not long thereafter. As he was dying, Bran commanded that his head should be cut off and buried in the White Mount looking out to sea, for he said that then no invader should ever prevail against the island of Britain. The head continued to talk and give wise counsel until it was so buried. There it remained until King Arthur's time, when he had it dug up, saying that Britain should not be defended by magic, but by the arms of her sons. William the Conqueror, grateful that this act of hubris had given him victory, built the Tower of London on the spot, to show how he thought Britain should be defended.

'Aberdovey Bells'

It is recounted by Peacock in *The Misfortunes of Elphin* that the lowland which is now Cardigan Bay was once fertile country, with the sea held back by dykes. But the steward of the dykes was the drunkard Seithenin ap Seithin Saidi, who neglected them in favour of making wassail. Consequently, the whole country was overwhelmed in a great storm, but the bells of Cantref Gwaelod, or 'Aberdovey Bells' can still be heard tolling under the waters of the bay.

The Three Lake Ladies

There were three lake ladies who lived in an upland lake near Aberdovey, with a pack of white hounds and a herd of white cows. One day a farmer caught one of the cows and took her home. She was the best of all cows, for milk, for butter, for cheese, for calves, and thanks to her the farmer's herds greatly increased.

However, the farmer was greedy, and after several years of increasing prosperity he saw that the cow was getting old. So instead of putting her to grass, he fattened her for meat. She fattened marvellously, and all the neighbours came on the killing day when he summoned the butcher. But just as the butcher's hand was poised for the fatal blow, a piercing cry rang out, and there was one of the lake ladies singing her cow home.

Not only the cow, but all her progeny to the last generation immediately rushed to the lake, and none could stop them. At the point where each disappeared there grew a water lily, but as for the farmer, his herd was wiped out and he was a ruined man.

DISTINCTIVE FLAVOUR

According to Evelyn Waugh, if a woman is seen smoking at a festive event, the band will only play 'Men of Harlech'. This is because all the other tunes have religious significance, and to play them while such a thing was going on would be blasphemous. To countenance the blasphemy would put the immortal souls of the bandsmen in jeopardy, so if they are to do it, they require to be paid extra in compensation.

COUNTY DIARY

August: Merioneth County
Show, Harlech

MONMOUTHSHIRE

SIR FYNWY

COUNTY FACTS

Derivation of name: A translation of the early Welsh, Aper Mynwy, meaning mouth of the (River) Monnow.

First Recorded: 1086 as Monemude

Motto: Utrique Fedelis (Faithful to Both)

County Town: Monmouth

Towns: Aberbargoed, Abercarn, Abergavenny, Abersychan, Abertillery, Beaufort, Bedwas, Blackwood, Blaenavon, Blaina, Caerleon, Chepstow, Cwnbran, Ebbw Vale, Llanhilleth, Monmouth, Newbridge, Nantyglo, Newport, New Tredegar, Pontllanfraith, Pontnewydd, Pontypool, Rhymney, Risca, Rogerstone, Rumney, St Mellons, Tredegar, Usk.

Local Government

Gwent County Council, Mid Glamorgan County Council and South Glamorgan County Council and seven District Councils.

Welsh Bicknor is a detached part of Monmouthshire in Herefordshire, administered by Hereford and Worcester County Council.

HISTORY

In 1404 Monmouth Castle was unsuccessfully besieged by Owen Glendower.

INDUSTRY PAST AND PRESENT

Agriculture is mainly devoted to dairy farming in the Usk Valley and sheep on the higher ground. Abergavenny is a centre for printing. Coal mining, iron and steel play a declining part in the county's economy.

Up to the 19th century the county was a centre for the manufacture of knitted caps. Queen Elizabeth I is responsible for preserving that industry, since by an Act of hers (13 Elizabeth, cap 19) they were to be worn by all and sundry on Sundays and Holy days.

Tin mills and mining were important in the 19th century.

LANDMARKS

The remains of the Roman walled city of Venta (the only civilian one in Wales) are to

be seen at Caerwent. It was defended with a double ditch, and later a 30 foot stone wall against Irish pirates.

MONUMENTS

Tintern Abbey was founded in 1131, and was celebrated in verse by Wordsworth. The ruins are still in a very fine state of preservation, despite the attentions of various pilgrims drawn to them by the poem.

In **Troy House** the cradle of Henry V, who was born there, is preserved along with the armour he wore at Agincourt.

The Kymin is a round tower built on a hill in 1794. It was originally a dining club, but in 1802 the members erected a 'naval temple' where Nelson was received as guest of honour in 1804.

Raglan Castle was built at the end of the middle ages and was one of the most sophisticated and elegant castles of its time. Unfortunately it was ruined during the Civil War.

Llanthony Priory, an Augustinian house in a remote valley, is remarkably well preserved. One of its west towers now houses the bedrooms of an inn.

The Bridge at Monmouth is a rare survival as it retains its fortified gate intended to repel the uninvited – above all the Welsh.

Chepstow preserves two major medieval monuments – its castle, a full circuit of towers and its priory church, which may well have been one of the very first churches in Britain to receive a stone vault.

FAMOUS PEOPLE AND LOCAL CHARACTERS

Geoffrey of Monmouth is largely responsible for the legend of King Arthur as we know it today. He wrote it up as part of a four-volume *Historia Regum Brittaniae*, which he alleged to be a translation from a Latin original lent to him by the Archdeacon of Oxford. No original has ever been found, and the parallel between this and the much later *Book of Mormon* which is very similar in character though much inferior in literary style, is very marked. His writings are no longer much regarded from an historical point of view, except by

TOPOGRAPHY INCLUDING RIVERS

The county is bounded on the north by Herefordshire, on the east by Gloucestershire and the Wye, on the south by the Bristol Channel, and on the west by Breconshire and Glamorgan. The Black Mountains in the west are picturesque, but elsewhere the county is flat, with the southern littoral protected from the sea by dykes. The highest point is Chwarel-y-Fan, 2226 feet.

Rivers: Monnow, Usk, Wye, Ebbw, Rumney.

THE GATEHOUSE ON THE BRIDGE AT MONMOUTH

the declining sect of the British Israelites.

ART AND LITERATURE

'The Welshmen … wearing leekes in their Monmouth caps.'
Shakespeare

'No. Not for Cadwalader and all his goats.'
Shakespeare

'The best caps were formerly made at Monmouth, where the Cappers' Chapel doth still remain.'
Fuller
Worthies of England

'It is impossible to travel in Monmouthshire without being struck with the appearance of neatness and cheerfulness, which results from the custom of whitewashing the houses. On account of the abundance of lime, this operation is annually performed, both within and without, and greatly contributes to the health of the inhabitants. The white colour of these dwellings, scattered along the summits and sides of the hills, and surrounded with foliage of different hues, considerably heightens the picturesque effect of the diversified landscapes.'
William Coxe

LOCAL FOLKLORE

Cadwaladr

The great Cadwaladr, who is still remembered in the name of Llangadwaladr (Bishopstown), was an affectionate man, and had a favourite pet nanny-goat called Jenny. But one day she seemed to become hysterical, and fled into the mountains for no good or obvious reason. He went after her, and having thoroughly lost his temper going up and down ever steeper inclines, he saw her outlined against the sky and threw a rock at her. Unfortunately she was standing on the brink of a precipice, and the rock knocked her over it. Cadwaladr climbed down to the bottom, to find her apparently dying there. However, she still had strength to lift her head and kiss the hand that had flung the rock.

Cadwaladr burst into tears of remorse at this gesture from the dying goat, and cradled her head in his lap. As he did so, she was transformed into a beautiful and unwounded young woman, who gazed at him lovingly and breathed, 'Ah, Cadwaladr, have I found you at last?'

She then rose to her feet, took him by the hand, and led him over more mountains, till they came to a high place where there were many half-ghostly goats, who bleated horribly loud. One, who seemed to be the King of the Goats, approached Cadwaladr, and suddenly butted him in the belly, so that he went over a crag, just as poor Jenny had done. He came to his senses in the valley next morning, but he never saw Jenny (in either form) again – which was possibly just as well, he being a married man of middle years.

Sion Dafydd

Sion Dafydd was a wizard who lived in the hills above Avergavenny. He was in league with the Devil, and under the terms of his compact, he could never be taken to Hell if he kept hold of something rooted to the Earth. He managed to avoid losing contact until the day he died, but God took the view that he might be too clever for Hell, but he was certainly too evil for Heaven. He therefore remains in the environs of Earth to this day, as a will-o'-the-wisp.

DISTINCTIVE FLAVOUR

Monmouth was not included as part of England until the reign of Henry VIII, and its status as English or Welsh continued to be disputed until quite recent times and remains unresolved. However, the character of the county is more Welsh than English.

It is said that the **River Usk** is a natural boundary with Monmouthshire to the west of the river being predominantly Welsh and to the east being more English.

COUNTY DIARY

May:	International Music Festival, Llantilio Crossenny
July:	The Border Counties Show, Abergavenny
August:	The Monmouthshire County Show, Monmouth

MONTGOMERYSHIRE

SIR DREFALDWYN

COUNTY FACTS

Derivation of name: Named after himself by Sir Roger de Montgomerie, in Norman times
First recorded: 1086
Motto: Powys Paradwys Cymru (Powys, paradise of Wales)
County Town: Montgomery
Towns: Berriew, Caersws, Church Stoke, Commins-coch, Guilsfield, Llandinam, Llanfair Caereinion, Llanfyllin, Llangurig, Llanidloes, Llanrhaedr ym Mochnant, Llansantffraid ym Mechain, Machynlleth, Meifod, Montgomery, Newtown, Trefeglwys, Welshpool.

Local Government
Powys County Council and one District Council.
Powys is the ancient Welsh kingdom of which the present Montgomeryshire formed a part.

HISTORY

In 895 a Danish force under Hasten was besieged by King Alfred at Buttington, near Welshpool. He managed to break through and escape, though only at fearful cost.
In 1093 Roger de Montgomerie conquered the county, and ruled it in association with Madog ap Maredudd, who survived until 1160.
In 1294 the last battle between Welsh and English took place near Montgomery.

INDUSTRY PAST AND PRESENT

Agriculture is almost entirely devoted to animal husbandry, but one does find the cultivation of oats and mixed corn. There are no manufactures of any note except those processing the products of local forestry and tanneries.
Some lead, zinc and copper were worked in the 19th century, but were never important.

LANDMARKS

The sources of the Severn and the Wye are famous for being very close to each other near Plynlimmon. George Borrow was led from one to the other, drinking at both, in a quarter of an hour.
The Creiddin is an extensive Iron Age hill

TOPOGRAPHY INCLUDING RIVERS

The county is bounded in the north by Denbighshire, in the east by Shropshire, in the south by Radnorshire, in the west by Cardiganshire, and Merioneth. Most of the county is bleak moorland overlying slate, though there is also granite, greenstone, new red sandstone and conglomerate. The highest point is Mole Sych in the Berwyn Mountains, 2713 feet.
Rivers: Severn, Fyrnwy, Tirannon, Afon Garno, Mule, Rhiw, Camlet, Wye, Dovey.

fort, with multiple ramparts and escarpment
It was occupied until reduced by Suetoniu

MONUMENTS

Powys Castle Gardens are laid out in th formal Dutch manner, which was popular the 18th century, but of which few inta examples survive. Because of the mildness the climate they include some tropic varieties not normally seen outdoors Britain. There is also a 180 foot Douglas f and some outstanding topiary work.
Montgomery Castle offers only vestigi remains and is more important for the artifac excavated on its site, including some ra secular stained glass.

FAMOUS PEOPLE AND LOCAL CHARACTERS

Local Characters
Lord Edward Herbert of Cherbury was bo at Montgomery Castle in 1581. His your manhood was devoted to war (principally the staff of Maurice of Orange) and diplomac He was more successful at the former, bei praised for his daring, but as a diplomat l was short of tact, and in 1618, whi ambassador to Paris so insulted the Constab of Luynes that the King ordered his reca King James was more tolerant, and sent hi back to France once the Constable was dea It was there that he published his *Tractatu* the first exposition of Deism in the Briti tradition. In it he asserted the sufficiency natural religion, without recourse revelation or the miraculous. In the Civ War Lord Herbert sided with the King again Cromwell, to his considerab impoverishment, as he died in 1648. As we as several editions of his *Tractatus* he wro some historical works, and his *Memoirs*, th first extant autobiography in English. Th however, remained in manuscript until 176 when it was published by Horace Walpole

ART AND LITERATURE

'The Source of the Severn is a little pool of wat some twenty inches long, six wide, and abo three deep. It is covered at the bottom with sm

POWYS CASTLE

stones, from between which the water gushes up. It is on the left-hand side of the Nant, as you ascend close by the very top. An unsightly heap of black turf-earth stands right above it to the north. Turf-heaps, both large and small, are in abundance in the vicinity.'

George Borrow

LOCAL FOLKLORE

The bull of Hyssington Church

At Hyssington there was once a wicked squire who was notorious for ill-treating his workforce. One of them prayed that he should be turned into a bull, and this prayer was granted, but as a bull he was even more of a burden to the parish, which he thoroughly terrorised. However, the parson confronted the bull and read to it from the Bible, which caused it to shrink to the size of a small dog. But then the candle burnt out, and the bull grew back to its former monstrous size, so that it cracked the wall of the church (the cracks are still there).

However, next day he prayed at it again, and this time got it small enough to be put in a boot, which he then buried under the church doorstep. So if you want a bull of monstrous size and vicious temper, you know where to dig.

The Fairies' Twins

There was once a cottage in Trefeglwys where the couple were always quarrelling over whether their twin children were actually their own or fairy changelings. In time their quarrels became so bitter that they called on a local wizard to adjudicate. He told them to boil a single eggshell and offer the broth to all the men working on the harvest. If the babies reacted to this, they must be thrown at once into Llyn Ebyr.

The couple tried this, and as soon as the eggshell was put to boil, the babies began to chant,

> *'Acorns before oak I saw,*
> *An egg before a hen,*
> *But never from one eggshell stew*
> *Enough for harvest men.'*

They would doubtless have got to the bit about sultanas going crunch, given time, but this was enough. The couple took them to the lake and prepared to heave them in, at which the fairies immediately arrived to save them, and handed their own children back.

The Treasure at Moel Achles

A story from as late as 1929 states that a man had heard there was hidden treasure at Moel Achles. He consulted a magician at Llanddervel, though while they were speaking a furious storm of wind and rain sprang up from nowhere. Nevertheless the magician said the treasure should be sought at full moon, and promised to send a guide.

He set out in the moonlight with a friend, and after they had covered less than 100 yards, they saw a hare sitting in the road. As they drew nearer it moved slowly forward till it reached a certain spot where it vanished. There they started to dig, but were continually forced to seek shelter by a thunderstorm. After this finished they went back to the digging, but a huge black bull came roaring from the pit, and they had to run for their lives. They felt it imprudent to continue digging after that.

COUNTY DIARY

June:	Montgomeryshire County Show, Welshpool

PEMBROKESHIRE

SIR BENFRO

COUNTY FACTS

Derivation of name: From the Welsh penn bro meaning 'head of the district'. Pen bro or brog meaning 'end land' was mutated by the Normans to Penbroc. 'Pen' very common in Celtic areas such as Cornwall and Wales, meaning promontory or head.

First Recorded: 1180

Motto: Ex Unitate Vires (Strength From Unity)

County Town: Haverfordwest

Towns: Fishguard, Goodwick, Haverfordwest, Johnston, Letterston, Merlin's Bridge, Milford Haven, Narberth, Newport, Neyland, Pembroke, Pembroke Dock, St Davids, St Dogmaels, Saundersfoot, Tenby.

St Davids is the smallest city in Wales. Haverfordwest is a county of a town unto itself.

Local Government

Dyfed County Council and two District Councils.

HISTORY

In 1797 Britain was invaded for the last time, when a French force under an American adventurer called Tate landed at Strumble Head near Fishguard. They were far too few to accomplish anything on their own, but had hopes of stirring up a peasants' revolt. This was not forthcoming, so they did some desultory looting and drinking until Lord Cawdor advanced upon them with the Castlemartin Yeomanry. The defensive ranks were swelled by a number of local women led by Jemima Nicholas, who wrapped themselves in red cloaks so as to look like redcoats in the distance. The French were so terrified by the sight that they surrendered without a struggle on the beach below Goodwick. Jemima lived to tell the tale (many times) until 1832.

INDUSTRY PAST AND PRESENT

Fishguard is a major ferry port, with the best communications to Rosslare and Cork. Sea-trout are fished, strictly as a luxury item.

A little copper was worked in the 19th century, but it was never profitable. Lead and iron were scarcely more so. Some slate was also worked, but it was of poor quality.

TOPOGRAPHY INCLUDING RIVERS

The county is bounded in the east by Carmarthenshire and Cardiganshire, otherwise by the Bristol Channel and Irish Sea. The Preseli range of low mountains runs down the centre of the county, which is otherwise fairly flat. In the north the rocks are mainly slate, grit and shale; in the south there is old red sandstone and carboniferous limestone. The highest point is Prescelli Top, 1760 feet.

Rivers: Eastern Cleddau, Western Cleddau, Nevern, Gwann, Solva.

LANDMARKS

St David's Head has an exceptional promontory fort, with a stone rampart and two banks. Inside there are plenty of huts and other remains.

MONUMENTS

Pembroke Castle was built by Henry I, and the central tower still stands, though the castle was besieged and dismantled by Cromwell.

There is a cromlech of impressive size at **Penre-Evan**.

At **Carew Castle** there is a 14 foot carved Celtic cross.

Manorbier Castle walls are down now, but the inner court remains intact. It has never been besieged, not being on the way to anywhere, and was much used by smugglers in former times because of its secluded location.

St David's Cathedral is the finest in Wales and displays an ornate late Romanesque nave topped by a Tudor wooden ceiling of great complexity.

FAMOUS PEOPLE AND LOCAL CHARACTERS

Giraldus Cambrensis (Gerald du Barri) was born in Pembroke in 1147. He was destined for the Church, and educated at St David's and at Paris. He accompanied Prince (later King) John on his expedition to Ireland, which allowed him to write his *Topography of Ireland*, in 1185, and his *History of the Conquest of Ireland* the following year. This is a most valuable factual history, as Giraldus confines his imagination to speeches which he puts in the mouths of the protagonists, describing events realistically as they happened. In 1188 he accompanied the Archbishop of Canterbury on a crusading mission through Wales, which provided material for his *Itinerary of Wales*.

In 1189 he was elected to the See of St David's, but John intervened to withhold it from him, believing that he was too keen on Welsh independence to be trusted in such a position. Undeterred he pleaded his case all the way to Pope Innocent III in 1189, but the Pope sided with John, so Giraldus returned to England, where he continued to write, mainly on church history. However, he also wrote a history of his own times, which includes a great deal about the domestic affairs of Henry II and his sons that Henry and they might possibly have preferred to keep dark. It is not unfair to say that without Giraldus we would never have had Anouilh's *Becket* or *The Lion in Winter*.

Henry VII was born in Pembroke Castle in 1457.

Local Characters

In the 5th century **St Gowan** lived near St Gowan's head, in a cell only accessible by a narrow flight of over 60 exposed steps. It is uncertain how many there are, as the same person will count different numbers going up and down. People who went to the trouble of visiting him were sometimes rewarded with a miraculous cure. The cell is supposed to have opened up miraculously to receive St Gowan, and to have closed behind him if danger threatened. It may still be seen, and was visited by people hoping for cures into the 19th century.

ART AND LITERATURE

'St Govan still lies in his cell.
But his soul, long since, is free,
And one may wonder – and who can tell –
If good St Govan likes Heaven as well
As his cell by that sounding sea?'
    A.G. Prys-Jones

'Ye sailors bold both great and small
That navigate the ocean,
Who love a lass that's fair and tall,
Come hearken to my motion;
You must have heard of Milford Haven
All harbours it surpasses,
I know no port this side of Heaven
So famed for handsome lasses.'
    Lewis Morris

LOCAL FOLKLORE

There were three brothers called Wil, Siôn and Dai. They owned a farm which they all worked. One day Wil was ploughing when by accident he hit the ox a blow which killed it. He went home and told the others what had happened, but they disbelieved him, trussed him up, and threw him into the sea. However, their trussing was poor, and Wil struggled free. That night he crept home, skinned the ox and took the skin away with him.

In town he sold the hide, and hid the money in pennies and halfpennies at various spots outside the town. Meanwhile he cured and tamed a wounded bird that he found. When the bird was fully recovered he went walking with it, treating it with exaggerated care. People asked what he was doing with the bird, and at first he refused to say, but at length confessed that it was a magic bird, that could always find where money was lost or hidden. No one believed him, but he proved it by taking it round all the places where he had left the hide money. At each spot he surreptitiously tweaked the bird, so that it cried out, and then turned over the earth to disclose the money. Many people wanted to buy the bird, but he wouldn't sell till an old miser offered him £100 for it. He then made haste to the next town, where he spent the money on a drove of sheep.

Then he took the sheep back to the farm, where he greeted his brothers as if nothing had happened. At first they thought he was a drowned ghost, but when he was obviously still alive, they asked, how he had come by all those sheep?

'They run wild under the sea,' Wil said, 'but they're hard to catch. If I'd a couple of helpers, I could catch a lot more.'

'Where under the sea?' Siôn asked.

'Where the grass is best, like other sheep. And that's always where the water's deepest.'

So the three went down to a headland, where the sea was very deep, and Siôn jumped at once. Various bubbling and gurgling sounds arose.

'What's that noise?' Dai asked.

'That's Siôn, taking all the best sheep for himself. Best jump at once.'

Presently Wil went back to his farm. He had always wanted the place to himself.

DISTINCTIVE FLAVOUR

In the reign of Henry I **a colony of Flemings** took up residence in the extreme west of the county. Finding English much easier to learn than Welsh, they adopted it, and sustained their identity up to the beginning of the 20th century. Consequently that part was called 'Little England beyond Wales'.

Pembrokeshire potatoes are said to be the sweetest potatoes grown.

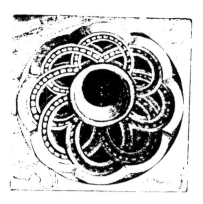

ST DAVID'S CATHEDRAL – ORNAMENTAL STONEWORK

COUNTY DIARY

On **Twelfth Night**, Hunting the Wren takes place in Pembrokeshire, to symbolise the end of winter. A wren is captured and put in the 'wren house', a wooden cage decorated with ribbons. It is then carried in pomp round the village, where the men sing ironical songs about the dangers of their hunt and the fearsomeness of the quarry. They stop at every house, and are given drinks or small amounts of money. The wren, if still alive, is released when the last man becomes insensible.

On **New Year's Day** at Tenby children sprinkle passers-by with fresh raindrops from twigs of box or holly. This is considered to be lucky, and those so favoured are expected to give the children money. Beware!

June 1st:
    Pembrokeshire Day

August: Pembrokeshire County Show, Withybush, Haverfordwest

RADNORSHIRE

SIR FAESYFED

HISTORY

Lord William de Breos of Llanbedr Painscastle led the army which in 1198 inflicted the most crushing of all defeats by the English on the Welsh. The River Bachawy ran red with the blood of over 3,000. The Welsh were led by Prince Gwenwynwyn, whose motives were personal as much as political, since Lord William had murdered his cousin, after first dragging him through Brecon tied to a horse's tail.

Lord William and his Maud both came to unhappy ends under King John. William was stripped of his land and titles and died a beggar, while in 1210 Maud and her son were imprisoned in the dungeons of Corfe Castle with only a sheaf of wheat and a piece of raw bacon between them. After only 11 days the dungeon was opened, and both were dead, Maud having started to eat the body of her son, beginning with the cheeks.

Maud was supposed to be a witch, and there is a stone in Lowes churchyard which she threw there from three miles away.

Radnor only achieved the status of a county under Henry VIII.

INDUSTRY PAST AND PRESENT

Reservoirs have been built in the valley of Elan to supply Birmingham. Agriculture runs largely to sheep farming, though vegetables are grown in the east. The soil is not mainly good enough for wheat, but oats, barley and potatoes are grown.

The county has never had much industry, and agriculture has had little scope for change since the introduction of the potato.

LANDMARKS

Offa's Dyke enters Radnorshire at Knighton and runs south to enter Herefordshire at Berva Bank.

MONUMENTS

Maesyronen Chapel is a perfectly-preserved Dissenting chapel from 1679.
Llananno Church has an exceptional Perpendicular rood screen, with a great deal of carved foliage.
Abbeycwmhir exhibits the remains of the Cistercian abbey of St Mary.

FAMOUS PEOPLE AND LOCAL CHARACTERS

Llewellyn, last Welsh Prince of Wales is according to legend, very much associated with Abbeycwmhir.

ART AND LITERATURE

'There's no more beautiful walk anywhere than the one from Tregaron to Abergwesyn. It's about fourteen miles, and the country is wonderfully varied, though all on a miniature almost domestic scale, with grassy mountains, rocky mountains, and finally a perfect hanging valley complete with waterfalls, and less than four miles long. It makes for a perfect morning, but the only trouble is, there's no pub in Abergwesyn, so you have to carry on another four miles into Llanwrtyd Wells, or over ten miles into Llandrindod Wells if you want a drink. That means covering three counties before lunch and qualifies you as a serious walker.'
N.C. Black

TOPOGRAPHY INCLUDING RIVERS

The county is bounded in the north by Montgomeryshire and Shropshire, in the east by Herefordshire, in the south by Breconshire, and in the west by Cardiganshire. The terrain is extremely mountainous, most of the geology being ancient crystalline rocks, though with some overlying slate and grit. Most of the lowland is bog or moor. The highest point is in Radnor Forest, 2166 feet.
Rivers: Wye, Elan, Ithon.

DISTINCTIVE FLAVOUR

Together with Breconshire, Radnorshire forms one of the largest parliamentary constituencies in the UK. It is a constant complaint from the agents of all parties that their unit **canvassing costs** are far greater than anyone else's, and no allowance is made for this in calculating their permitted budget.

Radnorshire regards itself as **the least Welsh part of Wales**, having been conquered by Harold Godwinson before the Normans ever came there. By 1931 Welsh-speakers were below 5%, not all of them very fluent. Consequently it holds aloof from the controversy between the 'North Walian' and 'South Walian' forms of the language, though the insistence on Welsh for many bureaucratic posts may have raised interest in the language.

COUNTY DIARY

July:	Llanelwedd, on the opposite bank of the River Wye to Builth Wells (Breconshire), hosts the great Royal Welsh Show every year.

The *Real* Counties of

Scotland

A BERDEENSHIRE

COUNTY FACTS

Derivation of name: Brittonic, At the mouth of the Don.
First Recorded: 1100
County Town: Aberdeen
Towns: Aberdeen, Ballater, Braemar, Bucksburn, Cults, Dyce, Ellon, Fraserburgh, Huntly, Inverurie, Maud, Mastrick, New Deer, New Pitsligo, Old Meldrum, Peterculter, Peterhead, Rosehearty, Strichen, Turriff. Aberdeen is a county of a city unto itself.

Local Government
Grampian Regional Council and four District Councils. In Armstrong's *Scotch Atlas* of 1777, that part of the ancient division of Buchan north of the River Ugie was included in Banffshire, locating towns such as Fraserburgh, Rosehearty, Strichen, New Pitsligo and Turriff in Banffshire.

HISTORY

The Sixth Earl of Mar raised the standard for the 1715 Jacobite Rebellion at Braemar on September 17 of that year, in support of James Stuart. This started favourably, but rapidly decayed into a morass of missed opportunities resulting from divided and ineffective command. The rebels took Perth, but failed to take Edinburgh, being foiled by a detachment sent by the Duke of Argyll. They took Leith instead, but it wasn't the same. They might also have taken Stirling, which was held by Argyll, but now with too small a force to hold out long. Instead they then marched on England, taking Lancaster on November 7 without opposition. Indeed they had no serious opposition until the Battle of Preston, where they were forced to surrender with the loss of 1,461 prisoners. On the same day their other forces were defeated by Argyll, who now had reinforcements, at Dunblane, and Lovat handed over the Pass of Inverness to the English.

Meanwhile, just as if he had won, James set himself up as James VIII and III at Peterhead, and set off on a progress round his kingdom. But by this time Argyll had had enough nonsense for one winter, and marched against them with a major force. Still with no further pitched battles, James retreated to Montrose and sailed into permanent exile, first in France later in Italy. He was buried in Rome, where his pretensions are graven on the stone of his sarcophagus in Latin of inexcusable barbarity. The noblemen who had supported him were less fortunate; some were beheaded, the rest disgraced and improverished. Of the common soldiers condemned to death and mainly hanged at Lancaster, 1,000 were reprieved to end their short and uncomfortable lives as plantation slaves.

INDUSTRY PAST AND PRESENT

Aberdeen is the centre of the Scottish fishing industry and a major seaport. It has become the centre of the British Oil Industry, with all the main companies basing themselves in the city. At one point property values were the highest in the whole of the British Isles and on par with the most exclusive parts of London, due to the oil boom. It also possesses an airport at Dyce, six miles to the north. Peterhead is the terminal for the Fulmar Flags and Frigg pipelines. Stockbreeding is done extensively in the county. Agriculture includes oats, barley, turnips and potatoes. Granite used to be quarried very extensively and Aberdeen was at one time a major centre for paper, linen and sailcloth. There was also paper-making and quarrying.

TOPOGRAPHY INCLUDING RIVERS

The county is bounded in the northeast and north by the sea, and on the south and west side by Perthshire and Angus, on the north by Inverness and Banffshire. The coastline is mainly convex, so that the points of Buchan Ness and Keith Inch are the easternmost in mainland Britain.

The surface is generally hilly, with cliffs of over 170 feet in many places, and the Grampians forming the southern boundary. The rock is chiefly grey granite, so that Aberdeen is sometimes called 'The Granite City'. Red granite is also present, especially near Stirlinghill. When nuclear installations are being considered, the effect on the people living nearby is often computed in terms of whether it would or would not be as great as if they had moved to Aberdeen. Elsewhere in the county there is abundant mica slate. The highest point above sea level is Ben Macdhui, 4296 feet.

Rivers: Don, Dee, Ythan, Ugie, Deveron.

LANDMARKS

Grampians – a large mountain range of granite outcrops.

MONUMENTS

Balmoral is the Scottish country residence of the Queen, where the spirits of Queen Victoria and Ghillie Brown linger yet, under the name of 'Balmorality'.

Braemar Castle was built in 1628 and has a gloomy underground pit.

Aberdeen Cathedral, dedicated to St Machar, retains 2 15th-century towers.

Aberdeen University is of unusual antiquity, and has that rare and lovely Scottish architectural device, a crown spire.

FAMOUS PEOPLE AND LOCAL CHARACTERS

John Arbuthnot was born in 1667, the son of a clergyman, and trained in medicine and mathematics. He excelled in medicine, and as an essayist on scientific subjects, becoming FRS and in 1709 Physician in Ordinary to Queen Anne. He took up with the Scriblerus Club, where he became friendly with Swift, Pope and Gay, and is credited with the invention of 'John Bull', the archetypal Englishman. His epitaph on the great rake, Colonel Charteris, represents the detached savagery of Augustan wit at its finest. Swift wrote in his 'Lines on the Death of Dr Swift',

> 'Poor Pope will mourn a month, and Gay
> A week, and Arbuthnot a day.'

Arbuthnot died in 1735, from chronic asthma.

Local Characters

Robert Hamilton, who taught mathematics at the university, was the original absent-minded professor. He had to be checked over each time he left home in the morning, to make sure he was completely dressed, and his students used to amuse themselves by shooting peas at him. On one occasion, however, one of them set off a firecracker, and he bolted out of the room, mistaking it for a shot.

As he stood quaking in the corridor a group of students emerged to apologise, and beg him to come back in. "Gentlemen," he said to them, "I have no objection to your peas, for I can easily protect myself with my hand, but I entreat you to spare my life." This so moved the students that they voluntarily denied themselves anything more lethal than peas thereafter.

ART AND LITERATURE

> 'Here lies the body of Mary Charlotte,
> Born a virgin, died a harlot.
> She was ay a virgin till aged fifteen,
> Which is a record for auld Aberdeen,'
> **Anon**

LOCAL FOLKLORE

The Church of Old Deer

When the church of Old Deer was to be built, on a small hill called Bissau, they found their work constantly impeded by supernatural obstacles. At length they summoned the Spirit of the River, which told them:

> 'It is not here, it is not here
> That ye shall build the church of Deer;
> But on Taptillery,
> Where many a corpse shall lie.'

So they transferred operations to Taptillery, where the church was completed.

There was a young man called John, the son of a crofter of Gairnside who had been walking out for over a year with a local girl. They used to meet at half-past ten every Sunday night behind a bush.

One night he was on his way to meet her when he was accosted by a white lady, who was leaning against a gate. She asked him where he was going.

"To meet my sweetheart."

"I know that," the lady said, "for I've been watching you over a year, and I can tell you, she's playing you false with another man."

"I don't believe you," he said.

"Then don't stop at the bush where you meet her, go to the bush further on, and you can hear for yourself."

So he went to the next bush, and here he heard a man's voice saying, "He's always carrying on with you."

Then he heard his own sweetheart answer, "And for that I'll need to be hurrying on now, for he's coming down to meet me, and I don't want to disappoint him."

John stood there, hearing all this coming from the bush, so he came away and went back to the gate where the lady was still leaning, "Now you've found out for yourself," she said.

"Yes," he said, "I've found out for myself."

"What are you going to do now?"

He shrugged. "I've nothing to do but go home again."

"Well," she said, "I know you've been meeting that girlfriend of yours for over a year. Could you meet me for a week?"

He could see no harm in meeting her for a week.

"Then I want you to meet me every night for a week at half-past ten. Can you do that?"

"I don't see what could hold me back, when I've been seeing the same girl for over a year."

"Then the bargain's made?"

"The bargain's made."

So John promised to meet her next day and set off home, but he was hurt and brooding about his sweetheart who had been false to him for a year, though he did not mention it

FYVIE CASTLE : THE SOUTH FRONT

Gold Armlet, found at Belhelvie, Aberdeenshire
(12 inches in length).

to his parents, and he did not sing or whistle as he normally did at work next morning.

His father noticed, and said to his mother there seemed something amiss with the lad. She reckoned it was nothing, but he went to the foreman, and asked how he was getting on in the field. The foreman said his work had fallen off, and he had noticed he was not whistling any more.

That night he had his supper and left the house, just as if he was going to meet his sweetheart. Once he was gone the old man asked, "Where's he off to?"

"Oh," his wife said, "you know what we were like when we were young. He's probably thinking of getting married."

"Oh. There might be something in that."

So off he went, meeting his new sweetheart every night, but it worried the father, because it seemed to him that John was getting more worn-out every day from meeting her. So he had a word with the foreman to follow him next time.

So next evening he had his supper and then off he went, and the foreman followed him. And after he had gone about a mile and a half or two miles down the road he saw John going along with his arm outstretched as if it was round a girl's waist, and talking to himself like a madman. "Well bless me!" he said to himself, "What's the matter with him? Has he lost his head?"

All this time the lad was talking to himself, like a man talking to his sweetheart, and then he came up to the gate, and went through it to an old ruined wash-house. There was nothing for the foreman to do but go home. Meanwhile John was in a cellar under the ruins, where the lady was entertaining him to a fine meal with the best of wines. But at about 11 o'clock she said to him, "Now it's time for you to be going, but I'll walk you home, part of the way."

John agreed to that, though it seemed to him rather odd that the lady should be walking the man home, which he had always taken to be the man's part. But he went with her as far as the wood, when she said, "I must be going back now, but be sure to be there tomorrow, for it's the last time."

And off she went. But as he was going through the wood he said to himself, "Perhaps, but I hope it's not a ghost I've been speaking to and making dates with."

"Oh no," he heard her voice say, "I'm not a ghost, I'm always here."

So he went home, and if he'd been brooding before, he was brooding twenty times more now. But next morning was to be the last time, but this time all three of them went – father and mother following the son. And they saw his arms going round her, but they couldn't see her, and they thought he must be going off his head and had murdered his sweetheart. So they went to the farm where she worked, and the farmer told them she was still there, and nothing amiss. And indeed, they met her, as she came in from the late milking.

But meanwhile John went into the ruin, and dined with the lady again. And at midnight she said, "This is the last time, and now you'd better be home. And don't come here again, for tomorrow I'll come for you."

So John went home again, more worried than ever about what she might be, but next morning he was having his breakfast when there came a rap on the door. His mother went to see who it was, and there was the white lady, fully visible.

"Who are you wanting?" she asked, for of course she didn't recognise her.

"You've a young man staying here."

"There's only one young man here, and that's my son."

"Indeed," she replied. "I'm the lady he's been walking out with."

So then they all came out, and they went to the old ruin where the two used to meet, but now the ruin was gone, and there was a big castle.

So John asked, "What's the idea of going down into the ruins, when all the time there's that castle there?"

"Oh," she said, "It's a long story, but a long time back I was a young lady, just as you see me now, and my brother was left that place, and he was a jealous brother. I was courting a young gentleman, and my brother was jealous, so he paid a witch to enchant me into a ghost. And the first man that could carry on and make love to me for a full week would break the spell, but nothing else could."

DISTINCTIVE FLAVOUR

The people delight in their reputation for **meanness**, and many stories are told of it. The most archetypal of all, according to J.B. Morton goes as follows:

'An Englishman, an Irishman and an Aberdonian were enjoying a drink in a pub, when it happened that three flies fell into the whisky which each had before him. The Englishman rang the bell and asked for a spoon. He then fished the fly out and ground it under his heel; the Irishman picked his out between thumb and forefinger, and threw it into the spittoon; but the Aberdonian picked his up and wrung it out.'

Aberdeen cutlet is old-fashioned slang for a dried haddock.

Aberdeen nips is a supper dish, made of smoked haddock in a white sauce.

Aberdeen rowies are light bread rolls with an unexpected similarity to croissants. As they contain a large amount of butter, they are eaten with jam only.

'Many a mickle makes a muckle' is a local variation on 'Look after the pennies and the pounds will look after themselves'.

COUNTY DIARY

August: Turriff Show

September:
    Royal Highland Games
    at Braemar

ANGUS
(FORFARSHIRE)

COUNTY FACTS

Derivation of name: Named after Angus, son of Fergus, an 8th century king of the Picts. Alternatively from Aeneus, brother of Kenneth II (c.838) who divided this part of Scotland between his two brothers Aeneus and Mekras as a reward for their wartime service. Also suggested is a Gaelic source from the tribe of the Oengus.

First Recorded: 1150

Motto: Lippen on Angus (Depend on Angus)

County Town: Forfar

Towns: Arbroath, Brechin, Broughty Ferry, Carnoustie, Dundee, Downfield, Edzell, Fintry, Forfar, Friockheim, Invergowrie, Kirriemuir, Lochee, Monifieth, Montrose, Southmuir. Dundee is a county of a city unto itself.

Local Government
Tayside Regional Council and two District Councils.

HISTORY

About 1460 a tribe of cannibals similar to Sawnie Bean and his family was flushed out of a cave near Fenisden. They were summarily executed, except for one child of about a year old, who was fostered in Dundee, until 'she came to a woman's years'. She was then tried for the crimes to which she had been party in her babyhood, and condemned to be burnt. This illustrates the generosity and kindliness of the people, since by allowing her the chance to repent they also allowed her soul a chance of Heaven. Note also that the fosterers could have no prospect of any return on their investment, but did it for love.

Regrettably, she spurned this kindness, and as she was being led away to execution she replied to the many women who lined the road, cursing her for her 'damnable deed', 'Whyfore chide you me, as if I had committed an unworthy act? Give me credence and understand, if you had experience of eating men and women's flesh, you would think it so delicious that you would never forbear again.' She was therefore publicly burnt, with no sign of repentance.

INDUSTRY PAST AND PRESENT

The county is mainly rural, with sheep being raised in the uplands, and cattle in the glens. It also produces high-grade seed potatoes for export. Whitefish curing is important in Arbroath, and Dundee has a range of engineering and minor ship building industries. Dundee and Montrose are famous for strawberry and raspberry jam.

In the last century the county was famous for the manufacture of coarse linen and jute. This is still carried on, but with more emphasis on quality.

LANDMARKS

Bell Rock Lighthouse, designed by R.L. Stevenson's father.

MONUMENTS

The rose window of the gutted **Arbroath Abbey** is known as the 'O' of Arbroath. **Glamis Castle**, now most celebrated for its links with Queen Elizabeth the Queen Mother, is an exceptionally lavish example of Scottish 17th-century architecture.

TOPOGRAPHY INCLUDING RIVERS

The county is bounded on the east by the sea, on the south by the Firth of Tay, in the west by Perthshire, and in the north by Aberdeen and Kincardineshires. There are a number of 'vitrified forts'. These are obviously artificial ramparts of granite that have been fused together by great heat, presumably in pre-historic times. They are a mystery, since though great deciduous forests are known to have been present at one time, and enormous oaks and ashes have been found in peat bogs, even if the entire country had been deforested to supply the fires, there would have been nothing like enough. At the same time, there were no coal-workings at such an early date. The highest point is Glas Maol, 3502 feet.

Rivers: Isla, Esk (North and South).

Edzell Castle, in ruins, dates from 1604. The charmingly named **Claypotts Castle**, built between 1569 and 1588, is remarkable for the eccentricity of its plan.

FAMOUS PEOPLE AND LOCAL CHARACTERS

St Margaret lived on a peninsula in Loch Brechin, at that time an island, but before that she was married to King Malcolm Ceannmor. She was a sister of Edgar Atheling, and made it her mission to anglify Scotland as far as lay in her power. Her main project was to persecute the Celtic Catholic Church in favour of the Roman, in which she was so successful that it effectively died out, in gratitude for which she was canonized in 1250.

'Lola Montez' (Maria Gilbert) was born at Montrose in 1820. She practised the art of exotic dancing with a flair rarely seen before or since, creating an especially favourable impression on King Ludwig of Bavaria (the Dream King). He made her his mistress, but unlike Nell Gwynn, she was unable to resist the lure of political dabbling. She was banished in 1848, but continued to perform all over the world (including Australia) until her death in New York in 1861.

James Graham, born 1612, First Marquis of Montrose, was one of the great romantic figures of history, fit to complete a trio with Alexander the Great and Sir Philip Sidney. None of the three lived to see his fortieth birthday.

Montrose's allegiance was always towards abstract freedom and justice, which inevitably alienated him from both sides in the bitter feuds of the King and the Covenanters. He signed the First Covenant, because he rejected Charles I's attempt to stifle religious freedom; but he turned against it because he equally rejected the Covenanters' attempt to usurp the political power of the King. This left him on the wrong side during Cromwell's ascendancy, and though he held Scotland for the King by means of a series of victories, he lost at Philiphaugh. Charles I surrendered to the Covenanters, which finished the first half of Montrose's military career.

The second half was disastrous. He took service on behalf of Charles II and invaded Scotland, but his fleet was wrecked in a storm, leaving him with next to nothing to fight the battle of Carbisdale, where he was routed by Colonel Strachan. He went into hiding, but was caught by MacLeod of Assynt, who turned him over to Colonel Leslie, who turned him over to the Covenanters, who hanged him at Edinburgh in 1650, in defiance of both chivalry and his rank, which entitled him to beheading. But he displayed the highest élan on that occasion, making it his chief concern to present a handsome and creditable figure, so that on the eve of his execution, Sir Archibald Johnstone upbraided him for being more concerned with the state of his hair than that of his soul. His reply was, "While my head is my own, I will dress and adorn it; but tomorrow when it becomes yours, you may treat it as you please."

He was hanged with his book on the civil wars and the manifesto he had issued to rally the Scots to him round his neck. His own testament is as follows:

'He either fears his fate too much,
Or his deserts are small,
That puts it not into the touch,
To win or lose it all.'

It is said that the executioner wept.

Local Characters

William McGonagall invented and perfected a type of poetry which still bears his name. The technique is based on continuing the line until a rhyme (or near rhyme) for the preceding one is found before starting the next, and McGonagall applied it mainly to subjects of public interest and concern. This one describes a dinner which he attended:

'The Banquet consisted of roast beef, potatoes and red wine,
Also hare soup and sherry, and grapes most fine,
And baked pudding and apples, lovely to be seen,
Also rich sweet milk and delicious cream.'

That McGonagall received no recognition from the literary establishment of the 1890s demonstrates that art was already becoming alienated from the people. If you go to any local literary society, or poetry workshop, you are likely to meet at least one and usually several followers of McGonagall, who employ the same technique to very much the same effect.

LOCAL FOLKLORE

The Laird of Balmachie's wife

In the olden times, when it was the fashion for gentlemen to wear swords, the Laird of Balmachie went one day to Dundee, leaving his wife at home ill in bed. Riding home in the twilight, he had occasion to leave the high road, and when crossing between some little romantic knolls, called the Cur-hills, in the neighbourhood of Carlungy, he encountered a troop of fairies supporting a kind of litter, upon which some person seemed to be borne. Being a man of dauntless courage, and, as he said, impelled by some internal impulse, he pushed his horse close to the litter, drew his sword, laid it across the vehicle, and in a firm tone exclaimed: 'In the name of God, release your captive.'

The tiny troop immediately disappeared, dropping the litter on the ground. The Laird dismounted, and found it contained his own wife, dressed in her bedclothes. Wrapping his coat around her, he placed her on the horse before him, and, having only a short distance to ride, arrived safely home.

Placing her in another room, under the care of an attentive friend, he immediately went to the chamber where he had left his wife in the morning, and there to all appearances she still lay, very sick of a fever. She was fretful and discontented, and complained much of having been neglected in his absence, at all of which the Laird affected great concern, and, pretending much sympathy, insisted on her rising to have her bed made. She said she was unable to rise, but her husband was peremptory and having ordered a large wood fire to warm the room, he lifted the impostor from the bed, and bearing her across the floor as if to a chair, which had been previously prepared, he threw her on the fire, from which she bounced like a sky-rocket, and went through the ceiling, and out of the roof of the house, leaving a hole in the slates.

He then brought in his own wife, a little recovered from her alarm, who said that some time after sunset, the nurse having left her to prepare a little caudle, a multitude of elves came in at the window, thronging like bees from a hive. They filled the room, and having lifted her from the bed, carried her through the window, after which she recollected nothing further, till she saw her husband standing over her on the Cur-hills, at the back of Carlungy. The hole in the roof, by which the female fairy made her escape, was mended, but could never be kept in repair, as a tempest of wind happened always once a year, which uncovered that particular spot, without injuring any other part of the roof.

The Campbell drummer

In 1640 the Duke of Argyle burned down the house of Airlie. A drummer of the Camerons had been posted in a watchtower to give warning, but he failed to give the alarm. The Ogilvie clansmen assumed this was a case of his own betrayal. rather than the superior cunning of the Campbells, and left him in the burning tower. He climbed up the battlement, still protesting his innocence, and went on drumming until overtaken by the flames.

Ever since then he has drummed before the death of each head of the family. In 1881 the 8th Earl died in America, and the drummer was heard to start drumming by Lady Dalkeith and the Countess of Latham, an hour before the actual event. He was also heard in the camp of the 9th Earl, before he was killed in action in 1900. It was a Sunday, and pious Boer prisoners complained at the profanation of the Sabbath by drumming, though there was no drummer in the camp.

The Pedlar

Some time in the 1880s a certain Irish clergyman was touring Scotland with his wife, when they stopped at an inn on the Perth Road, Dundee. There was only one room available, but it was clean and spacious, and the bed was well aired, so they took it happily enough. Among its other furnishings was a deep walk-in cupboard, which the lady poked into before going to bed.

But as bedtime approached, she began to feel somewhat uneasy, and wished for a candle to be left alight. However, her husband would not permit this, because of the danger of fire. He presently went to sleep, but she did not, and after a while she noticed an unpleasant smell which seemed to be coming from the cupboard. For a while she ignored it, but it grew stronger and stronger, and eventually it became too much, so she got out of bed and went to open the door. Inside she found a hideous, rotting, human head hanging in mid air, lit by the phosphorescence of its own decay. She was too appalled to move or make a sound, and as if this was not enough, it presently began to move towards her. Only then was the spell broken, and she rushed back to waken her husband.

The couple tried prayer, and he tried beating it back with his stick, but it continued to advance on them, the stick passing through without resistance. In their headlong retreat from it, they tripped over and fell in a heap on the floor, whereupon the head passed through them, through the floor and out of sight. The following morning they complained of this intrusion to the innkeeper, who at first ascribed it to a nightmare, then offered them free use of another room 'if only they would hold their tongues'. He finally confessed that he knew all about the haunting, which affected only that room, and then only one occupant in twenty. It was the head of a pedlar who had been murdered there over a century previously by two sailors, who had hidden the body under the wainscotting, and the head under the cupboard floor. As he said, he had the place on a twenty-year lease, and he could hardly shut it up for that.

Martin's Stone

At Kirkton of Strathmatine there is a boulder called Martin's Stone, marking the spot where a little-known hero called Martin killed a dragon. Carvings of the dragon are still to be found on it.

DISTINCTIVE FLAVOUR

Arbroath smokies are whole haddock, with just the guts and head removed. They are only lightly brined and then smoked until cooked by the heat of the smoke fire. They can be skinned and eaten as they are, or warmed and served in melted butter.

COUNTY DIARY

Carnoustie is on the golf circuit which hosts the British Open Championship.

THE ROUND TOWER, BRECHIN

ARGYLLSHIRE

HISTORY

In 1093 King Magnus Barefoot claimed that the Mull of Kintyre was an island. In support of this belief he had his ship dragged across the Isthmus of Tarbert while he sat at the helm, pretending to steer.

In 1614 there was a rebellion of the M'Donalds against the grant of Kintyre to the Earl of Argyll, which was put down with considerable bloodshed. It led to lasting enmity between the M'Donalds and the Campbells.

In 1691 William and Mary issued a proclamation of amnesty to every rebel who would swear to live peaceably, and submit by December 31. Chief Mac Ian of the M'Donalds of Glencoe was late submitting his, which was not received until January 6. He gave an excuse for his lateness, which was accepted, but this and his submission were suppressed by Sir John Dalrymple. In this way the Campbells obtained a warrant from the king to 'extirpate that set of thieves, the MacDonalds'. Accordingly a band of 120 soldiers marched on Glencoe, where they were received with friendship, and billeted in the village. They remained there twelve days, surveying the escape routes, and spent their nights drinking and playing cards with their hosts. The early morning of February 13 was fixed for the massacre, but probably because they had been up all night it was a

TOPOGRAPHY INCLUDING RIVERS

The county is bounded in the north by Inverness-shire, in the east by Perthshire, Loch Long, and the Firth of Clyde, elsewhere by the Atlantic. It also includes some of the Western Isles. The coast is heavily indented, with many narrow islands and the Mull of Kintyre, of which Mr Paul McCartney expressed such fervent approval. Highest point: Bidean nam Bian, 3766 feet.
Rivers: Urchay, Awe.

bungled job, with only 38 men, women and children being killed and the huts put to the torch. Another 300 got away in the confusion, though many of them were to die of hunger and exposure.

In July 1745 Charles Edward Stuart (also known as 'Bonnie Prince Charlie'), having taken over his father's claim to the English and Scottish thrones, landed at Barradale. He set about drawing the people to him, and achieved considerable success, especially at Perth. On this he built cautiously and intelligently. He took Edinburgh (though the Castle, under General Guest, held out against him) though he had not yet built up sufficient force for a credible invasion of England, and there had still been no major battle. That was to come at Prestonpans, where his army and Sir John Cope's manoeuvred against each other until, with the aid of superior local knowledge, Charles was able to engage Cope on favourable terms and routed him.

Charles retired to Edinburgh to consolidate further. Then, having got a large enough army, he marched on London, reaching Derby on December 4. There he learnt that a triple army, under the overall command of the Duke of Cumberland, was waiting for him at Lichfield, Coventry and Stafford, obviously hoping to execute a pincer movement against him. At this point he lost his nerve, and retreated north, hoping to meet further reinforcements. He failed in this, and returned to Scotland, where he enjoyed a number of minor successes, including the defeat of General Hawley at Falkirk. But Cumberland was moving ponderously northward, and by now Charles's headquarters was in Inverness. The final accounting came on April 15 at Culloden, in Nairn. On this occasion Cumberland had the superior local information, and launched the attack. He also had the superior discipline – the highlanders broke line and charged without proper cover, and were left exposed to Cumberland's artillery. Fatalities on Charles's side were only about 1,000, but loss of morale was total. Charles retreated to Gorthleck where he dismissed his army, giving the order *sauve qui peut*. Thenceforth he lived like a hunted animal until the end of June. Then

the medieval castle. Sir Walter Scott nevertheless admired its audacity.

Iona possesses its abbey, and more important, its three stone crosses – survivors of over 300 that stood till destroyed with characteristic fervour at the reformation.

Further evidence of religious zeal is furnished by the ruins of Dunaverty Castle, defended by 300 opponents of the Covenenters in 1647. Compelled by the agonies of Hurst to surrender, they were all immediately slaughtered.

FAMOUS PEOPLE AND LOCAL CHARACTERS

St Columba was born in Ireland in 521, but he made his chief mission to Scotland in 546, basing himself on Iona. He died, very much in the odour of sanctity, in 597.

In his propagation of the Gospel, Columba was particularly fond of using curses to overawe recalcitrant cathechumens. One which he applied to a rich man who refused him hospitality goes like this:

'The riches of that niggardly man who hath despised Christ in the strangers
who came to his gate as his guests will become less and less from this day; he
shall become a beggar; his son shall go from door to door with a half-empty
wallet, he shall be slain by a rival beggar in the pit of a threshing floor.'

Flora MacDonald, daughter of MacDonald of Melton, at great personal risk, conveyed him to the Isle of Skye, in travesty as her maid. From there he made his way, not without further tribulation, to France, spiritual home of the Stuart dynasty, and thence to Rome and his father's menage.

In the nineteenth century many of the inhabitants were exported (this is a more accurate term than 'emigrated') to Canada, with the assistance/coercion of the Duke.

INDUSTRY PAST AND PRESENT

Highland malt whisky is distilled in many places, that of the Isle of Jura being especially fine. There is also some farming, mainly of sheep and cattle, and a great deal of tourism, but less than 5% of the land is under cultivation.

Slate is mined at Ballachulish, but less so than previously. More modern industries are manufacture of woodpulp, chipboard, pit-props and building timbers. Afforestation is being undertaken. holy Loch is the home of the Polaris submarine fleet.

Silver, copper and lead used to be mined, and herring fishing was once of great importance. It has been almost totally replaced by whitefish.

LANDMARKS

Inner Hebrides and Iona – islands of exceptional beauty, where St Columba landed AD597.

Fingal's cave on the Isle of Staffa.

MONUMENTS

Inverary Castle is a poignant example of the 18th century's desire to create an almost wholly spurious and romanticised vision of

The saint always maintained that to be most effective curses should be pronounced from a high place in a loud voice. On the other hand, to nullify the effect of curses by rivals, Columbans used this charm:

'I appeal to Mary, aidful mother of men;
I appeal to Bride, foster-mother of Christ-omnipotent;
I appeal to Columba, apostle of shore and sea
I appeal to heaven,
To all saints and angels that be above.'

Sir Ewan Cameron was born in 1629 and brought up at Inverary in the hope of persuading him to favour the Covenanters, but he always hero-worshipped Montrose. As Chief of the Camerons he joined in the Royalist revolt of 1652, winning the personal commendation of Charles II. He harassed General Monk, including an ambush with only 38 men against a foraging party of 300 in 1654. During this engagement he was wrestled to the ground by an English officer much larger than himself, but prevailed by biting out the man's throat, which he subsequently referred to as 'the sweetest bite of my life'. Ultimately he concluded a truce with Monk and Morgan on terms of unparalleled generosity. Having quite run out of funds to prosecute the war, he was still so formidable that Monk remitted all taxes, paid compensation for damage to timber on his estate, and in return only required exchange of prisoners and his parole.

LOCAL FOLKLORE

Deirdre of the Sorrows

Deirdre, daughter of Phelim the Bard, fell under an evil omen, pronounced by Cathbad the Druid in the presence of Conor, King of Ulster, before she was born. He proclaimed that she would be of unequalled beauty, but three great heroes would die on her account. Conor therefore ruled that she should be raised alone on an island by Cathbad and Lady Lavercam until she was of an age to be his queen. But Lavercam told her that Naoise, not Conor, was the bravest and most beautiful of men. She also told Naoise of Deirdre. Naoise came with his brothers for Deirdre and captivated her, and carried her into his own country of Dalness, where they lived happily. Presently Conor sent as messengers, Connel, Cuchulain and Fergus to say that he forgave the elopement, and there should be peace between them. A dream came to warn Deirdre against believing this, but Naoise trusted the messengers, and they sailed into Erin to make peace with Conor. But the beauty of Deirdre drove Conor mad, so he surrounded their house, and fired it to drive them out.

Naoise and his brothers were trapped in a morass conjured by the magic of Cathbad, and Conor gave no quarter, but with a single stroke smote off their three heads as they stood. But when the time came to bury them, Deirdre leaped into Naoise's grave and clasped him in her arms, and then died of a broken heart. At the sight, Conor died of frenzy.

Captain Forrest

At the time of the Armada the body of a Spanish princess was washed ashore on the Isle of Mull. The people buried her without rites, but she could not lie easy, and her ghost went about the island crying

> 'Worm and beetle, they are whistling
> Through my brain – through my brain;
> Imps of darkness, they are shrieking
> Through my frame – through my frame.'

The King of Spain heard of this, so he sent a ship to avenge the affront to his daughter. It was commanded by Captain Forrest, master mariner and master of the Black Art, who swore he would sweep the island bare. The Lord of Duart heard of this, so he summoned all the witches of Mull to raise a wind to sink Forrest's ship. They did this by raising a stone quern on a rope of straw, and the higher rose the quern, the higher rose the wind. But Forrest worked counter magic, so that the quern could not be raised high enough, even with Black Donald, the strongest man in those parts, to help. Then they obtained the help of the strongest witch of all, Gormal of Moy, and she raised the quern to the roof, just in time, so that the wind rose so high, it blew the iron head off a magic axe Forrest sent to cut the straw rope. Forrest and all his men were drowned in Mull Bay, and the people sing

> 'Aha! Captain Forrest, thou didst boast
> Last year to desolate Mull's coast,
> But now, Hoo-hoo, thy ship is lost!'

DISTINCTIVE FLAVOUR

The people of Argyll take pride in their love of music, especially that of bagpipe, harp and fiddle. They still speak Gaelic (or 'The Doric') to a great extent.

In Lochaber in the late 19th century, the following method was used to avert **the Evil Eye** from a sick child. Two women stood opposite each other, holding an iron hoop vertically between them. The hoop was wrapped in straw, except where they held it, and burning briskly. Two other women stood on either side of the hoop, and passed the child backwards and forwards through the centre of the hoop. After a number of passes, the hoop was quenched by throwing it in the beck. The child's mother took no active part, but watched throughout.

The Isle of Islay produces the finest scallops in the world, and they are especially good smoked. Good restaurants in the area can also supply fresh scallops in creamy sauce.

Oval Bowl-shaped Brooch found in grave No. 2 at Ballinaby, Islay.

COUNTY DIARY

August:	Campbeltown Highland Games
August:	Argyllshire Highland Gathering, Oban

AYRSHIRE

COUNTY FACTS

Derivation of name: From Pict-Celtic name of the river.
First Recorded: 1177
Motto: God schaw the richt
County Town: Ayr
Towns: Ardrossan, Auchinleck, Ayr, Beith, Cumnock, Dalmellington, Dalry, Darvel, Galston, Girvan, Hurlford, Irvine, Kilbirnie, Kilmarnock, Kilmaurs, Kilwinning, Largs, Mauchline, Maybole, New Cumnock, Prestwick, Saltcoats, Stevenston, Stewarton, Troon, West Kilbride.

Local Government
Strathclyde Regional Council and four District Councils.

HISTORY

In 1263 Norwegian invaders were beaten off by Alexander II at the battle of Largs.
In 1570 Gilbert Kennedy, the fourth Earl of Cassilis, kidnapped Alan Stewart, the Commendator of Crossraguel Abbey, whose lands he coveted. Then he roasted him over a fire in the Black Vault of Dunure Castle until he signed over the lands to the Earl.

INDUSTRY PAST AND PRESENT

Coal-mining has been done since 1780, and remains important. Stockbreeding, of Ayrshire cattle among others, remains pre-eminent. The textile trade is centred on Irvine and Garnock.
Ayr was an important seaport until superceded by the Clyde ports. It still exports coal, phosphates and timber, mainly to Ireland. In the 19th century it was important for the manufacture of flowered muslin, tanning and shoemaking.
Many different kinds of stone have been quarried at various times, including freestone, whinstone, pudding-stone, blackstone (for ovens), whetstone and marl. Lead, antimony and copper have also been mined, but were never important.

LANDMARKS

The vitrified fort at Kildoon is an exceptionally handsome example, with a double rampart on the western side for more complete defence.

MONUMENTS

One of Ayrshire's few castles is **Maybole Castle**, a former home of the Earls of Cassilis. Alloway possesses the architecturally insignificant **Burns Cottage**, a museum dedicated to the poet.
Culzean Castle is a glorious Robert Adam house of the 1770's, incorporating an earlier more martial stronghold but mainly renowned for its furnishings that denote an age of comfort rather than conflict.

FAMOUS PEOPLE AND LOCAL CHARACTERS

Robert Burns was born in 1759 on a farm near Ayr, leased by his father, who was too poor to provide him with much education, and died young. He was left with his brother Gilbert to care for a large family, and although his rhymes won him some reputation in the locality, he was unable to publish until 1786. The publication cleared a small profit, and on the strength of it he went to Edinburgh, where he cleared £500. He invested it in a farm in Dumfries but it failed.
He had therefore to take up the occupation of excise officer in Dumfries, a post which paid only £50 per annum, not a great salary for a family man with a drink problem, even then. However, he was a man of little discretion, and though the indiscretions which led to his fathering perhaps as many as 14 illegitimate children were tolerantly regarded, his abandonment of political neutrality to the extent of purchasing weapons for the French revolutionary forces led to his enforced retirement 'on health grounds' in 1791. His poetry continued to provide him with a modest income until his death in 1796.

Robert the Bruce was born in 1274. His early career is ill-documented, but he seems to have played both sides against the middle very effectively vis-à-vis Wallace, Edward I,

TOPOGRAPHY INCLUDING RIVERS

The county is bounded on the west by the Firth of Clyde, on the east by Renfrew and Lanarkshires, and on the south by Dumfries, Kirkcudbright and Wigtonshires. The southern and eastern parts are hilly, elsewhere the clay is near the surface, but the mild climate means that cattle farming is practicable even on such poor soil. The highest point is Shalloch An Minnoch, 2520 feet.
Rivers: Ayr, Farnock, Irvine, Lugar, Doon, Girvan, Stinchar.

and John Baliol. However, in 1305 he tried it once too often and was caught double-crossing Edward by Comyn, who betrayed him. He barely escaped with his life on that occasion, but soon managed to engineer a brawl with Comyn (in the convent of the Minorite Friars) where he stabbed him to death (and his uncle, Sir Robert Comyn, for good measure). Since he could be certain that no one would trust him thereafter, he marched on Scone and proclaimed himself king.

His early attempts to secure his kingdom against Edward were unsuccessful, as he was unable to command sufficient popular adherence. He was hunted throughout the highlands, but never caught, and enjoyed considerable success in surprise attacks on isolated detachments. It is to this period that the apocryphal story about the spider belongs. But he was a man of some charisma, and after Edward died, Edward II lacked the personality and organising ability to triumph over him. He gradually won the country over, and was universally acknowledged in 1310.

He then took the offensive, and won his great victories at Stirling Bridge and Bannockburn, but his hardships had taken their toll, and he fell victim to what was described at the time as leprosy, but was probably psoriasis. He died in 1329.

John Loudon MacAdam who invented the macadam system of road-building, was born at Ayr in 1756. In his capacity as Trustee of the Scottish Roads he made an inestimable contribution to communications, for which he refused a knighthood. His name is immortalised in the word tarmac.

Local Characters

At the beginning of the 17th century **Alexander Kennedy**, Earl of Cassilis, married a woman very much his junior. He was very attached to her, and humoured her, and even took her walking on the Cassilis Downans by moonlight, so that she could 'watch the fairies dance'.

But one day in the absence of the Earl a troop of gipsies, including a handsome young man called Johnny Faa came to the Castle to earn a little money with a display of singing and dancing. The countess was so taken with this

that she eloped then and there with Faa. As soon as the count heard of this he gathered a band of retainers to go in pursuit. They caught up with the gipsies by the Doon, whipped them, and dragged the Countess back in disgrace. The Earl walled her up in a small tower which he had built at Maybole, and a row of stepping-stones laid across the Doon where they were taken is still called the Gipsy Steps.

ART AND LITERATURE

*'Auld Ayr, wham ne're a town surpasses
For honest men and bonny lasses.'*
Burns
Tam O'Shanter

LOCAL FOLKLORE

Sawney Bean was a disreputable character who lived with his girlfriend in a cave system in Ballantrae about the turn of the 15th to 16th centuries. They sustained themselves by highway robbery and murder, and as they retained and ate the corpses of their victims, it was many years before the disappearances on the road were attributed to a single factor. But their 14 children and 32 (incestuously conceived) grandchildren eventually became too much for the locally available food supply, so that they were forced to range further and were thus discovered. They were flushed our, and executed without process at Leith. Neither age nor sex was spared, the men being first castrated and then mutilated so that they bled to death, while the women were forced to look on. Then the women and children were burnt to death in three mass fires, being too numerous for one or two to accommodate.

This story has been perennially popular, and continues to surface in variant forms. The name Sweeney Todd is very likely derived from it, and in the film *The Hills Have Eyes* the story is updated and moved to the United States. H.P. Lovecraft's story, 'The Shunned House' explores a similar theme.

DISTINCTIVE FLAVOUR

The people take pride in the practice of the Presbyterian virtues of piety, decency and dignified behaviour. They maintain that Burns's 'Cottar's Saturday Night' describes them better than any of the other people of Scotland.

The 74th Foot has now been absorbed into Princess Margaret's Own Glasgow and Ayrshire Regiment. Its nickname is the Assaye Regiment, for its great victory at Assaye in 1803. There 2,000 British and 2,500 Sepoys defeated 50,000 Mahrattas.

Shortbread is made throughout Scotland, but it is better understood in Ayrshire than anywhere else. The basic formula is six/four/two – i.e. six ounces of flour, four of butter, two of caster sugar. Local variants are innumerable, but the science is a perfected science – no flavouring quite beats vanilla.

Ayrshire has long produced a special type of **bacon**. The rind is cut away after curing, then the meat is rolled and tied before slicing.

COUNTY DIARY

January 25:
Burns Night

April: The Ayr Show at the Racecourse.

Troon is on the circuit to host the British Open Golf Championship.

Regular race meetings are held at Ayr racecourse

COUNTY FACTS

Derivation of name: From Gaelic – Little pig, an affectionate name for the river Deveron.

First Recorded: 1150

County Town: Banff

Towns: Aberchirder, Banff, Buckie, Charlestown of Aberlour, Craigellachie, Cullen, Dufftown, Findochty, Ianstown, Keith, Marduff, Newmill, Portessie, Portgordon, Portknockie, Portsoy, Tomintoul, Seatown, Whitehills.

Local Government

Grampian Regional Council and two district councils.

HISTORY

In 1010 Viking invaders were defeated in the field of Bloody Pots, Gamrie. The bones of many of them were built into the walls of the church that was built to commemorate the event, and remained in use until 1830.

In 1637 Isobel Malcolm was charged before the Kirk Session of Strathbogle. She proved to be an exceptionally versatile witch. Among her skills were the making of 'corp criadh', an image of an enemy which is allowed to moulder or melt, causing the enemy to die of a wasting disease: the making of moon paste, which involved pulling the moon from the sky; a part of it was then mixed with certain herbs and water from seven different wells, and kneaded together by its own light in the kirkyard, whereafter it could be made into images to bring down curses on enemies or blessings on clients: and the affliction of erisipelas, by cutting red hair into snippets and casting it in the direction of one's enemies.

In 1645 Banff was plundered by the Duke of Montrose.

In *Armstrong's Scotch Atlas* of 1777 that part of the ancient division of Buchan north of the River Ugie was included in Banffshire. Locating towns such as Fraserburgh, Rosehearty, Strichen, New Pitsligo and Turriff in Banffshire. Due to the total complexity of the formation of Scottish county boundaries, this is being researched further.

INDUSTRY PAST AND PRESENT

There are the splendours of salmon fishing (mainly in the Spey). There is also fishing of a more mundane sort, considerable brewing and distilling, and an iron foundry. Agriculture consists mainly of oats, barley, root crops and livestock. There is also boat building, quarrying and the industries dependent on wool.

In the 12th century Banff was a thriving seaport and member of the Northern Hanseatic League. Its herring fishery has also declined.

LANDMARKS

Tomintoul claims to be the highest village in Scotland (1,120 feet).

The Cairngorm Mountains rise in the extreme south of the county.

MONUMENTS

Duff House, by Robert Adam, is an exceptionally fine example of 18th-century classical architecture. It is based on the Villa Borghese.

Banff itself is an unusually elegant town with 17th and 18th-century civic buildings.

FAMOUS PEOPLE AND LOCAL CHARACTERS

James MacPherson, who combined the characters of troubador and footpad, was

TOPOGRAPHY INCLUDING RIVERS

The county is bounded on the south by Aberdeenshire, on the west by Moray and on the north by the Moray Firth. The scenery is varied and undulating, with a great deal of first-class hunting and grazing country. The highest point is Ben Macdhui, 4296 feet.

Rivers: Devenon, Spey, Aven.

caught and sentenced to be hanged in 1700. While in jail he composed a march for himself, and played it while being led away to execution. Burns wrote the words, and it remains among the best-loved marches of the Scottish people.

Local Characters
James Sharp, a famous Presbyterian divine, was apostasized to the Church of Scotland and became Bishop of St Andrews. He persecuted the Covenanters with all the ardour of a convert, and it was said of him that, among other dirty deeds, he deliberately delayed the delivery of a reprieve signed by Charles II, so that a dozen would be hanged after all. He also had 200 battened under hatches in an unseaworthy old ship under pretence of transporting them to the colonies, but ordered the master to run the ship onto a rock. The master and all the crew escaped the wreck, but none of the unwilling passengers. He was murdered on Magus Moor in 1679, in protest at his infidelity and other crimes, real or imaginary.

LOCAL FOLKLORE
The Laird of Duffus
The Laird of Duffus was walking in his fields one day when a cloud of dust whirled past him, and from the midst of it he heard a shrill cry of 'Horse and Hattock'. Being a bold man, he repeated the cry, and immediately found himself whirled away in the air with a troop of fairies to the King of France's cellar. There they caroused all night so merrily that the Laird fell asleep and was left behind. The royal butler found him next day, still fast asleep, with a cup of curious workmanship in his hand. He was taken before the King, and told him all that had happened. The King pardoned him, and he returned home with the Fairy Cup, which was kept in his family for several generations.

Ben Macdhui
Ben Macdhui is haunted by an invisible ghost, Ferlas Mor (the Grey Man). He manifests himself by footsteps which are heard when no one else is present. The climber J. Norman

Collie was once taken with overwhelming panic while alone on the mountain and ran all the way down. He refused ever to climb it again.

DISTINCTIVE FLAVOUR
William Caine, in his novel *The Devil in Solution* had a much larger-than-life hero, Lord Mark Mucklethew, decuple blue, poet, lover, raconteur and MP - for Banff!

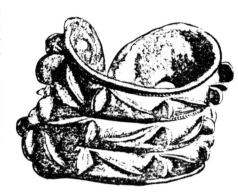

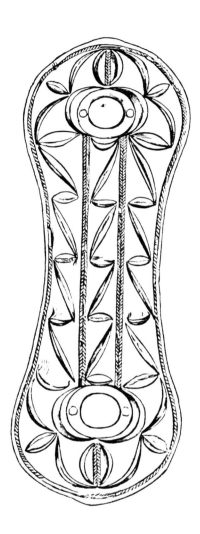

THE ORNAMENTATION ON A BRONZE ARMLET FOUND AT AUCHENBADIE, BANFFSHIRE

COUNTY DIARY

BERWICKSHIRE

COUNTY FACTS

Derivation of name: From Old English berewic – barley farm (bere = barley; wic = farm or dwelling).
First Recorded: 1097
County Town: Duns
Towns: Ayton, Chirnside, Coldingham, Coldstream, Duns, Earlston, Eyemouth, Greenlaw, Lauder, Swinton

Berwick upon Tweed, from which the county takes its name, was decreed to be neither in Berwickshire or Northumberland. It is a county within itself. An 1836 Act of Parliament placed Berwick in England, although that part of the town north of the river Tweed is naturally in Berwickshire.

Local Government

Borders Regional Council and one district council.

HISTORY

Berwick-upon-Tweed was a bone of contention between England and Scotland, changing hands 13 times between 1300 and 1482, when the present county and national border was settled in favour of the English.

INDUSTRY PAST AND PRESENT

The main crops are cereals and roots, and grain-processing, fish-packing and forestry are all done in the county. The Blackadder and Whiteadder are important trout streams. There are also attractive grouse moors, and others, with less heather and more grass for sheep.

In the 19th century there were attempts to mine copper, but there was insufficient ore to make it worthwhile. For a while gypsum was extracted near the Whiteadder, and slate from Lander.

LANDMARKS

Lammermoor Hills
St Abbs Head Wildlife Reserve

MONUMENTS

Mellerstain, home of the Earl of Haddington, was built by William Adam and his son Robert.
Dryburgh Abbey, one of the Scottish border abbeys, was ruined in the 16th century. Both Sir Walter Scott and Field Marshall Earl Haig are buried in it.
Thirlstane Castle is a notable example of a border fortress, altered in the 17th century.

FAMOUS PEOPLE AND LOCAL CHARACTERS

St Ebba, daughter of King Edelfrid of Northumberland, established a convent at Coldingham. This was presently threatened by Danish marauders, so St Ebba, to make herself and her sister nuns less attractive to improper advances, cut off her own nose and upper lip, and all of theirs. The Danes, displeased by the reproach to their manners implicit in this act, burnt them all alive and their convent with them.

Local Characters

Duns Scotus was born in Berwickshire (though this is disputed) in 1265, the fourth of the five great Schoolmen and proponent of the doctrine of the Immaculate Conception, finally proclaimed as an Article of faith by Pius IX in 1854, to the delight of the Dominicans and the discomfiture of the Jesuits.

Though fêted and honoured in Oxford, Paris and Cologne during his lifetime, his school of philosophy was subsequently eclipsed by that of Thomas Aquinas, hence the derivation of 'dunce' from his name – a wildly unsuitable monument to a logician of such skill. More recently his stock has risen; Gerard Manley Hopkins, despite his Jesuit affiliation, proclaimed that Scotus was his favourite philosopher, and the Irish paid him the rather doubtful compliment of putting his portrait on their currency.

TOPOGRAPHY INCLUDING RIVERS

The county is bounded on the east by the sea, on the west by Roxburgh, on the north by East and Mid Lothians, and on the south by the English border. The northwest is hilly, most of the rock being sandstone or slate. Much of the soil is rich in iron, but not sufficiently to be treated as workable ore. There is also a little coal, but too thin to be worth mining. The highest point is Meikle Says Law, 1749 feet.
Rivers: Tweed, Eye, Blackadder, Whiteadder, Dye.

LOCAL FOLKLORE

Thomas the Rhymer

Thomas the Rhymer lived at Ercildoun towards the end of the thirteenth century. At an early age he was carried off to Fairyland where he became a favourite of the Fairy Queen, who conferred upon him the gifts of poetry and prophecy. Both poems and prophecies survive, and of the prophecies it can be said that they are quite as accurate as Mother Shipton's, and easier to understand than those of Nostradamus. However, he was only permitted to return home for seven years, after which time the King and Queen of the fairies, in the form of a stag and a hind, came to summon him from a feast he was holding in his tower at Ercildoun. He followed them into the forest, and was never seen again.

Not far from where Thomas the Rhymer had lived there subsequently lived a jolly rattling horse-coper, named **Canobie Dick**. He was remarkable for his reckless and fearless temper, which made him the admiration and dread of his neighbours. One night he was riding over Bowden Moor, to the west of the Eildon Hills, and leading a pair of horses that he had been unable to sell at market, when he met an old man in antique garb, who enquired if the horses were for sale, and immediately started to bargain for them.

To Canobie Dick, one customer was as good as another – all he cared for was getting the best price he could, never mind how honestly, though he dealt with the Devil himself. At last they agreed on a price, and the stranger paid in good gold, though the pieces were all unicorns, bonnet-pieces, and other obsolete coins. But it was fine gold, which passes current everywhere, and Dick had made a good price, so he was not concerned. Indeed, he agreed to bring more horses to the same spot. He did this several times, and did not at all mind the stipulation that he always come alone and at night.

But after he had made several bargains this way, he began to be curious, so next time he began to complain that dry bargains were unlucky, and that since the old fellow obviously lived somewhere nearby, he ought to stand him a dram, as he would himself had the situation been reversed.

'You may see my dwelling if you will,' the stranger said, 'but if you lose courage at what you see there, you'll be sorry forever.'

Dick laughed at this, and, having secured his horse, followed the stranger up a narrow footpath which led to the odd minor peak between the southern and the central, which is called the 'Lucken Hare', because that is what it looks like. The place is almost as famous for witch-findings as the nearby windmill of Kippilaw, so Dick was more alarmed than surprised to see the stranger enter the hillside by a passage that he had never noticed before, though he knew the district well.

'You may still return', the stranger said, looking ominously back. But Dick was not about to show fear, so he strode on. They entered a very long range of loose boxes. In every stall stood a coal-black horse, and by every horse a knight in black armour, with a drawn sword in his hand, but all were as still as if they had been cast in black iron. Torches in sconces gave a gloomy light to the great hall, which was very long, but at last they came to the upper end, where a sword and a horn lay on an antique table.

'He that shall sound that horn, and draw that sword,' the old man said, 'shall, unless his heart fails him, be King over all broad Britain. So speaks the tongue that cannot lie. But all depends on courage, and on whether you take up sword or horn first.'

Dick recognised from the form of words that this must be Thomas the Rhymer himself, and he was inclined to take the sword, but his bold spirit was quenched by the supernatural horrors of the hall, and it occurred to him that to unsheath the sword without first announcing himself might give offence. So with a trembling hand he took the horn, and blew on it a poor, feeble note, but the best he could manage with his dry lips. There was a terrible answer. Thunder rolled, peal on peal, through the immense hall, as horses and men rose from slumber. The horses snorted and stamped, the warriors clashed their armour and brandished their swords. Dick was terrified to see the whole army about to rush him, so he made a feeble attempt to seize the sword. But as he did so, a fearsome voice pronounced these words:

'Woe to the coward, that ever he was born,
Who did not draw the sword, before he blew the horn!'

Then there came a whirlwind of great fury, which took up poor Dick, blew him from the mouth of the cavern, and cast him down a steep bank of stones. There shepherds found him in the morning, with barely breath enough in his body to tell this tale, before he expired.

DISTINCTIVE FLAVOUR

The great sport of Berwick is **motor-racing**, and at Duns there is a memorial to the driver Jim Clark, twice world champion, killed in 1968. This has not dampened the ardour of Andrew Cowan, the Paris/Dakar rallying champion, or Louise Aitken-Walker, the Ladies Rallying Champion.

Berwick Rangers F.C. is the only 'English' club to play in the Scottish League.

Scotland has a sweet tooth in general, but the **Eyemouth fruit tarts** are generally reckoned the finest anywhere.

COUNTY DIARY

July:	Eyemouth Herring Queen Festival
July:	Earlston Civic Week

BUTESHIRE

COUNTY FACTS

Derivation of name: Named from the island of Bute in the Firth of Clyde. The word Bute may derive from Both = a cell, or Ey Bhod = Island of corn (Gaelic). Alternatively, its source could be the Old Irish word Bòt meaning a fire or a beacon.

First Recorded: 1093

County Town: Rothesay

Towns: Brodick, Craigmore, Millport, Port Bannantyne, Rothesay, Whiting Bay.

Local Government
Strathclyde Regional Council and two District Councils.

HISTORY

Sir John Stewart led the Brandanes, and died fighting alongside Wallace at Falkirk in 1298. In 1544 the Earl of Lennox invaded Bute, intending to sell the island to Henry VIII.

In 1646 the Campbells, in pursuit of their quarrel with Sir James Lamont, made a surprise attack on his castles of Toward and Ascog, knowing he must be in one of them. They destroyed both, murdering everyone they found, either on the spot or by hanging at Dunoon, except Lamont himself, whom Archibald Campbell took to Inverary where he amused himself by torturing him. In 1661, with the Restoration, Campbell was beheaded for this.

In 1686 a new bell was ordered for the Tolbooth. After it was delivered in 1687, a belfry was ordered to accommodate it.

In 1699 the last expedition to the ill-fated colony of Darien sailed from Rothesay Bay. It consisted of four frigates and 1,200 immigrants.

In World War II Bute saw the last phases of two extraordinary feats of navigation and heroism. The tanker San Demetrio was set on fire by shells, and the crew took to the boats. However, the fire went out, so they reboarded. The bridge was burnt out, but they got the engines going and navigated home by dead reckoning and a school atlas, refusing an offer of a tow on the way and fetching up at Rothesay.

Another tanker, Imperial Transport, was actually split by a torpedo. Once again the crew got into lifeboats, but they noticed that the stern half was still afloat. They too reboarded, got the engines going, and finally beached their half ship at Kilchattan Bay. This incident may well be the inspiration for James White's moving novel, *The Watch Below*.

INDUSTRY PAST AND PRESENT

There is some fishing, and mixed farming too, but tourism is the only industry of any note, though crystals are to be found on Arran. There is also some shooting and distilling.

The honour guard of the ancient kings of Scotland was at one time made up wholly of 'Brandanes', or men of Bute.

The first cotton mill in Scotland took its water-power from Loch Fad.

A little coal and iron were worked on the island in the last century.

There was a submarine depot ship based at Bute until 1957.

TOPOGRAPHY INCLUDING RIVERS

The county consists of the islands of Bute, Arran, Great Cumbrae, Little Cumbrae, Inchmarnock, and Pladda. All are formed from ancient crystalline rocks. The highest point is Goatfell on Arran, 2866 feet.

Rivers: Buteshire is without major rivers.

LANDMARKS

The Kyles of Bute are a long narrow sound between Bute and the mainland, very popular with yachtsmen.

MONUMENTS

Rothesay Castle dates from the 13th century, and was added to by James IV and James V.
Rothesay Winter Gardens are a more modern tourist attraction.
Brodick Castle on Arran was the seat of the Duke of Hamilton.

St Blane's Chapel dates from the 11th century.

FAMOUS PEOPLE AND LOCAL CHARACTERS

Walter Stewart married Marjory, daughter of Robert Bruce, who died in childbirth in 1316. The baby, Robert, was therefore heir-presumptive after David Bruce. Walter died in battle in 1326, but Robert was active for independence under David II as soon as he was of age. After many battles and sieges, including the storming of Dunoon Castle and Rothesay Castle, he succeeded David as Robert II, first of the Stewart kings. He was a frequent visitor to Rothesay, and died there in 1390. The Exchequer Rolls of 1376 record that he had sent there 'Pipes of wine, fat cattle, lampreys from the Forth, honey from Blackness, and from Linlithgow many a jar of red Rhine wine to swill down the huntsman's venison'.

Edmund Kean, the famous but hard-drinking tragic actor, maintained a country seat on Bute, for when the city became too much.

Local Characters

Alexander Douglas Hamilton, the 10th Duke, took an extremely hospitable view of his feudal obligations on Arran, so much so that some of his visitors, finding that all they asked for was given free at his expense, decided never to leave. His principal concern in life was to be buried in a style worthy of his station, and to this end bought an Egyptian sarcophagus originally made for a princess. However, he was a very tall man, and though he practised lying at full length in it, he had still not solved the problem at the time of his death in 1852. His last words are said to have been, "Double me up! Double me up!" This alas proved impracticable as rigor mortis had set in, so before he could be buried his feet had to be cut off. Later scholarship proved that the sarcophagus had not belonged to a princess after all, but to her court jester.

LOCAL FOLKLORE

St Blane of Kingarth

The saint's mother, while yet a virgin, became pregnant by drinking water from a sacred well. Her family therefore cast her adrift in a coracle, but she came ashore on Bute where he was born and grew up to work many miracles. He was canonized in AD 1000.

DISTINCTIVE FLAVOUR

The county consists of two major islands, which make no claim to share any particular flavour. Arran will always be associated with **the Arran sweater**, while Bute has its strong naval and political associations.
Arran produces a version of Dunlop cheese, imaginatively named **Arran Dunlop**. Dunlop in general is considered to have a richer, more mellow flavour than Cheddar, another cheese produced in abundance in Scotland.

COUNTY DIARY

August: Bute Highland Games, Rothesay

CAITHNESS

COUNTY FACTS

Derivation of name: From the Celtic/ Norse = People who worship the Cat God.
First Recorded: 970
County Town: Wick
Towns: Castletown, Dunnet, Halkirk, Lybster, Thurso, Wick.

Local Government
Highland Regional Council and one district council.

HISTORY

In 1650 Montrose beseiged and took Dunheath Castle in two days on the way to his ultimate defeat at Carbisdale.

In 1680 the Sinclairs and the Campbells of Glenorchy met in battle to decide who should inherit the earldom of Caithness. The two armies met at Stirkoke, and prepared to fight the next morning, but the preparations of the Sinclairs were less thorough than those of the Campbells, since Campbell had arranged for a shipload of whisky to be wrecked where they could get at the cargo. Their hangovers proved fatal to some 200 of them in the ensuing battle. However, Campbell of Glenorchy was unable to retain the earldom against a hostile country, and had to give it up in 1686. He was granted the barony of Wick in compensation.

In 1792 occurred the Bliadhna nan Coariaich (year of the sheep) when crofters, terrified that they were to be dispossessed in favour of sheep runs, and angered at having to pay fines for the release of impounded cattle, rose with the purpose of driving every Cheviot and Linton sheep from the county – and further if necessary. Five men were tried for various offences in connection with this endeavour, but all were sprung from jail and disappeared.

In 1978 there was a blizzard in which three motorists lost their lives. One who survived was a traveller in ladies' underwear, who wrapped himself in layer upon layer of tights.

INDUSTRY PAST AND PRESENT

Traditional farming remains important, usually on a high-intensity farm of 15 acres or less. Whitefish fishing is also important. There is fish-packing, and at Thurso shellfish-processing, principally of lobsters.

Britain's first nuclear breeder reactor was built at Dounreay in 1955, and remains operational, though threatened with closure. Caithness glass is famous for its excellence, and always supplies the trophy for winning Mastermind.

John O'Groats is a tourist attraction, owned by Peter de Savary who has recently bought Land's End.

Distilling and the manufacture of stockings and protective clothing are carried out in Caithness.

LANDMARKS

The Merry Men of May, the name for the wild breakers in the Pentland Firth. By analogy, the Northern Lights are called 'the Merry Dancers'. The Firth also contains a minor maelström, called Salchie.

The Stalks of Duncansby, two freestone columns, much used by birds.

Ord Ness is a most impressive precipice.

MONUMENTS

John O'Groat's House is no longer extant, but the site is kept in good order for the convenience of people who wish to be photographed there.

May Castle is the residence of the Queen Mother in Caithness.

TOPOGRAPHY INCLUDING RIVERS

The county occupies the extreme northeast of Scotland, being bounded on the west by Sutherland and on all other sides by the sea. The coastline is extremely indented and the cliffs are high, so Caithness is basically a plateau. The highest point is Morven, 2313 feet.
Rivers: Thurso, Wick, Oikel.

FAMOUS PEOPLE AND LOCAL CHARACTERS

Adam Smith was a counterfeiter from Banff, who was caught and condemned to death. But he was also a craftsman of great skill, and while in prison he designed an ingenious lock that so impressed King James (who was an ingenious man himself, and admired it in others) that he pardoned him.

The Earl of Caithness offered him employment of an unspecified kind at Castle Sinclair, in a workshop to which only Smith and himself had access. Not very surprisingly, Sir Robert Gordon, brother of the Earl of Sutherland, soon discovered a flood of false coin covering Caithness, Orkney, Sutherland and Ross. He applied to the King for a warrant for Smith's arrest, which was granted in May 1612. He deputised Donald MacKay and John Gordon to carry it out, which they did, finding a large amount of false gold and silver coin in Smith's house.

But James Sinclair, nephew of the Earl, was furious at this and made an unsuccessful attack on Gordon, in the course of which Sinclair of Stirkage was killed. MacKay panicked and hurried back to offer unnecessary help to Gordon, leaving Smith in the care of his followers, who killed him 'to prevent him escaping'.

There followed a bitter legal wrangle between the Earls of Sutherland and Caithness, the latter alleging murder, and the former treason. They agreed to accept the arbitration of the Marquis of Huntly, but this broke down, so the matter had finally to be settled by the Privy Council. In December 1613 all charges were dropped, leaving the Sutherland party clear victors.

Local Characters

'Tuck o' drum' was the method used until 1792 to summon the people of Thurso to work in the Laird's fields. Those who failed were subject to 'poinding' [impounding] of their fire-tongs and the family's best blanket. During the minority of Sir John Sinclair, Lady Janet Sinclair had the drum sounded very frequently, to the improverishment of the people.

Eventually a certain **Sandy Murray** approached the drummer, and drove his staff through the drum, with a threat to do the same and worse to any other drum (and drummer) who dared to sound again.

Neil M. Gunn was born in Dunbeath in 1891. Though he went south to work as a civil servant, his novels reflect his early life in the county. One, *The Silver Darlings*, is named

for the local term for herring. He died in 1973.

ART AND LITERATURE

'The blighting wind that almost perpetually blights Caithness.'
Alexander Sutherland (1825)

'Its Steepness, and being all along on the very Brink of a Precipice, are the only Difficulties, for otherwise it is one of the finest Roads in the World, being so broad that in most places two Coaches might pass one another.'
Bishop Robert Forbes (1792)

In connection with this it should be mentioned that the Bishop walked beside his horse on the road across the Ord to Wick.

'The meanest of man's towns, and situate certainly on the baldest of God's bays.'
R.L. Stevenson, of Wick

'In communical life it is quite simply the recognition of others, the need to be one with them and to enjoy the work and games, to contribute what one can to increase the mutual delight.'
Neil M. Gunn

LOCAL FOLKLORE

'Fitheach'

There was a witch called Fitheach who lived in a turf hut near Latheron. You could tell she was a witch by all the strange things she had in her hut, such as hair ropes, ravens' feathers and various odd stones. She had an anti-social way of returning friendship, for when a family was kind to her it was noticed that they were putting out more cheeses to dry than ever before, while all the other people's cattle were running dry.

There was nothing to be done, even though Fitheach used to run round the farms at night in the form of a hare, no dog could catch her. One day a man set a snare for the hare, and kept watch over it. In time his patience was rewarded, when the hare ran into the snare. It promptly turned back into Fitheach, but all she did was give him the snare back, and tell him he had better not set it in her path again.

But a few months later he drowned in the Thurso.

DISTINCTIVE FLAVOUR

David II used the weights and measures of Caithness as the standard for the whole of Scotland.

H.V. Norton saw Caithness as a 'strong blonde Viking maiden at her spinning wheel'.

Bowl-shaped Brooch, found with a Skeleton Caithness (4½ inches in length).

COUNTY DIARY

July:	Thurso Gala Week

CLACKMANNANSHIRE

COUNTY FACTS

Derivation of name: From the Gaelic, meaning Stone of Manae, the name of a glacial rock in the town centre.
First Recorded: 1133
Motto: Look about ye
County Town: Alloa
Towns: Alloa, Alva, Clackmannan, Dollar, Menstrie, New Sauchie, Tillicoultry, Tullibody.

Local Government
Central Regional Council and one District Council

HISTORY

Castle Campbell was burned by Montrose in 1645.

INDUSTRY PAST AND PRESENT

The county is generally agricultural, though much of the land has been damaged by former coal working. Alloa has a mix of light industry. Alloa Glass Works was founded in 1750 by Lady Frances Erskine. The 18th century also saw wool-spinning and weaving, tanning, pottery, foundry and cabinet-making established in the town, as well as expansion of the brewing and distilling trades. This heritage is reflected in the present mix of light industry in the town.

The coalmines are now worked out, and the quarrying of granite, freestone and ironstone were never very profitable. Some attempts were made to extract silver, lead, copper and antimony from the hills, but the ore was too lean and too mixed to be worth refining.

LANDMARKS

The Ochil Hills are a gentle range, and afford good pasture for sheep.

MONUMENTS

Clackmannan Tower is a medieval structure which was added to in the 17th century.
Dollar Academy for poor children is a building of great dignity designed by Playfair.

FAMOUS PEOPLE AND LOCAL CHARACTERS

Robert the Bruce reputedly had Clackmannan Tower as his palace.

Local Characters
John Erskine, 6th Earl of Mar, was a great 'improver', who was responsible for the deepwater harbour on the Forth, and the road connecting it with the town. There he encouraged the establishment of shipbuilding and allied industries, including a sawmill, a ropeworks and sailmakers. He also constructed the reservoir at Gartmorn.
David Allan was born in 1744, the son of a shoremaster. He showed an early talent for caricature, which caused him to be known for a while as 'the Scottish Hogarth'. But he found that straight portraiture was more profitable, so that the productions of the later part of his career, as portraitist and illustrator, are worthy rather than inspiring.

TOPOGRAPHY INCLUDING RIVERS

The county is bounded in the south by the Firth of Forth, in the north and west by Perthshire, and in the east by Fife. Most of the surface is alluvial plain, rising to the Ochil Hills in the north. The highest point is Ben Cleugh, 2363 feet.
Rivers: Black Devon.

LOCAL FOLKLORE

The Doom of Mar
The First Earl suppressed the Abbey of Cambuskenneth, and used the stones to build a mansion for himself. The last abbot made the following prophecy:

'Proud Chief of Mar, thou shalt be raised still higher, until thou sittest in
place of the King.
Thou shalt rule and destroy, and thy work shall be called after thy name; but
thy work shall be the emblem of thy house, and shall teach mankind that he who
cruelly and haughtily raiseth himself upon

the ruins of the holy cannot prosper.

Thy work shall be cursed and shall never be finished.

But thou shalt have riches and greatness, and be true to thy sovereign, and

shall raise his banner on the field.

Then, when thou seemest to be highest; when thy power is mightiest, then

shall come thy fall; low shall be thy head amongst the nobles of thy people.

Deep shall be the moan among the children of dool.

Thy lands shall be given to the stranger; and thy titles shall lie amongst

the dead.

The branch that springs from thee shall see his dwelling burnt, in

which a king was nursed, his wife a sacrifice in the same flame; his

children numerous but of little honour; and three born and grown who

shall never see the light.

Yet shall thine ancient tower stand; for the brave and true cannot be

wholly forsaken. Thy proud head and daggered hand must dree thy weird

until horses shall be stabled in thy hall, and a weaver shall throw

his shuttle in thy chamber of state.

Thine ancient tower – a woman's dower – shall be a ruin and a beacon

until an ash sapling shall spring from its topmost stone. Then shall

thy sorrows be ended and the sunshine of Royalty shall beam on thee

once more. Thine honour shall be restored; and the kiss of peace shall

be given to thy Countess, though she seek it not, and the days of

peace shall return to thee and thine.

The line of Marr shall be broken, but not until its honours are

doubled, and its doom is ended.'

This prophecy came true over the generations with detailed accuracy, including the three children born blind, the squatting weaver and the ash sapling on the roof. The only false detail is that when Alloa House was burnt down in 1800, the lady was not killed, the master being a widower of two years' standing.

At Hawkhill, Alloa.

The following tale illustrates the dialect as well as the beliefs and moral tone of the seventeenth century:

In a small cottage, on the summit of Sheardale Braes, lived a man named **Patie M'Nichol**. He was a wee booly-backit body, and wore aye a blue coat, plush waistcoat and knee-breeks, and a 'Tam o'Shanter' bonnet, wi' a red tap. It was darkly hinted that he was in league with the witches. He never wrought ony, but he always had plenty. The Bible he would not read, nor allow a religious book to enter his door. The minister (Mr Couples) hearing this, went to him, and endeavoured to show him the errors of his ways; and so far succeeded as to get Patie to tak' the present o' a Bible! Every Sunday after this saw Patie at the kirk; and although the distance he had to walk was about three miles, yet he was never absent, unless sickness prevented him. He was quite a changed man. But mark his punishment. He had ga'en awa' oot, in the gray o' the gloamin', to tak' a walk. Suddenly a soughin' soun' cam ower his head, and immediately he felt himself lifted from the grun', and carried thro' the air wi' an awfu' velocity. Neist mornin' he was found, half dead wi' cauld and hunger, on the very tap o' Sea Mab, among the very highest o' the Ochils. He was ta'en hame, but he never got the better o' his unmercifu' treatment. He had na a day to thrive, and he dwined awa' like snaw aff a dyke, until he sunk into the grave.

The next object of their machinations was the worthie divine wha had been instrumental in bringing' Patie to a knowledge of the richt. Noises and lood screams were heard in a' the corners o' his house, and when he gaed to see what was the matter, he could see naething! Ae time, in particular, the noises were heard to such a degree that the minister was obliged to leave his hoose in the Middle Bank, wi' naething but his sark on. He ran doon to a sma' cot, ca'd the Willow Wands, a muckle black boar following him a' the way. Matters, however, did na end there, for on the Sunday following, as he was gaun awa' to the kirk, things like planks o' wood rowed doon afore him a great part o' his way' be he being a God-fearin' man, withstood a' thae demonstrations and baffled Satan completely.

The theory that **Clackmannanshire terriers** were originally bred to speed the eviction of recalcitrant crofters (by dropping three or four of them down the chimney or smokestack) is indignantly denied by the locals, who attribute it to a London journalist.

DISTINCTIVE FLAVOUR

Clackmannanshire is the **smallest county** in the British Isles, and as such inspires a unique affection and sense of local identity not possible in (for instance) larger counties such as Yorkshire or Inverness.

COUNTY DIARY

July:	Alva Highland Games
September:	
	Alloa Flower Show

DUMFRIESSHIRE

COUNTY FACTS

Derivation of name: Gaelic meaning the fort (Dun) of the copse or little wood (phreas).
First Recorded: 1183
County Town: Dumfries
Towns: Annan, Brydekirk, Cummertrees, Dornock, Dumfries, Eastriggs, Ecclefechan, Gretna, Gretna Green, Hightae, Kirkconnel, Langholm, Locharbriggs, Lochmaben, Lockerbie, Moffat, Moniaive, Sanquhar, Thornhill.

Local Government
Dumfries and Galloway Regional Council and two district councils.

HISTORY

In 1305, John Comyn, the heir of Lady Devorgilla, and a contender for the throne, was assassinated by Robert the Bruce, his rival for the throne.
In 1570 the town and castle were sacked by the Earl of Essex and Lord Scrope.
In 1989 Lockerbie was the site of the Pan-Am disaster, caused by a terrorist bomb.

INDUSTRY PAST AND PRESENT

The county is overwhelmingly agricultural, mixed farming predominating. Pigs are reared in many places. Dumfries itself is a textile town, specialising in hosiery and knitwear. Afforestation is practised and there is some quarrying for sandstone and limestone. Gold and silver have both been found in the county in the past, the silver in association with the lead at Leadhills, the gold nearby at Wanlockhead. The tweed-making industry has declined.

LANDMARKS

Defoe had this to say of the Pass of Enterkin: 'It is a Precipice horrible and terrifying; on the left the Hill rises almost perpendicular, like a Wall; till being come about half Way, you have a steep unpassable Height on the left, and a monstrous Chasm or Ditch on your Right; deep, almost as the Monument is high, and the Path, or way, just broad enough for you to lead your horse on it, and, if his Foot slips, you have nothing to do but let go of the Bridle, lest he pulls you with him, and then you will have the Satisfaction of seeing him dash'd to Pieces, and lye at the Bottom with his four Shoes uppermost.'

MONUMENTS

Robert Burn's House is now a museum.
The Mill at Maxwelltown is now a regional museum.
Gretna Green has a romantic reputation, due to its being just across the border from England, where laws governing marriage were more intricate and hindering. By Scottish law, a marriage could be legalised by a declaration from the two parties before witnesses. Though this was made illegal in 1940, the Grail of those hungering for immediate wedlock, the blacksmith's shop, is much visited by sentimental tourists.
Caerlaverock Castle is a triangular fortress that has a Renaissance palace within. Both are now ruinous.

TOPOGRAPHY INCLUDING RIVERS

The county is bounded in the south by the Solway Firth, in the north by Lanarkshire, Peebles-shire and Selkirkshire, in the east by Roxburghshire and in the west by Kirkcudbrightshire and Ayrshire. The surface is largely hilly where it is not actually mountainous, with many lakes, including Loch Skene, 1,300 feet above sea level. The highest point is White Coomb, 2695 feet.
Rivers: Nith, Annan, Esk.

FAMOUS PEOPLE AND LOCAL CHARACTERS

In the reign of James V the duty of guarding the Marches against the English devolved on **Sir John Charteris of Amisfield**, who was brave but lazy and corrupt.
At that time there was a young farmer in Annandale named **George Maxwell** who was very active against the English. They raided and plundered his house in reprisal, and drove off his livestock. He pursued them, but was killed in the skirmish that took place when he caught them, so his wife, Marion, was a widow and his nine-year-old son, Wallace, was an orphan.

Wallace grew up in reduced circumstances as servant of a large farmer, and in due course fell in love with another servant, a girl named Mary Morrison. They pledged troth, though they knew it would be long before they could marry.

It happened about this time that the son of a rich English borderer was taken in a raid and held to ransom by Charteris, who kept the money for himself. In the next raid, Wallace was taken, and the man who had paid for his son's release gave out that he would only return Wallace on payment of the same amount. There was no chance of this, of course, so Marion pleaded with Sir John to mount a rescue raid, but Sir John refused, saying Wallace was not worth the effort.

Next Mary tried, and this time Sir John said that such a rescue would be both too costly and too dangerous. On the other hand, he might himself pay Wallace's ransom in return for certain favours which Mary had been reserving for him at some later date. She refused this indignantly, whereupon Sir John said that Wallace could rot in the dungeon until disease or the English made an end of him.

Mary told the farmer about this interview, and asked leave to appeal to the King. This was forthcoming, as Sir John was by this time unpopular with everyone, on account of his insolence and neglect of his duties. King James agreed to receive them and hear their case when next he came to Annandale. However, he came in disguise, as was often his custom.

He contrived to meet Mary as she was washing linen in a stream, and feigned a distemper to see if she had a properly sympathetic nature towards the 'Gudeman of Ballengleich', as he called himself. He also discovered the general hatred in which Sir John was held.

Having achieved this, he set out for Dumfries, but left his retainers in Duncow, and set out alone for Amisfield, disguised as a beggar. There he asked the porter to get him an immediate interview with Sir John. The reply was that Sir John was at dinner, and would not be available in less than two or three hours. The King gave the man a groat, and asked him to tell Sir John the matter was urgent, but got the same answer. He then gave him two more groats, and told him this time to say that he had seen the English massing for an attack over the border, and he must light the beacons. Sir John replied (understandably), 'If he chooses to wait two hours I shall see whether he is a knave or a fool; but if he sends me such another impertinent message, you will both regret it.' The porter offered the stranger food and ale to pass the time, but the King gave him three groats this time, and told him to return and say that the 'Gudeman of Ballengleich' insisted on seeing him at once. As the man went with this last message, the King threw aside his beggar's disguise and blew his horn loudly, bringing his men-at-arms. Sir John came hurriedly, pleading ignorance of the King's presence, but the King replied that the meanest of his subjects had access to him at all times. He then set a date for examination of Sir John on various charges at Hoddam castle, adding that if Wallace Maxwell could not be produced within a week, Sir John would be hanged from a tree in front of his own window.

He also required him to entertain his entire retinue at his own expense until the time of the examination and provided Marion with a fine cow, blankets and other presents. And on the examination, he compelled him to establish Wallace in a fully-stocked farm of 50 acres, rent-free in his own lifetime and his wife's.

Thomas Carlyle was born in Ecclefechan, Annandale, in 1795. He showed an early characteristic literary style, based very much on the constructions of his own speech, which he harnessed to a powerful imagination and intellect. Though he had first to work as a schoolmaster, he became the father of social history, as it is currently understood, with his works *The French Revolution*, *Frederick The Great* and *Chartism* demonstrating both the need for and the potential of this new approach. However, he was always unashamedly partisan, regarding objectivity as a dangerous form of self-deception.

This has told against his later reputation; his denigration of Byron, and the entire medical profession, and his overt racism - he regarded slavery as the natural lot of the negro - were failings of his time and background, and in a man of genius appear monstrous. He also suffered the usual fate of visionaries who live long through turbulent times, which is to live to see many of their prophecies discredited. Moreover, his chronic indigestion made him an easy target; people could always attribute what they most disliked in his work to his intestines, much as Dr Johnson's scrofula and Marx's carbuncles were used to belabour their thoughts.

He died in 1881, and chose to be buried in the parish of his birth.

Local Characters

John de Balliol, son of the founder of Balliol College, Oxford, became King of Scotland on the death of the Maid of Norway in 1292. He was unable to hold the throne without the help of Edward III, but when Edward claimed judicial as well as feudal authority, he rebelled against him. However, he was unable to rouse the enthusiasm of the people, and was captured by Edward who threw him into the Tower of London. There he remained, until the Pope persuaded Edward to release him into exile in France. He died there in 1314.

Robert Burns was an exciseman in Dumfries in the latter part of his life. He died in Dumfries in 1796 and is buried in St Michael's Churchyard.

LOCAL FOLKLORE

The Vampire

A murderer from Yorkshire, who took refuge in the service of William De Brus of Annandale obstinately refused all the sacraments even to the day of his death. Nonetheless, De Brus ensured a Christian burial for him.

He became vampire, and used to leave his tomb to pass through the town at night, so that none dared come out; but this availed them nothing, for his passage filled the air with pestilence that killed the people. Those who were not killed fled, so that the town became depopulated.

Then there came a holy man, who gathered the remaining people, and held a colloquy on Palm Sunday. He then held a feast for all who were present, among them two brothers. These men had lost their father to the vampire and they agreed to leave the feast early to dig him out and burn him. At only a little depth they came on the corpse, but it had grown to enormous size, swollen and crimson, with the monstrous corpulence of ceaseless blood-sucking.

They set about the body with their spade, and huge jets of blood burst forth, soaking the ground. They dragged the body outside the town and built a pyre for it. There they cut out the heart with their blunt spade, for only so could heart and trunk be consumed. Then when both were reduced to ashes, they ran back to the dinner party, to tell what had been done.

From that day forth the pestilence abated, and the night air was foul no longer.

Bonnie Bodsbeck

There was a brownie who had lived, by his own account, at Leithin Hall for three centuries. He would show himself only once to each master, and other people only got to see his hand at most. There was one master whom the brownie loved greatly, so that when he died, he mourned grievously, and took no food for many days. Then the new laird came back into the country to take possession, and the brownie appeared to do him homage, but the new laird knew nothing of brownies, and was distressed at his starved and haggard appearance. He ordered a new livery, and meat and drink to be set, in the brownie's hearing. The brownie vanished, calling in a loud voice:

> 'Ca', cuttee, ca'!
> A' the luck o' Leithin Ha'
> Gangs wi' me to Bodsbeck Ha'.'

In a few years Leithin Hall was a ruin, but 'Bonnie Bodsbeck' began to earn its name from that time.

The Murder Hole

On the estate of Lord Cassilis lay a great moor, without trees or vegetation, where it was rumoured that many unwary travellers had been intercepted and murdered, though no investigation ever revealed what had happened to them.

People living in a nearby hamlet believed that in the dead of night they sometimes heard a cry of anguish; and a shepherd who had lost his way once declared that he had seen three mysterious figures struggling together until one of them, with a frightful scream, sank into the earth. No one lived there except an old woman and her two sons, who were too poor to flee. Travellers occasionally begged a night's lodging at their cottage, rather than continue their journey across the moor in darkness, and even by day no one travelled that way alone.

One stormy November night, a pedlar boy was overtaken by darkness on the moor. Terrified by the solitude, he repeated to himself the words of St Matthew, 'I was a stranger, you took me in', and so struggled towards the old cottage, which he had visited the year before in a large company of travellers,

and where he felt assured of a welcome. Its light guided him from afar, and he knocked at the door, but at first received no answer. He then peered through the window and saw the occupants at all their accustomed occupations: the old woman was scrubbing the floor and strewing it with sand; her two sons seemed to be thrusting something large and heavy into a great chest, which they locked with an air of haste which puzzled the watching boy.

He tapped lightly on the window, and they all started up, with consternation on their faces, and one of them suddenly darted out of the door, seized the boy roughly by the shoulder, and dragged him inside. He said, laughing nervously, 'I'm only the poor pedlar who visited you last year.'

'Are you alone?' cried the old woman in a harsh, deep voice.

'Alone here, and alone in the whole world,' replied the boy sadly.

'Then you are welcome,' said one of the men with a sneer. Their words filled the boy with alarm, and the confusion and the desolation of the formerly neat and orderly cottage seemed to show signs of recent violence.

The curtains had been torn away from the bed to which he was shown, and, though he begged for a light to burn until he fell asleep, his terror kept him long awake.

In the middle of the night he was awakened by a single cry of distress. He sat up and listened, but it was not repeated, and he would have lain down again, but suddenly his eye fell on a stream of blood slowly trickling under the door of his room. In terror he sprang to the door, and through a chink he saw that the victim outside was only a goat. But just then he overheard the voices of the two men, and their words transfixed him with horror. 'I wish all the throats we cut were that easy,' said one, 'Did you ever hear such a noise as the old gentleman made last night?'

'Ah, the Murder Hole's the thing for me,' said the other, 'one plunge and the fellow's dead and buried in a moment.'

'How do you mean to despatch the lad in there?' the old woman asked in a harsh whisper, and one of the men silently drew his bloody knife across his throat for answer.

The terrified boy crept to his window and managed to let himself down without a sound. But as he stood wondering which way to turn, a dreadful cry rang out: 'The boy has escaped – let loose the bloodhound!' He ran for his life, blindly, but all too soon he heard the dreadful baying of the hound and the voices of the men in pursuit. Suddenly he stumbled and fell on a heap of rough stones, which cut

him in every limb, so that his blood poured over the stones. He staggered to his feet and ran on; the hound was so near that he could almost feel its breath on his back. But suddenly it smelt the blood on the stones, and, thinking the chase at an end, it lay down and refused to go further after the same scent.

The boy fled on and on till morning, and when at last he reached a village, his pitiable state and fearful story roused such wrath that three gibbets were at once set upon the floor, and before night the three villains had been captured and confessed their guilt. The bones of their victims were later discovered, and with great difficulty brought up from the dreadful hole with its narrow aperture into which they had been thrust.

DISTINCTIVE FLAVOUR

The cheeses of Scotland are very largely cheddars of various kinds. They are hard, keep well, and dissolve easily into soufflés, soups and flans. Dumfries, as a sophisticated county, has the best expertise on this subject. Dishes comprising melted Dumfries cheddar and lobster-meat imported from the counties immediately north, especially when taken late at night after an evening of cellar-bar entertainment, can give rise to the most lively nightmares. Strong men and women come down to breakfast, and compare notes over laughter and black coffees. Weaklings remain a-bed, reading Freud.

COUNTY DIARY

August: Dumfries and Lockerbie Agricultural Show

DUNBARTONSHIRE

HISTORY

In 1603 the massacre of Glen Frewin took place, being an incident in the feud between the MacGregors and the Colquhouns. It is chiefly notable because the Colquhoun chieftain sued for quarter. He was promised safe conduct into England, and surrendered on those terms. The MacGregors honoured their bond to the extent of marching him under guard over the English border. Then they marched him straight back, and executed him at their leisure.

This was widely condemned as sharp practice, and led ultimately to the proscription of the clan. Many members changed their names to MacAlpin(e) or to Graham.

INDUSTRY PAST AND PRESENT

There is a major hydroelectric installation at Loch Sloy, and a deepwater oil-importing port at Finnart, Loch Long, connected by pipeline to the refinery and petrochemical plant at Grangemouth. There is forestry on the high ground, and vegetable-farming on the low, mainly to supply Glasgow. Whisky distilling and blending is done round Dumbarton.

The chief industry of Dumbarton was the manufacture of crown glass, until the abolition of the glass duty. Thereafter the town lost out to St Helens. Later there was shipbuilding in Dumbarton, but this has declined, as has the textile industry in the Vale of Leven.

Coal was mined at Langfauld, but it was of poor quality and not worth digging for to any depth. Granite and freestone were also extracted in the last century. It was also a major textile centre, with cotton-bleaching on the banks of the Leven, as well as turkey-red calico-dyeing and printing.

LANDMARKS

Loch Lomond, and the many islands thereupon.

MONUMENTS

The Antonine Wall, built by Antoninus Pius, marks the extreme northern boundary achieved by the Roman Empire.

Dumbarton Castle is set on a high rock, and was in its time one of the most impregnable castles in Scotland. It commands some spectacular views. Cobbett held that it was worth the journey from the Isle of Wight just to see it.

FAMOUS PEOPLE AND LOCAL CHARACTERS

John Logie Baird was born at Helensburgh in 1888, but he carried out his research at Hastings. It took him 18 years to produce his first TV picture in 1924, and a further five before it was ready for demonstration. He died in 1946, having pioneered colour transmission in 1941.

Local Characters
Tobias Smollett was born in Leven Valley in 1721. He was educated at Glasgow University, and trained as a surgeon's mate on a man o' war, subsequently spending some time in the

TOPOGRAPHY INCLUDING RIVERS

The county is in two parts, split by Loch Lomond. The western is bounded by Loch Long in the west, the Clyde in the south, Stirlingshire in the east and Perthshire in the north. The small, detached, eastern part is mainly enclosed by Stirlingshire to the north and Lanarkshire to the south. The country is extremely mountainous, and includes many lush glens. The highest point is Ben Vorlich, 3092 feet.
Rivers: Leven, Clyde.

West Indies. In 1748 he published *Roderick Random*, reflecting these experiences. He combined the careers of man of letters and physician, though with little financial success, up to the end of his life in 1771. His other novels include *Peregrine Pickle*, *The Adventures of Frederick*, *Count Fathom*, and *The Expedition of Humphrey Clinker*.

ART AND LITERATURE

'*Dumbarton is the lock of the highlands, but Stirling castle holds the key.*'
    Local Saying

LOCAL FOLKLORE

Dumbarton's Origin

When the witches chased St Patrick out of Scotland, they were unable to pursue him across running water, so they threw rocks after him instead. One of these is now the fortress of Dumbarton.

DISTINCTIVE FLAVOUR

Dumbarton, partly under its pre-Roman name of Alcluid, has the doubtful honour of figuring in James Branch Cabell's enormous *Life of Manuel* cycle, a work of fantasy and great learning, which is held to disparage every major religion and holy book from the Vedas to *Capital*.

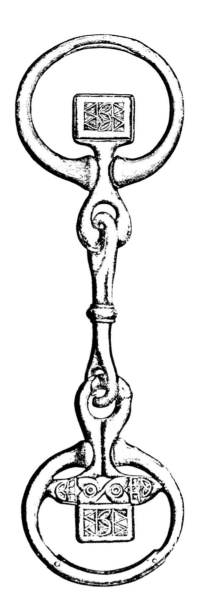

COUNTY DIARY

| July: | Balloch Highland Games |
| July: | Dumbarton District Festival |

EAST LOTHIAN
(HADDINGTONSHIRE)

COUNTY FACTS

Derivation of name: Named from Leudonus, and signifying his territory. No one knows who or what Leudonus was. It has been suggested, though with little confidence, that he may have been Loth, grandfather of St Mungo.
First Recorded: 970
County Town: Haddington
Towns: Aberlady, Belhaven, Cockenzie & Port Seton, Dunbar, East Linton, Elphinstone, Gullane, Haddington, Longniddry, Macmerry, North Berwick, Ormiston, Prestonpans, Tranent, West Barns, Wester Pencaitland.

Local Government
Lothian Regional Council and one District Council.

HISTORY

After the battle of Pinkie in 1547 Haddington was garrisoned by an English force, and sustained a prolonged siege.

In 1548 the parliament of Haddington convened to sanction the marriage of Queen Mary to the Dauphin, from which stemmed her pretentions to be queen not only of Scotland, but of France and England.

The battle of Prestonpans, in 1745, was the greatest triumph of Bonnie Prince Charlie.

INDUSTRY PAST AND PRESENT

The county has the distinction of containing 'Silicon Glen'. Golf is important at North Berwick. There is also some food and drink processing, and some textiles. Farming is mixed, with little specialisation except in the direction of turnips.

The former deep coal-mining industry, which dated from monkish workings in the 12th century, has declined during this century. The fishing, especially for trout and salmon, is not what it was, though eels are still to be found.

Pottery has declined, and herring salting is now a thing of the past.

TOPOGRAPHY INCLUDING RIVERS

The county is bounded to the south by Berwickshire, to the east by the sea, to the north by the Firth of Forth and to the west by Midlothian. The surface is varied, though not mountainous, and inclines gradually upwards to the Lammermuir Hills. The geology is very varied, and includes trap, porphyry, freestone and limestone. The highest point is in the Lammermuir Hills, 1733 feet.
Rivers: Tyne, Coalstone, Whitewater, Fastna, Peffer.

LANDMARKS

The Lammermuir Hills are inevitably associated with Scott's The Bride of Lammermoor (an alternative spelling) and Verdi's opera based thereupon.

For Stevenson, the Pentlands were 'the hills of home'. Yellow Craig Hill is the prototype for 'Spyglass Hill' in Treasure Island.

MONUMENTS

It was to **Hailes Castle** that Bothwell brought Mary Queen of Scots after their abduction/ marriage, following the assassination of Rizzio by Darnley in 1565. Knowing her character, he kept her in a water-gated dungeon, which can still be seen.

Much of **Tantallon Castle** remains extant. It is placed in a superb defensive position, and resisted siege in 1461 and 1528. But in 1651 General Monk broached its defences with cannon fire.

Dirleton Castle was stormed by Cromwell in 1650, but the drum towers remain.

Haddington Abbey Church is a large, cruciform church from the 14th century.

Dunbar Castle is still a splendid historic monument.

FAMOUS PEOPLE AND LOCAL CHARACTERS

John Knox is supposed to have been born in Haddington in 1505, though this is disputed by Gifford. He was ordained in 1530, and was from his earliest years a radical reformer. He attached himself to George Wishart, and, despite his cloth, carried a sword to protect him at public meetings. However, this was not sufficient to save him from being burned by Cardinal Beaton at St Andrews in March 1546. Beaton watched the event from his window, and Wishart called to him from the stake to appear shortly before the bar of God's Justice.

In May of that year Beaton was murdered in the same room from which he had watched the burning, an act in which Knox may have been involved, though the fatal blow was struck by Norman Lesley. Certainly, St Andrews became a hotbed of reform with Knox at its centre. However, the French took it by siege in 1547, and Knox was condemned to the galleys, where he endured 19 months of intense privation before being released.

Knox obtained rapid preferment, including the offer of several bishoprics, but chose to accept no office apart from chaplain to Edward VI. This meant that he had to flee to Switzerland to escape the Marian persecutions in 1554. He travelled extensively at this time, marrying his first wife, preaching and pamphleteering, his best-known work being *The First Blast of the Trumpet Against the Monstrous Regiment of Women*, directed against Mary Tudor, Mary Queen of Scots, and Catherine de Medici. He returned to Scotland in 1559, where his inflammatory sermons were the occasion for much ecclesiastical vandalism. He became effective head of the Kirk by 1560, but found he had to deal with Queen Mary in 1561. She arraigned him for treason in 1562 on account of his partisanship over the Holyrood riots, but he was acquitted.

A second marriage, to twenty-year-old Margaret Stewart, and his sixtieth birthday did nothing to quench Knox's love of controversy, and in 1567 he was demanding that Mary be arraigned for the murder of Darnley. This did not take place, but after Mary's fall from power he regained prominence. But by 1570 his powers were in decline. He suffered a stroke, and was unable to respond with his former resilience when an assassin set fire to his house in Edinburgh, and retired to St Andrews, dying in 1572.

Local Characters
John Napier was born at Merchistoun in 1550. Little is known of his early life, aside from his having matriculated into St Andrews University in 1562, but in common with Sir Isaac Newton, he combined brilliance at mathematics with an interest in the quirkier reaches of theology. His first known production was a *Plain Discovery of the Revelation of St John* (1593). The following year, however, found him well into the study of trigonometry which was to result in the publication of his natural logarithmic tables (log to base e) in 1614. He withheld his method of obtaining these for posthumous publication, which was carried out by his son

two years after his death in 1617. Napier's other achievements include the theorem of five circular parts, which provides a ready solution to all cases of right-angled spherical triangles, including, for instance, all those based on a line of latitude with their apex at a pole.

ART AND LITERATURE
'Some wyfis of the burrows-toun sa wondir vane ar, and wantoun, in warld thay att not quhat to weir,
On clathis they waist mony a croun, andall for newfangilnes of geir.
Sumtimes they will beir up thayre gown, to shaw thayre wilicoat hing- and doun,
And sumtimes baith they will upbeir, to shaw thayre hose of black or broun;
And all for newfanglines of geir.'

Sir Richard Maitland,
on the ladies of Haddington

'Musselburgh was a burgh when Edinburgh was nane;
Musselburgh will be a burgh when Edinburgh's gane!'

LOCAL FOLKLORE
Witchcraft
North Berwick was notorious for witchcraft, and greatly excited James VI. He believed that the cult was led by his own cousin, Francis, Earl of Bothwell. Certain local ladies were noticed sailing in a sieve round the ship bringing in his bride from Denmark, with the intention of wrecking it. It was in fact trapped off Bass Rock by a pocket storm. They were watched, and eventually caught at the Aulkd Kirk, dancing to the Jew's Harp, and kissing

the Devil's (or perhaps Lord Bothwell's) anus. At their trial in 1591 evidence was collected by the always effective method of tying a knotted rope round the temples and gradually tightening it with an iron bar. This persuaded 94 witches and 6 wizards to confess to such misdeeds as opening graves to steal the fingerbones of corpses.

The Duke of Lauderdale
The Duke of Lauderdale, who was Charles II's viceroy in Scotland is buried in St Mary's Church. There the Devil refuses him rest, and frequently tosses his coffin about in its vault.

DISTINCTIVE FLAVOUR
In 1598 there was a major fire in Haddington, after which for many years the Crier progressed through the town reciting a doggerel verse called '**Coal an' Can'le**', to remind the people to tend their fires and lights.

Dried fish is plentiful in East Lothian cuisine: Sir Walter Scott, when visiting the site of the battle of Prestonpans, 'dined.....on tiled haddocks very sumptuously'. Tiled haddock was dried in the sun as a rather optimistic curing process.

COUNTY DIARY

August: East Lothian Highland Games, Prestonpans
September:
   Edinburgh Races (Flat), Musselburgh

F^{IF}E

COUNTY FACTS

Derivation of name: Named from Fith, and signifying his territory. No one knows who or what Fith was.
First recorded: 590
Motto: Virtute et Opere (By Virtue and Industry)
County Town: Cupar
Towns: Auchterderran, Ballingry, Buckhaven, Burntisland, Cardenden, Cowdenbeath, Cupar, Dunfermline, Glenrothes, Inverkeithing, Kelty, Kennoway, Kincardine, Kirkcaldy, Leslie, Leven, Lochgelly, Methil, Newport-on-Tay, Rosyth, St. Andrews, Tayport.

Local Government
Fife Regional Council and three District Councils.

HISTORY

In 1599 John Knox effected the demolition of St Andrews Cathedral in a single day. Dunfermline was once the capital of Scotland.

INDUSTRY PAST AND PRESENT

Coal mining is still important, as is Ravenscraig Steelworks, the latter more probably for political than industrial reasons. Broadleaf forestry has been practised in Fife for two centuries. Other industries include linen making, engineering, quarrying and linoleum making.

Lead was mined at one time in the Lomond Hills. Lime was also extracted and exported, as a fertiliser of acid soil. Linen manufacture has declined.

LANDMARKS

The Firth of Tay was the scene of the notorious Tay Bridge disaster.
May Island Lighthouse is a very impressive example.

MONUMENTS

St Andrews University and golf course are two of the oldest and most distinguished of their kind in the country. St Andrews IS the oldest golf club in the world and where golf as a game began.

Falkland Castle is largely ruined, but the southern façade is still very impressive.

Dunfermline Abbey is one of the premier Romanesque buildings in Scotland. The columns of its nave, with their deeply grooved zig-zag ornamentation, echo very strongly those of Durham Cathedral.

St Andrews Cathedral was over 300 feet long and with Elgin, was arguably Scotlands finest medieval church. Its destruction at the Reformation was distressingly thorough.

FAMOUS PEOPLE AND LOCAL CHARACTERS

Alexander Selkirk was born at Largo in 1676. He was cited before the session in 1695 for laughing in church, and rather than suffer the gruesome penalties which could attach to that crime, ran away to sea. He was taken on by a semi-pirate called Straddles, who presently tired of his company and marooned him on the uninhabited island of Juan Fernandez with some survival equipment. There he remained for four years and four months, before being rescued by Captain Woods Rogers. He joined the navy, and ultimately reached the rank of lieutenant, dying in service aboard HMS Weymouth in 1723. He is believed to have given his diary to **Daniel Defoe**, who used it as the basis for *Robinson Crusoe*.

Adam Smith was born at Kirkcaldy in 1723 and it was there that he wrote his famous *Enquiry into the Nature and Causes of the Wealth of Nations*. In much the same way that all western philosophy has been described (by Whitehead) as 'writing footnotes to Plato',

TOPOGRAPHY INCLUDING RIVERS

The county is bounded in the south by the Firth of Forth, in the east by the sea, in the north by the Firth of Tay, and in the west by Clackmannanshire, Perthshire and Kinross-shire. There is a very high proportion of arable land. The highest point is West Lomond, 1712 feet. Rivers: Eden, Leven, Den.

all subsequent economists have either built on Smith's foundations, or attempted to undermine them. The underminers include Marx, whose obsession with money prevented him from understanding the concept of value-added, and Keynes, who wrote on the assumption that inflation was something that only happened in foreign countries. Attempts to operate economies on principles that would not have been familiar to Smith have been in every case disastrous.

Local Characters

Macduff, pivotal character in *Macbeth*, was Thane of Fife.

Charles I was born at Dunfermline.

In the reign of Queen Anne **Lord Burleigh** was enamoured of a local girl, who refused either to sleep with him or even to marry him, the former because she was too virtuous, and the latter because she was too much his social inferior. His family sent him on tour to get his mind off her, but before he left he swore to marry her on his return, or if she married another, to murder them both.

The lady discounted this vow, and married a local schoolmaster. However, on his return Lord Burleigh heard of the marriage, and went straight to the school house. There he was greeted by the master, but having made sure he had the right man, drew his pistol and shot him dead without further ado. He then cantered off.

A reward of £200 was set on his head, and he was presently captured and sentenced to death. However, his friends broke into the jail and though he was subsequently heard of in the Battle of Sherrifmuir, his ultimate fate is unknown.

Robert Adam was born in Kirkcaldy in 1728. He studied in Italy, where he derived the principles of neo-classicism. His name, along with those of Capability Brown, Vanbrugh, Grinling Gibbons and Inigo Jones remains synonymous with the most enduring aspects of 18th century taste.

ART AND LITERATURE

'There history and romance abide,
Martyr and saint, Pict, Scot, Culdees.
They dared, they fought, they suffered, dreamed and died,
Yet of their long wild centuries
Left but these stones their bodies beside.'
Walter de la Mare

LOCAL FOLKLORE

Largo Law

Somewhere under Largo Law there's got to be a gold mine, because, as the people point out, the sheep grazing in the hill pastures sometimes come back with their wool tinged yellow. This proves they have been lying above hidden gold.

Once, long ago, a Balmain shepherd came near to finding it. Balmain lies at the northwestern slope of Largo Law, and the shepherd had brooded over the gold for many years, watching the resting places of the sheep and trying to track down the source of the yellow tinge, but it eluded him. But there was a ghost haunting the valley, and the ghost was believed to have the secret, but it was a tongue-tied ghost, who could only speak if a living man questioned it. Many would have liked to do that, but when it came to the point, they were all too frightened.

The shepherd had seen the ghost several times, but without daring to approach it, but at last he plucked up courage and spoke. The answer was that the ghost was willing to yield its secret, but only if the shepherd would meet it at eight o'clock on a specified day, and subject to a doggerel condition:

'If Auchindowie cock disna craw,
And the herd of Balmain his horn disna blaw,
I'll tell ye where the gowd is in Largo Law.'

The shepherd imagined himself becoming as rich as the Laird of Largo, or the Earl of Montrose, even, and he was leaving nothing to chance. He secretly murdered every cock in Auchindowie. And he threatened Tammie Norrie, if he valued his life, not to blow the horn which he used to call the cows together to return to the pastures. The shepherd turned up for his appointment, and the ghost appeared at eight on the dot. Also at eight on the dot, Tammie blew his horn, for he was a cattleman, and everyone knows that no self-respecting cowboy lets himself be pushed around by a mere sheep-person.

The ghost was quite as annoyed as the shepherd, and spoke two more lines of doggerel:

'Woe to the man that blew the horn,
For out of that spot shall he never be borne!'

The shepherd found himself alone, and was never to see the ghost again. Nor was Tammie Norrie ever to call the cattle home to Balmain. The echoes of his blast had not died before he did, and no one was ever able to move his corpse for burial. Whoever touched it always

found the strength drained from his arms, and his legs moved as sluggishly as the legs of a dreaming man. So they gave up the task, and built a cairn over him instead.

As for the shepherd, he left the district. Parsimony is one thing, but he should not have been too mean to bribe poor Tammie.

St Andrews

St Andrews Cathedral was built on the bones of the eponymous saint, the very first stone being laid on his thighbone. They were imported especially from his former resting-place at Patras, on the Gulf of Lepanto, for this purpose.

DISTINCTIVE FLAVOUR

East Fife has the dubious distinction of having for several years returned a Communist MP to Westminster.

The Royal and Ancient is the most famous of all golf clubs, and the course goes back 500 years.

Fife is not known as a County but as the Kingdom of Fife.

The area of the five towns of St Monans, Pittenweem, Anstruther Easter, Anstruther West and Crail are known as the **Neuk of Fife**.

The town of **Auchtermuchty** received regular national prominence due to top Fleet Street editor Sir John Junor. He would regularly introduce the town into his column, using it as a yardstick for moral comment on modern behaviour – 'What *would* the ladies of Auchtermuchty say?'

Bannocks are found throughout Scotland. **Fife Bannocks** are typical of the genre, being an oatmeal and flour bun-like delicacy.

COUNTY DIARY

July:	'Breath of Scotland' Variety Show, St Andrews
July:	'Scots Night', St Andrews

INVERNESS-SHIRE

COUNTY FACTS

Derivation of name: From the Gaelic/Brittonic meaning the mouth of the Ness.

First Recorded: before 1300

Motto: Air son math na siorrachd (For the good of the county)

County Town: Inverness

Towns: Ardersier, Beauly, Broadford, Caol, Castlebay, Corpach, Dunvegan, Fort Augustus, Fort William, Inverness, Kingussie, Mallaig, Newtonmore, Portree, Tarbet.

The important distilling and fishing/tourism centre of Grantown-on-Spey is within the detached part of Inverness-shire within the County of Morayshire.

Local Government

Highland Regional Council and Western Isles Island Council, and four District Councils

HISTORY

The murder of King Duncan in the 11th century is alleged to have occurred at Inverness Castle, though this is disputed, both as to site and as to whether it was murder or a straight duel. The version in Shakespeare has no pretension to accuracy, and is actually modelled on the murder of King Duff by Chief Donwald and his wife at Forres Castle, Moray.

The heir to the chieftainship of Clan Ranald was called Ranald Gallda, or Stranger, because he had been brought up by the Lovats, and was unfamiliar with the ways of his people. As a result, at the time of his presentation and inauguration, he made what proved to be a costly gaffe. On being told that fifty bullocks had been slaughtered for the feast, he made a quick computation based on the numbers present and commented that fifty fowls would have been sufficient. This was such an insult to Highland hospitality that they rejected the 'Hen Chief' out of hand.

Lord Lovat attempted to heal the breach (forcibly), wherepon they joined with the Camerons to raid his lands at Glenelg, by way of teaching him to mind his own business. Lovat was not having that, so he assembled a mixed force of Frasers, Grants and MacIntoshes, and attacked Lochaber. At this point Huntly and Argyll stepped in, and persuaded the Camerons to cease hostilities. Lovat therefore dispersed his forces, so that the Frasers were alone when they reached Letterfinlay.

There took place on July 3 1544 the conflict called the 'Field of Shirts'. The Ranalds had not given up hostilities, and fell upon the Frasers. The day was exceedingly hot, so the men, whose tactics were based on the assumption that one fought in plaid, were fighting in their shirts. This may be part of the reason why in the ensuing battle virtually everyone on both sides was killed, nearly 800 in all, including Ranald Gallda, Lord Lovat and his son. Gallda, 'Hen Lord' or not, perished trying to save the dying Lord Lovat, who had ordered him off the field to save his life. On the 'winning' side, there were ten survivors, on the losing side, four.

In 1746 the army of 'Bonnie Prince Charlie' was routed in about half an hour on Culloden Moor.

INDUSTRY PAST AND PRESENT

Tourism is important, with special reference to the Loch Ness Monster. There are also oil-related industries on the west coast of the Moray Firth. There are extensive sheep farms, with cattle in the valleys. There has also been recent development of winter sports, rock-climbing and forestry. Ardesier is a centre for production of oil platforms. There is an airport at Dalcross, eight miles northeast of Inverness.

Conifer plantation took an early hold in the county.

Traditional industries of whisky distilling, woollen manufacture, and boat-building continue, while in the west, classical crofting is still practised, as a form of subsistence farming based on sheep, oats, potatoes, and some fishing.

The pioneer aluminium-smelting plant at Foyers has been superceded by more modern installations at Kinlochleven.

TOPOGRAPHY INCLUDING RIVERS

The largest county in Scotland, it is bounded on the north by Ross and the Moray Firth, on the east by Nairnshire, Morayshire, Banffshire and Aberdeenshire on the south by Perthshire and Argyllshire, and on the west by the Atlantic. It also covers many Western Isles, including Skye, Harris, Benbecula, North and South Uist, and Bara. The surface is extremely mountainous, and divided by the Great Glen (Glenmore). Nowhere in Britain is the evidence of glaciation more prominent. The highest point is Ben Nevis, 4406 feet.

LANDMARKS

The Great Glen contains the three lochs Lochy, Oich and Ness.
Ben Nevis is the highest peak in the United Kingdom, 4,406 feet.
Ben Alder Mountains
Culloden Moor.

MONUMENTS

The Caledonian Canal took from 1805 to 1822 to complete, and had to be extensively refurbished in 1847. The entire cost of construction was only £986,924, but it never caught on. Then and now, seamen prefer to go round the north of Scotland.

St Andrew's Cathedral, Inverness, is a fine example of the decorated Gothic style.

The Stone of Tubs (under the Forbes Memorial Fountain) is still to be seen in Inverness. It is so called because women carrying water from the river to their homes used to rest their tubs on it to break the journey.

FAMOUS PEOPLE AND LOCAL CHARACTERS

Thomas Telford, the great hydraulic engineer, was born in Dumfries in 1757, but in Scotland he is mainly associated with Inverness. Of all his canals the Caledonian Canal was the greatest, with locks 40 feet wide and up to 180 feet long. He was employed as a shepherd boy, and his engineering expertise was originally self-taught from books while tending sheep. His efforts included bridges, docks and tunnels as well as canals, and were so impressive that despite his total lack of formal training he became president of the Institute of Civil Engineers in 1820. He died in 1834.

Local Characters

After the 1745 rebellion, **Lord President Duncan Forbes of Culloden** tried to alleviate the sufferings of the Highlanders in the aftermath of defeat, mainly by curbing the atrocities perpetrated under Cumberland, so far as he could. He did this unadventurously by using the influence of his position at Court.

ART AND LITERATURE

[Of Ardnamarchan] *'A black, inhuman, fearful landscape.'*

Alasdair Maclean

LOCAL FOLKLORE

The Loch Ness Monster

Attempts to sight the Loch Ness Monster, sometimes familiarly referred to as 'Auld Nessie' by ill-bred persons, are possibly the greatest single gift to the tourist industry in any part of the world. The Pyramids have lasted longer and bring in more, but they rest on an incomparably more solid foundation. Mr Peter Scott has a long-standing wager with Mr Michael Watts that the monster does exist as a specific entity. It was only after the wager was ratified that Watts realised that as no time limit had been imposed, he could never win. This typifies the intellectual rigour with which the subject is approached. Among many theories brought forward to account for the (always poorly focussed) photographs of the monster are: that Loch Ness is the breeding ground for either the sea serpent or a surviving colony of ichthyosaurs or both; that columns of seals are often mistaken for the vertebrae of a single large creature; and that the Edinburgh Alligator-Fanciers Club illegally and clandestinely bring their pets there, to award prizes in their equivalent of Crufts, and to breed the next generation thereof.

Mr Nicholas Witchell is a firm protagonist of the monster.

St Torranan

When St Torranan brought Christianity to Benbecula he decided to build a church on the Knoll of the Hooded Crow, near Cailgeo. He and his converts began collecting materials, but every night they were all moved to a small island in a nearby loch. He thought this must be the work of the Devil, so he sprinkled holy water, but it made no difference. He therefore kept watch one night, and saw angels lifting the stones and carrying them to the island. He therefore set to work building the church there next day. The following morning he returned to find the church complete, except for the roof, as he had not got round to providing roofing materials.

The Cave of Raitts

The Cave of Raitts near Lynchat is seventy feet long, eight broad, and seven high. It was dug in a single night by giantesses, who carried the spoil down to the River Spey in their aprons, where they dumped it. Meanwhile their gigantic husbands were cutting the great slabs of rock which form the cave walls.

DISTINCTIVE FLAVOUR

The people of Inverness claim that theirs is the best spoken English in the United Kingdom, a claim that has been disputed by many, most notably Dr Johnson canvassing on behalf of Litchfield. In this connection, it should be noted that Gaelic is still spoken by many in the west of the county.

A mildly scatological song called '**The Ball at Killiemuir**' has as its first line, 'The four-and-twenty virgins came down from Inverness'. It is possible that it is still sung at or after Rugby Football matches in some of the less enlightened parts of the United Kingdom, and reference is made to it in Frank Marcus's play, *The Killing of Sister George*.

Inverness is the greatest of **salmon** counties. All types of salmon are best cooked the same way – poached whole in their skins. Having headed and gutted the fish, the type of stuffing and the amount of butter that you add are entirely your own concern. But it is absolutely crucial to cook the fish in a sealed container over a hot but not infernal fire, so that although some moisture may escape, the fish will not dehydrate. The matter of smoked salmon is – another matter.

COUNTY DIARY

July-September:
    Scots Ceilidh Night, Carrbridge
August: Glenurquhart Highland Gathering and Games, Drumnadrochit.

KINCARDINESHIRE

COUNTY FACTS

Derivation of name: From the Gaelic and Brittonic, signifying the end of a copse or a thicket, 'wood end'.
First Recorded: 1295 as Cinn Chàrdain
Motto: Laus Deo (Praise be to God)
County Town: Stonehaven
Towns: Banchory, Fettercairn, Gourdon, Inverbervie, Kincorth, Laurencekirk, Marykirk, St. Cyrus, Stonehaven, Torry.

Local Government
Grampian Regional Council and two District Councils

HISTORY

By 1652 Dunnottar Castle was the only one in Scotland still in royalist hands, so the Scottish regalia were stowed there for safe-keeping. The castle fell after eight months' siege, but the crown and sceptre were smuggled out before the surrender. They were then hidden in Kinneff Church, also in the county.

INDUSTRY PAST AND PRESENT

Present Industry
Limestone, granite and sandstone are quarried in various places. Agriculture is mixed.

Past Industry
In the last century the area was a centre of manufacture for wooden snuff-boxes. Herring fishing has declined.

LANDMARKS
The Grampians occupy the west of the county. Unlike many of the more impressive ranges in Scotland, they are of limestone rather than igneous rock.

TOPOGRAPHY INCLUDING RIVERS

The county is bounded in the north and north west by Aberdeenshire, in the south and south west by Angus, and in the east by the sea. The western third and much of the centre consists of the Grampians, but the rest is generally arable soil resting on old red sandstone. This is especially true of the Howe of the Mearns in the south east. The highest point is Mount Battock, 2555 feet.
Rivers: Dee, North Esk, Dye, Cowie, Carron, Bervie and Luther.

MONUMENTS
In Fettercairn is the shaft of the old **Kincardine Tower Cross**, notched to show the length of the standard Scottish ell. This is 37 inches, and should be borne in mind when witches in fairy stories are described as having noses 'three ells long'.
Crathes Castle gardens are arranged to display a variety of horticultural traditions.
Laurencekirk is a fine example of the 18th century planned village. It was commissioned by Lord Gardenstone.

FAMOUS PEOPLE AND LOCAL CHARACTERS
John Charles Walsham Reith was born at Stonehaven in 1889. As Director General of the BBC, he is credited with the Latin inscription in the main hall of the Portland Place Headquarters, which reads:
'This temple of the Arts and Muses is dedicated by the first governors of
broadcasting in 1931, Sir John Reith being Director General. It is their
prayer that good seeds sown may bring forth a good harvest, and that all
things hostile to peace or purity be banished from this house.'
Reith's austere influence was felt for decades at the BBC, and its passing is still deeply regretted. The annual Reith Lectures were founded to perpetuate his name in 1947, but he lived until 1971.

Local Characters
R.W. Thompson was born in Stonehaven in 1822. He was intended for the ministry, but as he showed no aptitude for the classics, he was sent to Charleston, Virginia, to acquire a mercantile education. On his return to Scotland he was employed by a demolition company on various projects, including the demolition of Dunbar Castle. It was there that he first conceived the technique for setting off explosives by electricity. Later he worked as a railway engineer with Robert Stephenson, which inspired him to invent and patent the rubber tyre in 1845. In 1851 he invented the fountain pen, and later designed the first portable crane. He died in 1873.

LOCAL FOLKLORE

Sir James Carnegie of Pittarro

The Earl of Southesk, known locally by his other title as Sir James Carnegie of Pittarro, was a great swordsman who had studied fencing at Padua. However, it was said locally that he had actually studied black magic under the Devil himself at Padua, and that this was how he acquired his skill. The Devil's payment for holding the classes was the body and soul of whichever student should be last out of the door when class was over, and on one occasion it was Sir James. But he argued that as his shadow, not himself, had actually been last out of the room, the Devil should take it instead.

The Devil was not taken in by this, but he chose to accept the bargain on the grounds that Sir James would do a whole lifetime of evil, and his soul would be just as secure at the end of it. So Sir James went back to persecute his tenants, oppress the poor, and occasionally kill people in duels, but he always walked in the shade if he could, as lack of a shadow embarrassed him.

DISTINCTIVE FLAVOUR

The people have a long-standing reputation for physical strength. A common tag runs, '*I can dae fat I dow, the men o' the Mearns (Kincardine) can dae nae mair.*'

COUNTY DIARY

December:
      Stonehaven Fireball
      Ceremony

KINROSS-SHIRE

COUNTY FACTS

Derivation of name: From the Gaelic, meaning the tip or end of a promontory. Alternatively, it may derive from the word ros, meaning a moor.
First Recorded: c. 1144
Motto: For All Time
County Town: Kinross
Towns: Cleish, Crook of Devon, Drum, Kinross, Milnathort, Scotlandwell.

Local Government
Tayside Regional Council and one District Council.

HISTORY

In 1303 Wallace with eight companions rowed to Castle Island, where they surprised and massacred the entire garrison, sparing only the women. He then cleared the corpses out of the way and held a feast, using the castle's supplies. It is unknown if the ladies were invited to partake.

The county of Kinross only achieved a separate identity in 1426. Before that it was once part of the Kingdom of Fife.

In 1567 Mary Queen of Scots signed her abdication on Castle Island in Loch Leven. The following year she escaped from it by using her womanly arts on the 18-year old nephew of the jailer, 'Daft Willie' Douglas, whom she persuaded to steal the keys. Once she was out she locked the gates and threw the keys in the loch. This was shortly before the battle of Langside.

In 1662 eleven women were accused of 'consorting with Satan, and sorcerie' at the church at Tullibole. They were tortured to make them confess, and subsequently burnt at Lamlaires.

INDUSTRY PAST AND PRESENT

The soil is mainly sand, gravel and clay, so that only oats, barley, root crops and cattle are practicable. Linen manufacturing used to be important but has declined over the years. Defoe commented on the planting of conifers in this area that it would 'in Time make Scotland a second Norway for Firr;' a sentiment that has since been echoed with markedly less enthusiasm.

Kinnesswood was at one time the only place where vellum and parchment were manufactured in Scotland. It is popularly believed that the National Covenant of 1638 was written on Kinnesswood parchment.

Such freestone quarrying as there was has now declined.

LANDMARKS

There are the ruins of a 15th century castle on an island in Loch Leven, but its gardens are of more interest to the modern tourist.

MONUMENTS

Burleigh Castle is now largely ruined, but parts of the 15th century keep are still to be seen, as is the tower house, from 1582.

Kinross House was built by Sir William Bruce, sometimes called the 'Scottish Wren'. Of it Dryden said:

> 'Strong Doric columns form the base,
> Corinthian fills the upper space;
> So all below is strength, and all above is grace.'

The alarmingly-named **Rumbling Bridge** spans a 120 foot chasm. A bridge from 1713 is to be seen beneath it.

FAMOUS PEOPLE AND LOCAL CHARACTERS

Robert Adam was MP for Kinross, 1768-74. He decorated the front of the Old Tolbooth

TOPOGRAPHY INCLUDING RIVERS

The county is bounded in the east and south by Fife, and in the north and west by Perthshire. Most of the county forms a natural hollow round Loch Leven. The highest point is Bishop Hill, 1492 feet. Rivers: Garney, North Queich, South Queich.

at his own expense. However, in 1818 Elizabeth Fry described it as

> *'Two miserable cells on the ground floor, one of which gave the occupant*
>> *a chance to chat with passers-by on the street, while the other was a*
>>> *dungeon without light or air except through a grated hole in the door.*
>>> *There was no exercise yard.'*

Regardless of this, there was only one occupant, a debtor who lived there from choice. An inspector who called on one occasion was unable to get in because the only prisoner had gone for a walk with the key in his pocket, having first locked up.

After he renounced his title of 14th Earl of Home in order to fight the 1964 General Electon, **Sir Alec Douglas Home** was MP for Kinross.

Local Characters

Michael Bruce, 'the gentle poet of Loch Leven', was born at Kinnesswood in 1746. Though he died in 1767, aged only 21, his verses show signs of a genius which might have flowered given more favourable circumstances. His best-known works are the paraphrase hymns 'O God of Bethel' and 'Behold, the mountain of the Lord'.

ART AND LITERATURE

'There's mair kail in Kinross than e're cam' oot o't.'
Scots saying

'Those never got luck that came to Lochleven.'
Old saying

LOCAL FOLKLORE

The **Auld Manse** was occupied from 1699 to 1719 by the Reverend Robert McGill. He reported various forms of poltergeist activity, including the disappearance of silver cutley which later turned up in a barn, with no attempt at concealment. There were also pins and needles found inside hard-boiled eggs. The place was rebuilt in 1769, but it is

still haunted, with footsteps being heard crossing the ceilings, and babies crying in unoccupied rooms.

DISTINCTIVE FLAVOUR

Kinross is referred to locally as '**the Sleepy Hollow of Scotland**'.

COUNTY DIARY

August: Kinross Show

KIRKCUDBRIGHTSHIRE

(GALLOWAY)

COUNTY FACTS

Derivation of name: Either from Caer-Cuabrit, the name given by the pre-Roman Novantae, or named from the church of St Cuthbert.

First Recorded: 1278 as The Church of St Cudberct

County Town: Kirkcudbright

Towns: Castle Douglas, Creetown, Dalbeattie, Dalry, Gatehouse of Fleet, Kirkcudbright, Maxwelltown (continuous to the west with the town of Dumfries), Minnigaff, New Galloway.

Local Government
Dumfries and Galloway Regional Countil and two District Councils.

HISTORY

In 1461, after his defeat at Towton, Henry VI sought refuge at Kirkcudbright.

In 1587 James VI visited the Royal Burgh, and presented it with a small cannon cast in silver, 'to encourage them in the use of firearms'. It was subsequently stolen and presumably melted down, but the thieves were never caught.

James VI's preoccupation with witches was well known, and continued to set the tone into the reign of Charles I. This brought about the sad end of the 'witch of Irongray', a widow who made a precarious living by spinning and weaving in a cottage near the Cluden. No direct accusation of harm was ever brought against her, but she was seen at odd times walking about gathering sticks, or talking to herself. Moreover, she owned a brassbound Bible, which people assumed to be a grimoire.

Apart from these things, she was visited by young women of the district, ostensibly for the purpose of buying stockings that she had made, and to share a dram or a pipe; but it was felt that the redness of their eyes, sometimes when they left, was the effect of neither tobacco, liquor nor woodsmoke, but of scrying. These things were made subject of a report to the Bishop of Galloway, who eventually bowed to public pressure, and brought her to trial. Though she protested her innocence, she was sentenced to be drowned in the Routing Burn. But the mob insisted that she should be tied up in a barrel of pitch, set on fire, and then rolled into the Cluden. Thus popular feeling was gratified, but the fate of the valuable brassbound Bible remains obscure.

Shortly after this Samuel Rutherford held the living of Anwoth. At that time the people were in the habit of visiting Mosscobin Farm to play football on the Sabbath, a practice denounced by Rutherford with great fury. There were also three standing stones there, and Rutherford called the three to 'stand witness' to his denunciation.

Subsequently a local man wanted to use the three stones to build a wall. Another warned him of the impiety of removing 'Rutherford's Witnesses', but he persisted, swearing he would remove them all before he had breakfast. He managed the first, but fell dead trying to move the second, which remained well into the 19th century.

INDUSTRY PAST AND PRESENT

There is a tradition of rearing Galloway cattle. The honey from Borgue is exceptionally good. Otherwise, agriculture is largely confined to potatoes, oats and turnips. These go mainly to feed cattle and pigs.

Some iron and lead were mined in the 19th century, but were never important. Salmon fishing is not what it was. Cheese making has declined.

LANDMARKS

There is a 50 foot circle of 28 standing stones at Glen Quicken.

MONUMENTS

At **Cairn Holy**, there are two chambered cairns, the larger being 170 feet long and 50 feet wide.

Threave Castle was built by Archibald the Grim, 3rd Earl of Douglas during the 14th century. It is ruined now, but there is a wildfowl refuge on the estate.

TOPOGRAPHY INCLUDING RIVERS

The county is bounded on the north and northwest by Ayrshire, east and northeast by Dumfriesshire, southwest by Wigtownshire, and south and southeast by the Solway Firth. The terrain is rocky, and the soil is thin. The highest point is Merrick Mountain, 2764 feet.
Rivers: Dee, Urr.

Sweetheart Abbey is now a roofless ruin, but still very beautiful. It is so called because the foundress, Devorgilla, had a deep affection for her husband, John Balliol. After he died in 1273 she kept his embalmed heart with her until her own death in 1290, after which it shared her coffin before the high altar.

Dundrennan Abbey, though ruined, is still one of the finest of all Scottish monasteries. Together with Melrose, Dryburgh and Kelso, it is one of the so-called Border Abbeys.

FAMOUS PEOPLE AND LOCAL CHARACTERS

Sir Thomas MacLellan was an ardent Covenanter, and commanded the South regiment, which fought and defeated the English at Newburn. In 1645 he raised a regiment of Galwegians at his own expense, which was instrumental in the defeat of Montrose at Philiphaugh. Patrick Gordon of Ruthven recounts what follows:

'With the whole baggage, which was exceedingly rich, there remained now but boys, cooks and a rabble of rascals, and women with children in their arms, all these without commiseration were cut to pieces; whereof there were three hundred women, that being the natives of Ireland, were the married wives of the Irish; there were many big with child, yet none of them were spared, but were cut to pieces with such usage and inhuman cruelty as neither Turk nor Scithean was ever heard to have done the like. For they ript up the bellies of the women with their swords, till the fruit of their womb, some in the embrion, some perfectly formed, and some ready for birth, fell upon the ground, weltering in the gory blood of their mangled mothers.'

Local Characters

Andrew Heron of Bargaulie was a highly respected botanist in the 18th century, who cultivated many rare plants on his estate. On one occasion he went to Kew, to see what the King had that he had not. A gardener there wanted to know what a rustic-looking Scotsman was doing, poking among the shrubs.

Heron told him in exhaustive detail what the shrubs were, and what were the special properties of all the others in sight, so that eventually the gardener asked him his name, which he gave, along with his address. The gardener had heard of the Bargaulie collection, and commented that he might have guessed, as only 'Bargaulie or the Devil' could have made such answers. 'Bargaulie or the Devil'

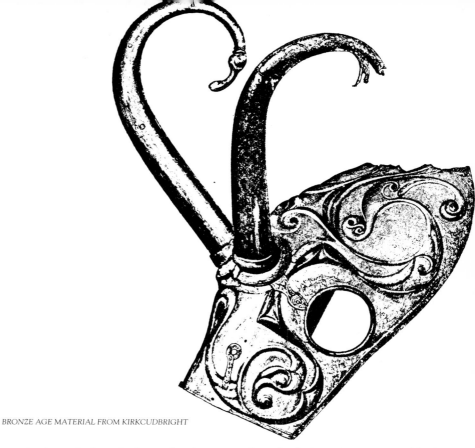

BRONZE AGE MATERIAL FROM KIRKCUDBRIGHT

remained a catch-phrase in the area for a long time after.

ART AND LITERATURE

'Here is a pleasant Situation, and yet nothing pleasant to be seen. Here is a Harbour without Ships, a Port without Trade, a Fishery without Nets, a People without Business.'
Daniel Defoe

LOCAL FOLKLORE

Jock Mulldroch

Jock Mulldroch, a fellow who lived at Craigwaggie, Galloway, used to lay eggs, larger than goose eggs, and strangely speckled black and yellow. He used to cackle too after he laid them. Once a fortnight he is said to have produced an egg, and his mother, after having sold a few of them as bonny goose eggs, set a couple of them beneath her favourite laying hen to hatch. The hen sat for a long time, but at last they chipped and out came two little lads dressed in green. The woman looked after them, and they throve under her care, so that they were known all over the south of Scotland as Willie and Wattie Birly. Everybody liked them, and they were

reckoned to be brownies, or mongrel fairies. But they vanished after forty years, which was in the year of the long storm. Perhaps they were swallowed up by a snowdrift, or a quagmire.

DISTINCTIVE FLAVOUR

The pronunciation of Kirkcudbright is Kircoobree, and it should properly be referred to not as a county but as the Stewartry of Kirkcudbright. Before the Reformation, the county possessed more monasteries than any other in Scotland.

Traditionally this has been regarded as an especially primitive part of Scotland, where the standard of rural life was very low, and the people subsisted on kail and oats, hand-ground in a quern, and dried in a pot, well into the 19th century.

COUNTY DIARY

August:	Stewartry Agricultural Show, Castle Douglas

LANARKSHIRE

COUNTY FACTS

Derivation of name: From the Brittonic word Llanerch meaning a glade or forest clearing.
First Recorded: 1116
Motto: Vigilantia (Vigilance)
County Town: Lanark
Towns: Airdrie, Baillieston, Bellshill, Blantyre, Biggar, Bishopbriggs, Cambuslang, Carluke, Carstairs, Cathcart, Coatbridge, Douglas, East Kilbride, Glasgow, Govan (partly in Renfrewshire), Hamilton, Lanark, Larkhill, Lesmahagow, Motherwell, Newmains, Partick, Pollockshields, Rutherglen, Shotts, Strathaven, Uddingston, Wishaw.

Local Government
Strathclyde Regional Council and ten District Councils.

HISTORY

In 1298 Sir William Wallace, while on honeymoon in Lanark with Lady Leamington, killed Sheriff Hazelrigg and expelled his soldiers from the town.
Building commenced on Glasgow Cathedral in 1123, and completed about the same time Glasgow University was founded, in 1450. Lanark had custody of the Scottish Standard Weights until they were superseded under the Act of 1826.

INDUSTRY PAST AND PRESENT

The industrial present and past of Glasgow cover virtually every phase since the beginning of the industrial revolution. In the late 19th century it was styled 'Second City of the Empire' and could compare to Liverpool for shipping, Newcastle for coal, and Wolverhampton for iron.
In the countryside breeding of Clydesdale draught horses is still done, and has recently returned to favour as shire horses have once more taken the popular imagination.
The decline of shipbuilding on the Clyde has given rise to many expressions of regret, some rather lachrymose. Lead and silver were mined in the 19th century, along with a little gold. The importance of New Lanark as a

textile centre is also much reduced, as is coal-mining.
In the 17th century rum was distilled from molasses, and was known as 'Glasgow brandy'.

LANDMARKS

Clydeside
Leadhills (1,323 feet) is the highest inhabited point in Scotland.

MONUMENTS

Barncluith House and gardens date from 1583, and were planned by John Hamilton. The great statue of **William Wallace** at Lanark was made by the self-taught sculptor, Robert Forrest.
Cadzow Castle, now in ruins, was once visited by Mary, Queen of Scots.
Glasgow Cathedral, dedicated to St Mungo, is one of the few undamaged medieval churches in Scotland. It has an unusually large crypt.
New Lanark is remarkable as a model town of the Industrial Revolution.

FAMOUS PEOPLE AND LOCAL CHARACTERS

In 1650 **Cromwell** entered Glasgow, and attended divine service in the High Church; but the Presbyterian divine who officiated poured forth, with more zeal than prudence, his indignation against the person, principles and cause of the Independent General. One of Cromwell's officer rose, and whispered to his commander who seemed to give a short and stern answer, and the sermon was concluded without interruption.
Among the crowd, assembled to gaze at the General as he came out of the Church, was a shoemaker, the son of one of James VI's Scottish footmen. This man had been born and bred in England, but, after his father's death, had settled in Glasgow. Cromwell eyed him among the crowd, and immediately called him by name. The man fled, but, at Cromwell's command one of his retinue followed him, and brought him to the General's lodgings. A number of the inhabitants remained at the door, awaiting the end of this extraordinary scene.
The shoemaker soon came out in high spirits,

TOPOGRAPHY INCLUDING RIVERS

The county is bounded on the north and northwest by Stirlingshire and Dunbartonshire, west and southwest with Renfrewshire and Ayrshire, east and southeast by West and Mid Lothian, and Peeblesshire, and on the south by Dumfriesshire. The terrain is very varied, with mountain, moorland, and arable.
The highest point is Culter Fell, 2454 feet.
Rivers: Clyde, Douglas, Avon, Calder.

and, showing some gold, declared that he was going to drink Cromwell's health. Many attended him, to hear the particulars of his interview. The shoemaker said he had been a playfellow of Cromwell, when they were both boys, their parents residing in the same street; that he had fled, when the General first called to him, thinking he might owe him some ill-will, on account of his father being in the service of the Royal Family. He added that Cromwell had been so very kind and familiar with him, that he ventured to ask him what the officer had said to him in the church.

"He proposed," said Cromwell, "to pull forth the minister by the ears; and I answered, that the preacher was a fool, and he was another." In the course of the day, Cromwell held an interview with the minister, and contrived to satisfy his scruples so effectually that the evening discourse, by the same man, was tuned to the praise and glory of the victor of Naseby.

Scott
Minstrelsey of the Border

Robert Owen was born in Montgomery in 1771, but settled in New Lanark after marrying a local mill-owner's daughter. He was shocked at the general demoralisation of the workforce, which he attributed to overwork and low pay. He set about improving them by providing infant schools, refurbishing their homes, restricting the sale of liquor, and setting up a subsidised shop.

These things were all very well, but his report to the committee on the Poor Law, which advocated arbitrarily dividing the entire population into communities of 1,200 people each, under the control of benevolent dictators modelled on himself, was less well received. Less popular still was his militant atheism.

In 1825 he attempted to put his ideas into practice, at an ideal colony on an estate in Indiana, which he named New Harmony. It rapidly degenerated into chaos, but Owen had by this time rejected atheism and taken up spiritualism instead. He published the fruits of this, which consisted of the conversations in which he had engaged a number of famous men, now deceased, by the laborious method of table rapping. They were highly supportive of his views and actions, especially Benjamin Franklin. Owen was active to the last, and died in 1858.

Local Characters

Sir James Douglas, (also known as 'Good Sir James' or 'The Black Douglas' according to which side you were on) was one of the great Scots Nationalists. His father was imprisoned by Edward I, and he was forced to retreat to France, but he returned to Scotland after three years to fight on behalf of Robert Bruce. He is said to have fought in seventy battles, including Bannockburn, where he commanded the left wing. He also found himself compelled to invest and take his own family home on three occasions, each time destroying the fortifications. His comment was that he did it 'loving better to hear the lark sing than the mouse squeak'.

By 1327 there was peace between Scotland and England, so after Bruce died Douglas set about the salvation of his own soul, by means of a pilgrimage to the Holy Land, bearing Bruce's heart in a silver casket. However, his soldierly qualities got the better of him, and he took service with King Alfonso of Leon and Castile in his war against Granada. He was overwhelmed and killed at the battle of Theba in 1330. When his body was found next morning, he was still clutching the casket with Bruce's heart.

David Livingstone was born in Blantyre in 1813. A man of intense application but slender means, he acquired an education by attending evening classes in Greek, medicine and theology. During the day he supported himself by operating a spinny jenny, with his book propped against it. In this way he could keep abreast of his studies (which he completed in 1840), and achieve his ambition of becoming a missionary in China.

In fact, the London Missionary Society sent him to Africa instead, but Livingstone was not put out. There he devoted his energies to missionary activity (at which he was very unsuccessful) and exploration (at which he excelled). In later life he became obsessed with the search for the source of the Nile, which he discovered (in Lake Tanganyika) just before his death in 1873.

Alan Ramsay was born in 1686 in Glengonar, and was apprenticed to a barber. But long before Burns or Scott, he came to an appreciation of the commercial potential of Scots poetry, which he transcribed and polished as necessary from the Banatyne manuscript in the Advocates' Library. He published these and his own work in a number

of collections and miscellanies with considerable success up to his death in 1758.

ART AND LITERATURE
*'I belong to Glasgow, dear old Glasgow town
There's something the matter with Glasgow, 'cos it's turning round and round,
I'm only a common old working chap, as you can easily see,
But when I've had a few on a Saturday night, Glasgow belongs to me.'*
    Traditional

LOCAL FOLKLORE
The Old Widow of Camp-del-more
There was an old widow who lived in the Camp-del-more of Strathaven, whose cattle were seized with a murrain, when there was an epidemic in the area. Need-fires were lit, and hallowed waters were procured, but to no effect. So she was forced to the conclusion that only the one infallible remedy, the juice of a dead head from the churchyard, would bring relief. This is not an easy remedy to obtain, as the head must be dug up single-handed at midnight, but she had a stout heart and a strong stomach, and besides, her need was greater than her natural feelings of delicacy and piety. So she hired a poor neighbour to accompany her and they set out together, a little before midnight, to cover the half mile.

At the churchyard her companion's courage failed her, but she promised to wait for her at the gate. The old lady therefore went in alone, chose a promising-looking grave, and began to dig. After much toil, she turned up a mouldering skull, and she was about to put it in a bag to take home, when a hollow voice exclaimed, "That's my head! Leave it alone!" Now the old lady found it hard to dispute title in the circumstances, so she put it down and carried on digging until she found another. But the same voice bellowed, "That's my father's head!"

This also was hard to dispute, so the old lady sighed, dropped it back in the hole and dug some more. But as soon as she found another, the same voice claimed it as his grandfather's skull. By this time the old lady was tired, it was getting cold, and she was disinclined to dig further. So she leaned back on her spade and said, "It may be your grandmother's skull as well, but you're still not getting it back till I've finished with it."

At this point the ghost appeared, starting out of the ground in unkempt cerements. "What

Ball of cast bronze, found at Walston, Lanarkshire (actual size).

do you say, you limmer?" it shouted, in great rage. "By the great oath, you'd better leave my granddad's head alone!"

The old lady decided that now was the time to start bargaining, so she got her pipe going, and told the ghost the whole story about the murrain on her cattle, and promised that if the ghost just let her borrow the skull, in a peaceable manner, she would restore it the following night. The ghost settled down to negotiate, and in the end she agreed to return it by cock-crow that morning, under a stiff penalty clause.

On coming out of the gate, she discovered to her disgust that her weak-livered companion, fearing she might be included in the various pains and penalties which the ghost threatened, had been taken with the vapours and was lying insensible. Moreover, she had not thought to bring any sal volatile. There were barely two hours to cock-crow in any case, so she lugged her to the nearest house and dumped her for the remainder of the night in the porchway. Then she set off home at her best speed, made 'dead bree' of the head, restored the skull (by now quite gleaming clean), and piled in the loose earth as the cocks crew around her.

Her perseverance was rewarded, for her cattle soon recovered, and while she had any dead bree left, they were never sick for long.

DISTINCTIVE FLAVOUR

In **Glasgow** support for rival football teams is largely a matter of religion. Protestants tend to follow Rangers, Catholics follow Celtic.

Glasgow people traditionally address men to whom they have not been introduced as '**Jimmy**', a custom which can be unnerving if your name happens to be James.

Glasgow Magistrates are herrings, so called for their sleek plumpness. Fillets of the fish are cooked in herbs and wine vinegar, then served hot with oatcakes.

COUNTY DIARY

September:
    Hamilton Races (Flat)
December:
    Biggar Ne'er Day Bonfire

MIDLOTHIAN
(EDINBURGHSHIRE)

COUNTY FACTS

Derivation of name: Named from Leudonus, and signifying his territory. No one knows who or what Leudonus was. It has been suggested, though with little confidence, that he may have been Loth, grandfather of St Mungo.

First Recorded: 1800

County Town: Edinburgh

The ancient name for Edinburgh is Dun-Edin, now celebrated in the name of the great New Zealand city on the South Island, called Dunedin.

Towns: Arniston, Bonnyrigg, Corstorphine, Cramond (partly in West Lothian), Currie, Dalkeith, Easthouses, Edinburgh, Eskbank, Gilmerton, Gorebridge, Granton, Lasswade, Leith, Liberton, Loanhead, Murrayfield, Musselburgh, Newtongrange, Penicuik, Portobello.

Edinburgh is a county of a city unto itself.

Local Government

Lothian Regional Council and two District Councils.

HISTORY

Edinburgh is named after King Edwin of Northumberland, and remained part of that kingdom until it was annexed by Scotland in 1020.

In 1385 Richard II burned down Edinburgh.

In 1436 James I was assassinated in Edinburgh, but it is from about this time that its status as capital became undisputed.

In 1537 Edinburgh was almost entirely destroyed by fire, and what remained was sacked by the Earl of Hertford.

In 1715 a band of Jacobites attempted to surprise the Castle, but without success. They did rather better in 1745, when they held the rest of the city and besieged the castle for six weeks, but it held out, and they joined the march on England.

In 1736 there was a disturbance at the execution of a smuggler called Wilson, and the mob attacked the executioner and the guard. Captain Porteous ordered the guard to fire on the crowd to disperse them, and six were killed. Porteous was tried before the High Court of the Judiciary, but got a royal reprieve. The mob therefore reassembled and broke into the jail where he was confined, dragged him out to the place of execution, and hanged him by torchlight on a dyer's pole. The actual perpetrators were never discovered, but the city was fined £2,000 to compensate his widow.

In 1826 two Irish labourers named Burke and Hare obtained lasting notoriety by their practice of luring vagrants and down-and-outs to their hostel in Tanners Close, where they would get them drunk and then strangle them, selling the bodies to the pioneer anatomist, Dr Knox, for up to £10 a time, according to condition. They came to grief partly through killing a pretty whore called Mary Patterson, whose body was all too familiar to several of Knox's students, and to Fergusson, his assistant (later Sir William Fergusson, Bart., Serjeant-Surgeon to Queen Victoria). Her body was such a fine specimen that Knox kept her pickled in a barrel of whisky for three months, to star in important demonstrations. The story has caught the public imagination in sundry sorts of verse. Dylan Thomas found it entirely suitable matter for a musical comedy, and Edinburgh children used to sing, to the tune of 'Girls and boys come out to play',

> 'Up the cloose an' doon the stair
> Gang yon cullions Burke an' Hare
> Burke's the murderer, Hare's the thief,
> And Knox the boy that buys the beef.'

A more dispassionate view is that

> 'History has been unfair
> To the memory of Hare.
> Early anatomical work
> Owes much to him and Burke.'

TOPOGRAPHY INCLUDING RIVERS

The county is bounded in the north by the Firth of Forth, in the north west by West Lothian, in the east by East Lothian and in the south by Lanarkshire, Peeblesshire, Selkirkshire and Roxburghshire. The Lammermuir (Moorfoot) and Pentland hills to the south are mainly Silurian gneiss. Relics of glaciation are the boulders deposited at their summits which came originally from Dunkeld and Ben Lomond. The highest point is Blackhope Scar, 2136 feet.

Rivers: Breich, Almond, North Esk, South Esk, Logan.

INDUSTRY PAST AND PRESENT

Most of the agriculture is arable and cereal farming, to supply Edinburgh and Leith.

Edinburgh is one of the world's greatest centres for life insurance. As the capital of Scotland, Edinburgh boasts all the cultural, commercial, diplomatic and industrial activities appropriate to its status. Elsewhere in the county one finds coal mining, quarrying, paper-making, distilling and those trades related to publishing.

In the 19th century Edinburgh was a centre for gunpowder manufacture. It was also well-known for the manufacture of paraffin and paraffin wax candles, bricks, and carpets.

Limestone and ironstone quarrying have greatly reduced in importance, and coal-mining is not what it was.

LANDMARKS

Lammermuir Hills
Pentland Hills
Arthur's Seat

MONUMENTS

Edinburgh Castle still contains the Honours of Scotland (i.e. the Scottish regalia). Despite its formidable appearance, it is not a defensible place even in medieval terms, and the fabric is almost all of more recent date, mainly from the reign of Charles II.

Edinburgh has two cathedrals. **St Giles's** with its marvellous crown-spire, was, in truth, only a cathedral for part of its existence. **St Mary's Cathedral** is a lavish Victorian structure whose trio of spires has led some to call it 'the Lichfield of the north'.

Roslin Chapel, a fine example of true Gothic architecture.

The **'Cat Stane'** near Kirkliston is conjectured to cover the remains of Hengist and Horsa's grandfather.

Holyrood House is the official residence of the Queen in Scotland.

FAMOUS PEOPLE AND LOCAL CHARACTERS

King Edwin of Northumbria, whose sway covered the greater part of Britain from the Thames to the Highland Line, built Edinburgh. His reign was one of unprecedented law and order, so that it was said that a mother and her suckling child could walk the length and breadth of it unmolested. (This is often given as 'a virgin with a bag of gold'.) He certainly set up massive bronze drinking cups where there were clean springs for travellers on the highways, and these were not stolen for scrap or souvenirs as it seems likely they would be now.

John Knox was for a while Minister of St Giles's Church, where he used to preach thrice daily and twice on Sundays.

David Hume, founder of the Scottish School of Metaphysics, was born in Edinburgh in 1711 and died there in 1776, though he travelled widely in between. His principal contributions to thought are to be found in his *Treatise of Human Nature*, which introduced the idea that the mind can only be approached as a series of mental states, so that he can be called the founder of psychology as a science. He also formalised the doctrine of unknowability, which has some startling

MONS MEG.

implications, for instance: we have no way of knowing if the universe in which we live is highly thought of among critics of universes. It may be prentice work of the creator, or the product of declining powers, but we have no standards of comparison. However, those same critics have no way of judging the quality of the larger universes of which themselves and our own universe form a part.

Hume was extremely influential on later philosophers of the Age of Reason, especially Rousseau, Kant and Tom Paine.

James I & VI was born in Edinburgh Castle. In 1637 Archbishop Laud attempted to impose the liturgy of the Church of England, in the form of a service-book, which he ordered to be read in St Giles's Church, Edinburgh. The church was filled with an angry crowd of Presbyterians, and when the Dean began to read a stall-woman called **Jenny Geddes** picked up her stool and flung it at him, shouting, "Villain! dost thou say mass at my lug?" The ensuing riot effectively finished the liturgy, and by the following year 95% of the nation had signed the National Covenant.

Jamie Duff's first claim to fame was his habit of entering himself in the Leith horseraces, running under his own colours. To encourage himself he whipped himself, but possibly because he ran barefoot instead of in racing shoes, he took no prizes. He therefore took up a second career as a professional mourner, and no important Edinburgh funeral was

complete without him. He made an especially strong impression at that of David Hume in 1776, with his weepers, black cravat, cape and black hat dyed even blacker for the occasion. It was an informal tradition that he should be paid 6d by the undertaker for lending such tone to the event.

This caused him a certain concern, because he feared that someday he would have pressed upon him the 'King's Shilling', and find himself drawn into the army. He therefore took his small nephew with him to accept the donations, as the boy was too young for conscription.

James Boswell, biographer and amanuensis to Dr Johnson, was born in Edinburgh in 1740. Apart from his famous biography, and the many anti-Scottish epigrams with which his presence inspired the great man, his diaries constitute an invaluable if somewhat louche sourcebook for many aspects of later 18th century society in London, as good for their period as that of Pepys for the reign of Charles II. It was his misfortune to be singularly susceptible both to loose women and to venereal disease, so that the tensions which this combination brought about in him made superb matter for a recent TV dramatisation. Regrettably, his excesses brought about his death in 1795.

Henry Raeburn was born in 1756 and apprenticed to a goldsmith. Finding this trade uncongenial, he taught himself to paint, specialising at first in miniatures and graduating to full-length portraits. He first exhibited at the Royal Academy in 1792, and thereafter his life was one of continuing recognition and good fortune, with RA in 1815, and a knighthood in 1822. He died in

1838.

Sir Walter Scott was born in 1771, and trained as an advocate, but took an interest in poetry and folklore from an early age. He met the ageing Burns, who encouraged him to develop his genius. His work, first in verse then in prose, caught the public imagination, though he has been accused of having invented much of the Highland tradition in order to provide material for his novels and poetry.

Robert Louis Stevenson was born in Edinburgh in 1850. His output was vast and diverse; his treatment of it always exciting, since his approach was always to view events through the eyes of a personality under stress. This allowed him to explore terror, madness and cruelty through the medium of the psychological novel, resulting in such masterpieces as *The Suicide Club, Dr Jeckyll and Mr Hyde*, and *The Wrong Box*. All of these contain strong elements of Grand Guignol humour, which have ensured that they continue to be read.

Gold Armlet found at Slateford, Midlothian.

ART AND LITERATURE

'Edinburgh society – as narrow as its wynds, as dull as its weather, as severe as its sermons, as prying as its excisemen's lanterns.'
Richard Gordon

'They have … the finest Bagnio in Britain; 'tis perfectly well contriv'd, and exactly well finish'd, no Expence being spar'd to make it both convenient and effectually useful.'
Daniel Defoe
A Tour thro' the Whole Island of Great Britain

LOCAL FOLKLORE

The House in Forrest Road

A certain single, titled lady took a house in Forrest Road about the turn of the last century. She had heard it was supposed to be haunted, but as the manifestations consisted only of an occasional untraceable smell, and certain dancing shadows seen from the corner of the eye, and these were only evident on Fridays, she was not put off.

However, as the summer progressed the Friday smell, which consisted partly of damp earth and partly of something sweetish but unpleasant, became stronger by the week. By late August it was so bad that the lady decided to seek out the ghost. She therefore gave the servants the day off, lit a candle, and followed her nose into the cellarage. In the cellar with the strongest smell she found only a large number of very active black beetles, but she noticed that though the air was exceedingly damp the walls were quite dry. She turned to leave the cellar, but as she did so the candle flame turned blue. Then she heard something fall with a crash, which made her start and drop the candle.

She made her way back to the steps, but when she reached them she saw, standing at the top, a squat, lank-haired, androgynous figure. It was clad in loose robes, and inexpressibly repulsive. As she gazed on it, the ceiling collapsed behind her and she fainted. When she recovered consciousness she returned to the main part of the house, and tried to put the incident from her mind.

The following Friday, at about three in the morning, she suddenly woke, for no obvious reason, and certainly not from a dream. She opened her eyes, and found, bending over her and looking at her, a huge and hideous face. The forehead receded sharply, and was partly covered with lank, black hair; the skin was as grey as lead, and it was so thoroughly emaciated that it had split, showing the naked cheekbones. The eyes were enormous and deeply sunken.

The lady was too frightened to shriek, but as she watched the face changed, the lower jaw fell open, exposing a bloated black tongue; the eyes rolled into the skull, showing only the whites; and a blast of putrid breath emerged from the mouth. The lady fainted again.

It proved on investigation that the house had been built on the site of a cottage which had been occupied by two sisters, both nurses. One had been suspected of poisoning the other, but there had not been sufficient evidence to bring a case, and one night the cottage had been blown down in a storm, killing the survivor.

DISTINCTIVE FLAVOUR

The original **'Heart of Midlothian'**, after which the football club was named, was the Old Tolbooth jail which used to stand opposite the Royal Exchange.

COUNTY DIARY

June:	Royal Highland Show, Newbridge
August:	The Edinburgh Military Tattoo
August:	The Edinburgh Festival

MORAYSHIRE
(ELGINSHIRE)

HISTORY

In 1390 the Earl of Buchan, a bastard son of Robert II, (also known as the Wolf of Badenoch) burnt down the cathedral in umbrage at being excommunicated. It was rebuilt, but in 1568 Regent Morton stripped off the lead for scrap so as to pay his troops, and it was allowed to fall into decay. However, it was insufficiently decayed for the Covenanters of 1640, who, under the leadership of the Reverend Gilbert Ross, tore down and then tore up the medieval paintings and smashed the rood screen for firewood, along with the choir stalls and the font lid. The 'Order (Ordeal) Pot', now filled in, was the last pond officially used for ducking witches and drowning thieves in Scotland.

INDUSTRY PAST AND PRESENT

Cereals, potatoes and beef cattle are all raised. The Forestry Commission has extensive larch plantations in Culbin Forest. Whisky distilling is important in Strathspey, as is salmon fishing, as part of the tourist industry. There is little first-class agricultural land, but oats and barley flourish in places. Turnips and potatoes are also grown. Whisky distilling is widespread.

Granite, slate and freestone have all been quarried at various times in the county. In the last century commercial salmon fishing sometimes grossed £100,000 per annum.

LANDMARKS

Glen Urquhart, famous for the Urquhart check, lies to the north of the county.

MONUMENTS

Elgin Cathedral, now ruined, is mainly 13th century. The presbytery façade is still very impressive.
Spynie Palace, also ruined, was a massive fortress of the Bishops of Moray.
Forres Castle was the royal residence of Duncan, and later Macbeth.

FAMOUS PEOPLE AND LOCAL CHARACTERS

Macbeth (MacBeathad MacFinlegh) was Moarmor (chieftain) of Moray, and married to the granddaughter of King Kenneth Macduff. After Malcolm II, who had murdered King Kenneth and usurped him, was succeeded by Duncan M'Crinan, his grandson, Macbeth took up arms against Duncan and killed him in battle near Elgin in 1039. He took the throne and reigned for fifteen years, displaying great energy and love of justice. But partisans of Duncan rose up against him and defeated him, first at Dunsinane in Perth, from which he escaped, and later in pitched battle at Lumphanan in Aberdeen, where he was killed in 1056. His wife, Gruach, was famous for her charitable and religious endowments.
James Ramsay MacDonald, first Labour Prime Minister, was born at Lossiemouth in 1866. His early career in politics was blighted by his pacifist stance during World War I, but he returned to prominence in 1922 as MP for Aberavon when he was elected leader of the Labour Party, and became Prime Minister and Foreign Secretary of a minority administration. A further election was held to clarify the situation, wherein he was defeated. This was partly because of the 'Zinoviev Letter' affair, a Russian literary hoax, which suggested that the British

TOPOGRAPHY INCLUDING RIVERS

The county is bounded in the north by the Moray Firth, in the west by Nairnshire, in the east and south east by Banffshire and in the south by Inverness-shire. The coastline is varied, with rocky cliffs and beaches, and the terrain is hilly, except in the Spey Valley. The highest point is Cromdale, 2329 feet.
Rivers: Spey, Lossie, Findhorn.

At Burghead

At Burghead

Communists were poised for bloody revolution, and the Labour Party was their stalking-horse.

MacDonald returned to power in 1929, but the stockmarket crash and recession left him in an impossible position as Prime Minister of the Tory dominated National Government. He hung onto it, while his political credibility and intellectual powers declined, until 1935, dying a broken man in 1937.

Local Characters

Isobel Goudie, the most famous of the North Scottish witches, was an attractive young woman, married to a dull farmer near Lochloy. She became friendly with Sir Robert Gordon, who initiated her into witchcraft. She claimed to have acquired the skill to turn a floating straw into a fine horse, to make all manner of wax images, to use flint 'fairy arrows', and to make moon paste. Curiously, these interesting pastimes lost their appeal after a while, and she confessed voluntarily to the church at Auldearn where she had renounced her baptism. Despite this repentance, she was sentenced to be strangled and then burnt at Elgin in 1646.

ART AND LITERATURE

'Now we had to bid adieu to sweet Moray. Oh! Thy pretty girls, thy fertile fields, and they delightful prospects will ever be dear to our remembrance. If Samuel Johnson had had eyes to have seen thy beauties, thou wouldst have saved Scotland all his sarcasms.'

Walter Thom, 1810

LOCAL FOLKLORE

Witchcraft

Michael Scott, the great wizard, had been inducted into the Black Art at Salamanca, and thus had no shadow. His wickedness was a matter of some pride in the county, as was that of Sir Robert Gordon:

> *'O who hasna heard o' that man o' renown,*
> *The Wizard, Sir Robert o' Gordonstoun!*
> *The wisest o' warlocks, the Morayshire chiel,*
> *The despot of Duffus, the frien o' the deil.'*

Unfortunately, his friend was unable to save his sundry disciples from wearing the 'harden goun'. This was a penitential garment kept in every parish, and made of the coarsest and heaviest unbleached linen. A sinner (of either sex) was required to wear this livery of shame for anything up to 16 days continuously, sitting on a penitential stool with two steps - the more serious sinners sat higher, those whose sins were of less consequence took the 'cock-stool'. But as nothing was to be worn underneath, and there is no record of a harden goun ever being washed, one can assume that the itch was the same for all grades of sinner. The cost of replacing harden gouns was borne by the poor-box, and most frequently arose at the occasion of a witch-burning, since the witches were burnt in them.

At Elgin the further refinement of a mitre was added, on which was catalogued the sins of the penitent – a tribute to the high level of literacy.

DISTINCTIVE FLAVOUR

The county of **Morayshire** is in no way connected with the **eels** of the same name. Moreover, the people maintain that no one – anywhere – ever – has succeeded in making a joke on those lines which was even remotely funny.

In the 19th century, the expression '**Moray coach**' was prevalent over much of Scotland, and meant a cart.

The county, like neighbouring Nairnshire, was famous for its early attainment of a high level of literacy.

Morayshire is part of the ancient province of Moray (whence its name) that stretched from Aberdeenshire through Banffshire, Morayshire and Nairnshire to coastal Inverness-shire.

Findhorn is the sight of a 'new age' community, where it is said that vegetables grow three or four times larger than their normal size, due to the mystical vibrations and ley lines.

COUNTY DIARY

December 31:
At Burghead, on the Moray Firth, a blazing tar-barrel, called a Claivie, is carried round the town.

NAIRNSHIRE

COUNTY FACTS

Derivation of name: Named from the local river, which in Gaelic is Uisage 'nEarn meaning River of the Alder trees. It is possible however that it derives from the Pre-Celtic language for 'flowing water'.

First Recorded: c.1200

Motto: Unite and be Mindful

County Town: Nairn

Towns: Auldearn, Cawdor, Ferness, Nairn

Local Government

Highland Regional Council and one District Council. There is one small detached part of the county within Morayshire, one detached part in Ross-shire and one within Inverness-shire. Apart from that part of Nairnshire within Morayshire administered by Grampian Regional Council, the rest are all controlled by Highland Regional Council.

HISTORY

Montrose defeated the Covenanters at Auldearn in 1645.

In 1746 the battle of Culloden took place on Drummossie Moor in a sleety snowstorm. It did not have the mark of a decisive battle, since both armies were seriously depleted, the Jacobites by the season (many had gone home for the spring sowing) and the Hanoverians by the fact of being well beyond the end of their supply lines.

The Hanoverians attacked, nonetheless, while Murray and Lochiel were still trying to persuade Hay and the Prince to take up a defensive position on the heights above the river. In fact, the Jacobites were outflanked. If they chose to defend, Cumberland could perfectly well ignore them and march on Inverness, by way of their baggage-train, incidentally. The moor was flat, favouring the Hanoverian tactics and superior artillery. The two armies manoeuvred against each other, something that Cumberland understood better than the Highlanders. Eventually the waiting was too much for the Mackintoshes, who broke and charged in traditional Highland fashion, the rest of the army following them in a ragged wave. It was the tactic that offered them least hope of success, and so it proved.

TOPOGRAPHY INCLUDING RIVERS

The county is bounded in the north by the Moray Firth, and in all other directions by Morayshire and Inverness-shire. Most of it is hilly with peaks above 2,000 feet, but there is level country up to six miles inland from the coast. The highest point is Carn-Glas-Choire, 2182 feet.

Rivers: Nairn, Findhorn.

INDUSTRY PAST AND PRESENT

Whisky-distilling remains important, and granite is quarried, but the main industry of Nairn is mixed farming.

Nairn was a bathing resort in the 19th century, but has been superceded by places further south. The salmon fishing is not what it was.

LANDMARKS

The field of Culloden is a somewhat melancholy tourist attraction, especially to those with Jacobite sympathies.

MONUMENTS

Cawdor Castle dates from 1454, and is in good condition. It is heavily restored but with a 15th-century tower, where Lord Lovat took refuge after the Battle of Culloden. He was the last man to be beheaded for treason in England, despite having asked to be hanged as a favour. This was not an expression of solidarity with the lower classes, but because he had hunched shoulders, which he feared might make his neck a difficult target. Gratifyingly, the executioner was sober, and his eye was in that day. He did not botch the shot.

Unfortunately the castle is not open to the public.

Boath Dovecote, built in the 17th century contains 546 nest-holes. It is an early example of factory-farming.

FAMOUS PEOPLE AND LOCAL CHARACTERS

Nairn has some exciting times ahead, according to the **Brahan Seer**:

'There shall be a hand with two thumbs at I-Stiana, in the Black Isle, a man with two navels at Dunean, and soldiers shall come from Carra Chalarsair on a chariot without horse or bridle, and the raven shall drink his three fulls of the blood of the Gael from the Stone of Fionn.'

His prophecies are not to be treated lightly. He also told the people of Milburn, near Culloden, that a day would come when their mill wheel would someday be turned three days by water red with the blood of men. Three days is doubtless an exaggeration, but this was a century before Culloden.

Local Characters

Johnnie Morgan the pigman was a well known sight in Nairn in the first half of this century. He used to travel about the town collecting discarded food, mainly from hotels, to feed his pigs and presumably himself and his pony, since he was never seen to buy any. The smell of his cart was so powerful, it was said to travel against the wind, but it was nothing to the smell of his pigsties or himself. Yet his pony was a beautiful blond Highland Garron, immaculately kept, and very sweet-tempered.

ART AND LITERATURE

'And in conclusion, I will say for good bathing Nairn is best
And besides its pleasant scenery is of historical interest.
And the climate gives health to many visitors while there.

Therefore I would recommend Nairn for balmy pure air.'
        William McGonagall

LOCAL FOLKLORE

The Bodach

Nairn is home to the Bodach, a shrivelled, little old man who lives up your chimney, inhaling the fumes of burning peat. If children make a fuss at bedtime, he notes it, and once the child is asleep he comes down to tweak its nose, toes and ears, and to give it nightmares. However, crafty children know that if you throw a pinch of salt on the fire, the Bodach will stay up.

The Kempock Stane

In 1662 in a witch trial at Auldearn, the witch confessed that she and her coven used to fly to Kempock Stane in Renfrew to raise the wind there: "When we raise the wind we take a rag of cloth and wet it in water, and we take a beetle (mallet) and knock the rag on a stone, and we say thrice over

> *I knock this rag upon this stane,*
> *To raise the wind in the devil's name.*
> *It shall not lie until I please again."*

MacQueen of Pollohcaig claimed to have killed the last wolf in Scotland, though this is disputed by Ewen Cameron of Lochiel.

Carved Stone found at Muckle Geddes, Nairn.

DISTINCTIVE FLAVOUR

In Nairnshire, as in many Highland counties, the **'Pure Box'** (Poor Box) was a powerful bone of contention betwen the natural piety and the natural parsimony of the people. The Kirk extracted fines, often very considerable ones, from people who were late for church, played golf on the Sabbath, or were caught in unhallowed forms of sexual behaviour. In Nairn, however, the greater sophistication of the clergy made the following kind of transaction more typical. After the service one Sunday, a well-to-do farmer appeared among the supplicants outside the church. The Minister heard his whispered confidences, and, in a very public manner, gave him a whole shilling from the box. This caused great speculation, as the farmer was not believed to be in want. However, the following day the farmer appeared before the Session on a charge of poaching. He pleaded guilty, having little option, and the magistrates retired to consider how great a fine should be imposed.

"What!" cried the Minister, "Fine that poor man? Did you not all see me give him something from the poor box on the Lord's Day? Admonish him, and let him go!"

The bench could hardly deny that they had seen such an event, but the profusion of venison and salmon on the Minister's table was the subject of some remark.

James VI used to boast that he had in his kingdom a town whose only street was so long that the people living at one end could not understand the tongue of the people at the other. This was Nairn, though of course the people were all bilingual in Gaelic and Lowland Scots.

COUNTY DIARY

July:	Craft and Country Fair, Nairn
July:	Vintage Car Rally, Nairn

ORKNEY

HISTORY

Orkney was a Danish possession until 1468, when they were used to secure a dowry of 60,000 florins in respect of the marriage of Princess Margaret to James III of Scotland. Only 2,000 were ever paid, and the time for settlement has now lapsed.

The German fleet was scuttled in Scapa Flow during World War I.

During World War II causeways were built between Mainland and the islands of Burray and South Ronaldsay, to prevent U-boats from getting into Scapa Flow.

INDUSTRY PAST AND PRESENT

The oil pipeline from the Claymore, Scapa and Highlander fields terminates at Flotta. An oil-related helicopter service operates out of Kirkwall. Trout fishing in the streams is popular, but they are not long enough to tempt salmon. Traditional sea-fishing is still very important.

The cultivation of oats and big barley have both declined with the advent of more profitable oil-based industries.

TOPOGRAPHY INCLUDING RIVERS

The county consists of a group of 73 islands, but some of these become peninsulas at low tide, and most are uninhabited. They are separated from the mainland of Caithness by the Pentland Firth. The largest is called Pomona, or Mainland. Those in the west have generally very steep beaches, and are hilly inland. They are quite treeless, owing to the high winds. Much of the land is peat and moor, but some small-scale, high-intensity agriculture, mainly of cattle and poultry, is beginning to encroach. The highest point is Ward Hill on Hoy, 1565 feet.
Rivers: Orkney has no rivers.

LANDMARKS

The Standing Stones of Stenness consist of three stone rings, one (at Bookan) a cairn, the others at Brodgar and Stenness are henges. There are Runic inscriptions on the one at Brodgar.
The Old Man of Hoy is a 450 foot rock stack.

MONUMENTS

Skara Brae, an underground village on West Mainland, is a complete neolithic relic.
The Cathedral of St Magnus was built by Christianised Norsemen in the 12th century.
Dwarfie Stane is a great block of sandstone, with cell tombs cut into either side.

FAMOUS PEOPLE AND LOCAL CHARACTERS

Sir Mordred, incestuously conceived son/ nephew of King Arthur by his half-sister, was born and raised in Orkney. He, more than any other, brought about the fall of Arthurian Britain.

Local Characters
Earl Rollo of Orkney conquered Normandy, and became the grandfather of William the Conqueror.
Eric Linklater was born in 1899. He was trained as a doctor, but his principal interests were literature and travel, which he combined by joining the staff of *The Times of India* for two years. In 1927 he became professor of English literature at Aberdeen University, but on the outbreak of war he returned to Orkney to command the fortress. After the war he took part in the war in Korea. He died in 1974.

ART AND LITERATURE

'No bloody sport, no bloody games,
        No bloody fun, the bloody dames
Won't even give their bloody names
        In bloody Orkney.'
                                Captain Hamish Blair

LOCAL FOLKLORE

Assipattle and the Stour Worm

Assipattle was the seventh son of a farmer. He was a good-for-nothing who spent all day lying in the warm ashes in front of the fire, and in the evening boasted about imaginary deeds of adventure.

But there came a time when the kingdom was ravaged by the Stour Worm, the worst of monsters. He could only be assuaged by young virgins, which he ate seven to the meal, and no hero could stand before him, though the king promised his daughter, Gem-de-Lovely, and his kingdom for dowry, and the great sword Skippersnapper, all for the man who killed him. Then the king's scald prophesied that the monster would only leave the land when Gem-de-Lovely was sacrificed to him.

When he heard this, Assipattle stole his father's horse, Teetgong, the fastest of horses, and came to the coast where the Stour Worm was sleeping. There he found a croft, where he took a smouldering turf in a bucket, and cozened a coracle from a fisherman. He rowed out to the head of the Worm, which was as large as a small island, and when the Worm yawned, he sucked in Assipattle, boat and all. Assipattle rowed deep into the Worm's guts, till he found his liver. There he drew his dagger, and cut himself a hole in the liver, broad and deep, and in it he stuffed the turf. Then he blew on the turf, till it burst into flame, and at last the liver itself took fire. He had killed the Worm, but its death-throes were long and awesome, for first it spewed out Assipattle and his boat: then it began to spew out its guts, and the first spew became the Orkney Islands; the second spew became the Shetland Islands; the last and furthest spew became the Faroe Islands; and at last the monster curled up and died, and his body is what we call Iceland now. But his liver has not gone out yet, which is why the mountains of Iceland still sometimes open up and leak out burning Worm-oil.

And as for Assipattle? He went off and married Gem-de-Lovely of course – if you were as lazy as he was, you wouldn't be going to that much trouble for nothing, now would you?

The King's Stone

John Kirkness farmed at Stove, and one morning in the 1530s he rose early to take up his barley which he had left to steep in the burn, to help it germinate. As he was about this, a young man with long red hair came striding over the hill. He approached John,

Ornamented Stone Ball found at Hillhead, near Kirkwall, Orkney. Obverse and Reverse (2¾ inches diameter).

greeted him, and asked if there was any work going on the farm.

John was Norse, and had little love of Scots, but he offered him breakfast, even though there was no work. However, the young man made a good impression on John's daughter, who pleaded with him to give the stranger a job keeping the geese out of the new-sown fields, and to pay him a decent wage for it: "Don't let a pound come between thee and him, faither!"

So the stranger got the job, and sat, day after day, watching the geese from a stone in the meadow. He was careful of his appearance, and used his comb a lot, and it was noticed from the sunlight falling on it that it was backed with gold. It was guessed that he must have been at one time a man of distinction, which aroused curiosity, which the stranger found irksome.

One day he announced that he had tarried long enough, and would be about his travels. He was indeed a man of consequence, which he would show by rewarding their kindness. Turning to John he bade him kneel, and knighted him on the spot, in the style of Sir John Kirkness, first of the hereditary line of the Belted Knights of Stove. He was, of course, James V.

Thereafter the stone in the meadow was called the King's Stone, and the family continued to prosper and hold the farm until

the 1860s, when the stone was moved to be used in the foundations of a new watermill, where it remained until the mill fell into disuse and was pulled down. It was then incorporated into a barn, but the family never had much luck once the stone was moved.

DISTINCTIVE FLAVOUR

During World War II 'Orkneyitis', or 'scapathy' was defined as 'that mental and moral depression that tends to ensue after one has been stationed for some time in the Orkneys.'

Orkney squid is a local delicacy. The squid are cooked in tomato sauce or with red wine.

Orkadians greatly dislike such expressions as 'Orkney Islands', 'Orkney Isles' or worst of all 'The Orkneys'. The name of the county is Orkney, *tout court*.

COUNTY DIARY

August: Festival of 'Horse and Boys' Ploughing Match, St Margaret's Hope
December: The Ba' Game, Kirkwall

PEEBLES-SHIRE

(TWEEDDALE)

HISTORY

In 1792 Peebles was the scene of riots, ascribed at the time of reformist clamour, but proving on investigation to be in protest against local landowners for turning so much land over to sheep.

INDUSTRY PAST AND PRESENT

The county is mainly devoted to mixed farming, but there is a major tweed mill in the town.

The only noteworthy industry the county has ever possessed is woollens, and though this has changed emphasis with fashion and the sort of competition met with from other fabrics, it continues to hold its dominant position.

LANDMARKS

Cademuir Hill has two notable forts, which seem to have remained in use until the Romans occupied the country.

MONUMENTS

Portions of **Peebles town walls** are still in place.

Neidpath Castle is now in ruins, but it has the distinction of never having surrendered to Cromwell's forces, though it was besieged in 1650.

Traquair House was used by Mary Queen of Scots and Lord Darnley in 1566. It contains many relics of Scottish history from the 12th century onwards.

It was in the kitchen (now bar) of the **Crook Inn** at Tweedsmuir that Burns wrote *Willoe Wastle's Wife*.

FAMOUS PEOPLE AND LOCAL CHARACTERS

Alexander III made Peebles his rural seat.

John Buchan was born in Perth in 1875, but is much more closely associated with the Tweeddale area, which was his mother's country. His home was at Bank House, and the family legal firm still occupies it. In 1935 he gave the March Riding address as 'Warden of Neidpath'. In 1895, the year of his first novel *Sir Quixote of the Moors* he won a scholarship to Oxford, where he took a First in Greats, the Newdigate, and the Stanhope prize as well as becoming president of the Union. He was called to the Bar in 1901, but immediately joined the staff of Lord Milner in South Africa.

In 1910 he published *Prester John*, the first of a wide output of novels, poems, history and biography. He entered Parliament in 1927, but was moved to the Lords in 1935 so that he could become Governor General of Canada. There he was popular with both the many Scots-descended Canadians, and with the French, to whom he was able to speak fluently in their own tongue. His death in 1940 was largely attributed to overwork.

Local Characters

The brothers **William and Robert Chambers** were born in 1800 and 1802 respectively. Their early life was unsettled, as their father, who was in the cotton trade, suffered severe

TOPOGRAPHY INCLUDING RIVERS

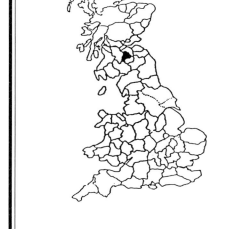

The county is bounded to the north by Midlothian, to the west by Lanarkshire, and to the east and south by Selkirkshire and Dumfriesshire. The ground is high, for a lowland county, and much of the soil is heavy clay. The highest point is Broad Law, 2754 feet.

Rivers: Tweed, Lyne, Manner, Leithen, Quair.

financial setbacks. They were therefore both forced to support themselves from an early age, and independently decided to do so through bookselling. First separately and then together, they built up the publishing firm of W. & R. Chambers which survives to this day, their *Twentieth Century Dictionary* being the preferred source for crossword puzzle enthusiasts. William was the businessman, Robert being the more literary of the two. His most famous work is *Vestiges of the Natural History of Creation*, one of the books that led towards Darwin's theory of evolution. Robert died in 1871, William in 1883.

David Ritchie, known locally as 'Bowed Davie', was the original for Scott's *Black Dwarf*. Scott visited him in 1797, and his cottage is still to be seen on Muckelstane Moor.

ART AND LITERATURE

Defoe has a commentary on two locals:
'Here are two Monuments in the Country, all Scotland not affording the like, of the Vanity of worldly Glory. The one is in the Foundation of a Royal Palace, or Seat of a nobleman, once the first man in Scotland, next the King: It is a prodigious Building, too great for a Subject, begun by the Earl of Morton, whose Head being afterwards lay'd in the Dust, his Design perish'd; and the Building has not been carry'd on, and I suppose never will.
The other is the Palace of Traquair, built and finish'd by the late Earl of Traquair, for some Years Lord High Treasurer of Scotland, and a person in the highest Posts, both of Honour and Profit in the Kingdom, who yet fell from it all, by the Adversity of the Times; for his Conduct under his majesty King Charles I being generally censur'd, and himself universally hated, he sunk into the most abject and lowest part of human Life.'

LOCAL FOLKLORE

A Prophecy

Thomas the Rhymer made the following prophecy:

> *When Tweed and Powsail meet at Merlin's grave,*
> *Scotland and English shall one monarch have.*

It was reported that on the day of James VI's coronation as James I of England, the Tweed rose to such a level that it ran into Powsail Burn.

COUNTY DIARY

The Beltane Festival takes place in the third week of June.

At Innerleithen St Ronan's Games are held in July, culminating in the Cleikun Ceremony, when there is a firework display on Caerlee Hill and the Devil is burned in effigy.

PERTHSHIRE

COUNTY FACTS

Derivation of name: Brittonic (a branch of the Celtic language) for a thicket or copse.
First Recorded: c. 1128
Motto: Pro Lege Et Libertate (For Freedom And Liberty)
County Town: Perth
Towns: Aberfeldy, Abernethy, Alyth, Auchterarder, Blackford, Blairgowrie, Bridge of Earn, Callander, Comrie, Coupar Angus, Doune, Dunblane, Errol, Killin, Longforgan, Methven, New Scone, Perth, Pitlochry, Rattray, Stanley.

Local Government
Tayside Regional Council and one District Council.

HISTORY

The first church built in Perth after the conversion of the people was dedicated to St John the Baptist, and until the 17th century it was often known as St John's Town. It was capital of Scotland until 1452.

In 1054 Macbeth was defeated in the Battle of Dunsinane, but escaped.

In 1689 Viscount Graham of Claverhouse with 2,500 men won the Battle of Killiecrankie against the English under MacKay, who had 4,000, but at the cost of his own life, being shot by a musketeer in the closing minutes of the battle.

The old name for Perth is St Johnstone retained in the name of the city's football club.

INDUSTRY PAST AND PRESENT

As a river port, Perth exports seed potatoes, and imports fertilizers. It is also a centre for the dyeing and distilling industries, and the manufacture of jute, twine and glass. But it is pre-eminent as a market city, and famous for its livestock sales.

Fruits, especially raspberries, are cultivated on the low ground near the rivers, locally called the carses. There is also land suitable for sugar beet, potatoes, cattle and sheep.

Salmon and trout are abundant.

The Tummel-Garry hydro-electric scheme operates ten power stations, and is the largest in Scotland.

Blackford is the centre for Highland Spring mineral water, the Scottish 'Perrier'.

The Perth textile industry, which included cotton, linen and silk, has all but disappeared. The quarrying of freestone, marble and slate is much reduced also, while coal, lead and copper are no longer mined at all.

Perth glove-making, once very strong, died out in the 19th century, along with shipbuilding.

LANDMARKS

Drummond Castle gardens are open to the public and quite exceptional, though the castle itself is not open.

The earthworks of Ardoch Roman camp are in the grounds of Ardoch House. It was large enough to accommodate 40,000 soldiers.

The Trossachs are the most distinguished feature of the landscape.

In addition to its historical interest, the Pass of Killiecrankie is a great beauty-spot.

MONUMENTS

Scone Palace was the ancient resting place of the Stone of Destiny, brought there by King Kenneth I in 843. It remained there until 1296, when it was captured by Edward I.

A fine prison was built in **Perth** to accommodate French prisoners taken in the Napoleonic Wards, and still stands. French prisoner-of-war work, made by these men from the most wretched materials to pay for small luxuries, is now greatly prized by collectors.

FAMOUS PEOPLE AND LOCAL CHARACTERS

John MacNaughton of Glen Lyon was in the service of James Menzies of Culdares, who was taken prisoner at Preston in 1715, but reprieved. In respect of the reprieve, he felt unable to follow Bonnie Prince Charlie's colours in 1745, but to show where his heart lay, he sent MacNaughton after Charles,

TOPOGRAPHY INCLUDING RIVERS

The county is bounded in the north by Inverness-shire and Aberdeenshire, east by Angus, south by Clackmannanshire and Stirlingshire, southwest by Stirlingshire and Dunbartonshire, and west by Argyllshire. The terrain consists mainly of hills and straths inclining towards the River Tay. Many of the peaks exceed 3,000 feet. The highest point is Ben Lawers, 4004 feet.
Rivers: Tay, Garry.

with the gift of a fine white charger. MacNaughton handed over the horse, but was caught and imprisoned after Culloden. The judges could see well enough that the horse had not come from MacNaughton himself, so they offered to spare his life if he gave evidence against whomever had sent it. NacNaughton refused, saying gravely that it would compromise the honour that exists between master and servant to reveal such a secret. On the actual scaffold he was given a last chance to change his mind, but indignantly refused, appearing more upset at the affront to his honour than the threat to his life, which ended not long thereafter.

Local Characters

James Robertson was a champion of the Jacobite Cause, who had actually fought in 1745, for which he was briefly imprisoned, but released as harmless. This greatly upset him, and he went to considerable lengths to be re-arrested and tried for high treason, by such means as proclaiming noisy toasts to 'Charles III' in public houses. The authorities ignored him, and the only way he could get back in jail was to refuse to pay his rent.

By this time the locals had entered into the spirit of the thing, and his rent was paid by public subscription. Robertson then dug his heels in, and refused to vacate his cell except to face a charge of high treason, so two soldiers were sent to present themselves as his escorts to the court. But as soon as they had him outside the prison gates they released him and sprang back inside. Then the gates were quickly slammed shut.

LOCAL FOLKLORE

The Devil at Little Dunkeld Manse

A long time ago there was a servant lassie, who worked for the Minister at Little Dunkeld. She was a quiet lass, who had no mind for dances or such follies, and she liked fine to go for long walks on Birnam Hill.

After a time she told the Minister that she had met a grand gentleman there, who used to walk and talk with her, and he was courting her. The Minister thought that a fine gentleman would be dangerous company for the lass, and he told her to bring him to the Manse, and let him see what kind of man he was.

The lassie was pleased enough, and next Saturday she brought in her beau.

He was a grand-looking gentleman, sure enough, and pleasant-spoken, but when the Minister looked down at his feet, the blood ran cold in his veins, for he saw that he had cloven hoofs, and he knew that there was just one person that had that. So, when the stranger had gone, he said to the lassie, 'That's a braw man, yon, but did you see the feet of him?'

'Aye, did I,' said the lass, 'and bonnie feet he has, with braw shining boots.'

'Take another look on them, when you see him again,' said the Minister.

But nothing he could say made any difference. She was still terribly taken up with him. At last it came to this, that the braw gentleman asked her to marry with him. When the Minister heard that, he was sorely put about, but at length he said, 'Well, you may be married on one condition, that none shall wed you but me, and that the wedding shall be in the Manse.'

The lassie was well enough pleased at that, for it would be a grand wedding for her, and when the day came, half the parish came to see it. All the guests were waiting, and the bride in her bonnie new gown, and there was no sign of the bridegroom. But at length they heard a great rumbling, and a chariot drove up to the door, with six black horses. In comes my fine gentleman, bowing and smiling around him. The guests were terribly taken up with him, but the Minister saw the cloven hoofs of him as plain as ever.

So the Minister took a candle, and he lighted it at both ends, as they do for an auction, and he said, 'Now, when this candle is burnt out I'll marry you, and not a minute before.'

The stranger looked black at this; but the Minister held the candle steadily between his two fingers, while the bride cried, and the bridegroom scowled, and the guests shuffled their feet and whispered. The wax dripped and dropped, and the candle burnt and burnt, till the one flame was about two inches from the other. Then, whilst it was still burning, the Minister put it into his mouth and swallowed it.

'Now,' he said, 'the candle will never burn out, and you will never be married.'

With that the stranger gave the most awesome shriek, and leapt out of the window, and vanished into the earth, and his coach and six with him. And outside Little Dunkeld Manse there is a black spot of earth where they say no grass will grow to this day.

K.M. Briggs (collected 1926)

Witches' Stone

There is a Witches' Stone near the slate quarries at Aberfoyle, where fairies and witches dance together by the light of the Beltane Fire.

Donaldgowrie House

In the latter half of the last century Donaldgowrie House, Perth, was bought at a bargain price by William Whittingen, a retired grocer with a grown-up family of two sons (Ernest and Hervey) and three daughters (Martha, Mary and Ruth). Ernest was recently ordained and married, Hervey was articled to a firm of solicitors, and the three girls were on the lookout for husbands.

In their first September, Mary left a croquet party to bring some photographs from her bedroom, and when she did not come back, Martha went after her to find out what was keeping her. On the way to the room she encountered a man dressed as a highland piper, coming from her sister's bedroom. His face was a livid grey, and his eyes glowed with a baleful light. Moreover, the look of him took her breath away so that she was unable to shout or scream, even when he walked straight through her. She hurried into the bedroom, where she found Mary lying in a dead faint.

When Mary recovered she recounted how the piper had surprised her in her bedroom and marched round it, playing a dirge on the pipes - very loudly, which had frightened her into a swoon. No one else had heard anything, and only Martha had seen him as well, and the servants emphatically denied having admitted him. The family therefore kept quiet about the incident, which might reflect ill on their sanity.

But a week later, Mary was running across the croquet lawn when she tripped on a hoop. As she fell, she ran a hat-pin into her scalp. Septicaemia set in, and she shortly died.

Three months later, and nearing Christmas, the family was round the fire when there came the sound of a heavy coach coming up the drive at high speed, followed by a terrific knocking on the front door. But the servants apparently heard nothing, but the footman did not go to open it. Then the door opened of itself, and heavy footsteps were heard approaching. Martha was the only one not rooted to the spot, and she got up to lock the door. Then the whole family started to pray. But the door opened, despite the lock, and there appeared the blurred outlines of a ghastly group of figures, bearing a grotesque object which no one could subsequently describe. At this point Ruth fainted, the group turned away, and presently the invisible coach was heard driving away.

A fortnight later Ruth contracted acute appendicitis, peritonitis set in, and she died under the surgeon's knife.

Over a year later Hervey came to stay with them, bringing his wife and new baby boy. It happened that one day Martha found herself alone in the upper part of the house with her nephew. There she was taken with a sudden compulsion to pick up a pair of scissors and use them to cut the baby's throat. She dismissed this as morbid and ridiculous, but to her horror it gradually became stronger and stronger. She attempted to leave the room, but found her way barred by the highland piper, who guided her hand so as to complete the horrid deed. Once it was over he danced a minuet in the moonbeams, much in the manner subsequently adopted by the Pink Panther; then he piped himself out with a mournful dirge heard only by Martha.

Martha was now released from his grip, and screamed. but it was too late for herself or the baby. She was certified criminally insane, and died shortly afterwards in an asylum. Her father decided that this was really too much, and fearing further depletion of his family, sold the house for the best price he could get.

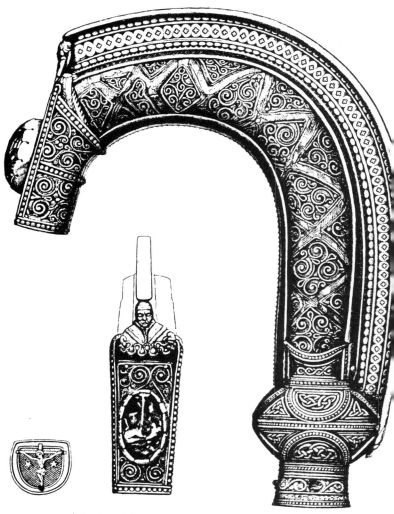

Side view of the external case of the Crosier of St. Fillan. View of the front or pendent portion of the Crook, and of its terminal plate.

DISTINCTIVE FLAVOUR

The 2nd Battalion Cameronian (Scottish Rifles) were in the 19th century the 90th (Perthshire Volunteers) Foot. They were known as the Perthshire Greybreeks on account of their grey trousers, white being the colour of most foot regiments at that time.

Perth styled itself 'the fair city', on account of the beauty of the view over its ten-arched bridge.

Atholl brose is a mixture of whisky, honey and oatmeal, and is said to have been invented by the Duke of Atholl at the time of a rebellion in 1475. He knew which well his enemies were accustomed to drink from, so he filled it with the mixture. It made them so drunk that he was able to capture them all.

An alternative story is that the forest of Atholl was at one time haunted by a fearsome satyr. The thought of encountering him so alarmed the heiress of Tullibardine that she promised her own hand in marriage to anyone who could capture him. A yeoman who had noticed that the satyr always drank from the same stone basin diverted the rill that fed it, emptied it, and refilled it with the brose. He then manacled the satyr while he lay in a drunken stupor. The manacled satyr is still to be seen on the arms of the Dukes of Atholl.

COUNTY DIARY

The Pitlochry Arts Festival

RENFREWSHIRE

COUNTY FACTS

Derivation of name: From the Welsh rhyn frwd, meaning 'point of current'.
Motto: Avito Viret Honore (He Flourishes by Ancestral Honour)
County Town: Renfrew
Towns: Barrhead, Bishopton, Bridge of Weir, Busby (partly in Lanarkshire), Clarkston, Eaglesham, Elderslie, Erskine, Giffnock, Gourock, Greenock, Inchinnan, Johnstone, Kilbarchan, Kilmalcolm, Linwood, Neilston, Newton Mearns, Paisley, Port Glasgow, Renfrew.

Local Government
Strathclyde Regional Council and three District Council.

HISTORY

In 1164 Malcolm IV defeated and killed Somerled, Lord of the Western Isles.

In 1316 Marjorie, daughter of Robert Bruce suffered an accident while pregnant and was brought to Paisley Abbey. There she gave birth to the future King Robert II, who was the founder of the Stewart line. Hence the title of the Abbey.

In 1697, on the evidence of the eleven-year-old Christine Shaw, daughter of the Laird, 21 people were indicted of witchcraft, and seven of them burned. It began in August 1696, when she went into a series of fits, and swore that it was the work of a young woman called Katherine Campbell, whom she had caught stealing milk, and an old woman called Agnes Naismith, whom she had insulted and was now taking revenge. She also vomited various common but inedible substances, such as cinders, bones, candle-wax and hair.

Encouraged by the attention this got her, she accused a further seven people of bewitching her, including her father, two cousins, and two upper class townswomen, Margaret Lang, and her daughter, Martha Semple. Some of the people she accused implicated others, bringing the total to 21. Only Margaret Lang kept a totally cool head, and said, 'Let them quake that dread and frar that nee; but I will not gang.'

Others of more hysterical persuasion gave accounts of visits to sabbats, cannibalism, murder etc. The Lord Advocate led the eventual prosecution, which brought in seven guilty verdicts (one on a boy of 14) and included Margaret and Martha. All seven were burned, and a horseshoe in George Street marks the spot.

Christine, apparently satisfied, stopped vomiting feathers, etc., and later married a local minister. She subsequently achieved a considerable fortune by introducing from Holland the machinery for the manufacture of fine sewing thread, called after her family name, 'Bargarran'.

It is believed that she introduced the feathers, etc., into her bedroom by thread through a small hole in the wall under her bed.

INDUSTRY PAST AND PRESENT

Renfrew is very much a centre of what remains of Scotland's heavy industry, including boilermaking and shipbuilding. It also manufactures rubber and paint. Sanitary ceramics are made at Barrhead.

Fresh milk and vegetables are cultivated for Glasgow.

Copper was mined in the 19th century, and coal was also very important. Barrhead was once a centre for textile printing, with cotton, plaid and flannel also being produced.

LANDMARKS

Eaglesham is an 18th-century experiment in town-planning, having been designed by the 10th Earl of Eglington in 1769. It takes an unusual triangular form.

TOPOGRAPHY INCLUDING RIVERS

The county is bounded on the north by Dunbartonshire, on the northeast and east by Lanarkshire, on the south and southwest by Ayrshire and on the west by the Firth of Clyde. The county is mainly in the basin of the Clyde with the hilly parts in the west and south. The highest point is the Hill of Stake, 1711 feet.
Rivers: Rotten Burn, Black Cart, White Cart, Gryffe

MONUMENTS

Paisley Abbey, 'Cradle of the Stewart Kings' was founded in 1163, but the present church is 14th and 15th-century work, restored in the 19th century.

Newark Castle, Port Glasgow, was begun in 1597 by Patrick Maxwell.

FAMOUS PEOPLE AND LOCAL CHARACTERS

William Wallace was born in Auchinbothie in 1270. He rose to prominence in 1297 by the raid on Lanark, supporting the claim of the deposed John Balliol against Edward I. He raised the army which then defeated Edward's forces at Stirling Bridge and invented for himself the title of Guardian of Scotland, which was regarded by most as tantamount to king. He fought again at Falkirk, losing on this occasion, but leaving the English army too badly mauled to consolidate, so that it had to fall back on Carlisle.

This was the beginning of the end for him, however, and after the fall of Stirling Castle in 1304 he had to go into hiding, Edward having specifically excluded him from the general amnesty. His valet, John Short, betrayed his hiding-place in Glasgow to Monteith, who brought him in chains to London. There Edward, wishing to make an example of him, invented the novel punishment of hanging, drawing and quartering, including the details of castration and burning of the entrails on a brazier, specifically for Wallace. It did nothing to deter the rebelliousness of the Scots, of course; but the English were quick to recognize the appeal of a new outdoor spectator-sport, and practised it for the next four centuries.

The poem of 11,861 lines on the subject of Wallace's life, by 'Blind Harry' the minstrel, is almost wholly fictitious.

Local Characters

James Watt was born in Greenock in 1776. He showed from his earliest years an interest in electricity and chemistry, so that he became instrument-maker to Glasgow University in 1757, where he was asked to repair a scale model of Newcomen's steam engine, which was not working well. Watt identified the trouble as design faults, which he eliminated, thereby greatly improving steam technology. He patented an improved design in 1769, and set up a company to exploit it with a Dr Roebuck, who was subsequently bought out by Matthew Boulton.

Watt continued to contribute to engineering science almost to the end of his life, in 1819.

ART AND LITERATURE

'All the people seemed to be in the streets; all going their way to different churches; no noise of any sort; no dirtily-dressed person; and not a soul to be seen who did not seem seriously engaged in the business for which the day was set apart.'

William Cobbett, 1832

LOCAL FOLKLORE

Maria Selwyn

Maria Selwyn, a rich farmer's daughter from near Exeter, fell in love with a local shepherd, and against her father's wishes refused to have anything to do with the far more eligible husband he obtained for her. The father and the slighted suitor therefore murdered the shepherd by shooting him from an ambush. However, they did not make a very clean job of it, and Maria, coming to keep a tryst with him, found him dying but still conscious. He told her how he had come by his end.

Some servants of her father's came to drag her home, at the same time that a dozen sheep came to seek their master. He looked up, and said with his dying breath, 'These are my flock and my all, Maria! Take my crook, and these sheep will follow you wherever you go.' With that he expired.

Maria was dragged home by the servants, but when she got there, so fearsome were the curses which she called down on her father and her suitor, that they dared not keep her from the spot where her lover had died, and the sheep still waited. She took the crook, and said, 'Follow me.' The sheep followed her, and she made a gradual trek northwards, living by what charity she could get, and accompanied by the sheep, until she reached Dumfries in 1767, by which time three had died. She carried on, wandering through the south of Scotland, until in 1771 she was found dead near Loch Goin, with the last three sheep beside her.

Local shepherds buried her on the spot, and tried to appropriate the sheep, but they always came back to it, and shortly afterwards all three were found dead, one on and the other two beside, the grave of their mistress.

DISTINCTIVE FLAVOUR

The Paisley pattern, used on innumerable ties, bears a strong resemblance to some of the most beautiful aspects of the Mandelbrot Set (drawn on the plane of complex numbers) which has become the emblem of the new science of Chaos.

COUNTY DIARY

August:	Port Glasgow Festival
August:	Galloway Games
	European Heavy Events
	Open Championships,
	Stranraer

COUNTY FACTS

Derivation of name
Cromarty: from the Gaelic, meaning a promontory or bay with a crooked coastline (crom meaning crooked; bàdh meaning bay).
Ross: From the Gaelic, meaning 'the high, upsurging rocky moorland where nothing but heather will grow'.
First Recorded:
Cromarty 1257; Ross ante 1100
Motto: Dread God And Do Well
County Towns: Cromarty and Dingwall
Towns: Alness, Avoch, Balallan, Barres, Carloway, Cononbridge, Cromarty, Dingwall, Evanton, Fortrose, Gairloch, Invergordon, Kyle of Lochalsh, Munlochy, Muir of Ord, Portmahomack, Strathpeffer, Stornoway, Tain, Ullapool.
Cromarty is the only town that lies totally within its own county. The town of Ullapool to the north has the majority of its area within Cromartyshire, but parts of it spill into Ross-shire.
Ross is peppered with detached parts of Cromarty, hence the sense in uniting the two counties into one. Whether it can be classed as one geographical county is debatable, as they are two distinct counties which have a right to separate identity. But the directive from the Association of British Counties says that a detached part of one county, which is an island completely cut off from its parent county and surrounded geographically by another, is within the geographical bounds of the county it lies in.

Local Government
Highland Regional Council and the Western Isles Island Council. One District Council.

HISTORY

The title of Earl of Ross was united with that of Lord of the Isles, and in 1476 both were absorbed by Robert III. The current holder is the Prince of Wales.

The counties of Ross and Cromarty were amalgamated in 1861, for obvious reasons. Ross comprehended a considerable area of mainland Scotland, together with the large island of Lewis. Cromarty was a large number of detached portions, either interspersed among the inland parts of Ross or lying along its border. The differences between them had always been artificial, and depended on which areas were more strongly influenced by the chieftains of Ross, and which by the Earls of Cromarty.

In 1922 there was a fishing party on Loch Maree, which saw the first identified outbreak of botulism in Britain. The early symptoms were not nausea or cramps, as one might expect from food-poisoning, but double vision and giddiness, so the initial reaction of the unaffected guests was to make leaden jokes about the amount of beer and whisky consumed over lunch. The many deaths which ensued were eventually traced to a single jar of wild duck pâté. The Coroner's jury made history with the first known agitation for 'sell-by' dates on preserved foods.

INDUSTRY PAST AND PRESENT

The main crops are cereals and potatoes, though cattle and sheep are raised on the higher ground.
There is a major aluminium smeltery at Invergordon, and submarine ports there and at Nigg.
When the navy moved from Invergordon to Scapa Flow it caused widespread unemployment among both sexes.

LANDMARKS
Mam Soul (3,862 feet)
Beinn Eighe and Inverpolly are National Nature Reserves.

MONUMENTS
Inverewe House and Gardens were first laid out in 1862 by Osgood Mackenzie. They contain a huge variety of extraordinary tropical and sub-tropical plants, including high-altitude magnolias, bush daisies, and giant forget-me-nots.

FAMOUS PEOPLE AND LOCAL CHARACTERS
The Seer of Brahan pronounced the following

TOPOGRAPHY INCLUDING RIVERS

The counties are bounded by Sutherland in the north, by the Atlantic in the west, and by Inverness-shire, Morayshire, and the Moray Firth in the south and east. The coastline has many deep lochs. The terrain consists of groups of granite and mica slate mountains divided by glens and ravines. Consequently, there is comparatively little agriculture, but deer, foxes, badgers, weasels and polecats are still common. Martens are less so than formerly. The highest point is Càrn Elge, 3877 feet.
Rivers: Oikel, Repath (Carron).

curse on the Seaforths, which came true in every detail, including the various disabilities specified:

'I see into the far future, and I read the doom of the race of the oppressor. The long-descended line of Seaforth will, ere many generations have passed, end in extinction and in sorrow. I see a chief, the last of his house; both deaf and dumb. He will be the father or four fair sons, all of whom he will follow to the tomb. He will live careworn and die mourning, knowing that the honours of his line are extinguished forever, and that no future chief of the Mackenzies shall bear rule at Brahan or Kintail. After lamenting over the last and most promising of his sons, he himself shall sink into the grave, and the remnant of his possessions shall be inherited by a white-coifed lassie from the east, and she is to kill her sister. And as a sign by which it may be known that these things are coming to pass, there shall be four great lairds in the days of the last deaf and dumb Seaforth – Gairloch, Chisholm, Grant and Ramsay – of whom one shall be buck-toothed, another hare-lipped, another half-witted and the fourth a stammerer. Chiefs distinguished by these personal marks shall be the allies and neighbours of the last Seaforth, and when he looks around and sees them he may know that his sons are doomed to death; and the broad lands shall pass away to the stranger, and that his race shall come to an end.'

Local Characters

When Christianity was first introduced to Lewis by **St Kieran**, the older inhabitants of the island, who were giants, refused to listen to him. He therefore turned them into a set of standing stones, and so they remain to this day.

LOCAL FOLKLORE

The Haunted Cottage

A shepherd's wife was taken ill, in an isolated house, and the doctor was sent for. It was midwinter, when the days are short, but the doctor thought he knew the way. However, the night overtook him, and he lost the track. He carried on looking for the track, but the sky was overcast, so he lost his sense of

direction as well. Eventually he saw a light which must indicate a cottage where he hoped to ask the way.

He headed towards the cottage, but before he reached it the light went out. However, he found it at last, and stood his horse in the byre. Then he knocked on the door, but there was no answer. He was getting desperate, so he pushed on it, and to his surprise it came open. Clearly it was not the cottage where the light had been, as it had obviously been unoccupied for many years, with dust thick on all the furniture. He decided to give up his journey and make the best he could of the night.

He managed to light a fire in the grate, and by its light lay down on the musty bed, first taking off his watch and chain, which he placed on the bedside table, along with his purse of money. He was just falling asleep when he heard the voices of two men coming from the kitchen. They seemed to be in contention over something. He crept to the kitchen door, where he was very surprised to see two villainous-looking men sitting at the table playing cards. It seemed that each was accusing the other of cheating. As one bent to pick a card off the floor, the other drew a knife and stabbed him to death. This so frightened the unarmed doctor that he crept back to the bed, where he lay in terror.

But presently the murderer came into the bedroom, looked the place over, and picked up the valuables, while the doctor feigned profound slumber. Despite his terror, he must have drifted into sleep, for he woke to broad daylight. As he opened his eyes he saw to his great surprise that his watch, chain and purse were on the table where he had left them. He rose and peeped into the kitchen, where he could see no sign of the previous night's events - no bloodstains, no cards, no footprints, and certainly no corpse.

He also found his horse unmolested, and now that it was daylight he soon found the track and carried on with his mission to the sick woman. When he got there he described his experience to the shepherd, who said he knew the cottage, which had been empty for many years. But the drainers had used it last, and one had murdered his mate and fled, never to be heard of again. It had been haunted since then.

Infertility

If a barren woman goes to sit all night on the stone in Brahan Wood near Dingwall, she will be fertile by the morning. Alternatively, she can make her way to the stone on Black Isle, near Arpafeelie, which has a natural basin on its surface, and wash in the water collected therein, with the same effect.

The Kelpie

The river Conon is haunted by a kelpie, who was once seen by a party of Highlanders who were cutting corn near a ruined church. It was noon, and the kelpie appeared, standing in a false ford. This is a deep black pool, but a trick of turbulence gives it a constant ripple, so that it looks like shallow water. The kelpie called, "The hour, but not the man, has come." It called the same message again, before disappearing under the water.

They were wondering what it might mean, when a horseman came down the hill, very fast, and made for the false ford. They cried out to warn him of his danger, but he would not listen, so to save him from himself they dragged him from his horse and locked him in the ruined church. They determined to keep him there until the fatal hour of the kelpie was past.

However, when they opened the church again, they found the man drowned, with his head in a stone trough that had been used for holy water. He had suffered a fit, so it seemed, and collapsed above the trough.

DISTINCTIVE FLAVOUR

The people take most pride in their **reticence and hardihood**.

The 78th Foot, now absorbed into the Queen's Own Highlanders (Seaforths and Camerons) are known as the **Ross-shire Buffs**, on account of their buff facings.

COUNTY DIARY

August:	Black Isle Show, Muir of Ord

ROXBURGHSHIRE

COUNTY FACTS

Derivation of name: From the Old English, meaning Fortress of Hroc – Hroc being the rook.
Motto: Ne Cede Malis Sed Contra Audentior Ito (Yield Not To Adversity But Oppose It More Boldly)
County Town: Jedburgh
Towns: Darnick, Denholm, Hawick, Jedburgh, Kelso, Maxwellheugh, Melrose, Newcastleton, Newton St Boswells, Roxburgh, St Boswells, Town Yetholm.

Local Government
Borders Regional Council and two District Councils

HISTORY

In 1460, during a battle with the English, James II was killed by the bursting of a cannon. The castle was subsequently destroyed, and the town fell into disuse.

In 1544, as part of Henry VIII's attempt to pacify Scotland, he made a grant of the whole of the counties of Berwick and Roxburgh to Sir Ralph Evers and Sir Brian Latour, who were to hold them in freehold of the English crown. They came to take possession with 5,000 men. At first Angus was unable to resist the encroachment; they burnt Jedburgh, and when Angus attacked them with a small force he was driven off. But he received reinforcements from the Leslies and the Lindsays, and from Buccleuch, who attacked them near Ancrum. At this point the unreliability of border troops became apparent, as 600 of them changed sides and attacked the English formation from within. Neither Evers nor Latour survived the defeat.

INDUSTRY PAST AND PRESENT

The county is largely devoted to mixed farming, and all types are to be found, including sheep on the highest land and orchards in the valleys.

The textile industry has greatly declined.

TOPOGRAPHY INCLUDING RIVERS

The county is bounded on the north by Berwickshire, east and southeast by the English border, southwest by Dumfriesshire, west by Selkirkshire, and northwest by Midlothian. The terrain is uneven, especially in the south, where it merges into the Cheviots. Most of the county is in the basin of the Tweed. The soil is mainly clay, though better in the Tweed and Teviot valleys. The highest point is near Auchop Cairn, 2422 feet.
Rivers: Tweed, Teviot, Liddel, Jed, Ettrick, Gala, Leader, Eden.

LANDMARKS

Woden Law is a multivallate fort, which still shows evidence of Roman siege-works. These are believed not to have been built in anger, but as a training exercise.

Eildon Hillfort and signal station is a very fine example, covering 40 acres. It was used both by the Selgovae and by the Romans, who built the ditch.

MONUMENTS

Melrose Abbey was founded by David I in 1136, and it eventually became one of the richest in Scotland. However, its situation on the border meant that it was in the front line when any sacking of ecclesiastical buildings was on the English agenda, as occurred in 1322 (by Edward II), 1385 (by Richard II) and in 1547 (by the Duke of Somerset). This last occasion was fatal, though the church continued in use until 1810.

Floors Castle is a superb example of the Scottish Baronial style by Playfair.

Hermitage Castle, dating from the 14th century, was owned by Bothwell, the ruffianly lover of Mary Queen of Scots. She was sufficiently enamoured of him to ride forty miles there and back from Jedburgh to visit him.

Jedburgh Abbey is the best preserved of the Border Abbeys, as its church was in use as a parish kirk for some considerable time after the Reformation. Its very long nave is virtually intact.

Kelso Abbey is more dilapidated. Nonetheless it is a dramatic fragment, and the martial massing of its western tower and transepts has inspired innumerable watercolourists.

Abbotsford is architecturally not of the first rank, but as the home of Sir Walter Scott, its importance is literary rather than art-historical.

FAMOUS PEOPLE AND LOCAL CHARACTERS

Sir James Murray was born in 1837. He can claim to have been the greatest of British philologists and a pioneer of phonetics, and he superintended the compilation of the

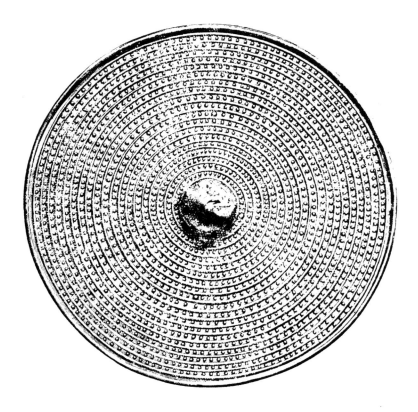

Bronze Shield found at Yetholm

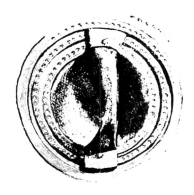

LOCAL FOLKLORE

The Dragon of Linton

The Dragon of Linton had a den in Linton Hill, but occasionally he would crawl out and coil himself round Wormington Hill. It was there that he was killed, and as he died he contracted round the hill with such force that the spiral impressions can still be seen going up the hill.

DISTINCTIVE FLAVOUR

The **local pronunciation** of Jedburgh is 'Jeddart', and the expression 'Jeddart Justice' means 'hang first, then hold a fair trial'. It refers to the short local way with moss-troopers and border raiders, lest they escape while due process pursued its serpentine course.

The people have always been famous for their **martial qualities**, the halbard also being known as the 'Jeddart staff'.

There is very little left of the **original town** of Roxburgh which has declined to almost nothing and is now quite extinct.

Oxford New English Dictionary on Historical Principles. This monumental work of scholarship set out to record every use of every word which has passed current in English from AD 1150 onwards, and is supported by over 2,000,000 quotations. There have been many supplements, but no new edition until 1989. Henry Bradley commented that it would have been a 'national disaster' had anyone else been charged with this responsibility. It is widely held that lacking Murray's guiding genius, there could have been no new edition at all without the help of computers. The book is still sometimes referred to as 'Murray' by older scholars, though in fact Murray died in 1915 before it was completed. However, he was the direct and personal editor of the letters A – D, H – K, O, and P – T.

Local Characters

Mary Somerville was born in 1780, daughter of Sir William Fairfax. She took an early interest in mathematics, which had to be self-taught, as she had no encouragement from her father or her husband, Samuel Grieg. After he died she married Dr Somerville, who introduced her into the highest scientific society. Her work on ultra-violet light obtained for her honorary membership of the Royal Society, and Somerville College, Oxford is named after her. She was active to the last, and died in 1872.

ART AND LITERATURE

'If thou would'st view fair Melrose right,
Go visit it by the pale moonlight;
For the gay beams of lightsome day
Gild, but do flout, the ruins grey.'
Traditional.

COUNTY DIARY

July:	The Border Union Show, Springwood Park, Kelso

SELKIRKSHIRE

COUNTY FACTS

Derivation of name: From the Old English, sele-chyrche, meaning 'blessed church' (built for the king's use while hunting in Ettrick Forest). An alternative suggestion has the name meaning 'hall church' (sele being Old English for hall).

First Recorded: 1113

Motto: Leal to the Border

County Town: Selkirk

Towns: Ashkirk, Ettrickbridge, Foulshiels, Galashiels, Selkirk.

Local Government
Borders Regional Council and one District Council.
There is a small detached part of Selkirkshire in Roxburghshire around Sinton.

HISTORY

In 1645 the Royalists under Montrose were defeated by Covenanters under Leslie at the battle of Philiphaugh.

INDUSTRY PAST AND PRESENT

The country is mainly unsuitable for agriculture except of clover and hay, but cattle are pastured in all parts.
Tweed mills were major employers in the 19th century. At an earlier date the town was so famous for shoemaking that the burgesses were all called souters (shoemakers).

LANDMARKS

Ettrick Forest is mainly famous for being the site of James Hogg's early travails.

MONUMENTS

Selkirk Church goes back to the early 15th century.

TOPOGRAPHY INCLUDING RIVERS

The county is bounded in the north by Midlothian, in the east and southeast by Roxburghshire, in the south and southwest by Dumfriesshire, and in the west and northwest by Peeblesshire. The terrain is hilly, especially in the south and west, and mainly of slate, granite and porphyry. The highest point is Ettrick Pen, 2269 feet.

Rivers: Ettrick, Yarrow, Cawder

FAMOUS PEOPLE AND LOCAL CHARACTERS

Mungo Park was born in 1771 and apprenticed to a surgeon, subsequently qualifying at Edinburgh. His principal interest was botany, however, and to further this he took passage as ship's surgeon on a voyage to Sumatra. Having enjoyed this, he got himself appointed leader of the Africa Association expedition up the Gambia in 1795. This led him into many misfortunes, including imprisonment by the Moorish commander of Yarra, from which he escaped quite destitute, but nonetheless carried on exploring. At the end of his mission (Sego) he was laid up for five months with a fever.

His book *Travels in the Interior of Africa* was highly regarded, so in 1805 he set out to repeat his triumph, by testing the hypothesis that the rivers Congo and Niger were branches of the same stream. He failed to return from this expedition, so whether he suffered another fever, was drowned or was killed by the locals is unknown.

Andrew Lang was born in 1812 at Selkirk. That he had a multi-faceted intellect was obvious from very early in his life, and it was no surprise when he took a double first in Greats at Balliol College. He obtained a fellowship at Merton, but soon gave it up in favour of less formal scholarship and journalism, mainly in folklore and the occult sciences. He contributed many papers on these subjects to the famous 9th edition of the *Encyclopaedia Britannica*. From there he proceeded to anthropology and Scottish history, which he approached from a determinedly Jacobite viewpoint so that his writings on this topic have lost favour of recent decades.

He is chiefly remembered for his series of variously coloured 'Fairy Books', in which old stories from many places are re-told for children in a style which shows respect for

the sources but does not condescend to his audience. However, he omitted some of the more gruesome details, which reduces their value to the scholar.

Local Characters

James Hogg, called the 'Ettrick Shepherd', was born in Ettrick Forest in 1770. His childhood was unsettled, with his father going bankrupt when he was seven, so that he received little education and had to work as a shepherd from an early age. He entered the service of William Laidlaw, a friend of Sir Walter Scott, who encouraged his interest in literature. His first poems were published in 1794, and more followed over the next 13 years, netting him £300, which he invested in a sheep farm in Dumfries.

This failed, so Hogg made his way to Edinburgh in 1810. He gradually built up a reputation, and in 1817 was left a life interest in a small farm at Altrive by the Duke of Buccleuch. There he remained, combining literature with agriculture, until his death in 1835.

LOCAL FOLKLORE

The Blacksmith of Yarrowfoot

The blacksmith of Yarrowfoot took on two brothers as apprentices, but though he treated them both well, only the elder prospered

while the younger grew thin and pale.

The elder asked him what was the matter, and eventually the younger confessed that it was the blacksmith's wife who was wearing him out. Every night she came to his room and threw a bridle on him, which turned him into a horse. Then she rode him off bareback to the Witches' Sabbath, and afterwards rode him back, and what with a full day's work next morning it was all too much.

The elder brother quite fancied a spot of bareback riding with his mistress, so he offered to change places that night. But to his chagrin, when the lady came in she threw the bridle over him and rode away on his back, just as described. This time the witches were meeting in the Laird's cellar, where they made free with his claret and sack, but the horse found he could rid himself of the bridle by rubbing against the wall, which turned him back into a man again. Then he waited until his mistress returned, but this time he threw the bridle over her instead, and turned her into a fine grey mare. He mounted her, and rode home, but he noticed one of her foreshoes was loose, so he lit up the smithy and changed them both. Then he slipped off the bridle, giving them both just time enough to get back into bed before the smith woke up.

That morning the lady complained of being ill, so the smith sent for the doctor. The first thing he did was to ask to take her pulse, but she refused, until the smith grew impatient and pulled the bedclothes off. There her hands were revealed, with the shoes still nailed on very tight, for the elder brother had done a good job.

So the whole story came out, and the woman was tried by the magistrates at Selkirk, and condemned to be burnt on a stone at Bullsheigh.

DISTINCTIVE FLAVOUR

Selkirk Bannock is a rich, yeasty bannock which was a particular favourite with Queen Victoria. It should contain raisins as well as sultanas.

COUNTY DIARY

June:	Braw Lads' Gathering, Galashiels

SHETLAND

COUNTY FACTS

Derivation of name: From the Old Norse Hjaltland, meaning 'High land', thence Yealtland, Yetland and Zetland.
First Recorded: 1289
Motto: Med Lögum Skal Land Byggja (By Law Is The Land Built Up)
County Town: Lerwick
Towns: Burravoe, Hamnavoe, Lerwick, Otters Wick, Scalloway.

Local Government
Shetland Island Council

HISTORY

The Shetlands are securing the same debt as the Orkneys.

In 1868 the 'Lessing' out of Bremen was wrecked on Fairisle, and all 465 passengers rescued by the islanders. The following year the 'Gazelle', met the same fate, and again all on board were rescued.

In 1959 a most extraordinary hoard of silver brooches and communion furniture was discovered on the peninsula of St Ninian's Isle.

INDUSTRY PAST AND PRESENT

The Brent and Ninian pipelines terminate at Sullom Voe. The craft of traditional sweater making still proves remunerative.

The Lerwick herring industry has largely been superceded by whitefish. There was some copper-mining at Sandwick in the 18th and 19th centuries.

LANDMARKS

Roeness Hill is the greatest elevation on the islands.

Fairisle is an important centre for birdwatching.

TOPOGRAPHY INCLUDING RIVERS

The county consists of over 100 islands, islets and skerries, of which well under half are inhabited. The largest is Mainland, but of the rest only Yell and Unst are of any size. They are the most northerly group of the British Isles. Their coasts are generally very ragged, with deep bays or voes. The highest point is Ronas Hill, Northmaven, 1475 feet.
Rivers: There are no rivers.

MONUMENTS

Muckle Flugga Lighthouse is the most northerly point in Britain, less than 400 miles from the Arctic Circle, and well north of the southern tip of Greenland.

Brochs, tapering circular dry stone towers, litter the islands. Of considerable antiquity, their exact purpose is still the cause of some energetic debate. The most spectacular is the Broch of Mousa.

FAMOUS PEOPLE AND LOCAL CHARACTERS

Arthur Anderson was born in 1772 and began work at 11 as a beach boy, turning cod set out to dry. When he was old enough he entered the navy, but he survived the Napoleonic Wars, going into partnership in 1837 with **John Willcox** to found the Peninsula Steam Company. He was active in liberal politics as MP for Shetland, and campaigned with Cobden and Bright against the Corn Laws.

As the Peninsula Company expanded it contracted to run the mail service to India, and renamed itself Peninsula and Oriental, a name it retains. On Shetland Anderson is principally remembered for his philanthropic works, including the Anderson Educational Institute at Lerwick. He also instituted a pension scheme for his employees. Anderson died, Chairman of P & O, in 1869.

Local Characters
Margaret was the daughter of the same Earl Hakon who murdered St Magnus. She married Earl Maddad of Atholl and had a son, Harald. When her son was 19 Maddad died, and she returned to Orkney. There she enjoyed an affair with a brother of Sweyn Asleifsson, by whom she had another child. Next she eloped with the Shetland chieftain **Erlend Ungi**, who carried her off to a broch on Mousa. Harald was becoming embarrassed by this louche behaviour on the part of his mother, and followed them there, where he proposed to lay siege to the place. But it was too tough a nut to crack, so he gave the couple permission to marry. The broch is still to be seen.

-Exterior View of the Broch of Mousa, Shetland.

ART AND LITERATURE

James Tudor recommended anyone visiting Fairisle towards the end of the 19th century to take with him a pocket enema, as the local diet was *'apt to bring on violent constipation, which purgatives seem at times to increase instead of dispersing'*.

Sir John Buchanan, justifying his action in burning down the Dutch fishermen's bothies spoke of *'the great abominatioun and wickednes committit yeirlie be the Hollanderis and cuntrie people, godles and prophane persones repairing to thame at the houssis of Lerwick quilk is a desert place.'* He objected to the drunkenness and bloodshed arising from the sale of beer, and to the *'manifold adulterie and fornicatioun'* practised there by women who came under the pretext of selling socks.

LOCAL FOLKLORE

A Circle of Trolls

In Fetlar there is a circle of trolls, who were so taken with the music of a fiddler that they were caught, still dancing, by sunrise. Unfortunately the fiddler and his wife were contagiously petrified, and are still to be seen at the centre of the circle.

Tree Geese

Tree geese grow in the Shetlands. Unlike other geese, they hatch not from eggs but from the fruit of a tree that grows by the water's edge. The fruit is about the size of an

ostrich egg, and is green and bitter when unripe. However, it is impossible to gather ripe ones as they will only ripen in darkness and unseen. On ripening they immediately fall into the water and break, releasing the chicks, which swim away.

It is a matter of controversy whether tree geese should be roasted like birds, boiled like vegetables, or fried like fish.

Michael Page & Robert Inkpen

DISTINCTIVE FLAVOUR

The islands have been called the 'skeleton of a departed country'. The people are more seafarers than landsmen, whose homes are best regarded as harbours. There characteristic boat is the '**Shetland Model**', a double-ended boat.

This is the only part of the British Isles from which the **Northern Lights** can be seen regularly, and where it is possible to play golf at midnight.

According to N.C. Black, the **Shetland pony** was first produced by boil-washing a drayhorse. Further boil-washing is not recommended, as it will produce successively a Skye terrier, a woolly bear caterpillar, and the contents of a working-man's navel at the end of a long day.

Fairisle sweaters are said first to have been knitted in imitation of the embroidered doublets found on the corpses of Spanish sailors washed up from the wrecks of the Armada ship 'El Gran Grifon' in 1588.

COUNTY DIARY

January: Up-Helly-Aa is a Norse fire-raising ceremony which culminates in the burning of an imitation longship. It takes place on the last Tuesday in January.

STIRLINGSHIRE

COUNTY FACTS

Derivation of name: The name possibly derives from Strevelin, meaning the dwelling of Velyn, though no clear explanation has come to light. It may be related to the name of the river on whose banks the town of Stirling stands.

First Recorded: ante 1124

County Town: Stirling

Towns: Avonbridge, Bainsford, Balfron, Banknock, Bannockburn, Bearsden, Bridge of Allan, Bonnybridge, Brightons, Cambusbarron, Camelon, Cowie, Denny, Dennyloanhead, Falkirk, Grangemouth, Kilsyth, Larbert, Laurieston, Lennoxtown, Maddiston, Milngavie, Polmont, Redding, St Ninians, Slamannan, Stenhousemuir, Stirling.

Local Government

Central Regional Council and Strathclyde Regional Council and three District Councils

HISTORY

In 1297 William Wallace defeated the English under Edward I in pitched battle under Stirling Castle, but Edward took it by siege in 1304. In 1314 the Battle of Bannockburn was a decisive victory for Robert Bruce, and is held to be only the second time that the 'British Square' of infantry against heavy cavalry was deployed. (The first time was by Wallace at Falkirk, but Edward I broke it.) On this occasion, of the original English force of at least 30,000, only 500 survived to fall back on Dunbar with Edward II.

In 1452 James II, in a momentary frenzy, murdered the Earl of Douglas, who had come to parley at Stirling Castle under a safe conduct.

In 1488, at Sauchie, James III was defeated by a rebel army and fell from his horse into the Bannock. There he was murdered in cold blood by a rebel trooper, who, being in Holy Orders, offered to hear the King's confession before delivering the *coup de grace*.

In 1567 James VI, being only one year old, was crowned in Stirling Castle by John Knox, following the forced abdication of Mary Queen of Scots.

INDUSTRY PAST AND PRESENT

Around Falkirk and Grangemouth there is a major petrochemical complex. Other industries in the county include brewing, malting, distilling, tanning and papermaking. There is an ironworks at Carron. Farm machinery is produced at Stirling.

The coal seams are now all worked out.

LANDMARKS

Ben Lomond.

The Campsie Fells, adjacent to the Lennox Hills, consist of large tabular masses of black, volcanic trap.

MONUMENTS

Stirling Castle, 'the key to Scotland'. It is stipulated in the Act of Union that Stirling Castle should always be kept in repair.

The Antonine Wall, really an earthwork, continues through Stirlingshire. It is known locally as Grim's Dyke.

Bore Stone is said to mark the spot where Robert Bruce raised his standard at Bannockburn.

The National Wallace Monument at Abbey Craig was built in 1869 to overlook the site of Stirling Bridge, where Wallace's greatest victory took place.

TOPOGRAPHY INCLUDING RIVERS

The county is bounded in the north by Perthshire, in the north east by Clackmannanshire and Perthshire, in the east and south east by West Lothian and in the south by Lanarkshire and Dunbartonshire. The north western extremity is mountainous, and includes the highest point, Ben Lomond, (3,192 feet) – this declines to the volcanic Lennox Hills and Campsie Fells. The county is drained partly by the Clyde and partly by the Forth, though only the Forth is actually in the county.

In the north western highlands annual rainfall can be in excess of 100".

Rivers: Bannockburn, Carron, Avon, Teith, Allan, Devon, Enfrick, Kelvin.

FAMOUS PEOPLE AND LOCAL CHARACTERS

James II and **James V** were both born in Stirling Castle.

George Buchanan was born in Killearn in 1506. He and his family were poor relations in the clan, but his promise was quickly recognised, and he was educated at Paris and St Andrews. His learning was acknowledged by Lord Cassilis, who appointed him tutor to James Stuart, a bastard of James V, in 1537. This gave him leisure to begin serious writing, which he began with *Somnium*, a satire against the clergy. Two others followed, which aroused sufficient notice to get him imprisoned for heresy. Cardinal Beaton was sufficiently incensed to offer the King a bribe to sign his death-warrant so that he could burn him. The King refused, and Buchanan escaped to Paris, only to find Cardinal Beaton taking up residence there shortly afterwards. He therefore accepted an appointment at Bordeaux, where his reputation as a Latinist, already high, was even further enhanced. On the strength of it he accepted the position of Principal of the University of Coimbra, Portugal. However, he was again imprisoned for heresy, and took the opportunity to compose his version of the Psalms.

On his release in 1553 he travelled in France, returning to Scotland in 1560. In 1562 he renewed his links with the Stuarts, becoming classical tutor to Mary Queen of Scots. In 1570 he took up the same position *vis-à-vis* her son, James VI.

He continued his career of religious reform, education and classical scholarship until his death in 1582, having just lived to see his *magnum opus*, a history of Scotland, published. It was still the standard work on the subject in the mid 18th century.

STIRLING CASTLE

Local Characters

Dougal Graham was born in Stirling in 1724. He was a hunchback, and made a precarious living as a pedlar and jobbing printer. His big break came in 1745, when he joined the rebellion as a camp-follower, and virtually invented the profession of war-correspondent. After Culloden he returned to Glasgow, where he wrote and published a doggerel chronicle of the entire rebellion. Graham continued to produce and sell chap-books until his death in 1779, but the rest were on less elevated subjects, with such titles as *The Courtship and Wedding of Jocky and Maggy*, and *The Coalman's Courtship of the Creel Wife's Daughter*. They are full of drinking bouts and homely wit, such as the following: 'Never marry a widow's only son, for a' the wifely gates in the world will be in him for want o' a father to teach him manly actions.'

LOCAL FOLKLORE

The 'White Lady'

Rownam Manor House, near Stirling, was a fine 16th century mansion that belonged in the early part of the 19th century to a laird who was known as 'Auld dour crab', or 'The laird deil'. This was largely on account of the ferocity with which he enforced the game laws against poachers.

The mansion was approached by a magnificent avenue of elms, oaks and beeches, that swarmed with rabbits and squirrels, and

a certain small boy was very fond of trespassing there to hunt small game. He had discovered an oak which was very easy to climb, and if he heard the laird or the keepers in the distance, he would hide in it. The place was also alleged to be haunted by a 'White Lady', who of course only appeared at night, and whose identity was disputed. The most popular theory was that she was a young wife whom the laird had taken in his youth, and driven to the grave with his ill-treatment.

The boy determined to see her for himself, and one night went into the estate to watch for her. He stayed there a long time, hiding in the tree from the keepers, until at last the ghost appeared. She was a lady of unearthly beauty, dressed in what he instantly recognised from his conversations with the undertaker's son as a winding-sheet. He looked on her with awe, as she shone with a supernatural phosphorescence. Only then did he notice the dark figure of the laird by her side, but he looked very changed from his usual aspect. Instead of his customary scowl, his expression was one of the deepest love. This more than anything surprised the boy, and he leaned too far out from the tree and fell.

When he recovered his senses he expected to find himself in the custody of the laird, and about to be punished for trespassing. But instead he was alone in the avenue. He made his way back home, and crept into bed. The following day he learnt that the laird's body had been found in the avenue shortly

after sunrise, having apparently died from syncope, most likely brought on by severe nervous shock, at much the same time that the boy had been falling out of the tree.

DISTINCTIVE FLAVOUR

Stirling measure, in the form of Stirling (pint) Jug is preserved in the Smith Institute, along with the Linlithgow wheat firlot and the standard wheat bushel of 1824. Stirling also claims to have given to the country the firlot (via Linlithgow), the ell (via Edinburgh) the reel (via Perth) and the pound (via Lanark).

COUNTY DIARY

June:	Museum Workshop Open Week, Grangemouth
September:	Drymen Garden Club Show

SUTHERLAND

COUNTY FACTS

Derivation of name: From the Old Norse meaning Southern land (to Norseman from Scandinavia).
First Recorded: c. 1040 as Sudrland
Motto: Dluth Lean Do Dhuthchas Le Durachd (Cling To Thy Heritage With Diligence)
County Town: Dornoch
Towns: Brora, Dornoch, Durness, Helmsdale, Golspie, Lairg, Lochinver, Melvich, Tongue.

Local Government
Highland Regional Council and one District Council.

HISTORY

The minority of James V was a lawless time in Scotland, and the further north, the worse it was. It was typical that in 1517, as soon as Adam, Earl of Sutherland, went to Edinburgh on business, the MacKays of Strathnaver began a series of raids, laying the surrounding country waste. The Countess of Sutherland therefore raised the clan to try conclusions with them. They enlisted many Sinclairs from Caithness, and the two armies met at Torran-Dubh. The Sutherlands won decisively, but John McKay blamed neither his own generalship nor the luck of the day, but his ally John Murray of Aberscours. He launched an expedition against him, but was defeated again at Loch Salkie. He tried yet a third time, on this occasion raiding Murray's town of Pitfourand and was routed again.

For all this aggravation and loss of life he was not formally punished at all, but his power being largely broken, he was forced to submit to the Earl of Sutherland on his return from Edinburgh in 1518.

The last witch-burning in Scotland took place in Sutherland in 1722. The records in Forres include an item, 'To carting two loads of peat for the burning of ane witch at the Mercat cros, aichteen pence.' She had been so tortured to make her confess, that she held out her hands to the burning faggots, saying, 'Welcome, Death.'

In 1811 the Duke of Sutherland carried out the 'Sutherland Clearances', which consisted of turning a large number of poor tenant farmers off their land and exiling them to Canada. He then turned the country over to sheep, to his own great profit. This was undoubtedly high-handed and accompanied by much casual brutality, and has been represented as a major abuse of feudal power. However, it can be defended on the grounds that those dispossessed were the poorest of the poor, living on land from which it was impossible to wring a tolerable living for such numbers. Certainly, within a generation the new Canadians had achieved a level of prosperity which their fathers could never have dreamed of.

TOPOGRAPHY INCLUDING RIVERS

The county is bounded in the north by the sea, in the northeast by Caithness, in the west by the Minch, and in the south by Ross and Cromarty. It also takes in some islands to the north and west. Cape Wrath is the northern extremity of mainland Britain. Most of the county is very broken and wild, culminating in Ben More of Assynt (3,431 feet), though there is quieter country in the southeast. The northwestern coastline is very ragged, with many cliffs, while the eastern has sandy beaches. Most of the underlying geology is ancient crystalline rock, with some sandstone and limestone on top.
Rivers: Eanack, Carron, Oykill, Cassley, Shin, Fleet, Brora, Helmsdale, Halladale, Strathey, Naver, Torrisdale, Hope, Dionard, Inchford, Laxford, Inver, Kircaig.

INDUSTRY PAST AND PRESENT

There is some manufacture of woollens, and whisky distilling, but the principal industry of the county is up market tourism, especially salmon-fishing, grouse-shooting and deer-stalking. Forestry has taken on an increasing importance of recent years.
In the last century gold was mined in the Strath of Kildonan, but not enough was found to make it viable.

LANDMARKS

The Stach and Skerries Islands are the scene of the haunting folksong 'Silkie'

MONUMENTS

The Duke of Sutherland's Statue: after the first duke died the family commissioned an immense statue of him to adorn the summit of Beinn a'Bhragaidh. The inscription reads in part 'A MOURNING AND GRATEFUL TENANTRY, UNITING WITH THE INHABITANTS OF THE NEIGHBOURHOOD, ERECTED THIS PILLAR AD 1834.' This was immediately after many crofters had been evicted to make room for sheep.

Dunrobin Castle is now partly used as a boys's school, but the principal rooms open to the public contain some impressive furniture and artworks, as well as sundry stuffed animals shot by the 5th Duke.

Learable Hill has many cairns and stone-rows, though it is unknown if they were constructed by the same people in the same era of pre-history.

FAMOUS PEOPLE AND LOCAL CHARACTERS

The 3rd Duke of Sutherland was chairman and major shareholders of the Sutherland Railway Company, which had extended the line as far as Culrain by 1871, going up to Lairg in the hope of stimulating development of the country. The third-class fare by the train across the viaduct between Culrain and Invershin was held at $^1/_2$d until 1917, the cheapest ticket in the United Kingdom.

Local Characters
When the Countess of Cromartie died in 1888, her husband, the 3rd Duke of Sutherland lost no time in marrying again, this time to a widow called Mary Blair. He also altered his will to make her his principal heir. After he himself died, in 1892, his son contested the will in a court-case of venomous acrimony. At one point the Dowager Duchess was fined £250 and imprisoned for 40 days in Holloway Jail. After the case was settled she re-married and set about the construction of a castle even more pretentious than Dunrobin, at Carbisdale. The place was not completed until 1914, and is now a youth hostel.

LOCAL FOLKLORE

Mountain-building
When the world was new the gods came to Sutherland to practise the art of mountain-

building. They raised Quinag, Suilven and the Stack, which they felt was enough to get their eyes in, after which they set about the serious business of building the mountains of Norway.

The Monstrous Hare
A man called Donald was cutting peat one day, when a monstrous hare rushed into view, pursued by two hounds. He raised his spade and brought it down on the hare's back as it went past, cutting it in two. But as he watched, the hare took on the appearance of the wife of a neighbour, who was reputed to be a witch. Donald fled away, but as he did he looked over his shoulder, and neither hounds nor hare/woman were to be seen. When he got home his wife told him that their neighbour had been killed by a kick from a sheltie pony. Donald said nothing, but he realised he had seen the soul of the witch being chased by the hounds of Hell.

The rhyme to change a woman into a hare goes as follows:

'When we go in shape of hare
Say 'I shall go into the hare
With sorrow and syck and meikle care';
And I shall go in the Devil's name
And will till I come home again.'

DISTINCTIVE FLAVOUR

Sutherland is pre-eminent for deerstalking.

Brooch of Silver, plated with gold, found at Rogart, Sutherlandshire

COUNTY DIARY

September:
  Invercharron
  Traditional Highland
  Games, Bonar Bridge

WEST LOTHIAN

(LINLITHGOWSHIRE)

COUNTY FACTS

Derivation of name: Named from Leudonus, and signifying his territory. No one knows who or what Leudonus was. It has been suggested, though with little confidence, that he may have been Loth, grandfather of St Mungo.

First Recorded: c. 970 as Lothian

County Town: Linlithgow

Towns: Armadale, Bathgate, Blackburn, Blackridge, Bo'ness (Borrowstounness), Broxburn, Dalmeny, Fauldhouse, Grangepans, Kirkliston, Linlithgow, Livingston, South Queensferry, Stoneyburn, Torpichen, Uphall, Whitburn, Winchburgh.

Local Government

Lothian Regional Council and two District Councils.

HISTORY

The county had been part of the kingdom of Northumbria, but was conquered and annexed to Scotland by Kenneth MacAlpine in 1020. In 1746 Linlithgow Palace was burned down by troops under General Hawley, whether by accident or arson is uncertain.

INDUSTRY PAST AND PRESENT

The agriculture is largely devoted to cereals, potatoes and fodder crops, though dairy farming is increasing in importance. Oil refining came early to this part of Scotland. In the 18th century porpoises were hunted out of Queensferry, and rendered for their blubber.

Local oil shale used to be worked and refined, but has been superceded by better quality feedstock from the North Sea.

LANDMARKS

Cairnapple Hill has been used for mortuary purposes from very early times. There are cairns, henges and Bronze Age crematory urns. Subsequently the cairns were reopened for Iron Age intrusions.

Abercorn Standing Stones

MONUMENTS

Linlithgow Palace was begun in the 12th century, and completed by James VI in 1617.

The Parish Church is 182 feet long, 100 feet broad, and 90 feet high, not counting the steeple.

Torpichen Church was built on the site of the Hospital of St John of Jerusalem in the 16th century. The tower and nave incorporate parts of the older structure.

The Cross Well at Linlithgow, has thirteen grotesque figures.

The Forth Bridge, completed in 1890, was hailed as one of the wonders of the modern world. In fact, it is heavily over-engineered, and created no tradition. This has given rise to the incessant painting required to keep it in good repair.

FAMOUS PEOPLE AND LOCAL CHARACTERS

James 'Paraffin' Young was born in Glasgow, the son of an undertaker. He showed early interest in scientific matters, particularly chemistry, and became scientific advisor to Tennants Chemical Works, Manchester at a young age. In that capacity he received a letter from Lyon Playfair, describing an underground spring of combustible fluid that he had found in a Derby coal mine. He recognised it as a possible superior substitute for whale oil, and set about investigating its potential.

He moved to Bathgate, where he set up the first experimental oil refinery, at first using oil coal as feedstock. He later realised the potential of oil shale, and marketed paraffin wax for candles as well as paraffin for lamps.

Local Characters

Mary Queen of Scots was born at Linlithgow Palace in 1542.

Henry Bell was born at Torpichen Mill in 1767, and was apprenticed to the shipbuilding firm of Shaw and Hart at Bo'ness. He subsequently became an enthusiast for steam, and designed steam machinery for milling and pumping water, but his great achievement was the completion of the first practical steamship, the Comet, built at Port Glasgow in 1811.

TOPOGRAPHY INCLUDING RIVERS

The county is bounded in the north by the Firth of Forth; in the west, south west and north west by Stirlingshire and Lanarkshire, and in the south east by Midlothian. The country is mainly level on the coast, becoming hilly inland. The highest point is The Knock, 1023 feet. Rivers: Avon.

ART AND LITERATURE

'Of all the palaces so fair,
Built for the royal dwelling,
In Scotland, far beyond compare,
Linlithgow is excelling.'
Sir Walter Scott,
Marmion.

LOCAL FOLKLORE

General Tam Dalyell

General Tam Dalyell of the Binns had what can only be called a love-hate relationship with the Devil. He was an arch Royalist, who refused to cut his hair at any time between the execution of Charles I and the Restoration, and according to the Covenanters, the Devil was always there to deflect the many bullets fired at him during his life, no matter how well aimed.

The Devil also invented various tortures, in which he instructed Dalyell, and which he practised on Covenanter prisoners. These included thumbscrews, the boot, and a special oven for slow roasting alive.

But there was another side to their relationship, for both were foul-tempered and frequently forgot themselves over the card table, which had a heavy marble top. On one occasion, the Devil (who was losing) picked up the tabletop and threw it out of the window into a nearby deep pond. There it remained for over 250 years, until an exceptionally hot summer, when the level sank low enough for it to be dragged out by horses of the Royal Scots Greys, which coincidentally Dalyell had founded in 1861.

On another occasion the Devil threatened to blow the Binns away, and Dalyell took him seriously enough to have a wall built round the place, but the Devil said he would just have to blow a little harder, that was all. So Dalyell had to have them pinned down at all the corners with turreted towers.

Inevitably, Dalyell still haunts the Binns on a grey charger, which he rides into the dining room, though what sort of relationship he enjoys with the other ghost, a kelpie who inhabits the tabletop pond, is unknown.

Flodden

It was in Linlithgow parish church that James IV witnessed an apparition that warned him against proceeding with his plan of campaign against the English. He disregarded it, to the great cost of Scottish chivalry (not to mention his own life), at Flodden.

COUNTY DIARY

August: Bo'ness and Kinneil
Railway Steam Trains
Event

WIGTOWNSHIRE
(GALLOWAY WEST)

COUNTY FACTS

Derivation of name: Wigtown is the Old English for a manor 'town'. It has to be said that this explanation is not entirely satisfactory.
First Recorded: 1266 as Wigeton
County Town: Wigtown
Towns: Drummore, Garlieston, Glenluce, Kirkcolm, Newton Stewart, Spittal, Stranraer, Port Patrick, Port William, Whithorn, Wigtown.

Local Government
Dumfries and Galloway Regional Council and one District Council.

HISTORY

In 1685 the two 'Martyred Margarets', Margaret M'Laughlan (63) and Margaret Wilson (18), were drowned in the tidal part of the river for holding to the Covenant. They are still held in honour locally, and the Wilson family, to which President Woodrow Wilson was connected, continues to name many of its daughters after them.

INDUSTRY PAST AND PRESENT

The climate and terrain are most suited to sheep-farming, though cattle are fattened on the low ground. Pigs are also popular.
A little iron and copper were extracted in the 19th century. 'Galloway Nags', a tractable breed of all-purpose horses, were formerly famous, but have now mainly been ousted by more specialised types.

LANDMARKS

From the hills above Port Patrick it is possible to see England, Ireland and the Isle of Man, as well as the Mull of Kintyre.
The Cave of St Ninian, who introduced Christianity to Scotland, is a current tourist attraction.

The Mull of Galloway extends to 70 miles south of the northern tip of England. It is therefore sometimes called the 'Scottish Land's End'.

MONUMENTS

The Torhouse Standing Stones are a perfect circle, 60 feet across, and dating from the Bronze Age.
Glenluce Abbey dates from 1190, and is now a ruin, except for the Chapter House.
Drummore is Scotland's most southerly village.

FAMOUS PEOPLE AND LOCAL CHARACTERS

St Ninian, son of a local chieftain who converted to Christianity, travelled to Rome where he was consecrated Bishop of the Picts. In about 390 AD he returned to found a religious centre at Whitehorn dedicated to the memory of Martin of Tours. This shrine became very popular, and all the kings of Scotland from 1000 AD until the Reformation came there to pray for a blessing on their reign.

Local Characters
Admiral Sir John Ross was born at Balsarroch in 1777. His naval career began early and was distinguished, so that in 1818 he was sent in search of the Northwest Passage, getting as far as Lancaster Sound. In 1829 he was commissioned to try again, privately on this occasion by Sir Felix Booth. He got as far as Prince Regent's inlet.
His nephew, Sir James Ross, carried on the tradition, but in the Antarctic. He commanded the expedition of the Erebus and Terror from 1839 to 1843. This expedition was notable for the singular lack of fatalities among the crew, despite spending much of the time iced up.

TOPOGRAPHY INCLUDING RIVERS

The county is bounded in the east by Wigtown Bay, in the northeast by Kirkcudbrightshire, in the north by Ayrshire, and in the west and south by the Irish Sea. The coastline is heavily indented, with Luce Bay running 15 miles inland, Wigtown Bay ten miles, the Mull of Galloway 15 miles, and Loch Ryan eight miles. The country is rolling, but generally low-lying. Much of it is covered with alluvial soil. The highest point is Craigairie Fell, 1025 feet.
Rivers: Cree, Luce, Bladenoch.

ART AND LITERATURE

'Know we not the Galloway nags?'
Shakespeare

LOCAL FOLKLORE

Sir Godfrey MacCulloch

As Sir Godfrey MacCulloch was riding one day, not far from his own house, a little old man in green, and riding a white palfrey, accosted him. After an exchange of amenities the old man told Sir Godfrey that he lived under his own house, and he was unhappy because of the common sewer that vented itself directly into his drawing room. Sir Godfrey was greatly surprised to hear this complaint; but realising what sort of person he had to deal with, he assured the old man very courteously that the direction of the drain should be altered, and he set it in train. Many years later, Sir Godfrey had the misfortune to kill another gentleman in a brawl. He was indicted, convicted, and condemned to death. The scaffold for his beheading was built on Edinburgh Castle hill, but just as he reached it, the old man rode through the crowd on his white palfrey and called to Sir Godfrey to jump up behind him. Sir Godfrey jumped up behind his neighbour, who spurred down the steep bank, and neither was ever seen again.

Provost Coltrane

Provost Coltrane had been in nominal charge at the time of the martyrdom of the Margarets, though he was attending to business in Edinburgh at the time. He was still in office in 1708, when he visited Stranraer. On that occasion Margaret M'Laughlan's daughter came to her Minister in great distress, saying that her mother had appeared to her in a dream, looking just as she had looked at the time of her drowning. She had given warning that Coltrane must repent at once, for he was about to be summoned by God. Shortly after this a message was received that Coltrane had been taken with apoplexy at Stranraer. He was carried home, but died without regaining consciousness. At the moment of his death, all the windows of his house (still standing in Bank Street) blazed with unnatural fire, as the Devil came to take his own.

Saucepan of Roman form found in Dowalton Loch

habitually fought 'berserk', i.e., bare to the sark, or shirt. At the Battle of Northallerton they were ranked with King David against the English. The King wanted to put armoured men in the front rank, as the English did, but the Galwegians pleaded their ancient right in these terms: 'Why are you so fearful? Why do you dread those iron tunics? Our sides are iron, our breasts are bronze, our feet have never known flight, nor our backs a wound.' By this the King was persuaded.

However, there was a less admirable side to the Galwegian character. In the same campaign they enjoyed a reputation for tossing little children to catch on their spearpoints, and for drinking the blood of dying enemies, centuries before the same inelegant habit was ascribed to the Bashi-Bazhuks.

Incidentally, the Battle of Northallerton was a decisive victory for the English.

In modern times the local character has taken on a less disquieting aspect. It appears that people visiting the area, from whatever part of the world they come, meet their neighbours or cousins. Even if it is for the first time, they always seem to encounter a friend's friend, or when they leave, meet someone else who has met everyone they met there.

Wigtown is the official spelling in order to distinguish the county town from **Wigton** in Cumberland.

DISTINCTIVE FLAVOUR

In olden times the men of **Galloway**, which is divided between Wigtown and Kirkcudbright, were famous warriors, who